W. T. (William Torrens) McCullagh Torrens

The Marquess Wellesley, Architect of Empire

W. T. (William Torrens) McCullagh Torrens

The Marquess Wellesley, Architect of Empire

ISBN/EAN: 9783743326361

Manufactured in Europe, USA, Canada, Australia, Japa

Cover: Foto ©ninafisch / pixelio.de

Manufactured and distributed by brebook publishing software (www.brebook.com)

W. T. (William Torrens) McCullagh Torrens

The Marquess Wellesley, Architect of Empire

THE
MARQUESS WELLESLEY

Architect of Empire

AN HISTORIC PORTRAIT

BY

W. M. TORRENS, M.P.

London
CHATTO & WINDUS, PICCADILLY
1880

[The right of translation is reserved]

PREFACE.

OF the eminent men whom in earlier years I had many opportunities of closely observing, none seem to me so characteristically representative of the two races long alienated by evil laws as those whose likeness I have sought to trace in these volumes. The ideas and usages of a dominant caste, taught from childhood to believe themselves indispensable to the maintenance of authority, and alone qualified for the duties and privileges of freedom, have passed away; and with them the mute subjection, murmuring complaint, deferential remonstrance, partial enfranchisement, and at length organised agitation, by which the two estranged communities were rendered one in the eye of the law. Wellesley and O'Connell, each in his separate way, signally contributed to the gradual revolution which occupied in its accomplishment well-nigh the whole period of their lives, and to which their best efforts were devoted. Yet a greater contrast cannot be conceived than that presented by their dissimilar ways of life, habits of thought, and impressive powers of expression. Without flattery or disparagement I wish simply to recall how the illustrious statesman and the unrivalled leader of the people each lived and moved and had his being. As they were seldom in direct contact or antagonism I have had no temptation to resort to antithesis, which in spite of what is deemed conspicuous success in many well-known instances I must be permitted to think fallacious and misleading in historic portraiture.

CONTENTS.

CHAPTER	PAGE
I. From Welles-Leigh to Dangan. 1125-1760	1
II. Harrow and Eton. 1770-1778	20
III. Irish House of Lords. 1781-1783	33
IV. Old St. Stephen's Chapel. 1784-1788	55
V. College Green and Carlton House. 1788-1791	74
VI. Board of Control. 1792-1794	89
VII. Holwood and Walmer. 1795-1797	111
VIII. The Voyage out. 1798	132
IX. Fort William. 1798	149
X. Seringapatam. 1799	176
XI. Leadenhall Street. 1799-1800	203
XII. Paramount Power. 1801	224
XIII. Bassein. 1802-1803	247
XIV. Bhurtpore. 1804-1805	274
XV. Portsmouth and Putney. 1806	298
XVI. Nowhere. 1806-1808	322
XVII. Seville. 1809	346
XVIII. The Foreign Office. 1810	387
XIX. Torres Vedras. 1810	421
XX. Oatlands and Dorking. 1811-1812	449
XXI. Threshold of the Treasury. 1812	487

MARQUESS WELLESLEY.

CHAPTER I.

FROM WELLES-LEIGH TO DANGAN.

1125—1760.

In the parting of forfeit lands among the soldiers of the Conquest, and the re-enfeoffment of the old possessors that recked not who was king so they might hold their own and dwell in peace, Henry I. confirmed to Avenant of Welles-leigh in Somersetshire the lordship of his manor there; and granted him beside the grand serjeantry of all the country eastward of the river Parret as far as Bristol Bridge. His son, according to tradition, accompanied Henry II. as standard-bearer into Ireland; as an old flag preserved with reverent care till recent times was held to prove, warranting the emblazonry of St. George's banner in the family arms. In the next century the English heritage descended in the female line, and the name became territorially extinct. Meanwhile a younger branch struck root in Leinster, and, grafting with more than one vigorous stock of like planter origin, helped to form a stubborn and thorny fence along the borders of the Pale.

Sir William de Wellesley had writ of summons as a baron to the Irish Parliament of 1339, in right of his Castle of Kildare, granted him by Edward II. on condition of his holding it fast against the native enemy, and paying twenty pounds a year for the pastures round the same. Later on the FitzGeralds ousted him, as they did all their rivals in Leighlin and Offaly; and the evicted favourite of royalty was compensated by Edward III. in 1342 with the manor of Demor. Sir John, his son, was active in the English interest, and wrought wide havoc among the sept of the O'Tooles, whose chief he caused to suffer on the scaffold. His descendants dwelt at Paynestown in Meath, where in the fifteenth century they had great possessions; often serving the office of sheriff and sitting in Parliament, sometimes for the hamlets bidden by the Crown to send burgesses to the Lower House, and sometimes in the Upper as Barons of Norragh.

Walter Wellesley was Abbot of Kildare and Master of the Rolls, and in 1531, at the request of Henry VIII., he was appointed bishop of the diocese by Clement VII. in reward for his services in obtaining the release of Delvin, the Lord Deputy, taken prisoner by O'Conor. Many intermarriages took place with the Cusakes, Plunkets, and Cowleys, who were neighbouring lords of the Pale. A great-granddaughter of Sir William and the fair Ismay Plunket was wedded to Sir Henry Cowley, whose progenitor, a trusted officer of Elizabeth under Lord Sydney, espoused the daughter of Lord Chancellor Cusake; and is said by Hooker to have been one of the chief foes of the malcontent FitzGeralds. In the troubled times of the Stuarts the Wesleys, as they had come to be called, dwelt at Dangan; and the Colleys, as they chose their name to be written, slumbered on at Castle Carbery; neither family losing or gaining by the vicissitudes of the period. In 1700 Richard Colley, who is spoken of as a youth of genial temperament, not overweighted with learning but much given to practice on the violin, unexpectedly succeeded to his brother's patrimony: and fortune though he knew it not, had in store still greater gifts for him. Of his relatives in Meath he knew but little. Garret Wesley and his wife (a daughter of Sir Dudley Colley) sometimes visited Dublin; but for the most part their childless days were spent at the old house near Trim. It was but an evening's walk from Laracor, the secluded village where Swift spent some of his happiest years. Thither he had persuaded Mrs. Dingley and Stella to accompany him when, in chagrin at the ingratitude of Whig patrons, he tried to take to the life of a country pastor without flock to tend; and where for a time he amused himself with small garden improvements, desultory writing in prose and verse, and playing whist with his nearest neighbours.

Garret Wesley was but too glad to have for a companion the man of all his countrymen worth knowing as a guest or friend. Swift in 1699 had accompanied Lord Berkley to Ireland as private secretary and chaplain. One of his household, Bushe, having had sufficient influence to supplant him in the former place, the Viceroy promised him the best preferment that fell vacant. The deanery of Derry, of considerable value, would have made him content for life; but Bushe asked 1,000*l*. for securing it to him; and Swift not having the money, it was sold to another for that sum. Jonathan, in a rage, exclaimed, 'Confound you both for a couple of scoundrels,' and quitted his Excellency's service. Berkley, afraid of his resentment, gave him the living of Agher and the vicarages of Rathbeggan and Laracor, which, with the prebend of Dunlavin, yielded an income of 400*l*. a year: and this was all he had, while plausible Addison continued to be Secretary for Ireland, and Godolphin to be Lord Treasurer. Mr. Perceval, Sir Arthur Langford, Garret Wesley and his wife, were his most intimate friends. Congregation beside he had none, and even these not always. So, like Sterne in his remote incumbency, 'he strove to beguile the time with mirth;' and on wet days put the finishing strokes to 'The Tale of a Tub.' Dangan never failed in welcome and good cheer; and though Glasnevin was a three hours' ride, and Addison the most dignified of hosts, community of tastes, and of political associations, often drew him in 1709 to the house of his right promiseful friend. Just opposite on the other side of the brook, he loved to linger under the evergreen oaks of Delville, where later on, at a private press in the garden, were printed the once famous 'Drapier's Letters.' Before the fall of the Whigs, Wharton who had succeeded Berkley, strove to rekindle faith in failing friends and held out hopes anew to the no longer forgotten Vicar of Laracor: for 'The Tale of a Tub' had made a sensation, and there were symptoms of coming change in the humour of the Court. Somers too and Halifax were eager to take up over-due promises; but the bitterness of neglect had entered the wayward soul, and Swift turned for satisfaction, if not for sympathy, to the society of Pope and St. John. By the former he was introduced to Harley, with whom he quickly became intimate, and through whom he would probably have obtained a mitre but for the insuperable antipathy of the Queen. The Wesleys seem to have resided occasionally in London, and Swift's friendship is indicated by his leaving a ministerial dinner-table to read evening prayers to his kind hostess of Dangan when in declining health.

Her husband, whom she left childless and who thought himself too old to marry again, looked round in search of some young kinsman to whom he might bequeath his fair possessions. A clergyman of his name was for many years incumbent of Epworth in Lincolnshire, and had gained some reputation as a controversialist in defence of the Revolution and the Toleration Act. His fanatical parishioners burnt his parsonage over his head, and his wife and children were with difficulty rescued from the flames. The eldest John, was destined to become the Savonarola of the English Church. While his younger brother Charles was at Westminster their father received a letter from Garret Wesley offering to adopt the boy, and by way of earnest to provide for the payment of his school bills. One day his unknown namesake called at Dean's Yard and asked the youth if he was willing to live with him in Ireland. After some hesitation Charles whose mind was bent on Christ Church, gratefully declined; and John, destined with his help to attain religious influence so memorable and lasting, noted the fact with the characteristic comment, that his brother had thus had a fair escape from the snares of the world.[1]

Though balked at first in quest of an heir, he still was bent on making choice in his lifetime of a successor and witnessing the anticipated joy to be by his will conferred. Cousin Richard, who had married a daughter of Dr. Sale Registrar of the Archdiocese of Dublin, received from him an unexpected visit at Butlerstown in Kildare, where was wont to gather round him the musical circle whose clear and innocent laughter still rings in the pleasant recollections of the pretty diarist of Delville.[2] Without preface or circumlocution Garret Wesley unfolded his kind purpose. As heaven had not blest him with posterity, he wished that after he was gone the different branches of the family should be knit together under his kinsman, whom with his young wife he should like betimes to make at home at Dangan, and treat as children of his own. One condition only he insisted on—that Richard Colley should adopt his name and arms. The easy covenant was willingly accepted; and save as a prefatory surname, Colley of Castle Carbery disappeared from the muster roll of Leinster gentry.

[1] Southey's *Life of Wesley.*
[2] *Life and Correspondence of Mrs. Delany.*

By will in March 1727, the last descendant in the male line of the lords of the manor of Welles-Leigh, bequeathed to his kinsman the mansion and estate of Dangan and all that appertained thereto; and on his death soon afterwards, the heritages of both branches of the family were united in the hand of one possessor. Richard's heart enlarged with his fortune, and his house became the seat for many years of unaffected and unstinted hospitality. It was in its way pretentious, and withal commodious, but the situation was not attractive from the want of wood and water. These deficiencies the new owner set himself to remedy; planting trees of great variety in well chosen spots, and taking advantage of the undulations of the ground to form ponds and what were then called canals between. By help of drainage from the hills around and the contributory aid of skies too often given to weep, the artificial lakes widened and deepened till at length a miniature royal yacht carrying its due complement of guns, with all sail set and pennant streaming (meant for a present to the Duke of Cumberland) was safely launched upon the amplest of the park waters; in another swam a barge, the 'Pretty Betty,' which on a picnic could accommodate a dozen people. How much arboriculture is helped and hastened by the humid atmosphere of the Green Land they best can tell who in a few years have seen bald hill-sides clothed with luxuriant foliage, and valleys through which the ocean breeze swept and soughed unpityingly, converted into sheltered dells as if to catch and hold the fleeting sunshine. In long after years a more illustrious owner of Dangan loved to recite laughingly the lines of an eccentric rhymester all but locally forgotten:

> Erin, thy weather's like a modish wife,
> Thy words and tears for ever are at strife;
> To gain her end she every method tries,
> And when she can no longer scold, she cries;

> Like her, consistency thy whim disdains,
> And when it can no longer blow it rains.

Swift no longer dwelt at Laracor, but he came occasionally from his deanery of St. Patrick's to recall genial memories, and to gladden his old friends in Meath with his quaint and sardonic pleasantry. Dr. Delany came too from Delville, fascinated early by the winning ways and bewitching smiles of Mrs. Pendarves, who for the first time visited Ireland in 1731 on the invitation of her cousin Lord Carteret, and who has left in her letters many amusing traits of the place and of the family, with whom she became an especial favourite.

Allegoric names and accessories were the fashion of the day; and the pastimes of a country house were marshalled in fantastic order supposed to be classical.

'Mr. Wesley (alias *Paris*) has provided each of his visitors with a walking staff whereon is fixed the Parnassus name. Mr. Usher, *Vulcan*; young Murray Don, *Mars*; and Mr. Kit Don, *Neptune*. Our staffs are white, and when we take our walks we make a most surprising appearance, somewhat like the sheriffs' men at the assizes!'[1]

'In his garden there is a fir-grove dedicated to Vesta, in the midst of which is her statue; at some distance from it is a mound covered with evergreens, on which is placed a temple with the statues of Apollo, Neptune, Proserpine, and Diana; all have due honours paid them.'

The style of living was that of cheerful luxury without ceremony or ostentation. In the large old hall were an organ and harpsichord, where all the company met when they had a mind, and where music, dancing, shuttlecock, draughts, and prayers took their turn between the three o'clock dinner and the convivial supper-time of ten.

[1] From Dangan, April 5, 1733.

By her friends Mrs. Wesley was evidently much beloved; she had very engaging qualities, and a very easy temper, though her merits were scarce equal to her husband's. 'He has certainly,' says Mrs. Delany, 'more virtues and fewer faults than any man I know; a proper mixture of good and agreeable qualities: his wife, his children, his friends, his poor and rich neighbours, can testify the truth of what I say. He values his riches only as they are the means of making all about him happy; no ostentation, no taste merely for grandeur. He improves his estate and all the country around him as much as if he had a son to enjoy it, which there seems no great probability of his having.' The youthful daughters of the house were its supreme grace and joy; 'engaging little creatures, and improving every day.' One only blessing was hitherto denied him; that of a son, and the inheritance seemed to be once more destined to pass in reversion to a stranger, if not a personal enemy. Youngest born [1] of his children came at last a son, baptized Garret, in grateful memory of the donor of the house, and early destined to gladden his father's heart by rare indications of a bright and playful intelligence, and of a susceptibility to musical impressions still more rare. Even in babyhood he gave, 'twas said, tokens of sympathy in his father's fiddling of which the parent loved to boast; but after Dubourg, the well-known violinist, had been to Dangan, the boy refused to listen to any other touch, and used to creep in childish adulation to the musician's feet, and gently pray him to keep on. Then came the time for his own wanderings among the strings,—cruel inflictions doubtless on all ears less lenient than those of his eldest sister, whose chief trouble with him was to keep his fingers off the harpsichord. From his tiny inner consciousness he was incorrigibly bent on making out tunes for himself: dimly giving discernible promise of the

[1] July 19, 1735.

melody to come which every true lover of catch and glee cherishes with fondness.

Dubourg was the favourite pupil of the once celebrated Geminiani, who seems to have felt so much sympathy in his professional success, that in his old age he came to visit him at Dublin, and tarried there till he died. Richard Wesley probably became acquainted with Dubourg after his appointment in 1728 as Master of the Castle Band, in which successive Viceroys took much interest and spared no pains to make perfect in its way. The Irish capital had little politics in Carteret's and Chesterfield's time, but it was full of merriment and music. Several societies existed for the cultivation of the tuneful art among the educated classes, each of which had its special object of local benevolence, to which the profits from its amateur exertions combined with professional aid were devoted. Mercer's Hospital, of which Mr. Wesley was a governor, and the City Infirmary, were prominent among these; and an association whose mercy was not less needed of another kind, namely, one for the release of unfortunate debtors of small amount, then a numerous class of sufferers. The violinist had become intimate with Handel when *maestro di cappella* at Canons, the palatial residence of the Duke of Chandos, near Stanmore. Thither he drew all London fashion on fine Sunday mornings to hear him play, as none ever played before, in the little chapel where his magnificent patron said his prayers, and where were revived for the first time since the exile of the Stuarts, orchestral accompaniments to sacred song. Handel composed twelve anthems and more than one 'Te Deum' for his patron the ex-Paymaster of the Forces, who gave him a thousand pounds for the oratorio of 'Esther.' His subsequent career as composer and director of operas at the King's Theatre, and the long story of his triumphs and his troubles, ending in temporary dethronement and the shutting up of the Haymarket House, have been often told. When at his lowest depth of disappointment in the summer of 1741, Dubourg, who never wavered in his devotion to his friend, urged him to pay a visit to the land of his own adoption, where his works, he said, were all well known and dearly loved, and where he promised him such a welcome as would kindle hope and joy in him again. The Duke of Devonshire, then Viceroy, was induced to send him a courtly invitation. Handel hesitated. He was busy with what he called 'something new,' which he thought would please, and which he could not break away from incomplete ere quitting home. Something new indeed—the like of which was never heard by human ears before or since that day. Some weeks in August and September he spent chiefly alone, piling up with rapidity inconceivable the matchless melodies and harmonies of his great masterpiece. When the score of the 'Messiah' was complete, he prepared to set out for Dublin, where Dubourg had negotiated for him engagements likely to be remunerative without operatic risks or cares. But in the shortening days the journey looked a long one, when he heard it took the King's Lieutenant with sixteen relays of horses five days upon the road from Piccadilly to Park Gate; and sometimes as many at sea. The letters of the violinist were however more and more persuasive: Handel was already in Ireland so well known, and the best people would be sure to make so much of him. At last he made up his mind, and engaging three or four artists on whom he could rely to follow him by the middle of November, he quitted home.

Weatherbound at Chester on his way, he bethought him of his precious manuscript, and inquired for a chorister who could read score at sight, that he might try over some of the passages which were running in his head as he smoked his long pipe at the inn. Jansen, a house-painter, was said to be just the sort of man he wanted; and when his outdoor work was done it was agreed they should begin. But the irritable bard quickly grew impatient at the blunders and hesitations of his half-taught assistant, and broke out in profanest polyglot of objurgation. 'You scoundrel; *pourquoi* you tell me you could read music at *soight?*'—'So I can,' said the decorator, 'but not at first sight.' The soft answer turned away wrath. The author of 'Saul' and 'Israel in Egypt' burst out laughing, and they got on very tolerably for the rest of the time.

At Dublin his welcome, in compliment and cash, was far more than he had bargained for. The Ducal Court did him all honour; the Bar and University added their homage; and the fashionable world of music went fairly mad with joy.

In a letter to his friend who wrote the libretto of his lighter pieces and adapted the Scriptural words of his oratorios, he tells how 'the nobility did make amongst themselves a subscription for six nights which did fill a room of six hundred persons, so that he needed not sell one single ticket at the door: and without vanity the performance was received with a general approbation. Signora Avolio, which he brought with him from London, pleased extraordinary. He found a tenor voice which gave great satisfaction; the basses and counter-tenors were very good, and the rest of the chorus singers by his direction did exceedingly well; as for the instruments they were excellent, Mr. Dubourg being at the head of them; and the music sounded delightfully in their charming room, which puts him in such spirits, and his health being so good, that he exerted himself on his organ with more than usual success. They opened with the 'Allegro,' 'Penseroso,' and 'Il Moderato,' and he assured his friend that his words of the 'Moderato' were vastly admired. The audience being composed besides the flower of the ladies of distinction and other people of the greatest quality; of so many bishops, deans, heads of the College, and the most eminent people in the law, as the Chancellor, Auditor-General, &c.; all which were very much taken with the poetry, so that he was desired to perform it again the next time.' He could not sufficiently express the kind treatment he received; but the politeness of this generous nation could not be unknown to his friend, who might judge of the satisfaction he enjoyed.

The instrument above alluded to he had brought with him from London in his anxiety to insure the due effect of his performances. It was given by him to Mr. Wesley on his leaving Ireland, and was long afterwards presented by his son to the old Church of St. Paul, on the rebuilding of which it was transferred to the Dublin Blue-Coat School.[1]

Years and vexations had not dimmed Handel's sense of humour, which never malicious, played freely among friends and acquaintances as well as critics and rivals. During a rehearsal, Dubourg who sometimes took a trip without leave into the tempting field of improvisation, lost his way, and had obvious difficulty in regaining the key from which he had wandered. Having at length succeeded, he tried to cover his escape with a brilliant shake; Handel murmured, ' Welcome home, Mr. Dubourg.'

Mr. Wesley was enchanted, as were his children, when he carried with him both the eminent musicians to Dangan, and invited all his neighbours of the country round to hear Handel play upon the organ in the great hall. Who can tell the depth of the impression made upon the precocious son, then a child, as he watched the fingers of the magician press the keys and bring forth tones of pathos and of power such as his boyish fancy had never dreamed of or imagined.

Dr. Quin, who was a leading member of the local Academy of Music, loved long afterwards to tell how Handel during

[1] Townsend; on the authority of Mr. Geary, organist of the Chapel.

his visit to Ireland, lived in the utmost degree of friendship and familiarity with many noble families.[1] His concerts were repeated during the spring, and with undiminished *éclat*. The enthusiasm he found among all classes for melody, native and foreign, gave him infinite pleasure. He noted carefully many of the popular airs which were sung to accompaniments on the harp; and though Carolan was dead, there were still not a few of the minstrels trained in his school who were devoted to the national instrument.

Everyone pressed the illustrious stranger to prolong his stay, and amid easy gains and flattering hospitalities he was nothing loth. But what was to become of the Royal princesses and their lessons on the harpsichord? for George II. had only given him leave of absence for a few weeks' excursion across the Channel. The Lord Lieutenant undertook to obtain an extension of time, which was granted, and thus Dubourg secured his heart's desire, that the *chef-d'œuvre* of his friend should be produced in Ireland for the first time under his direction. Mrs. Cibber and Signora Avolio were willing to remain, having reaped their full meed of profit and praise.

Society in Dublin was then full of cultivated taste, and hospitality was its ordinary way of life. Handel longed to hear the 'Messiah,' and Dubourg encouraged him to pay his Celtic friends the compliment of its first production. Singers for the chief parts were not wanting, and for an orchestra of sufficient range and skill the local societies would readily contribute their best performers. But fitting choruses there could not be unless the deans of the two cathedrals could be induced to lend their choirs. Here was a difficulty. Swift not long before had in a querulous fit made an order against his choristers 'hiring their voices to clubs of fiddlers.' What was indecorous at St. Patrick's, the singing men and boys of Christ Church could not be expected to do, and all the

[1] Burney, *History of Music*.

strength of both was wanted. Swift still lived, but was by this time past objecting. 'Dead at top,' he was no longer able to discharge his accustomed duties, or even to enjoy the conversation of old friends. His functions had devolved on the sub-dean and precentor, Doctor Wynne, who happened to be trustee and treasurer of Mercer's Hospital, the funds of which would be further benefited by the new enterprise should it succeed; and fortunately the Dean of Christ Church, Charles Cobbe,[1] was a lover of music, liberal and enlightened like himself. Dubourg persuaded both to let their choirs practise together the choruses of the 'Messiah;' and Handel spent February and March in drilling his Celtic cherubim when their surplices were doffed. The best players of the confederate orchestra set about practising diligently their parts. On April 30 it was announced that the 'Messiah' would be performed, and in a hall crowded to excess by nobles, fair women, dignitaries, and *dilettanti*, was for the first time heard 'Comfort ye, my people.' Who can realise the wonder and ecstasy of the hour? Handel's own account is simple and touching, giving praise to all concerned except himself. Mr. Wesley, Dr. Delany, and all their circle, save Swift alone, were there; and the doctor, though not apt to yield to emotion, was so carried away by the pathos of Mrs. Cibber, that he audibly exclaimed, 'Woman, for this be all thy sins forgiven.'

In 1743 Delany had the good fortune to win the hand of Mrs. Pendarves, whose residence thenceforth in the neighbourhood of Dublin added a new charm to the society in which Wesley moved. By her taste and skill Delville was decorated and its grounds improved, until, for the size of it, it came to be the most coveted spot in all the suburbs round. Its mistress seems never to have been spoiled by the popu-

---

[1] Chaplain to the Duke of Bolton 1717; and in 1743 Archbishop Dublin.

larity she enjoyed, and never tired of contriving how to make others happy. When her cousin became Premier, Chesterfield went to Ireland as Viceroy, and in his neverending hospitalities he was glad to pay especial devotion to his fair friend. In one of her letters she describes with a playful air of affectation the fuss at Glasnevin when his Excellency offered to come to breakfast with his lady wife, and how much he admired her shell-work, embroidery, and all the rest. Mr. Wesley, who was certainly not a man to push his way among the time-serving great, lost nothing in the eyes of Philip the Magnificent by her known esteem for him. The friends of his own station in life with whom he was most intimate had been chiefly in sympathy with Opposition during the administration of Walpole; and it needed little persuasion by Chesterfield to induce Lord Granville to name him for an Irish peerage as one whom he might remember during his own Lieutenancy to be a worthy gentleman of good estate, the owner of an obedient borough, and possessing not a little influence in his county. He was accordingly created by Privy Seal Baron Mornington, a dignity which he lived to enjoy for several years.[1] The cause of his elevation is not distinctly noticed in any of the journals of the time, and may probably be ascribed to his social popularity and the support his family had for generations given without much show of political preference, to the executive of the day. The Irish House of Lords was then the least exciting of assemblies, and few vestiges remain of its desultory deliberations. Of the senatorial sayings of the new peer, if he ever said anything, nothing is preserved. The votes of the member for Trim were of inappreciable value during the first half of the century, and could hardly have weighed in the scale; for there was then no debate in the dull provincial taxing-house on any question of greater

[1] Patent bears date July 10, 1746,

interest to the world than the tithe of agistment or the phraseology of an address to a carousing Viceroy, which some neglected lawyer strove to pepper skilfully with sarcasm.

The new peer had hardly entered upon the enjoyment of his honours, when through some accident unknown, the old house at Dangan was discovered to be on fire, and the greater portion of it was destroyed; but enough was saved of furniture and valuables to make the offices temporarily habitable while the work of rebuilding went on. Familiar friends came and made merry all the same. Mrs. Delany wrote in terms of admiration of the improvements made in all the surroundings since she had first been there.

'The place is really magnificent. The park consists of between eight and nine hundred acres; the walk from the house to the lake is six hundred yards long and fifty-two feet broad. The lake covers twenty-six acres, with a fort and islands full of wildfowl. My godson Garret is governor of the fort, and lord high admiral; he hoisted all his colours for my reception, and was not a little mortified that I declined the compliment of being saluted from the fort and ship. The ground as far as you can see every way is waving in hills and dales, and every remarkable point has either a tuft of trees, a statue, a seat, an obelisk or a pillar. How great a satisfaction it is to see so fine a place in the possession of a man so worthy of it.'

Lord Mornington was the same good-humoured agreeable man he had been seventeen years before. His eldest daughter, who had married Chichester Fortescue of Dromeskin in Louth, had become an invalid, and her sister, Miss Wesley, did the honours of the table. 'My godson is a most extraordinary boy; he is thirteen, a very good scholar, and whatever study he undertakes he masters it surprisingly. He began with the fiddle last year and now he plays everything at sight. He is a child among children and as tractable and complying to his sisters and all that should have any authority over him.' One of the stories oft recalled of the young musician's enthusiastic devotion to the art was, that when he was told that a new organ had been ordered for the hall, he eagerly offered for the post of organist; and for answer got the promise that he should have it if, when the instrument was finished, he could play on it a hymn. When the time came he not only proved able to comply with the condition, but, to his father's wonder and delight, performed a voluntary full of pleasant harmony and much variety, of his own composition. Thenceforth his aim in life was fixed; and with the aid of native and foreign teachers he became, as is well known, one of the leading amateurs of his day. The memory of Handel's visit was fondly cherished at Dangan; and when his youthful admirer was old enough to accompany his father to London, it was his chief delight to hear the great composer play at the Foundling,[1] which he did regularly on Sunday morning for several years; even after he had been smitten with blindness;[2] or to gaze on him with tender admiration as he conducted on the organ the performance of the 'Messiah,' and saw his tears drop upon the notes in the piercing wail of Samson mourning his loss of sight.[3]

Garret Wesley was educated at Trinity College, and obtained an honorary degree as doctor of music from the Irish University. At three-and-twenty he succeeded to the patrimonial inheritance, and thenceforth devoted his chief thoughts to the pursuit of his favourite art. One of the first undertakings of the harmonious peer was the reconstitution in Dublin of an Academy for the mutual culture of music by amateurs of good wealth and good breeding. In the good old times of the Irish metropolis when it

---

[1] Ladies were told to come without hoops and gentlemen without their swords.   [2] In 1753.   [3] Schœlcher.

possessed a Parliament and a West End of its own, and was full of the flutter and fashion of lavish landlords who rode hard, drank deep, were never at a loss for a repartee, or for a second at short notice in a duel, and dark-eyed, low-voiced loveable women who circulated from one another's pleasant mansions throughout the winter in gilded sedans, and on a Sunday morning effectively wept at a charity sermon at St. Ann's or St. Patrick's and left their bracelets or lockets on the plate; in those days when Dublin was a city ill-watched and watered, but delightful to live in among those who understood how to live, the young lord and his companions swam down stream loving and beloved, the gayest of the gay. Music more than ever was his fancy and his forte. The rules of the new Academy excluded all kinds of professional help. Listeners were admitted by tickets one evening in every month; and as many as three hundred sometimes came in ruffles and brocade. To show they were not proud, once every year the sons and daughters of Orpheus played for money, when anyone might pay at the doors: the proceeds being duly applied to the Indigent Room-Keepers and the Infirmary. Lord Mornington officiated generally as conductor of the orchestra, and prominent among his fellow-fiddlers was Sackville Hamilton, and pre-eminent for dainty pleasings on the lute, the Lord Lucan of his day. Mrs. Monck and Lady Caroline Russell warbled divinely; while Lady Tyrone matronised the younger vocalists of her sex, as Sappho might have done had she been married to a Beresford of an Earl's degree. Admission to membership was by strictest ballot, the subscription being high, and the improbable contingency of a surplus being provided for by its appropriation beforehand to a loan fund for distressed tradesmen.

The noble *maestro* was for a time the accepted lover of Lady Louisa Lennox, sister of Lady Kildare, and he seemed to have found favour at Carton. But after a little while Mr.

Conolly of Celbridge, with half his wit and twice his fortune, crossed his path and made away with the prize. Consolation for his wounded spirit soon presented itself in the person of the fair daughter of Arthur Hill, of Belvoir in the county of Down, who was afterwards created Viscount Dungannon. The lady brought him no great fortune, but he settled 1,400*l.* a year on her as jointure and 500*l.* a year as pin money. The Meath estates yielded at the time 8,000*l.* a year, and were expected to produce considerably more; but encumbrances had already begun to take root in the soil; and during his life-tenancy they throve apace. In Grafton Street, at an old mansion rented from the Corporation, which he purposed buying in order to rebuild, on the 20th June, 1760, his eldest son Richard was born. Not long afterwards he acquired the additional dignities of Viscount Wellesley of Dangan, and Earl of Mornington in the county of Meath;[1] and in her bridal year Lady Mornington walked as an Irish Countess at the coronation of George III.

[1] 20th October, 1760.

CHAPTER II.

HARROW AND ETON.

1761—1781.

It is easy to imagine with what pride the heir of Dangan was regarded by his youthful parents and their sympathising circle. Features are proverbially apt to change and the thousand accidents and maladies to which immaturity is liable, forbid parental confidence that beauty in the cradle will be followed, after a score years of growth, by manly grace and nobleness of bearing. But there are faces which when we look upon them even in maturity, and forms we gaze upon even in trembling age, that we feel instinctively must have been from the beginning perfect of their kind. No babylikeness has survived to tell how symmetrical were the tiny lineaments or rounded limbs that first engaged a mother's care; and we know scarce anything of how the first ten childish years were passed. But who shall say how much the impressionable nature of the boy was moulded by what he saw and heard around him? His father's house in town was a place of festivity and fashion. Life among the higher classes of society in Dublin was not perhaps more volatile or voluptuous than in other capitals. But with the exception of the enthusiasm for the culture and practice of music, there was little to redeem it from the character of frivolity: and we know that, when looking back after an interval of half a century upon the days of his bringing up, the statesman sighed to think how few advantages of mental training he had enjoyed in his early home. In winter time the family residence was Merrion Street,[1] near the lawn of Leinster House, where Arthur, destined to fill even a greater place in history than his eldest brother, came into the world.

But the long summer tide and perhaps still more enjoyable autumn, were spent by the little lord—for he was about the smallest Viscount in the realm—on the pleasant uplands of the Boyne; rambling in the dells and woods of Dangan, and casually on pony-back loitering to the preparatory school at Trim, where he learned as little as the delicate son of a fine gentleman might be expected to do. His after recollections of the period are but too reproachful of his parents' negligence, although there is not a word indicative of unkindness on the part of either.

Within the park-gates all bespoke the lavish ways of luxury: without, everything the penury of serfhood and the misery of squalor. Could a susceptible nature be unaffected by the contrast, all the more because unconsciously, or by the daily and hourly lesson it taught of the ineffable disparity of caste and creed? A boy does not philosophise or reason about such things; but ever, as in Lacedæmon, in Venice, in Virginia till the other day, imbibes impressions and ideas of unspeakable superiority to the subject community amid whom he dwells, and whom he takes for a type of the bulk of mankind. Everywhere the goodlooking, quickwitted firstborn of a noble house is immeshed in the wiles of adulation; but nowhere more so than in Ireland even to-day: what then must it have been a century ago?

His next brother William,[2] being two years younger,

---

[1] The house afterwards became the property of the Miltown family, and eventually was purchased for the office of the Ecclesiastical Commission.

[2] Born 1763: adopted by a relative named Pole, for some years representative of Trim, subsequently Chief Secretary for Ireland and created Earl of Maryborough.

was only beginning to be companionable when their father made up his mind that Richard should be sent to Harrow. His then only sister Anne and his younger brother Arthur were still in the nursery: and though the English school was a long way off and he knew that all around him would at first be strange, the boy had self-control enough even before eleven to disdain the suspicion of regret at quitting home. The Diocesan School of Meath sufficed for the younger members of the family. The building formed a portion of the old Castle of Trim, where Lord Deputy Talbot liked to rest in the intervals of his campaigns in France. The repute of the county academy for discipline or learning has not survived, but probably it was fortunate for himself and for his country that Arthur was not suffered too long to linger there.

For some years the musical Earl continued to hold his honorary professorship in the University of Dublin, delivering annually a course of lectures on vocal and orchestral harmony, said to have been attended by well-bred votaries of the art. During this period he published the catch, ' 'Twas you, Sir,' and several glees and madrigals that caught the popular ear. But it was not until a somewhat later period that he entered into competition with the best writers of vocal music in England, and justly earned a considerable reputation. Among his best glees were, ' What is life and all its pride?' ' See, the bowl sparkles;' ' Hail, hallowed fane;' ' Come, fairest nymph;', ' When for the world's repose;' and ' Here in cool grot,' which in 1779 won the gold medal. Of his madrigals, ' As it fell upon a day;' ' Come, shepherds, come away;' and ' Orpheus with his lute,' are perhaps the best remembered.

Either from a falling off in the attendance at his lectures or a sense of weariness not inexcusable at the restraint upon his otherwise complete freedom of artistic whim, he resigned his office, which for some time remained consequently vacant. As a member of the English Madrigal Society, and the old Glee Club, he cultivated the society of Mr. Lock and Dr. Callcott, vieing with Lord Sandwich and other persons of quality in kindly and useful sympathy with younger followers of the profession. A good deal of his time was spent in London, and he continued indefatigably to compete with professional and amateur composers for honourable distinction, and not unfrequently with cheerfully acknowledged success.

Richard went to Harrow in 1770, where he chiefly distinguished himself as forward in the memorable barring-out of a new head master Dr. Heath, because he was an Etonian, and therefore in Harrovian eyes an intruder and usurper. Daniel Roderick, one of the assistant-masters, wrote a full account of the affair.[1]

On the death of Dr. Sumner in September 1771, Samuel Parr who stood next in authority by general consent of his colleagues and pupils, offered himself for the vacant post. He was but five-and-twenty and as he had not taken his M.A. at Cambridge the governors objected to his want of standing, in preference leaning to Mr. Heath. The upper form considered it as an indignity to have an Eton assistant put over them when they had in their own school a person of superior learning; and a petition well drawn up and signed by every boy in the school, was presented to the governors on the subject. Dr. Bucknell's carriage was dragged from the inn yard and completely demolished, and Roderick had difficulty in dissuading some of the mutineers from breaking the windows of Mr. Horn, one of the governors, for which they had armed themselves with stones. Parr who believed that his real disqualification was a vote he had given for John Wilkes in Middlesex, made no secret of his sense of the injustice done him. He threw up the place

[1] Johnstone's *Life of Dr. Parr*, i. p. 58.

he had occupied with great credit for five years previously, and opened a school of his own at Stanmore, to which forty of his pupils followed him. Many more quitted Harrow without leave, not caring to face the retributive wrath of successfully vindicated authority. Heath called on their parents to send them back for exemplary chastisement. The tiny but intrepid insurgent returned to Dangan, where his mother tried her best to look shocked at his incorrigible impenitence, but shrunk from recommending that he should be delivered over to the tormentors: and his father though not given to Whig notions of discipline, agreed that he should be transferred to Eton, where speedily forgetting the jealousy out of which the strange affray had sprung, he soon grew happy and studious, and learned to love the place with a fervour savouring of romance that burned undimmed to his dying day. The election of Heath and the subsequent disturbance took place October 3, 1771.

Having by his own account profited very little by any previous teaching, he was fortunate enough to fix the attention and win the attachment of a youthful compatriot three or four years older than himself, but who remained long enough at the college to render him inestimable service. John Newport was the son of a Waterford gentleman, of small fortune but of good standing and public spirit, whose chief ambition was to see his son occupy a higher station than his own, and qualified for sustaining it. From childhood he had shown much facility in acquiring knowledge, and later on the aptitude for imparting it to others with a persuasive force and grace which made him in maturer years the valued ally of influential and distinguished men. The new comer whose singular features rivetted his gaze, struck him as ill-suited for the rougher sports of his companions in the lower form, and as having in his look something of promise rarely seen, with all the weakness and waywardness of a spoiled child. At home he had been made to learn nothing and to obey nobody. He was sensitive, passionate, and full of the self-importance which the eldest-born in the country-house of an Earl is pretty certain to acquire when left to the companionship of hangers-on and the flattery of servants. Luckily for him he happened to be Newport's fag, and in this relationship his shortcomings and the signs of good that was in him became daily noticeable; and then began that transformation of his mental nature which, as he himself loved to tell, was the foundation of all his subsequent success in life.

'Under Mrs. Young's great tree at Eton the brotherhood, for such it truly was, of Wellesley, Grenville, and Newport commenced, lasting undiminished through every vicissitude of political life, and still subsisted vigorously in the declining years of the survivors—proof against the estrangement usually created by elevation in rank and remoteness of removal.'[1]

Looking back at this period after the long fight of life was done, wherein he achieved much more than most of his contemporaries, he gratefully laid at the feet of Newport, as the founder of his public character, the credit of it all. The letter in which he asks his early guide and life-long friend to recount to him all that he remembers of the time they passed at Eton, is almost feminine in tenderness. There is in it that dash of romance and morbid egotism which is traceable throughout his whole career; and which unquestionably was the frequent source of unhappiness and error.

'You found me an idle boy, and by your instruction and example I was made diligent and studious, and inspired with that glorious passion for solid fame, that noble ambition to obtain power and honour by deserving them, which has been my " star of Arcadie," my " Tyrian cynosure," through my

[1] From Sir J. Newport, 23rd March, 1840.

long and active life, which has raised me to a station impregnable by slander, malice, or faction. I acknowledge this—I am proud to acknowledge it, and I have everywhere and on all occasions boasted that to you I owe the foundation of my public character.'

The closing words are curious:—' You must remember that you accompanied me from Eton to Dangan Castle, the seat of my ancestors, where you passed some time with my father and mother; alas! frivolous and careless personages, like most of the Irish nobility of that time. You taught them to respect me and my literary pursuits, and to encourage me in the career of honour and glory to which you had first directed my steps. You were to me what my father might have been:

> Tu, pater! es rerum inventor; tu patria nobis
> Subpeditas præcepta.

Be assured that I can never forget my duty towards you.'[1]

Ere he left Eton he had mastered the difficulties of Greek; and Goodall, one of his contemporaries, used to recall his rare facility in Latin verse, in which he thought him infinitely superior to Porson.[2]

He was a frequent contributor to the 'Musæ Etonenses,' where his first ambitious effusions are preserved. In metrical balance and the collocation of sweet-sounding syllables they may still be read with pleasure: for was he not born with music in his soul, and was not every childish memory linked with warbled cadence or with choral hymn? To the end he was wont to marshal all his words and thoughts in processional harmony. At Christ Church, where he matriculated in December 1778, he pursued his studies during three years.

---

[1] Letter to Sir J. Newport; Kingston House, Knightsbridge, 28th February, 1840.

[2] Evidence of Dr. Goodall, head master of Eton, before Education Committee of House of Commons in 1818.

His tutor William Jackson, afterwards Bishop of Oxford, urged him to compete for the prize in Latin hexameters, which he won in 1780, the subject being the death of Captain Cook. Among his class fellows, not a few of whom in after life rose to eminence, the diligent and dainty *filius nobilis* was less of a favourite than a competitor open to criticism and banter for his pretentious bearing; but he was more than compensated by the praise of friends whom he had the faculty of attaching in a singular degree. Of these in every way the most notable was William afterwards Lord Grenville.

How soon far-off scenes of public excitement fired his youthful curiosity and ambition cannot certainly be known; but they were made more real, one can imagine, by the older aspirations and conjectures of Newport, and the glimpses of political life caught through the companionship of Grenville, who had stories to tell about Lord Chatham and wistful anticipations of what his cousin William Pitt might do in Parliament. But vacations spent at Dangan did not abound in stimulants to exertion, and though at his father's house in Dublin he met men of legal reputation like Burgh and Yelverton, or of growing popularity like Brownlow, Gardner, and Grattan, there is no reason to suppose that the little Viscount, equally proud of his good looks and prize verses, cherished any idea of precipitate immersion in the struggle and fray of public controversy in Ireland. The state of affairs in that land of chequered fortune during his sojourn at Oxford was indeed hard to comprehend, even by those who were most conversant with it.

Rumours of American privateers hovering on the coast had prevailed in 1777, but were treated with official disdain: and when nothing came of the supposed peril the defenceless towns went asleep again, and the populace laughed at the scare. But when in April 1778, Paul Jones appeared in the Channel, and landing at Whitehaven, where a crowd of merchantmen lay at anchor, levied a heavy ransom, spiked the guns in the fort, and next day fought and took the sloop 'Drake' of twenty guns, affairs looked more serious: and anxious inquiries were made of Government by the few who in those days had access to authority, as to the means of resistance available at the outports should the dreaded rover swoop down upon them. Next year reinforced from Brest, he again swept the Channel, making prey of not a few merchantmen and menacing now and then troop and store-ships as they crept along the shore. On September 24, 1779, he attacked the Baltic fleet sailing under convoy off Flamborough Head, and took the 'Serapis' and 'Countess of Scarborough' after a sharp encounter, bearing them as prizes into the Texel; thence he again issued in December, and spread once more the terror of his name along the southern coast.

During the year amateur soldiering went on throughout the greater part of Ireland; Government not venturing to be nice in the sanction given to its spontaneous organisation. Every county had its regiment, of which the most popular proprietor was by acclamation chosen colonel, and the leading gentry officers. Some counties had several corps; and the towns and cities were not backward in furnishing their quota. Lord Charlemont took the initiative in the movement and by common consent was named commander; and the enthusiasm spreading he found himself ere long the elected general of a self-enrolled militia of from 80,000 to 100,000 men. As the war went on, most of the regular troops were sent beyond sea to succour the outnumbered armies of the King, daily harder pressed by the French and American forces under Rochambeau and Washington, until at last little more than six thousand regulars were left in Ireland. Charlemont loyally made the tender of his unpaid levies to take their place in the performance of garrison duty. The Viceroy muttered thanks, hesitated to refuse, and wrote for definite instructions to Whitehall,—instructions which never came.

The first fruits of the unlooked-for condition of things which had thus arisen was the exaction in Parliament of important concessions long demanded in vain. The tariff of exports and imports imposed by the English legislature by virtue of Poynings' law had but one purpose, namely to crush any attempt at commercial competition on the part of the weaker country. No disguise was affected in the purpose, and no scruple in the rigour of the repressive means employed. Flood, after some years of opposition, had entered the Viceregal Cabinet in the hope of effecting by expostulation in council some mitigation of the injustice under which his country pined; and he consequently incurred the distrust of his best friends, and no little obloquy out of doors. Conviction of the futility of his attempt was hastened by the unlooked-for resort of the community to arms, and resigning his office of Vice-Treasurer he resumed his former place as head of the popular party in the Commons. Meanwhile a younger and showier aspirant to pre-eminence in that assembly, whom he himself had helped to bring into notice, began to assert the magic power of an eloquence singularly adapted to fascinate an excitable and imaginative people. Flood would have hardly admitted to himself that he could be jealous of Grattan; yet jealous he certainly became; and their subsequent rivalry exercised no doubt a baneful influence over the cause which both of them sincerely had at heart. Both, however, in 1779 contributed materially to wring from the administration of Lord North a measure of commercial freedom which opened the trade with the Colonies and the Continent to Irish enterprise; and which, from its novel and specious sound, an inexperienced people without capital, shipping, or habits of business, fancied would prove a charter of national employment and wealth.

Dublin illuminated; Cork and Waterford were full of joy; and Belfast and Derry counted up beforehand how much they had to be thankful for. Grattan elated with his share of the triumph, and with a notoriety easily and pleasantly earned, pressed eagerly forward and urged, as did many others, the demand for legislative independence. Flood, who was not easily carried away, would fain have gone more slowly, and have tried to consolidate year by year the advantages gained and likely to be gained. But the course of events in America and the decrepitude of the administration in England put caution out of countenance, and wrought men of all parties and dispositions to a pitch of panic, hope, and venture, in which anything and everything seemed possible and practicable. Disaster followed disaster to the royal arms abroad; and when the last reserves in garrison were withdrawn for America, Charlemont by desire of the chief men in the Volunteer army, waited on the Viceroy to tender once more their services as a mobilised force for the maintenance of the State.[1] Ere the offer could be formally accepted, tidings came of Cornwallis's surrender with 7,000 men to Washington and Rochambeau at York Town. Humbled and paralysed, Government had no longer the nerve to maintain a tone of administrative dignity, and betrayed its inability to resist further concessions. Grattan sat down to draught a Bill of Rights, and Flood to mature a limited Mutiny Bill for Ireland on the English model. Such was the strangely exceptional condition of things in which the young Oxonian found himself suddenly called on to take a part.

Lord Mornington had never been a politician, and he continued throughout life absorbed in measures of music rather than measures of State. Attendance in the Irish House of Lords was simply to him a bore. Society in London had long had paramount attractions, and he passed a consider-

[1] September 1781.

able part of every year in town. He was living at Kensington in the spring of 1781, occupied chiefly in completing his last compositions, 'Bacchus, sprightly god of wine,' and 'Gently hear me, charming maid,' when he was seized with an illness which in a few weeks proved fatal. Richard was summoned from Christ Church to his father's death-bed, and by his decease on May 22, 1781, he became Earl of Mornington. He was scarce of age when he was thus called away from collegiate studies and associations to enter upon the responsible duties of life.

The first act of the young peer was to devolve the management of the family estate to his mother. Heavy encumbrances absorbed a great portion of the rental, and for the younger children scant provision had been made. His brother Arthur seems to have been the object of his chief domestic care: the school at Trim could do little to fit him for the profession to which he was destined; so at twelve years old he was sent to Angers, then a place of high repute for military training. Mornington continued to reside with his mother and sisters for some time, first at Dublin and afterwards in London.

The Irish House of Lords had ordinarily little to attract a young man of quick temperament and good parts. The chamber, somewhat Venetian in its quiet gloom, was about thirty feet in width by forty feet long; the roof supported by Corinthian columns, and the walls on each side hung with tapestries recording the civil conflicts of Derry and the Boyne. Of the Irish peers one-half dwelt in England, where their estates chiefly lay; and of the residents in Ireland comparatively few, except the bishops and the occupants of the judicial bench, were ever seen within its portals. Some twenty great proprietors came on particular occasions to record their votes or to qualify themselves to act by proxy; and some half-dozen of the needier sort found it a convenient place to make themselves troublesome or useful to the Castle. But as a national senate there was an air of unreality about its whole proceedings, which resembled usually those of a select committee when real business was doing, or of a fashionable debating club where the members quoted Latin and waxed loud in bag-wigs and swords. He took the oaths and his seat at the beginning of the most memorable session of Parliament held in Ireland since that of Kilkenny under the last of the Stuarts. For generations the provincial legislature had been exclusively sectarian and submissively subordinate. Molyneux, Swift, and Lucas had striven hard, but striven in vain, to stir in the nobles and gentry a sense of the humiliation of their class and country. But not until one of themselves began to mutter aloud words of mutiny could even a few of them be persuaded that an independent Parliament might, and if it could, should and ought to make laws, levy taxes, and call ministers to account in Ireland. It took Henry Flood five years to mature his plans of legislative revolt, and to organise a party capable of attempting it. Beyond the exaction of a right of free trade with the Colonies, which the tottering administration of Lord North was fain to yield in 1779, even Flood in the one House and Charlemont in the other did not venture to insist. But before America had won her independence in fair fight Ireland was almost denuded of troops, and her defence was left to self-organised corps of Volunteers. An unlooked-for opportunity seemed to have come. From the lips of Grattan a voice as the breath of the whirlwind broke forth, the like of which courtiers or country gentlemen had never heard before. Even the subject multitude, disfranchised and hitherto dumb, caught up the echoes and made as though they too would speak. Without money to buy, or troops to bully, or talents to cajole, Government had to give way; and the legislative freedom of Ireland was obtained.

CHAPTER III.

IRISH HOUSE OF LORDS.

1781–1783.

THE first trial of strength in the session of 1781-2 was on the Mutiny Act, which, contrary to the Revolution model, had heretofore been in Ireland perpetual, and which it was now proposed to make annual. But Government were strong enough in the Lords to resist the claim by forty-three to ten, the minority, as was the custom, protesting. It was on this occasion that young Mornington, at the instance of Grattan, was named by Charlemont, Opposition Whip in the Peers. One can easily fancy the pleasure his self-importance took in this early initiation into public business. What letters he wrote and what visits he paid to his luxurious and lazy but not very numerous party; how many reports of his doubts and perplexities he brought to Marino, and how profane were his denunciations of those who were missing when wanted, tradition fails to tell. It was one of his functions to have the best reasons ready in the best language, and in the best round hand for his out-voted friends to sign. At two-and-twenty what better could an Oxonian prizeman wish for than formulating in finest English a small State paper on some constitutional question? There is no mistaking the handiwork of the protest on the Mutiny Bill, which presents a full length portrait of patrician virtue in the manner of Vandyke. Six peers signed, and there were as many reasons as peers; all stepping daintily and with dignity, with every curl of wisdom and buckle of logic in due order; arguments keen and true as the rapiers they wore, and about as useless for any practical purpose.[1] They were dissentient, 'Because we hold it to be an essential principle of constitutional safety that Parliament should for ever retain in its own hands the power of creating, limiting, and controlling the army, since no other privilege or franchise can safely exist without recourse being had to the most desperate remedies if the absolute and uncontrolled power of the sword be lodged in the hands of the executive; and though it may be alleged that while Parliament retains the exclusive right of dispensing the public money for the creation and maintenance of the army, and of refusing such supplies as may be necessary for this purpose, no danger is to be apprehended on the part of the Crown; yet we conceive that in a matter of this momentous nature, where the essence of our rights and of our liberties is at stake, it is dangerously absurd to part with one defence merely because another remains in our possession, or wantonly to give up the strong important and tenable outworks of our constitution, from an idea, perhaps ill-grounded, of the security of its internal strength. We say perhaps ill-grounded because that, as in this kingdom His Majesty possesses an hereditary revenue, already dangerously considerable, and which like those maladies which grow upon our health and strength, must necessarily grow and increase in proportion to the prosperity and commerce of the country, it appears to us by no means impossible that at some future day the Sovereign may be in possession of finances so fatally extensive as to enable him to raise, or at least to subsist, a considerable army without having recourse to Parliament for any additional duties; not to mention that in an extreme, though improbable case,

[1] The signatures were—Westmeath, Arran, Mountgarret, Aldborough, Charlemont, and Mornington.

points may arise with respect to which the revenues of another country may be made subservient to the support of an army in this kingdom for purposes the most fatal to the constitution thereof. Our affection also for our sister kingdom, and our unalterable regard and watchful attachment to its rights and liberties, with which our own are so strictly interwoven, has concurred to induce us, with all our weight, to endeavour the limitation of a law which, in its present perpetual form, by enabling some future prince to make this country a place of arms, and to raise and maintain therein an uncontrolled and unconstitutional army, may endanger the liberty not only of Ireland but of Great Britain also.'

The fifth clause dealt with the ministerial suggestion that if two Mutiny Bills must be passed annually the Irish might at some time differ from the English, which was only met by the plea that as both required the royal assent the difficulty could not arise.

Clause 6 ran thus:—

' Because this last-mentioned argument, if such it can be called, only excepted, all the other reasonings which we have heard in behalf of the measure, have endeavoured no more than to prove that the Act in its present form is not pernicious, without pretending to show that it can be attended by any salutary consequence, or that a temporary law would not be preferable; so that at most, the perpetuating clause is, by those who support it, deemed unimportant; while on the other hand, we who have opposed it are determined in our belief, and have endeavoured to prove that it is fatally dangerous; an opinion in which we are joined by the people at large, whose minds are in the highest degree agitated upon this subject; a fact which we know to be true, and which is clearly evinced by the many instructions presented to their representatives in Parliament by the constituencies of this kingdom. Is it, then, reasonable or expedient that a measure deemed unimportant by those who support it, and which its warmest abettors have only endeavoured to prove inoffensive, should be so obstinately maintained against the fixed opinion of those who have loudly declared their apprehensions, and against the sense of a brave and loyal people agitated and alarmed by a firm persuasion that, from the consequences of this law in its present form, all that is dear to them is at stake? And ought not rather an unimportant point to be yielded and given up, in order to calm those fears, which to us appear but too well-founded, and to quiet the minds of the people?'[1]

It was natural that a long subservient oligarchy on the eve of revolt should look round anxiously for adherents and auxiliaries. They had won freedom for trade, and the traders were loud in their thanks; but manufactures would take time to revive and capitalists were few. The Bar were garrulous and enthusiastic at having something like constitutional realities to talk about instead of a mere caricature of legislative business: but politics with the Bar have always been too closely mixed up with promotion and profit; and the whole profession were but a small importunate throng of recruits waiting for party enlistment. But what of the outlawed nation,—not yet a century bereft of citizenship?

Some of the nobler and truer spirits of the dominant race were for Catholic enfranchisement, not only because it was right, but because it was the only means of establishing insular autonomy. How could national claims, if yielded, be realised into national possession, without a nation? Luke Gardner, a squire of good estate in Tyrone, asked leave to bring in a Bill permitting Catholics to vote at elections, which Grattan, Ponsonby, and Hussey-Burgh supported eloquently, but which was rejected by 145 to 56 on the advice of Flood. Charlemont, who understood the inveterate prejudices of his order only too well, thought the stirring of the

[1] 8th December, 1781. *Lords' Journals*, vol. v. pp. 249, 250.

religious question would irreparably mar the immature coalescence which was beginning to take place among all classes of the community.[1]

It is creditable to the sagacity and courage of Mornington that, with all his regard and reverence for his leader in the Peers, he was ready from the outset to avow his devotion to the great principle of religious liberty; and that throughout all the changes and vicissitudes of after life he remained unfaltering in his early faith.

A Bill to relieve Protestant Dissenters from various disabilities passed the Commons, but was warmly resisted in the Peers by the episcopal bench; and only carried by thirty-five to twenty-three—Mornington telling for the majority.[2]

Upon the fall of Lord North's administration, in March 1782, the Irish Whigs saw the opportunity had come for exacting guarantees of legislative independence. Charlemont, Yelverton, Flood, and Grattan pressed the claim with vehemence. The new Cabinet, through General Fitzpatrick and the Duke of Portland, tried fair words, and asked for time to consider. For a few weeks there were parleyings and negotiations; but at length Grattan gave notice that he would move the adoption of a Declaration of Rights. Lord Rockingham and his colleagues could not easily be made to understand how a body that had so long proved themselves so submissive and compliant, could have become informed by any genuine spirit of nationality. Even though they were in earnest, what mattered a minority of spendthrift nobles and commoners strutting up and down the corridors of their handsome Palaver-house, declaiming platitudes about inherent right and the insolence of Poynings' law, which the salaried or pensioned majority of their colleagues would not stay from dinner to hear? The example of America was indeed obvious

---

[1] Letter to Flood, 7th January, 1782.
[2] *Lords' Journals*, 3rd May, 1782.

and suggestive. But the insurgent Colonies were seven weeks off by sea, with a trackless back country behind them, and with French fleets and armies to foster their sedition. Ireland lay within sight of the paramount State; and so long as the Governor of Dublin Castle had 5,000 troops under a perpetual Mutiny Act at his command, and a viceregal civil list with a secret service fund at his disposal, who could seriously believe in the existence of an independent Irish party insisting on self-government? Fox had been too busy fighting his way into office in spite of the King, or losing his money at midnight play, to study the question; and even Burke, with all his universality of observation, was only fretted and vexed when Rockingham and Fitzwilliam looked anxious on receipt of letters from Ireland. In a fit of bureaucratic impatience he curtly wrote, 'Can no one stop that madman Grattan?' Mad indeed he was to all intents and purposes of corrupt and overbearing domination; for was he not in bewildering rhetoric challenging an old country, full of wealth, strength and freedom, to own the legislative equality of a pauperised realm whose soil had been confiscated, whose people decimated, whose franchises forfeited, whose church despoiled, and whose very revenues, such as they were, were in the hands of its rival? Nevertheless, Grattan, deaf to all dissuasives, finally fixed the day for bringing forward his memorable resolution. The Viceroy at the last moment sent him word that Government gave in; and instead of a fierce contention, courtiers and opposition assembled only to listen to a matchless song of triumph.

'Spirit of Molyneux, Swift, and Lucas, your genius has prevailed! Yesterday a province, I now salute a nation. I stand here with a letter of Henry and the charter of John, the aggregate opinions of the nobles of the land and all the passions of the people.' The extinguisher had taken fire, and the whole realm was wrapped in patriotic flame. For Grattan the enthusiasm was ineffable. He stood the central figure in a state of things incomprehensible by more staid communities, whose liberty has been accomplished step by step and not by a sudden breaking out from the twilight of subserviency into the dazzling morn of national day. It was a paroxysm of self-rule; but paroxysms are not lasting.

Grattan, still in early prime, was an object of special sympathy with the younger men of the day; and Mornington was one of his most fervent worshippers. At his father's house, during Oxford vacations, he had early become known to the great rhetorician, whose quivering lip, glittering eye, and quaint theatrical expression, fascinated him beyond measure, and who was not insensible to the admiration and sympathy of one so full of promise. He succeeded his father as colonel of the regiment of Volunteers raised at Trim; and for a time continued to take an active part in their musterings for parade or drill. But the inherent liability of a force so constituted to dislocation by the conflict of opinions social and political which prevailed around it, too soon grew manifest. Even in the heyday of triumph, when the future looked golden, it was not easy to preserve the rules of discipline. At a review of certain Leinster regiments in the Phœnix Park, their general sent an order to a light battalion to deploy, and wondered that it was not obeyed. The same direction was repeated by a second aide-de-camp; but the corps did not budge. Riding down the line, Charlemont demanded in person why his order had not been obeyed; and, piqued at the silent obduracy he could not understand, he was about indignantly to leave the ground, when a lance-corporal stepped from the ranks and respectfully exclaimed,— 'My lord, we mean no offence to you, but none of us happen to be on speaking terms with the colonel.' Greater perplexities were to come.

Flood had uniformly expressed grave and reasonable

doubts whether the simple repeal of the Act of George I. by the English Parliament, and the declaratory repudiation by the Irish Parliament of its overruling pretensions, brought the constitutional controversy to an end. The same power that had formerly chosen to assert paramount authority, and in an hour of weakness and embarrassment to revoke its assertion, might re-assert its injurious pretensions at some future day. Something more of specific renunciation on the part of Great Britain was needed to make the work of legislative emancipation complete. Mr. Walsh, a man of rare ability and learning who sat for the University, took the same view, and in a minority of four divided against a congratulatory address to the Throne, which pronounced all constitutional differences between the two countries to be at an end. Their foresight and warning of difficulties to come was ascribed to a jealous and grudging spirit by their sanguine colleagues; and Grattan who had been voted fifty thousand pounds in reward for his services, was impatient of cavil regarding them. Yet within a month of the declaration of legislative independence, Lord Mansfield gave judgment in the King's Bench at Westminster in a case which had some time before been brought by writ of error from one of the Irish Courts. Flood's misgivings seemed thus more than justified, and the cry arose that unless the old jurisdiction of conquest were formally renounced by Great Britain, the quarrel (as in America after the repeal of the Stamp Act) would break forth anew. Fox was indignant at the good faith of the Cabinet being distrusted. Ponsonby and Yelverton plausibly deprecated the expression of any doubt regarding the sufficiency of what had been done; and Charlemont, who was in the confidence of the Whig ministry, was angry at the distrust of their good faith, and wrote in a paroxysm of chagrin asking Flood what he was about, to inflame a groundless popular suspicion.[1]

[1] 28th June, 1782.

Grattan, irritated by an address of remonstrance from the Dublin Volunteers, threw up his colonelcy. From that day the fine gold of his popularity grew dim, while that of his great rival gradually regained its lustre. But at heart he and his friends were disquieted by the unrebuked re-assertion of appellate jurisdiction of the Courts at Westminster.

Early in the winter of 1782 Mornington visited London, and became the channel of several unofficial communications between men in power and their political supporters in Ireland. His letters to Grattan describe the state of parties at the opening of the session while negotiations for peace with America were still pending.

'I seize the first opportunity of offering my sincere congratulations to you upon the recovery of Miss Fitzgerald, which I heard of last night from O'Beirne. I have felt very anxiously both for your situation and hers; and believe me, nobody rejoices more thoroughly in the prospect of happiness, which the return of her health has opened to you both.

'I sent a hasty account of the first day's business in the House of Commons to Ogle; the debate was very uninteresting, and did not deserve to be particularised; since that day nothing has passed of any consequence. The report of a peace gains ground every hour; this morning it was believed to have been signed, and that Gibraltar was ceded for Porto Rico and Minorca. The cession of Gibraltar will be an unpopular measure; it was but hinted on the first day, and the very suggestion threw the House into a ferment. The language generally held is, that our successes in the last campaign entitle us to an honourable peace; and that if France should be unreasonable in her demands, the war must be prosecuted with vigour.

'The situation of the ministry seems to be very singular;

the number of their *devoted* friends is certainly inferior to that of their declared enemies; but their enemies are divided. Lord North's party are certainly the strongest in the House; but Lord North is equally averse to Shelburne and to Fox. Lord North's language is, that he will support Government as far as may be necessary for the strengthening of the nation's hands against foreign enemies; but that he will suffer no alterations in the constitution. You can easily conceive what a scene of confusion the contest between these three parties must afford—Fox, Lord North, and Pitt equally, and by turns, opposed to each other. As yet there has been no division in Parliament, so that I cannot with any accuracy state the numbers of these parties.

'Not one word has been said in debate upon Irish affairs; the subject is touched as you will see, very cautiously, both in the Speech and addresses.

'I have seen both the Duke of Portland and Fitzpatrick, and have from both received the most firm assurance of their intention, and that of Mr. Fox, to stand by the settlement of last session. I was just proceeding to mention the matter relative to Lord Mansfield and the Irish writ of error, when I received your obliging letter. I will give you as well as I am able under a total ignorance of law in general, the state of that business as it has been represented to me.

'The case had been, as I understand, entered for hearing before the time of the operation of the Irish Act, and it was by some accident delayed until this last term. The reason why it was not dismissed when it came before the Court, subsequently to the operation of the Irish Act, was that the time had elapsed for pleading against the competency of the Court, as pleadings had already begun upon the matter of the suit. The legal expression, I am told, is, that as the parties had already pleaded in chief, they could not afterwards plead to the writ. Now at the time the cause was entered, the Irish

Act had not passed, and therefore the objection to the competency of the Court did not exist at the only period when it could have been admitted, consistently with the practice of the Court. I do not know whether I have made myself understood, but what I have stated comprehends all that I have been able to collect upon the subject. I should observe that Lord Mansfield himself gave no sort of reason for his decision, but decided as a matter of course, without taking any notice of the particularity of the case. The argument I have alluded to was never touched by him. I think his silence alarming; and I do not think the reasoning I have stated at all satisfactory.'[1]

Some days later he wrote again to his friend.

'I conversed last night with Mr. Fox on this subject; he told me that when he was framing the repeal of the 6th of George I., he expressed doubts to the Attorney[2] and Solicitor General here, whether that Act would extinguish the appeal by writ of error to the King's Bench of Great Britain, unless there was an express clause for the purpose. He told me that both those great lawyers assured him that the simple repeal would utterly terminate all jurisdiction of the English courts of justice over Ireland. He seems now to think something further necessary, and to apprehend that Lord Mansfield could not have done otherwise than he did. I hold with you, that Lord Mansfield should have attended to the Irish law, which in reason ought to be paramount to the little forms of his Court. I should be very glad to know from you what remedy you propose for the extirpation of this sort of questions. I feel strongly the necessity of some future procedure, perhaps a bill here, declaring that the judicature is confined to Ireland and forbidding the inter-

---

[1] 9th December, 1782.
[2] Lloyd Kenyon, afterwards Lord Kenyon, and John Lee.

ference of the English Courts. You must see—and I think every man of common discernment in Ireland must see—that if Mr. Flood's Bill of Rights had passed in Ireland, and his Renunciation in Great Britain, this very case would still have happened; so that Mr. Flood has no reason to plume himself upon it as an example confirming his doctrine. I am just come from the House of Commons, where a hundred and ten thousand men have been voted for the navy this year; peace seems to become every hour more doubtful. Lord Shelburne cannot stand; everybody seems to be of this opinion; but who will succeed or what is to be the system, is dubious. The prevalent opinion is, that Lord North and the old party will return.

Yours sincerely,
MORNINGTON.'

Fiscal Acts had been passed since 1779 in England indirectly limiting the trade of Ireland; and Flood therefore brought in a bill asserting the sole and exclusive right of the Parliament of Ireland to make laws for that country, internal and external. Grattan strongly opposed it, and moved that to utter doubts of the supremacy of the Irish Parliament was inimical to the honour and welfare of both countries. But Fox, though he chafed and grumbled at the distrust shown of English good faith, introduced a measure to quench all further doubts regarding the constitutional parity of the two kingdoms;[1] and William Grenville seconded the motion, speaking from his observation of Ireland while Chief Secretary the year before.

During the brief administration of Shelburne, he had served in that capacity under Lord Temple; and Mornington lived much with his old class-fellow while he stayed in Ireland. It cannot be doubted that to the influence of

[1] January, 1783.

their friendship may be traced many of the changes in the personal history of both. Mornington continued to act under his old leaders in Ireland; but he soon began to look towards a different field of enterprise and ambition.

To appease in some measure the jealousy felt by the great Irish nobles at their almost invariable exclusion from the distinction of the Garter, George III. consented to institute a new order of knighthood equally limited in numbers. The first knight of St. Patrick was Edward Duke of Kent, and one of his nineteen brethren in heraldic arms was the already prominent though youthful lord of Dangan.[1] As might have been expected, the wounded self-love of those who were left out was far more active than the satisfaction of the comparative few who were preferred. One of the grand seigneurs who never alighted from a carriage drawn by fewer than six horses at the door of the House of Peers was the querulous and fantastic Lord Bellamont, who had fought a duel with Lord Townshend when Viceroy, for having turned his back on him in company. He was a man of considerable parts and great possessions, but among well-born coxcombs merited the title given him by Sir Hercules Langrishe of 'Vanity of Vanities.' He did not grudge the star of the Shamrock to Leinster or Inchiquin, Clanrickarde or Tyrone; but rivals of later creation moved him to exceeding wrath, and though Wesley and Colley traced a lineage more feudal than his own, he sniffed and scoffed at territorial revenues so far inferior, and at the grandson of a commoner being preferred to him. In reply to a speech of Mornington on moving an address to Earl Temple when quitting Ireland, he complained petulantly of the neglect which he and other persons of consequence had suffered in the choice of knights of St. Patrick. A sharp rejoinder promptly followed, which elicited a courtly disclaimer of offence, and averted

[1] By letters patent, 5th February, 1783.

the necessity of a personal encounter:[1] for the duty of sending and accepting a challenge on any occasion of affront in debate was a traditional Standing Order of Parliament on the other as on this side of the Channel, then and long afterwards.

Grenville writing to Temple in Ireland on the break up of the Shelburne Cabinet, frequently mentions young Mornington's name, and says: ' Pray communicate a little with him about your resignation; it will flatter him, and he is beyond measure disposed to you both in Ireland and *here*, to which he looks in a short time; but you must not let him know I have told you that.'[2]

Mornington spoke at length on the vote of thanks to Lord Temple, which he moved in the Irish House of Lords. He described the Act of Renunciation as having produced an instantaneous calm in Ireland. He specially dwelt upon Temple's administrative probity and energy in breaking up the evil system of corruption he had found in all branches of the Irish executive. He would appeal to those whose high stations and confidential offices gave them constant access to the person and councils of the Viceroy, to testify to his ability and assiduity in business, the extent of his researches, the vigilance with which he had penetrated into the secrets of departments, where the most gross rapine and peculation had been practised for ages with impunity, and particularly the firm integrity with which he resisted all jobs however speciously concealed or powerfully recommended.[3]

A further safeguard of independence was sought in a Bill requiring that in Ireland, as in England, Parliament should be summoned to meet every year. The measure was proposed by Lord Mountmorres, and supported by the subject of this Memoir.

---

[1] 23rd October, 1783.   [2] From Pall Mall, 27th March, 1783.
[3] Debate in the Irish House of Lords, 18th April, 1783.

Not a little perplexing to his friends was the conduct of Flood. As if unsatisfied with having obtained the Renunciation Act, and eager to secure his old ascendency as a party leader, or desirous of *rapprochement* with Pitt and those who had been left out of the Coalition, he sought to obtain a seat at Westminster. In September he visited the Duke of Chandos at Avington ; and for a sum of 4,000*l.* bargained for the influence of his Grace at Winchester, which was to be vacated for him previous to the ensuing session. He canvassed the borough in person, and lodged the money with an agent at Lincoln's Inn : returning to Dublin in October, in time to move for a reduction of the regular army on grounds of economy. It was then that the long gathering sense of mutual aversion between him and his illustrious rival broke forth in the terrible encounter of which the record is perhaps without parallel for condensed bitterness of reproach and sarcasm. As a ministerialist, Grattan sneered at a new-born zeal for economy hardly compatible with prolonged silence under a more prodigal administration. Flood boldly asserted that he had rendered his country more service in office than others had talked of doing who had never been there : and he recalled the fact of his resignation when his advice was neglected. Then scornfully alluding to the parliamentary grant to his assailant, he exclaimed : ' A man does not necessarily cease to be a patriot in office ; if he be true to himself and his country, he may be all the more a patriot for being there. I am the unpurchased friend of Ireland, and I will add of England, but I am not the bondslave even of my countrymen : I should not love the condition.' [1]

To the ever-pondering mind of Burke the idea of two

---

[1] In the published account of this memorable altercation the latter phrase does not occur, but it is to be found in the MS. report taken in shorthand for the Government of the day, and now in the State Library at Washington.

co-equal and co-ordinate Parliaments in the same realm seemed a mere solecism in terms;—a thing that in experiment must prove to be an illusion. He would not have had his countrymen make the rash attempt; but having made it, he would have had them rest and be thankful at the point of vantage gained; and set about the indispensable work of consolidating their strength and freedom by enfranchising all who professed and called themselves Christians. This would indeed have been the most effectual way to put bone and sinew into nationality, which without it, as the issue proved, was but an imposing phantom. Ponsonby, Hussey-Burgh, Yelverton, and Gardner were all zealous for the prompt enrolment of the bulk of the people to defend the claim of nationhood. In their hearts they felt that nothing less than this would do. But Flood, whose influence and experience outweighed all theirs, inexorably argued that with an independent Parliament, chosen by a preponderantly Catholic constituency, the dire feud of 1688 would be reopened; and that all the pride of England, political and religious, would be stirred to another life-and-death struggle for ascendency, in which Ireland must be inevitably not only beaten, but once more utterly crushed. 'I see my way,' he exclaimed, 'to Catholic constituencies; but who will answer for a Catholic House of Commons.' And Charlemont reluctantly went with him.

Flood felt, indeed, the perilous instability of the position. He would, in fact, have been content to let legislative emancipation come more gradually and less provocatively of the slumbering power of the paramount State. But events had hurried them all on faster and further than anyone had foreseen; and the question was, how to make the best of it. If religious equality could not be ventured on, what remained to fill the hollow panoply of nationalism with something like the vital forces of popular manhood? Nothing but Parliamentary reform. For this species of organic change there seemed to be rising on the eastern side of the Channel an unprecedented feeling. The Duke of Richmond pronounced for household suffrage, and Mr. Pitt on May 7 brought forward a scheme for diminishing the number of close boroughs and greatly extending the franchise in Great Britain. Why not move in parallel lines? The Volunteers, being chiefly Protestant in their regimental staff and in the bulk of their rank and file, would certainly prefer such a course to one which they were told would tend to subvert the Settlement of 1688, and which might eventually disquiet titles to the forfeited estates not yet a century old. Charlemont hesitated to embark in this new venture. He was ready, like others of patriotic spirit, to sacrifice his influence as a borough owner without compensation or compromise, in order to facilitate the restoring of the representation to its presumed original reality. But he feared the adoption of wild and subversive schemes by irresponsible delegates of armed corps; and he was persuaded to act as President of a Volunteer Convention for Reform chiefly to exclude a competitor who was believed to be eagerly ambitious of that station. A man like himself, of cultured taste and amenity of bearing, and one, from his peculiar position, commanding a degree of social influence little inferior to his own, was the noble and ir-reverend but energetic Lord Bristol Bishop of Derry, son of the minister whom Pope impaled on the epithet of Sporus. He was a man of undoubted talent and courage, but eccentric in disposition, dissolute in life, a sceptic at the altar, and insatiable of notoriety and applause.

Escorted by a brilliant staff, he rode from his palace at Downhill to Dublin, a distance of 120 miles, to attend the Convention of Delegates from the unpaid national army, which was more like a Polish Diet on the eve of electing a king than anything ever seen before or since within the Four

Seas. Lord Bristol urged that reform should include all creeds and conditions; a few supported him, and his faults and foibles were forgotten in the excitement of the hour; but his physical weakness disabled him from undergoing the fatigues of popular discussion. His counsel was rejected, and the guidance of the self-styled national assembly devolved on Flood.

Not all his reverence for Charlemont or his admiration for Grattan could blind Mornington to the usurping spirit of the movement. He kept Grenville informed by letter of each step in the proceeding; and was fortified by him in the conviction that at any risk of unpopularity it ought to be opposed.

After a certain show of deliberation the members of the Convention who happened to be members of Parliament undertook to present at the bar the demand for reform; and, true to the melodramatic spirit of the time, they walked in uniform, amid the cheers of an undoubting multitude from the Rotunda to College Green. Government, having for their spokesman Yelverton, then Attorney General, denounced the proceeding as an open attempt to overawe Parliament by presenting arms.

In the passionate interchange of threats and taunts, warnings and reproaches which ensued, Molyneux, Brownlow, Newenham, Parsons, O'Neil, Ogle, Curran, and Grattan supported the proposition, while Langrishe, Ponsonby, Fitzgibbon, and Wesley Pole—who had just been returned for the family borough—opposed it. 'I live,' said the member for Trim, 'in a part of the country where there are perhaps five hundred Volunteers; there has been a meeting for an address on this business; eleven people met and ten of them named me as their delegate. I refused to undertake the commission because I do not admit the necessity of any alteration in the existing system. I venerate the constitution which it is now attempted to subvert, and no man, how great soever his force of eloquence, can influence me to desert it. If this House should be so pusillanimous as to adopt this Bill, I thank Heaven I can go to a country where I can enjoy the liberties of Parliament; but first I will endeavour to support them here.'[1]

By 153 to 49 Flood was refused leave to bring in his Bill.

In the Upper House an attempt equally ineffectual was made to obtain consideration for the proposed scheme of reform. An address to the Crown, condemning the demeanour of the Convention as subversive of all semblance of legislative freedom, was warmly supported by many lords, spiritual and temporal, and by none with more animation than Mornington.

'This address comes from the Commons, and they desire your lordships to concur in it. The assembly of the Volunteers have sat for near three weeks with all the forms of Parliament; and will any noble lord say they have no intention to infringe the privileges of Parliament, and, perhaps, to compass the total extinction of the legislature? Have not both Houses of Parliament been surrounded by armed mobs; and will any man pretend to say, it is not time for this House to interfere? Can any noble lord, high in office though not in confidence, or any noble lord in confidence though not in office, not have a sense of the danger of the times, as the House of Commons seem to have? I am for this address, and upon this ground, that it offers to His Majesty a sufficient and necessary pledge of our loyalty and affection to his person and the constitution of the country; and to the people it speaks our firmness: for Parliament will not be robbed of its privileges, even by its own children; and we cannot for the sake of our posterity, suffer it. We

[1] *Irish Debates*, ii. 234.

ought to give Government our assistance when its instability may require it, to support the constitution. A great deal has been said relative to the Volunteers; there is no man that admires and respects them and reveres their services more than I do. Their past temper and moderation has made the greatest impression on my mind. But I am not blind to their imperfections when I find they have gone beyond the original idea of their institution. If the constitution is suffered to be infringed, I will not remain to be a witness of it, but leave the country. If the constitution is not supported, no body of people can be happy.'

Lord Mountmorres, with the ambition but without the ability to play a leading part, called the youthful Whip sharply to account for his Maccaroni airs and prematurity of tone.

'To all the big words and inflated expressions which I have heard, of danger to the constitution and insults from conventions of armed men, I answer in two short emphatic words— prove it. If formidable spectres portending the downfall of the constitution were to appear in this House, I admit the noble lord is frightened with a becoming dignity; the ancient Roscius or the modern Garrick could not start with better grace at the appearance of a spectre. But I, my lords, who am a plain man and of not so lively a fancy, cannot see them; and I have still to ask what these dangers are, or how fancy can torture into danger two respectable members of the other House of Parliament asking to bring in a Bill for the improvement of the constitution?'

At three-and-twenty it indeed required no little self-possession to oppose on such a question many of the ablest and best of his political friends: and it may be that even the approval of the Coalition Government would hardly have induced Mornington to take so vehement a part, had he intended to devote his time and attention exclusively to Irish parliamentary life. But already he was silently revolving other efforts and designs.

Men awoke to the danger of a military revolution narrowly escaped; the Convention adjourned [1] never to meet again; and the crazy Bishop of Derry went back by the way that he came, to scandalise his clergy by Voltairian jests and to amuse himself with inditing fantastical lampoons.

In reply there appeared some Conservative verses which ended with the couplet :—

> Motley Hervey, adieu; go home to your wife,
> And begin a reform of your own wicked life.

A gentleman who had in a certain degree acquired his confidence without sharing his erratic notions warned him that he had been placed under espionage by the authorities at the Castle, and that his favourite body-servant was in their pay. 'I have long been of the same opinion,' said the un-pious Prelate, smiling, ' and I write long letters from time to time which I give him to post for the purpose of bewildering the shabby sons of Ascalon.' But when the tide of sectarian nationality went down he grew tired of unnotoriety; and residence not being required of a pagan patrician who happened to be a bishop in those days, he emigrated to Rome, where he spent the residue of his days in the pursuits of a refined voluptuary.

The debate on reform over, Flood hastened to take his seat at St. Stephen's. Arriving late, and forgetting the fatigue of his journey, he was tempted without due preparation to speak on the second reading of Fox's India Bill,[2] which on constitutional grounds he condemned. The provincial pre-eminence in council and debate which he had long been used to find accorded him, misled him into the imprudent boast that he was unattached to any party, and that

---

[1] 1st December, 1783. [2] 3rd December, 1783.

he spoke no sentiments but his own. This was exactly what a House already tired of the best that could be said on both sides was disposed only to yawn or laugh at. When the fate of parties trembles in the balance and men are grown impatient for a decision, few care to ask what will this new babbler say; and when Mr. Courtenay (a fellow-countryman whom he had some years previously snubbed as counsel before a select committee) rose from behind Lord North to answer him, and proceeded with ready wit to ridicule his pretension to speak with authority self-derived, a good many on both sides laughed aloud : and the disappointed orator was constrained to own that he had made too free with his reputation. There was nothing for it but to return to Ireland and bide his time.

CHAPTER IV.

OLD ST. STEPHEN'S CHAPEL.

1784–1788.

MORNINGTON was already beginning to grow disenchanted with the vacillation and violence of provincial affairs when an opening occurred for his entrance on a wider and greater field of action. The overthrow of the Coalition and recall of Mr. Pitt to power enabled Grenville to suggest his class-fellow's name to his relative as an eligible adherent who might be attached by the offer of a seat at St. Stephen's. After some negotiations, the particulars of which would be hardly worth knowing if they could be exhumed, it was arranged to have him nominated as a representative for the Cornish borough of Beeralston. The village contained about forty houses, and under an old tree a court was yearly held to choose the port-reeve, and at election time the members to serve in Parliament. Three or four score inhabitants were endowed with the nominal rights of burgage tenure, which they were expected to renounce after each election. Without local interest arising from family connection, landed property or trade, a young man of ability, however great, had no chance, a century ago, of gaining admission to the House of Commons except through the quiet postern of a close borough; and even men who had attained legislative eminence sometimes preferred, after a Parliament or two, this way of re-entrance, to the more costly and troublesome one that lay through the uproar, treating and corruption of a contest for votes at the open poll.

William Grenville, with whom the sympathies of ambition rather than temperament bound him in maturing ties of friendship, was a near relative and confidant of Mr. Pitt, and by him he was personally made known to the youthful Chancellor of the Exchequer, on whom the eyes of men were set in curious expectation. From the outset it was observable, if not at the time observed, how the instinct of self-reliance prompted the aspiring son of Chatham to look for friends among men of his own age rather than amongst his elders and betters in political experience, to whom his unbending spirit would not suffer him to affect a deference he did not feel. In his cousin's class-fellow he saw much that he coveted as an adherent —youth, presence, culture, energy, talent, fortune less than he wanted, and, above all, freedom from the ties and prejudices of rival parliamentary connections. By birth and bringing up a Whig, Pitt was ready to serve under Shelburne as a King's friend; or when his bark foundered, to be captain himself of a mixed Tory and Whig crew. Mornington was just the man for him, and on learning his wish for a seat at Westminster, while retaining his place at College Green, he induced Lord Beverley to nominate him at the general election of 1784. Like Flood he was returned as a burgess to serve in the Parliament of Great Britain.[1]

Other men whose fortunes could bear the cost, and whose bodily strength the fatigue, had sat in both Parliaments at the same time; but they were comparatively few, and chiefly to be found among the younger Irish peers, who, finding no political career before them in their own country, availed themselves of their eligibility as commoners in England to seek admission to the representative chamber at Westmin-

[1] 1784.

ster. Such were Lords Ossory and Ongley, who sat for Bedfordshire, Lord Down for Petersfield, Lord Middleton for Whitchurch, Lord Galway for York, the Earl of Tyrconnel for Scarborough, the Earl of Inchiquin for Richmond, Lord Palmerston for Boroughbridge, the Earl of Lisburn for Cardiganshire, Lord Milford for Haverfordwest, Lord Melbourne for Luggershall, Lord Hood for Westminster. But none of these were at the trouble of crossing the Channel to take the oaths and their seats in the provincial senate, even to qualify themselves for voting by proxy. Their residences, and for the most part their properties, were in England, and a passage which in bad weather sometimes lasted several days was in itself a consideration with most of them in declining the performance of a duty whose obligation they would probably have regarded as rather a dull joke. But Mornington, full of the elasticity of youth and of eagerness for distinction, was only too glad to turn opportunities to account ; and he readily gave up winter days and nights of tedious travel to the discharge of his twofold legislative functions.[1]

Flood again brought forward his scheme of Reform in the Irish representation, hoping for support from Pitt's friends, who were pledged to all its principles. But a majority as great as before refused to consider the question, though means were taken to keep out of sight or hearing reference to Volunteer arms. The effect was seen in public meetings petitioning the King to dissolve Parliament, broaching projects of Catholic enfranchisement, and at last proposing an elective congress to sit in Dublin to consult for the public welfare. The Lord Lieutenant, in July 1784, refused his sanction to the Dublin petition to the King, and in September the minister told the Belfast petitioners that though still for reform he thought their

---

[1] Leave of absence to Lord Mornington, leaving his proxy, 18th December, 1783. Protested against postponement of Bill disqualifying revenue officers at elections, 22nd July, 1782. *Irish Lords' Journals.*

scheme would create greater evils than those they sought to remedy. Soon afterwards Lord Charlemont refused to acquiesce in a vote of the Ulster Regiments in favour of emancipation. The Attorney General warned the sheriffs not to hold elections for congress under threat of criminal prosecution. Meetings were held and delegates chosen without the authority of the sheriffs, and strong denunciations passed of the conduct of Government. Mr. H. S. Riley, high sheriff of the county of Dublin, having called a meeting of freeholders to instruct their delegates, was attached in the King's Bench, fined 3l. 6s. 8d., and imprisoned for a week. The magistrates of Roscommon and Leitrim were indicted by *ex officio* information, with the printers and publishers of the journals who circulated resolutions. Regardless of these measures, on January 2, 1785, the representatives of twenty-seven counties and ninety cities and towns— 200 in number—assembled; and sat by adjournment till April 20; and on May 12 their Bill, which left all details of reform to the judgment of Parliament, was once more brought in by Flood, and again rejected.

Meanwhile the failure of the free-trade enactments of 1779 to call up industry like Jonah's gourd, had caused ignorant belief that the previous long want of employment was owing to the import of British manufactures; and an agitation ripening at length into tumult and disorder arose, by which it was hoped that exclusive consumption of linen fabrics and the imposition of preferential duties amounting to prohibition might be exacted from the Irish Parliament. Disinterested and humane men like Mr. Gardner imagined that by adopting in vague generality the ideas of the populace, they might avert other movements and direct the storm. But their spells of rhetoric and evasion would work no charm either on ministry or mob; and the only apparent result of the outcry was a counterblast of Protection from the manufacturing towns of England, where the exclusion of Irish linens worth 1,500,000*l.* a year, was sturdily demanded.

Pitt, having done with Electoral Reform, took up instead the notion of commercial union. He had read Adam Smith and listened to Dr. Price until, in theory, he had become a free-trader before his time; and persuaded, no doubt sincerely, that a fiscal union of the three kingdoms would lay broad and solid foundations of imperial prosperity, he set about devising a plan of reciprocal relaxations of duty, having in view the ultimate extinction of prohibitory and even of preferential duties, and the placing his improved system by legislation completely beyond the reach of transient gusts of popular jealousy on either side of the Channel.

In the session of 1785 ministers essayed to carry what they designated as a commercial treaty regulating the fiscal relations of the two kingdoms; but which, from the necessity of the case, was in fact a Customs Bill, acquiring the sanction simultaneously of both legislatures. Eleven resolutions, professedly framed to secure to Irish commerce freer competition with that of England on terms of reciprocal advantage only, were hastily adopted on the recommendation of Mr. Orde, who filled the office of Chief Secretary. And to the English Commons, they were explained by Mr. Pitt, as forming a basis of mutual prosperity, and as tending to draw closer the ties of intercourse and friendship between communities heretofore estranged by complicated tariffs.

On February 7 Mr. Orde brought forward his eleven resolutions, which after some criticism were adopted. No picture of Eldorado glistened with light so golden as that wherewith he laboured to allay the fears of English competition. Foreign trade would, through mere geographical necessity, flow through the western isle, and 'Cork would become the emporium of the empire.' Liverpool and Bristol took the alarm, and asked to be heard by counsel at the bar. Political economy had yet but few disciples, and Fox and North raised a storm of opposition out of doors by their protestations that English commerce and manufactures were in danger of being sacrificed to the free-trade fantasies of Adam Smith and Dr. Price. The representatives of great towns urged innumerable objections in detail; and in the attempt to meet or mitigate their force, the minister yielded on so many points, and added so many provisoes, that the eleven resolutions became twenty-two, and the Opposition leaders revelled in raillery at the practical inexperience shown by their inexpert rivals. Fox taunted ministers [1] with the allegation of their Irish Chief Secretary, who, though in London some days before, had prudently kept away from the House in which he had a seat, lest he should have either to repudiate or avow the phrase.

After many discussions and divisions the twenty-two resolutions were carried by large majorities in both Houses, and finally passed on July 25. Leave was then given to bring in a Bill; but no progress was attempted to be made until the acquiescence of the Irish Parliament had been secured.

One of the changes made in the scheme, in a vain attempt to appease English jealousy, was a permanent appropriation of the surplus territorial revenue accruing to the Crown in Ireland, which was to be devoted to the maintenance of the Navy. Fox denounced this as a covert resumption of the power on the part of the English Parliament to tax Ireland; and when the altered scheme was laid before the Irish Commons, late in the session, parties broke their ranks and habitual supporters of Government coalesced with Opposition. Grattan and Flood agreed to bury in oblivion their past differences, and at the eleventh hour the success of the project seemed to be in danger. Mornington, who was

[1] Debate, 12th May, 1785.

becoming more and more attached to Pitt, wrote to Grattan from Stratford Place, June 20, 1785:—

'I was very sorry to see by the papers, that you had found it necessary to take so strong a part against the propositions, the more so as I cannot, after a very attentive consideration, discover how they affect the rights of Ireland as established in 1782. It would give me infinite pain to differ from you on so important a question, but I declare I cannot discern the danger you seem to apprehend. I am persuaded that the administration here never had the invasion of the independence of Ireland in contemplation, and I know that they are disposed to give every consideration to any doubts which you may entertain, and to remove your difficulties if possible. I should be happy to receive your opinion, and to know in what part of the propositions you see a subversion of Irish right. The question is of the first magnitude, and most materially concerns the peace of both countries; those whose object is to disturb that peace have expressed themselves with the greatest triumph in consequence of your speech, and are now endeavouring to turn it to purposes which I know must ever be remote from your mind. Pray let me have the pleasure of hearing from you soon. The propositions are now with the Lords, and likely to remain there till the end of this month. Pray give my best compliments to Mrs. Grattan. My brother desires his to you and her. We intend to come to Ireland with the propositions.

Believe me, dear Grattan,
Yours most sincerely,
Mornington.'

Plausibly Mr. Orde endeavoured to persuade the Irish Commons to regard their previous vote of February as but the ground plan of a work matured at Westminster, and still subject to their approval or rejection; but which they could best examine and modify by adopting the twenty-two English resolutions into which their original eleven had been commuted, and allowing him to bring in the Bill embodying them as it had been passed in England.

'The two nations acting in good temper and good faith, should proceed to draw closer the bonds of union, and if it were possible that anything he had introduced into the Bill could be interpreted as trenching on the freedom and independence of Ireland, he declared that he had no authority for doing so; on the contrary, were he to do so he would be acting against authority.'[1] 'From the revolution which had taken place in commerce and politics by the establishment of the American States, it had become necessary to draw the bonds of union between Great Britain and Ireland as close as possible. By a rivalship in trade, both countries would be injured; foreigners only could profit or rejoice. The resolutions therefore were framed upon the grounds of promoting the interest of the two countries, as of one united empire; to open each country to the other; to remove the prohibitions which the jealousy of England had established in order to keep her trade to herself; to form a scale of equal benefits and admit Ireland to every advantage which she enjoyed. In a word, that each country should prefer the other to all the world beside.'[2]

But the grounds on which the alteration had been made at Westminster were not to be mistaken. By constructive words deftly interpolated, a complicated harness was sought to be imposed on the foreign trade conceded or extended six years before. No share in this was in future to be claimed by Irish merchants, but upon conditions of port dues and abstinence from infringement upon the chartered privileges of the East India and other Companies, which

[1] *Irish Debates*, v. 331. [2] *Irish Debates*, v. 340.

virtually amounted to maritime monopoly. It would be a perpetual money bill, granting to the Crown the hereditary revenues now subject to local control.

Ponsonby and Grattan assented. Flood, who had been reproached with being in a minority of one in opposing the scheme, exulted in the numbers who finally came to oppose it.

At Westminster the 'Propositions,' for opening and regulating the trade between England and Ireland, were still vehemently though ineffectually opposed by the Opposition. In the protracted debates on this subject Mr. Eden took a prominent part, and by his knowledge of finance, and the skill and temper he displayed, gained the applause of the House of Commons and the confidence of the merchants and manufacturers, who were violently opposed to Mr. Pitt's measures. The Minister persisted and was sanguine of success.

While the issue was still doubtful Mornington and his brother, on their way from London to take their respective parts, as they believed, in carrying the ministerial plan through its last stage, were delayed by contrary winds in the Channel. Among their fellow-passengers was Mr. Woodfall, who asked if Lord Muncaster and other Irish peers who leaned to the Treasury Bench were going over likewise. 'The Earl said, "Oh no, you will see that we want no recruits."[1] So little was the event expected in Downing Street. They arrived in time for the debate, in which Newenham, O'Neil, and Curran denounced the modified proposal as an ill-concealed departure from the terms of reciprocity offered six months before. Flood more than ever proved his superiority in practical acquaintance with all the industrial interests of the country which he argued were about to be sacrificed under a specious show of equal dealings. Grattan tore to pieces the ambiguous stipulations

[1] Letter from Dublin (16th August, 1785) to Mr. Eden.

of the so-called treaty shred by shred, but relied chiefly on the constitutional objection suggested by Fox, that it would work a defeasance of the financial severalty and commercial freedom lately guaranteed to Ireland. The good faith of national equality would be broken if the greater country was to prescribe and the lesser to obey. The scheme in its development was but 'a contrivance for raising in Ireland an imperial revenue, to be subscribed by her Parliament without its consent, and in despite of her people.' Wesley Pole charged the Opposition with flinging away offers of closer connection, and with pointing the way to separation.

At the close of a sitting which lasted seventeen hours, Government only obtained 127 to 108 votes in favour of bringing in the Bill. This being equivalent to a defeat, its further consideration was postponed to a future day—a day which never came. Woodfall met Mornington soon afterwards behind the throne in the House of Lords, and had some conversation with him on the subject. He owned 'the extreme surprise he felt at the fate of the resolutions, and said he thought matters wore a most gloomy aspect in Dublin;'[1] so early had the fine gold become dim which he had had himself a hand in burnishing. Before returning to England, in acknowledgment of his fidelity to the cause of Government, he was admitted to a seat in the Irish Privy Council.

His first speech in the House of Commons[2] was brief and ineffective, and was delivered in reply to Lord North, who as minister had defended the reappointment of Warren Hastings after the Rohilla war. The topic was an enticing one: Burke had indicted the ex-Governor-General as a great offender, 'guilty of gross, enormous, and flagitious crimes,' and Francis crucified his reputation with pitiless proofs that he had

---

[1] Letter from Mr. Eden, afterwards Lord Auckland, 16th August, 1785.
[2] On the 1st June, 1786.

made a solemn compact with the Nawab of Oude to exterminate a people numerous and happy, habituated to industry, possessing a cultivated and prolific country, and capable of sending 60,000 men into the field.'

Pitt, oscillating mutely between what he knew to be the strong feeling of the King in favour of the oppressor, and his own high sense of public honour and justice, left it an open question amongst his supporters. Powys and Wilberforce assented to the motion; Dundas and Grenville opposed it on party grounds, but without venturing to justify Hastings: so did Mornington. He saucily twitted the ex-Premier with the ignorance he had avowed of the circumstances under which Rohilcund had been subjugated and sold to the Vizier of Oude. But impetuous and partial as were the feelings of the hour, the House of Commons was not disposed to give much heed to taunting criticism by a coxcomb of four-and-twenty, however fluent and well-bred, known by all to know nothing of his own knowledge of the matter in hand. Lord North succinctly but successfully defended himself with his habitual good-humour; and no subsequent speaker in a protracted debate seems to have thought the flippancies of his youthful censor worthy of notice. Could he have foreseen that in the revolving turn of fortune, he would himself be set in the midst of those many and great dangers in which by reason of the frailty of our nature we cannot always stand upright, he might have been less reserved in his implied palliation of the daring pro-consul. But when his day of reckoning as conqueror and annexor of territory came twenty years later, he had the satisfaction of feeling how great was the contrast in all personal respects between himself and Hastings.

Burke though supported by Windham, Elliot and Anstruther, was beaten by two to one: but ten days afterwards the too lenient ministerialists were disconcerted by

Pitt's assenting to the motion of Fox respecting the Rajah of Benares. 'Our victory,' wrote Elliot, 'has given me the greatest satisfaction and comfort. It may perhaps lead to little good in India, and will probably not carry such unwilling converts much farther; but it has saved the House of Commons from the disgrace of approving another villainy. Dundas voted in the majority: but Powney, who is called the King's member, as he was brought in for Windsor by the King's interest with his neighbours there, voted for Hastings.'[1] Can anybody doubt that on the minds of both the future rulers of India that were to be, the vote of the conscience-stricken minister made an impression not to be forgotten?

When the session was over, Mornington was appointed Junior Lord of the Treasury; and in October the new Commission was gazetted which included his name. He ascribed his first official appointment to Lord Buckingham's influence and to William Grenville's friendship, which had been exerted with his usual warmth and sincerity on this occasion; and who, having been at the same time named Vice-President of the Board of Trade, desired that his old class-fellow should enter office with him.[2]

Rumours now prevailed of a project of Union. Charlemont wrote to Flood:—'The English papers have been lately infested with the idea of a Union, but except from them I know nothing of it; neither can I suppose it possible that any such notion can have entered the heads even of our present administration. When we had no Constitution the idea was scarcely admissible: what then must it be now? I hope and believe, however, that it is merely the inflammatory lie of the day.'[3]

Lord Beverley, affronted with what he deemed neglect of

---

[1] To Lady Elliot, 15th June, 1786.
[2] Letter to the Marquess of Buckingham, 10th August, 1786.
[3] 12th November, 1786.

his political claims, refused to return Mornington again for Beeralston, whereby he was driven to seek for a seat in the less compliant borough of Saltash. There was in fact a contest, and he was returned by a small majority. In the debate, February 21, 1787, on the conditions of the commercial treaty with France (negotiated by Eden as one of the English commissioners) he was put up to answer Burke, and got through his task satisfactorily. With proper feelings of deference for the great statesman, he deprecated his jealousy of the liberal concessions which had been made to conciliate French merchants and manufacturers. 'It had been said with the eloquence of great authority that whatever its commercial merits might be, the treaty in a political point of view laid the country at the feet of France, and deposed Great Britain from her European throne. He answered that the true majesty of Great Britain was her trade; and that the fittest object of her ambition was the throne of the commerce of the world. The industry and ingenuity of our manufacturers, the opulence which these had diffused through various channels, the substantial foundation of capital on which they had placed our trade (capital which had that night been well described as predominant over the trade of the whole world), —all these, as they had been our best consolation in defeat, were the most promising sources of future victory: and to cultivate, to strengthen, and to augment these could not be inconsistent with the glory of the kingdom.'

A petition meanwhile had been presented by his opponent at Saltash against his return; and a committee, after due investigation, reversing the decision at the poll, on May 6, declared Mr. Lemon, whose family considered the suffrages of the inhabitants part of their property, to have been duly elected. He was thus left without a seat for more than a year, and it was during this period he became enamoured of the beautiful Hyacinthe Gabrielle, daughter of Monsieur Roland, the fascination of whose charms exercised over him a spell so lasting.

On the Duke of Rutland's death the Premier named his cousin Lord Buckingham to succeed him in the government of Ireland; and on his staff, at the request of Lady Mornington, His Excellency appointed Arthur Wesley, then in his nineteenth year and just returned from the completion of his military studies in France. The new Viceroy wrote that he must 'buy his men from the Charing Cross crimp that he might not be spoilt by recruiting: but he was happy that he could name him as aide-de-camp.' Such was the start in military life of the illustrious commander. His brother, who never ceased to take the liveliest interest in his career, wrote to the Lord Lieutenant:—

'You may well believe with what pleasure I received your appointment of my brother to a place in your family, not only as being a most kind mark of your regard for me, but as the greatest advantage to him. I am persuaded that under your eye he will not be exposed to any of those risks which in other times have accompanied the situation he will hold. I can assure you sincerely that he has every disposition which can render so young a boy deserving of your notice; and if he does not engage your protection by his conduct, I am much mistaken in his character. My mother expects him every hour in London, and before this time I should hope that he had himself waited on you. Once more, my dear lord, before I close this part of my letter, let me thank you most warmly for this flattering instance of your friendship. Grenville, I hope, has shown you my letter, in which I declare that I would not have asked you for this favour, knowing your inclination to attend to my requests, and apprehending that you might suffer your regard for me to interfere to the prejudice of your government; but certainly this object for my brother was very near my heart, and I accept it with a gratitude proportioned to the anxiety with which I desired it, and to the most friendly manner in which it has been given.'[1]

The Secretary-at-War at first demurred to the young officers on the Viceregal staff retaining their full pay. The Earl in a fraternal rage flew at the great man, who 'hoped he would deign to temper his anger with a little common sense; if not he threatened to send his brother with his newly raised men to join his regiment in India, which would of course be very unfortunate for Arthur, as he had concluded an agreement for an exchange now only awaiting the mighty fiat of the Secretary-at-War.'[2] Sir William Young yielded,[3] and instead of premature exposure to a tropical sun before his bones were knit, the young ensign betook himself to Dublin Castle, where during the next two years his military education proceeded in the salon of Lady Buckingham and the hunting field of his Excellency.

A new question, of more and better than party interest, now began to stir the minds of men. Clarkson and Wilberforce had hitherto pleaded, as was said in vain, for the abolition of the Slave Trade. Royalty, high birth, prelacy, and great possessions were set in the scale against what was nicknamed 'Utopian philanthropy' by practical men. The West Indian interest was one of the most widely ramified throughout the community. It kept great houses, race-horses, and rotten boroughs, and was equally strong in the City and at Westminster. Historically it had much to say for itself, for it could invoke the sanction of Elizabeth, the encouragement of Cromwell, and the approval of all the statesmen who maintained the Assiento Treaty. A crusade against kidnapping, slave-dealing, and the making of money out of innocent blood,

---

[1] 4th November, 1787.
[2] To the Marquis of Buckingham, 8th January, 1788.
[3] Secretary-at-War, 20th February, 1788.

seemed in 1787 to be one of the wildest speculations ever entertained, and the appeals by which it was stimulated in pamphlets and at public meetings suggested analogies so subversive of the established order of things that many otherwise humane men held the conviction that, whencesoever hewn, slavery was the keystone of the arch, perilous to remove, on which the national prosperity rested. Happily, not all this prejudice or the political influence arrayed on the wrong side, could deter young men of noble aspirations, in and out of office, from giving their adhesion, in private first and afterwards in public, to the righteous cause. Sheridan and Fox, Pitt and Granville Sharpe encouraged Wilberforce to bring the subject under discussion, and Mornington, though he knew how deeply his friends Lord Buckingham and William Grenville objected to the movement, told them frankly how much he sympathised with it. 'We are all very eagerly engaged,' he wrote, ' in considering a plan for the abolition of the Slave Trade which is to be soon brought forward by Wilberforce. I hear that Burke is to prove slavery to be an excellent thing for negroes, and that there is a great distinction between an Indian Begum and an African Wowski.'[1] This was, indeed, a strange mistake. Burke came forward on the very first occasion to declare that he wished for the abolition on principles of humanity and justice. If opposition of interests should render its total abolition impossible, it ought to be regulated, and that immediately. The Slave Trade was directly contrary to the interests of humanity, and the state of slavery however mitigated, was so degrading and so ruinous to the feelings and capacities of human nature that it ought not to be suffered to exist.[2]

In June 1788 another seat was found for him at Windsor, which he continued to represent in more than one Parliament.

---

[1] From London to the Lord-Lieutenant of Ireland, January, 1788.
[2] *Parl. Hist.*, xxvii., May 9, 1788.

During the prolonged debates on the Declaratory Bill respecting the Board of Control, his friends constantly urged him to speak, but from day to day his resolution failed him when the House was thin and the Speaker would have given him an opportunity ; and when listeners thronged the benches and Opposition taunts stung his ambition into eagerness to try, men of longer standing rose, and he had to gulp down his regrets as best he might. Grenville was so anxious that he should make a figure, that he begged his brother in Ireland to write to him urgently on the subject; lest the session should pass away without the realisation of his purpose.

In view of a general election the Marquess offered him a seat for Buckinghamshire, a kindness he warmly acknowledged; but he 'thought himself bound, by respect for the Person who placed him at Windsor, to endeavour to preserve that seat for him, that he might find his own friends where he was pleased to leave them, whenever he might happen to recover his reason. He might fail perhaps in this attempt to maintain the trust reposed in him, and the expense might be such as to disable him from purchasing any other seat: in that case the offer of the county would be most acceptable. He thought his brother Pole had found an opening at Grimsby, long the property of Anderson Pelham; and Pitt would thus have two seats at that place for about 5,000*l*. W. Pole was able to advance 1,000*l*: and he meant to give 1,500*l*., which would bring him in: another friend of Pitt's, R. Wood, agreeing to pay the remaining money for the other seat.'[1] The dissolution did not take place till 1790, when Wood and Pole found seats at East Looe in Cornwall.

At Holwood, purchased by Pitt from Mr. Rendall, he was, with Dundas and Eden, frequently a guest.

The old house was a small stuccoed brick building, near the old high road to Westerham, which had successively

[1] From Hertford Street, 15th November, 1788.

been occupied as a hunting-box by several persons who rode with the Duke of Grafton's hounds. Mr. Calcraft made it a sort of a quiet rendezvous for the heads of his party. A rich ship-builder named Rendall bought it of Burrow, and in autumn 1785 sold it to Pitt, who was a native of the adjoining parish, and by whom the ornamental grounds were chiefly formed.[1]

It is situated fourteen miles from London, in the parish of Keston, a name derived from the castrum of Cæsar on Holwood Hill, on the southern entrenchment of which the mansion stands.[2] The outlook from the house extends from Sydenham to Knockholt Beeches on the other side.

Lord Stanhope says the last instalment of the purchase-money, 8,950*l*., was not paid till 1794. In 1786 Pitt raised 4,000*l*. on a mortgage of the land.

There, as at Downing Street, Pitt sat late, and sought to stimulate his languid circulation in the morning by long rides on horseback, or quick walks with his woodmen, lopping sapless boughs and cutting new paths through the plantations. To the park, which was not originally of great extent, he added half as much more by help of certain provisions in a local Act stopping the direct road over the hill and making the new highway skirt it for a considerable distance round. The intervening portion of the common, about one hundred and twenty acres, was thus enclosed, and by way of compensation to those who dwelt hard by, they were specially exempted from paying turnpike for their carts and horses, and everyone was freed from toll coming or going to Keston Church on Sunday.[3] To the mansion he added a large dining room and a library on the other side, rendering the

---

[1] Decimus Burton possessed a sketch of the old house pulled down by Mr. John Ward. It had undergone little alteration.

[2] Neale: *English Seats*, vol. iv.

[3] 29 Geo. III. chap. 85, in the collection of Road Acts in the Library of the House of Lords.

edifice rather more picturesque than fitted for permanency.
Architectural pretension it had none, and what became of
the patched edifice after his time, he was too engrossed with
public business and the relaxations of the table to care.
Hayes, Chevening and Camden Place were not far off: and
from town not a few persons of wit, worth or distinction, came
at intervals to join his hospitable board; Addington, Grenville, and Dundas, full of serious politics; Malmesbury,
Eden, Gower, laden with confidential gossip from Paris and
Berlin; Wilberforce, not yet a power in the senate, but
brimming over with enthusiasm for religious and social
measures of improvement in which he tried his best to
engage the sympathy of the minister. A medallion on ivory
still depicts the young man of fashion in embroidered coat,
ruffles, and pigtail; and though without colour preserves the
delicate beauty of feature combined with intensity of will
which characterise later pictures. On the back is written in
his own hand—'*Le meilleur portrait de moi, selon l'avis
de toutes mes belles.*'

CHAPTER V.

COLLEGE GREEN AND CARLTON HOUSE.

1788-1791.

DURING the autumn of 1788 the condition of the King's health rendered it necessary to provide by some specific measure for the exercise of the royal functions. Pitt hesitated long about making any formal communication to Parliament. The emergency was unprovided for by statute; the jealousy with which George III. regarded the confidential advisers of his son was well known; and the expectation universally prevailed that under him the policy of the Government and the persons composing it would be altogether changed. Few were taken into council beforehand as to what should be done; but one of them was Mornington: for it was manifestly desirable to secure if possible, concurrent action by the legislatures of the two realms, if any conditions of Regency were to be imposed. When the aberration of the royal intellect could no longer be concealed, ministers proposed resolutions declaring the exercise of the sovereign authority to be in abeyance; and that it was the duty of Parliament to make temporary provision for the exigency by appointing the Prince of Wales Regent of Great Britain; but limiting the delegated prerogative for the space of one year regarding dismissals from the Household, the granting of pensions out of hereditary revenue, and the creating of peers. Fox, North, and Burke precipitately committed themselves to the assertion that the Heir Apparent was as fully entitled to take upon him the state and power of royalty as if his father were physically dead; and consequently, that he ought to be allowed to do so without limitations. But Pitt argued from precedent and principle, that the constitution recognised no such right by assumption; that every Protector or Regent in past times had been named by Parliament, with an Executive Council; whereby practically a check was imposed on all acts of importance; and that in every case on record the provisional trust was to cease and determine by a given time. From the peculiar nature of a case so unforeseen, no definite period could be set to the proposed locum-tenency; and the difficulties in the way of naming a Council under existing circumstances could not be easily overcome. As the sworn testimony of the physicians warranted the Privy Council in anticipating the King's recovery within a reasonable time, they were bound to take measures as far as possible for preserving to him, against that day, the discretion he had hitherto enjoyed in the bestowal of honours and emoluments. By a large majority [1] these views were accepted; and a Bill founded upon them was before Christmas brought in accordingly.

Pitt claimed for Parliament, in which he had a secure predominance, the absolute right to nominate a Regent and to limit his powers. Burke argued ingeniously that this was in point of principle to do what the Convention had done in 1689; namely, to declare that the royal authority had lapsed to whomsoever they might choose to appoint, and on whatsoever terms, with this only difference, that James II. had wantonly forfeited his office, and that Parliament had no alternative but to supply his place: whereas George III. was simply derelict by natural infirmity, which furnished no excuse for deviating from the rule of hereditary succession.

[1] By 268 to 204; 16th December, 78.

Already the advancing shadow of subversive change was cast over his anticipative mind; and had the question not arisen until somewhat later, when monarchy was overthrown by the misapplication of Pitt's theory in France, Burke would have prevailed. But the King's friends who had placed the minister in office, were ready to keep him there, regardless of theoretically possible consequences, which not even the seer of Beaconsfield as yet thought imminent. What he did foresee as likely to ensue, if the Whig view prevailed, was the overthrow of Toryism, under the dictatorship of Pitt; and it was this rather than any profound dread of unconstitutional results that animated Fox and Sheridan, Loughborough and Erskine, to contend as they did pertinaciously and long. They were ready in point of fact to come to terms of limitation after their defeat on the ultra-legitimist ground taken at the outset by Burke,—that to all political intents and purposes the throne was vacant, only until, as in the case of sickness unto death, the Heir-Apparent should feel justified in calling on the estates of the realm to acknowledge him as head of the State by inheritance, not election. They soon found that their reactionary notions would not go down with the public at large; and they made such haste to explain them away that Burke in a frenzy complained that his advice was discarded, and that consistency had forsaken the earth. To the end he persisted in his own view, calling the Limited Regency Bill disloyal, and all who voted for it traitors. But his violence did not turn votes. Sir William Young wrote to Lord Buckingham, after one of his unsuccessful invocations of obsolete tradition, ' He is folly personified, shaking his cap and bells under the laurels of genius.' With the exception of Windham and perhaps Francis, none of the leading men of his party went with him; and Gilbert Elliot thought with Pitt.

But under the gallery sat one on whom his invectives and

adjurations acted as a spell. Grattan had come over from Ireland to confer with Fox and the Duke of Portland. He too was willing to take the high prerogative line in favour of the Prince; and the attempts at compromise proving futile he went back disposed rather to adhere to the course at first advocated by Burke. Still it is possible that wiser counsels might have had sway if the Government by their mode of dealing with it in Ireland had not entangled the question with that of legislative independence. Renewed discussion at each stage and upon every clause delayed the passing of the Regency Bill through the Lower House at Westminster for several weeks; and it was not until the 12th of February that it was carried to the Lords. Meanwhile tidings came that in Ireland the arguments in favour of unconditional Regency were, irrespectively of party ties, likely to prevail. In opening the session on 5th February, 1789, the Marquess of Buckingham was content to communicate the fact that for some time he had been left without instructions from the King in consequence of the malady from which His Majesty was suffering; and that full information would in due time be submitted on the subject. The Chief Secretary, Mr. FitzHerbert, suggested that its consideration should be postponed for a fortnight, obviously with the hope of having by that time the English measure before them in its completed form. Grattan started: was this a new suggestion of legislative subserviency? if so, it was their duty to contravene and crush it by initiating an independent course of action. An early day being named for the purpose, Mr. Connolly, foremost of the country gentlemen, moved, and Mr. O'Neill who likewise possessed great influence, seconded, an address to the Prince, requesting him to take upon himself, during his father's illness, the executive authority in Ireland.

Mr. FitzHerbert, a fair but feeble man, was no match

for the varied talent and energy arrayed against him. The Chancellor of the Exchequer was equally out of his depth in the controversy; and the brunt of the battle fell on the Attorney General, who desired nothing better than from his crown brief to urge any topic that would please the minister or draw his opponents into untenable positions. With the indifference to historic consistency and to ulterior consequences which too frequently characterises law officers in debate, FitzGibbon bluntly stigmatised what he called the proposed Government under an unlimited Regency, as a criminal violation of the Act of Settlement which the Government to be still carried on in the King's name in Great Britain, would not tolerate or allow. He affrontingly told his hearers that their business was to move obediently within the lines traced for them by the Imperial Parliament, providing for the exercise of regal functions; because the crown of Ireland was appendant to the Imperial Crown; and because the Great Seal of England affixed to a Bill for conditional Regency would give it undoubted validity on both sides of the Channel. If, exceeding their privilege and duty, they affected in Ireland to clothe the Prince with prerogatives incompatible with those he might possess elsewhere, they meant to risk separation; and in the face of such a danger no alternative would remain but that of a legislative Union. Such a result he professed to deprecate, but sooner or later, if they persisted in assuming co-equal legislative authority, it would become inevitable. The immediate effect of such language was to pique every illogical and high-spirited waverer into swelling the ranks of Grattan, who with Ponsonby, Langrishe, and Curran hurled back the ministerial threats and taunts amid a tempest of patriotic cheers. Flood looked on moodily in silence; while his relative, Sir Frederick, protested, like other country gentlemen, at the wanton insolence of the ministerial tone: and not a few of the habitual adherents of Government went away. Wesley Pole, acting in concert with his brother, was one of the few unofficial members who ventured to stand their ground. 'Pensions,' he argued, 'might be granted, peerages bestowed, and places given in reversion to designing men who had wormed themselves into the confidence of his Royal Highness.' He passed the highest panegyric on the ability, virtue and integrity of Mr. Pitt, but Government did not venture to divide, and the address was sent up to the Lords for their concurrence.[1]

The over-masted ship, with all sails set, every defiant flag unfurled, and firing significantly minute guns, made head for the rapids. Had Flood's hand been on the helm he would sooner have run her ashore than risk a catastrophe. He would have preferred compromise to collision; and would have offered terms of accommodation, making partial concessions to the irresistible majority at Westminster: relying on the help of the minority there to modify the proposed limitations. This would have been a course worthy of a statesman. But Grattan was a political poet who thought dramatically, whose eloquence was epigram and whose logic antithesis, matchless since that of Demosthenes and practically as unavailing. He loved what the playwrights call a striking situation; and rather than lower his ambitious aim he was ready to hazard its failure.

So little had the vote of the Commons been expected, that Mornington and other Irish peers were content to send their proxies in the confident belief that in their House at all events the influence of the Castle would as usual prevail. But the pride of nationality, though of late it seemed dying out, flashed up anew. Sanguine expectations of novelty that must be improvement were concentrated in the Prince of Wales, with how little discernment or reason time was

[1] 12th February, 1789.

ere long to show. Lord Buckingham's popularity was unable to control or guide the movement, which for the moment carried away many on whose stability he had hitherto relied.

In terms identical with those of the Commons, the address to the Prince was adopted by a majority of nineteen in the Peers; and his Excellency was requested by a joint deputation to transmit the same officially to his Royal Highness.

The Viceroy replied 'that under the impressions he felt of his official duty, and of the oath he had taken, he did not consider himself warranted to lay before the Prince an address purporting to invest him with power to take upon him the government of that realm, before he should be enabled by law so to do.'

The peers and commoners reassembled in their respective chambers to denounce the affront thus offered to their legislative dignity; and long and stormy were the discussions that ensued. That Lord Buckingham did his duty to those whose policy and purpose he was sent to administer was plain: but not the less palpable was it that his act was one of open defiance of the Irish Parliament. It was felt, as it was meant to be, an assertion summary and stern of paramount authority. Submission after the course that had been taken would involve irredeemable humiliation; yet resistance in a time of peace abroad, and without preparation of any kind at home was an alternative not to be thought of. The showy scabbard of independence had been rattled in vain, for within there was no popular sword. Mr. Pitt understood well how thoroughly the vain-glorious patriotism of a provincial oligarchy was honeycombed by personal greed and social aspirations. How he would have dealt with them had there been occasion, we may infer by what happened later on. In the crisis of 1789 he probably did not take the trouble to think with regard to individuals or details; but it was an opportunity rare as unforeseen for avenging the affront put upon him in 1785, and he used it with a ruthless hand. A Roman tyrant had vainly wished that his refractory subjects had but one neck, that he might at a blow silence their sedition: the English Minister saw his opportunity and seized it without hesitation or scruple for humbling an unrepresentative parliament that dared without counting the cost to be unamenable. Sooner than succumb, the two Houses simultaneously resolved to try issues with the Executive Government. The Duke of Leinster and Lord Charlemont, with Ponsonby, Stewart, Connolly and O'Neill, were named commissioners and ordered to take ship and hie forthwith to London, there to lay the national desire at the feet of the heir to the Crown.

On February 20, Grattan moved, 'That the Lord Lieutenant's answer to the request of the two Houses of Parliament that he would transmit their Address to His Royal Highness the Prince of Wales has, ill-advised, contained an unwarranted and unconstitutional censure on the proceedings of both Houses of Parliament, and attempted to question the undoubted rights and privileges of the Lords, spiritual and temporal, and the Commons of Ireland.' After some debate but 83 voted against and 115 for the resolution. The Lords on the same day adopted a similar course by 40 to 21, including proxies. Nor was this all. The sense of exasperation still ravening for food, Grattan on the same day moved, 'That in addressing the Prince of Wales to take upon himself the government of Ireland, on the behalf, and in the name of his Majesty, during his indisposition, and no longer, the Lords and Commons of Ireland had exercised an undoubted right, and discharged an indispensable duty, to which in the actual emergency they alone were competent.' After another threatening notice from the Attorney General to the country gentlemen against embarking in what he termed a pernicious and perilous speculation, the resolution was carried by 130 to 74; and the House then voted that 'the Lord Lieutenant's answer was ill-advised, contained an unwarranted and unconstitutional censure on the proceedings of both Houses of Parliament, and attempted to question their undoubted rights and privileges.'

A vote of censure on the Lord Lieutenant in deliberate and dignified terms, but if possible laying still more bare the direct antagonism between the rival powers of the State, was passed in the Upper House by 37 to 31; whereupon a final protest, subscribed by Mornington and most of the ministerial peers, boldly challenged the autonomous authority of the body to which they belonged—

'Because,' the undoubted right and the indispensable duty, 'declared in the said resolution to have been exercised and discharged by the Lords and Commons of Ireland, do not in any legal or sound sense appear to us to have any existence; and because the assuming a right to confer the government of the kingdom upon the Prince of Wales, under the style and title of Prince Regent of Ireland, before he be enabled by law to do so, seems altogether unwarrantable and highly dangerous in its tendency to disturb and break the constitutional union whereby the realm of Ireland is for ever knit and united to the imperial Crown of England, on which connection the happiness of both kingdoms essentially depends.'[1] Amongst the dissentients were Lords Tyrone, Hillsborough, Longford, Bective, Bellamont, and Conyngham.

The Duke and his colleagues, reinforced by the principal landed proprietors[2] then in town who were connected with Ireland, proceeded to Carlton House, where they were received by the Prince with effusive acknowledgments of

[1] *Lords' Journals*, February, 1789.
[2] Among the peers were: Devonshire, Inchiquin, Fitzwilliam, Darnley,

gratitude and affection to the loyal and generous people of Ireland which he felt indelibly imprinted on his heart. But his Royal Highness was delighted to be able to inform them that favourable symptoms had lately been observed in the condition of his Majesty, and that a formal reply on his part to their solicitations must therefore be postponed. Lord Thurlow had, in fact, announced from the Woolsack the evening before, that George III. was convalescent, and that in consequence the Regency Bill would be proceeded with no further. The imminent hazard of an open collision between the legislative authorities of the two realms was thereby averted; and the waters of bitterness seemed to subside once more into their customary channels. But the impression made upon the minds of all who were capable of reflection or forethought was not to be effaced.

Mornington, who lived very much with the Grenvilles, was in close correspondence with the Lord Lieutenant throughout the controversy. His sentiments were doubtless well known to the friends in Ireland from whom he differed, and perhaps he was glad to be spared the pain of personal collision with them on what they deemed a point of honour. His name is appended to the several protests entered by the minority in the journals of the peers; and it has thence been inferred that some of these vigorous denunciations of Whig Jacobitism were from his pen. It has even been said that he took part, as he was well qualified to do, in the memorable discussion.[1] But all uncertainty on the point is set at rest by the fact that in every instance his signature is recorded with those of Lords Altamont, Carysfort, and Courtown as having been annexed ' by proxy.'

It is hardly too much to say, that in these once notable,

Galway, Besborough, Middleton, Ludlow, Rawdon, Lucan, and among the commoners, Sheridan, Pelham, Burke, Conway, Courtney, Francis, &c.

[1] *Pierce*, vol. i. p. 37.

but soon overlaid inscriptions may be traced sharply and clearly cut, the date and design of Pitt's annexing policy. Consolidation and extension of empire was the dominant idea of his life. About the means he was not nice, about the cost indifferent. With him the purpose fixed and supreme was everything; party ties, private friendship, disaffection of followers, popular suffering, royal ill-humour, even the pride of his own apparent personal consistency—nothing. Without unification of the three old realms for defence and for aggression he saw plainly that Ireland could never be peaceable, Scotland could never be rich, and that England could never again be great: and come what might he was bent on accomplishing that which was indispensable to all these ends. The rebuff he had received in 1785 from the Irish Parliament, on his scheme for fiscal union, served but to put a keener edge on his resolve; and the untenable position taken on the Regency Question by the majority of both Houses gave him the opportunity he was not slow to seize, of reading them a lesson on the suicidal sin of contumacy. The protest of the Lords was a white flag of surrender held forth from the topmost pinnacle of a citadel, many posterns of which he had already in his hands. From that day the hearts of the most sanguine sunk within them as to its eventual maintenance. Had swords never been actually crossed they might have been pointed and brandished boastfully for many a day, popular credulity being undispelled as to the invincibility of the shorter and the lighter one. But in a passionate hour conclusions had been rashly tried, and without drawing blood the glittering weapon was struck out of the weaker hand. The Crown of Ireland, by those who had most to lose within her confines, was confessed anew to be a pendant on the Crown of England; and as the English executive, by the very constitution of a free government, must be ever responsible in men and measures to the Parliament of Westminster, a parliament in Dublin could never effectually resist the one or change the other. No vote of theirs expressing want of confidence could enforce the recall of a viceroy if the Prime Minister chose to disregard it: how much less could a vote conferring sovereignty on a Prince of the Blood not already sovereign in Great Britain, make him virtually a King? It would be incredible if the record did not remain, that men so gifted and accomplished as many of the Peers and Commoners of 1789, should have failed to see what now looks like an obvious truth, or that they should have openly provoked the imperious statesman whom they suspected to be bent on the subversion of their legislative importance, to show to all the world the indefensibility of their position.

The sudden recovery of George III. delivered them from the immediate embarrassment of their situation; but the wound inflicted on their dignity in the eyes of the people and in their own, though it bled slowly and unobserved, was even unto death. From that day faith in the stability of the system began silently to fade away; and long before any project of absorption or annexation was even officiously put forward by the scouts and pioneers of power, the more thinking minds of the community had become prepared to receive it as a thing eventually inevitable.

George III., on coming to himself, favoured openly all who had resisted the pretensions of his son, and the young Irish peer especially for the active part he had taken.

It is hard to believe that a mind with the historic culture, comprehensive grasp, and instinctive forethought of Flood should have continued to regard the Constitution of 1782 as capable of long endurance. His bold attempt to reduce theoretic right into actual possession by the creation of a substantial constituency in Ireland had failed; but he was not a man to change his opinions or abandon his purpose at the bidding of either senate or mob. He saw that Reform had no chance of being adopted in Ireland while it was still refused in Great Britain; and having a seat in each Parliament, he strove in both consistently to win adherents to his fixed and definite doctrine of household suffrage.

One of the first decrees of the National Assembly in France had more than acknowledged the principle of direct representation, imparting thereby a new impulse of incalculable force to the movement of public opinion in its favour. The recoil of the Revolution was not yet come, or even apprehended by ordinary men, though already the scrutinising intellect of Burke had begun to be disturbed and distressed by its ominous utterances. Of what might become of the already damaged experiment of Irish legislative independence Burke took little heed, and probably thought of it, when he thought of it at all, as a mere transitional state of things which must sooner or later be commuted for something more durable and real. At heart Flood thought so too; but his reputation had grown to maturity on the western side of the Channel, and he was too old to learn indifference to the quasi-nationalism to which the best hours of his youth and prime had been devoted. He clutched at electoral reform as a common good which the popular party in both countries might seek simultaneously to gain, persuaded that out of its attainment might be safely left to grow, as in the younger States beyond the ocean, mutual guarantees of imperial strength and local liberty. His last speech at Westminster was for leave to bring in a Bill to put an end to rotten boroughs, and to enfranchise every resident holder of a separate dwelling paying rates and taxes; and although ineffectual then it may still be read with profit and pleasure by everyone who cares to trace the just and generous proportions of representative freedom. What decades of discontent and disaffection would have been saved had the Parliament of 1790 listened to his proposal, which in principle and detail Fox declared to be the best he had ever heard suggested. But Burke and Windham had become panic-stricken at what was taking place in France; Grenville vehemently protested he would never under any circumstances agree to democratic change, and to the last he kept his word; Pitt, without repenting of his early pleadings for Reform, warily asked for a more convenient season. It would have been useless to hazard a division. Flood saw the realisation of his hope afar off, and was glad; but it came not in his day. At the general election in autumn he was not again returned as an English member, and in the winter of the following year he had sunk to rest. Few more thoughtful and courageous men took part in the affairs of his time; and few of his contemporaries have left behind them nobler sentiments crystallised in nobler language.

His death[1] removed a serious obstacle to Ministerial schemes of Union, for with all his faults and prejudices, Flood retained to the last great influence among the educated classes in Ireland, and gifts, rare amongst them in his day, of persistent application to the study of great subjects, and of eloquently logical exposition.

Disparity of years, and a still greater difference in their ways of life, precluded an intimacy between Flood and Mornington; and there was a time when the latter was so carried away by party feeling as to speak of him as the 'arch-enemy of Ireland.' The young earl's preference for Grattan contributed, no doubt, to keep them apart. But when by experience he learned the value of the temperament which distinguished Flood from a community so impression-

---

[1] At the age of fifty-nine, 2nd December, 1791.

able and volatile as that to which he belonged, he not unfrequently reverted in a certain tone of reverence to his elevated and self-reliant character, and spoke of him as among the not very numerous statesmen he had known whose antagonism or support was always worth estimating for its own intrinsic weight.

CHAPTER VI.

BOARD OF CONTROL.

1792—1794.

For the first ten years it was the pride of the egotistic Minister to rely upon himself almost alone for the defence of his measures in debate. Of his Cabinet colleagues in the Lower House, Dundas only was capable of encountering the formidable adversaries arrayed against them. But all the more Pitt liked to afford opportunities of distinction to the younger men of his party occupying less responsible positions. The aspiring Lord of the Treasury desired nothing better than to be allowed to show what he could do; and his chief, who liked his classic taste in the choice of words, and the general tone of elevation in his thoughts and arguments, was not unwilling he should have his turn.

Wilberforce had kindled such a sense of shame at the continuance of the slave trade, that after it had been abolished by the edicts of the French National Assembly, English statesmen of humanity and wisdom felt it had become impossible to defend further participation in the odious traffic. Whigs and Tories vied with one another in fervency of denunciation; and though the rival leaders were unable to overcome the sordid instincts of many of their followers, they rallied to the cause of abolition the best intellects of their younger partizans. Mornington was among the foremost, moving as an amendment to Dundas's plan of deferred and gradual emancipation, that 'the trade should wholly cease on the 1st of January next ensuing.'

Lord Sheffield, a man of some reputation in his day as a political writer, undertook the palliation of the evil practice, and the proof that it was the interest after all of the much maligned crimps of the Gold Coast to bring their human herds to market in good condition, and the interest of the calumniated planters to keep them, like other stock, in usable and profitable plight. To interdict the trade, and send cruisers out to watch and chase the ships that carried negroes across the ocean, would only tend to worsen their chance of reaching shore alive; and under civilised and Christian masters they would be saved from all the casualties and cruelties of barbarism; they were certain to be well-housed, well-fed, and well looked after.

Mornington in reply, disdained to palter with these special pleas for wrong. He rejoiced in the blow given to the slave trade, which however modified was in his opinion no longer entitled to legalised existence. Modifications of right or of wrong were in the nature of things inadmissible; and the true question was whether we could, in strict justice, permit the duration for any space of time however short, of a commerce acknowledged to be repugnant to every principle of equity.

The slave trade, as actually exercised, was in direct violation of the law by which the merchants traded on the coast of Africa. That law strictly prohibited them, under the penalty of 100*l*. for each offence, 'from taking or procuring any African slave through force, violence, fraud, or any indirect means whatever.' Such were the words of the statute pleaded in favour of the slave trade. But who that knew in what manner that trade was really carried on would dare to assert that the statute was not habitually violated? Could such a traffic then claim the sanction of the legislature, in defiance of whose will it notoriously broke through the most essential restrictions laid upon it?

Parliament having recorded in general terms its condemnation of the traffic, 'it was no longer invective to call it inhuman and unjust. The question, therefore, now was, not whether the slave trade should be abolished, but how long should we continue to be unjust? How long should we carry on a practice which we had declared to be unjust and inhuman? Some thought that we should be unjust for ten years more, and some for seven; that at least the remainder of the century should continue in disgrace, and that justice was to commence its operation with the opening of another; but this, he trusted, would not be the sentiment of the Parliament of Great Britain.' He moved that the traffic should wholly cease in the ensuing year, but he was beaten by a majority of forty-nine.[1]

Encouraged however by the Prime Minister, he subsequently proposed to fix January 1, 1795, as the day of abolition, and pleaded the cause of humanity in a tone of heightened zeal, and what his opponents chose to designate fantastic declamation.

'He was sorry that so infamous a traffic should be respited for an hour. Being hated by all good men, and as far as regarded its justice or humanity, abandoned by its own advocates, what could be urged for its prolongation? It was said that time should be allowed the planters to cool, and to discover the truth of those who contended that the abolition would ultimately be for their advantage. What length of time it would take them to cool and for truth to make its way it was impossible for him to say. If he were to put the question mathematically he would say: "The force of truth being given, and the hardness of a planter's head being

[1] *Parl. Hist.* April 25, 1792, 29, 1229.

ascertained, in what space of time will the former be able to penetrate the latter?" He was willing to give them two years; and he thought that heads which could not take in or consider a truth in two years were not likely to be penetrated by it in seven. He would therefore move that the trade should cease from the 1st of January, 1795.' Lord Carhampton, for himself and his fellow-planters and the merchants of Bristol and Liverpool, scoffed at philanthropy borrowed from Republican France, whose random decrees had caused the ruin of St. Domingo; and inveighed passionately against the robbery about to be committed on the owners of West Indian property for doing only what Parliament had sanctioned for two centuries and a half. Dundas, by way of compromise, offered to fix the date of abolition at the beginning of 1796, and Mornington was defeated by forty, though supported by Pitt, Sheridan, and Fox.[1] It ended in Dundas agreeing to December 1796 as the period of compromise.

Grenville, having charge of the Bill in the Upper House, pleaded as earnestly for its passing as his friend had done; but the slave trade being an open question in the Government, a majority of the peers had no compunction about voting its continuance; and though Pitt spoke 'like one inspired'[2] for truth and right, as for freedom of trade and electoral reform, he was content to live and die in office without its legislative recognition.

It must be owned that the question of Reform had assumed an aspect never contemplated by his father or by him. It was no longer, in the public mind, the renovation of ancient usage or the awaking from the sleep of centuries old ways of procedure; but the setting up of an untried system modelled on that of Republican France, and chiefly recommended for English adoption in cheap editions of Paine's *Rights of Man*.

[1] *Parl. Hist.*, April 27, 1792.   [2] *Life of Wilberforce*, vol. ii.

It was there promulgated less for its own sake than as a requisite preliminary to the breaking up of estates, the destruction of Christianity and the subversion of the throne. All who speculated on the attainment of any of these ends ardently combined in demanding reform. Affiliated societies under various names were organised as early as 1790 for securing this indispensable means of further action. Various plans, more or less closely copied from the Paris pattern, found favour with the Constitutional Club, the Friends of the People, and lastly the Corresponding Society to which several persons of distinction were induced to belong. Sheridan, Francis, Whitbread, and Grey were ready to embark on the current of new opinions. But from the publication of Burke's memorable pamphlet on the French Revolution [1] large and influential numbers of their party took the alarm as at the sound of the fire-bell at the dead of night; and though deprecating open schism or the loosening of personal ties, hesitated with daily increasing reluctance to aid or sustain demands they had theretofore approved.

In private Burke 'received from the old stamina of the Whigs a most full approbation of the principles of his work.'[2] Fox on the other hand disapproved, and took no pains to conceal his disapprobation. He seemed to be daily drawn more and more away from Burke, filling his best friends thereby with sorrow and dismay. Fond as they were of the man, and lenient to his foibles, 'in this it was impossible,' wrote Elliot, 'for the reputable and weighty part of his supporters to follow him.'[3] After the violent scene in Parliament, in which Burke openly repudiated the friendship of Fox, the breach widened till it became irreparable. The Dukes of Devonshire and Portland, Lords Fitzwilliam and Spencer, Windham, Elliot, and a large section of the once powerful

---

[1] October, 1790.   [2] Letter from Sir G. Elliot, December 4, 1790.
[3] Idem, December 5.

Opposition, aghast at the sanguinary progress of the Revolution abroad, seceded from the ranks of Reform, believing that property and religion were in danger, and that in the face of the storm they could not with prudence advocate the transformation of the State. In the excitement of the period both sections drifted farther from their old moorings than either intended or would have believed possible, and the democratic associations on whose working the whole crew of agitators by trade subsisted in turbulent idleness, were still able to claim as leaders the most eloquent and able men in the House of Commons.

Regardless of the earnest remonstrances of the English and Austrian ambassadors in Paris, Louis XVI. and his ill-fated consort were brought to the scaffold. Pitt, who to the last had clung to the policy of peace, was at length constrained to give way. M. Chauvelin was told by Grenville in a peremptory note,[1] that his character as plenipotentiary having ceased in consequence of the death of his royal master, he must quit the realm within eight days. A message from the King four days later denounced the atrocious act lately perpetrated at Paris, and called for augmentation of forces by sea and land, as necessary to secure general peace, threatened by encroaching and subversive schemes. France thereupon declared war. In a second message George III. appealed to both Houses to support him 'in prosecuting a just and necessary war to oppose an effectual barrier to the further progress of a system which struck at the safety and peace of all independent nations, and the security and tranquillity of Europe.'

Grey adhered to Fox, and undertook to bring forward the subject of Reform in a practical and comprehensive series of proposals. Erskine seconded, and Windham opposed his motion to refer a petition from the Friends of the People to a

[1] January 24, 1793.

committee. Jenkinson and Anstruther opposed; also Mr. Stanley and Mr. Buxton unwilling to refuse, but thinking the time inopportune. Sir P. Francis supported : Mornington answering him, alluded to the rise of the nation from the depression following the American War,

> More glorious and more dread than from no fall,
> And trusts herself to fear no second fate.

Francis had presented a petition from sundry inhabitants of London, Westminster, and the vicinity, praying for universal suffrage as the only effectual, permanent, and practicable plan of Reform. The first signature was that of Thomas Hardy, a name obscure in this country, but not unknown to the National Convention of France, for in the November preceding he had signed, as secretary to the Corresponding Society, an Address, so fervently embracing the cause of the French Republic, and full of so warm a zeal for the destruction of the British Government, as to be circulated throughout all the departments and all the armies of the enemy. 'The desire which was universally professed by every one of these societies in the cause of Parliamentary Reform was mainly subsidiary to the great object of introducing their favourite maxim in the most advantageous shape. A change in the system of representation was not the real end of their efforts, but was pursued as affording the most favourable means of facilitating the total subversion of the monarchy itself, which would ever appear impracticable, even to the most adventurous and misguided zealots while the constitution of Parliament should remain unimpaired.' He then epitomised and derided Rousseau's principle of personal participation by all citizens in the business of government after the manner of the ancient democracies of Greece, where the daily work of the community could only be done by the maintenance of slaves. 'Here then the petitioners might see the Rights of Man carried to the extreme point of perfection, and might learn that, according to their own principles strictly and fairly pursued, civil slavery is the only solid basis of true political liberty. This is the natural course of all those who attempt to raise constitutions of Government on visionary speculations of abstract and indefinite right. They commence their career with some specious and plausible theory in view, but in endeavouring to pursue it they are continually driven from difficulties in practice, to contradictions in principle, and they find no resting-place until they have reached some monstrous and insurmountable absurdity. From thence they are compelled to trace back their steps, and to seek the real substance of liberty where alone it is to be found, within the just limits of expediency and experience. However extravagant and ridiculous his notions may seem, and however associated they are in his writings with the most profligate maxims of immorality and irreligion, Rousseau has been canonised by the people of France, and is now one of the few saints remaining on their calendar. Their admiration of his works and their reverence for his memory have not been inactive; they have imitated with the utmost success his systematic dishonesty and his zealous impiety; and they have neither been less earnest nor less successful in establishing his principles of political anarchy on the most permanent foundations, and in securing their full operation by most effectual provisions.'

In this spirit Mornington resisted the proposal of Mr. Grey, which was avowedly meant to change the basis of representation, and which was undoubtedly calculated to encourage and strengthen those who cherished subversive designs. The country, he argued, had thriven with its existing institutions; and if there were anomalies and defects they were far less evil than the risk of tempting the people to try the experiment which empirics had set for demoralised and bewildered France. His objections applied to the whole spirit and substance of the measure which was the subject of debate. It appears to be no less than to change the very genius and spirit of the British Government. In a speech of great length and ability he exerted himself to prove that the benefits actually enjoyed by the nation were invaluable; that no proof either had been, or could be, adduced of their being unconnected with the existing constitution of Parliament; and that there was the strongest presumption of an intimate connection subsisting between them: that in comparison with these benefits the grievances alleged were trivial and insignificant, and that they could in no degree be imputed to the alleged defects in the representation; above all that the new constitution likely to be given to us in exchange for what we then possessed, so far from securing any one practical good, or alleviating any alleged or practical evil, would utterly subvert every foundation of our present happiness and prosperity; would aggravate every evil of which any one could complain, and introduce many others of infinitely greater magnitude and of far more mischievous consequences.

For these reasons chiefly, though not exclusively, he concluded that no essential alterations should be made in the existing frame of Parliament.

Fox, in his reply, quoted the well-known lines—

> Let that be wrought which Mat doth say.
> Yea, quoth the Earl, but not to-day;

and lavished all the wealth of his eloquence in urging the general right of the industrial community to a restoration of their ancestral share in the representation, which once conceded, discontent would cease. But the spectre of the guillotine dripping with the best blood of France was not to be conjured away; and 282 to 41 refused even to refer the petition for reform to a committee.[1]

Compliments on the excellent tone and well-sustained

[1] Elliot's letters, May 1793.

reasoning of his speech came from colleagues and superiors in office, and led him to look for some advancement and for removal from the obscure routine of formalities at the Treasury to some department affording scope for the exercise of the talents he felt he possessed. His feminine sensitiveness would not suffer him to risk the mortification of refusal, and he consequently forbore to ask what he longed to have. But the same delicacy did not prevent his reminding those who had influence at the Horse Guards, that his brother Arthur aspired to regimental promotion, and though as yet without experience in the field had qualities that would not discredit those who trusted him. In May he had the satisfaction of receiving an intimation that Major Wesley had been appointed Lieutenant-Colonel of the 33rd Foot, then under orders for embarkation at Cork, to join the army in the Low Countries. The untoward incidents of the campaign and the eventual failure of the expedition were happily veiled from his, as from other eyes.

When forty years of popular disenchantment had elapsed, Paine and the *contrat social* forgotten, and the tide of equality and fraternity had subsided within bounds not incompatible with respect for property, toleration of thought, and Christianity, Wellesley was ready to join with Grey in a measure disfranchising close boroughs and giving a wide suffrage in counties and towns.

A few weeks after the debate in question he was sworn a member of the Privy Council, and on June 28, 1793, a new commission was issued constituting Mr. Dundas, the Duke of Montrose, the Earl of Mornington, Lord Belgrave, Lord Apsley, the Honourable S. Eliot, and the Honourable Richard Jenkinson, a Board for the regulation and control of the East India Company's affairs. The junior commissioners had practically little to do which deputies and clerks were not more competent to perform. The President had for twenty years exercised unshared power in the department, the patronage of which was more lucrative and varied than that of any other Minister except the Chancellor; and in return he devoted to his office the best energies of an intellect not the purest or the highest, but penetrating, subtle, versatile, and shrewd. He wanted no younger thoughts or suggestions, and met the offer whenever it was made to relieve him of part of his laborious duties with a cynical smile not calculated to encourage future presumption of the kind. Nevertheless, Mornington found it less irksome to study reports and elaborate minutes, received with a broad joke and apparently never thought of more, than intermittently to give perfunctory attendance, and to admit to himself that he was fit for nothing but a sinecure, that was harder than any amount of work; and when the permanent officials left his table bare day after day, he sent for books out of the limited library which then existed, and occasionally for copies of documents of importance from the archives, and from these set about compiling, in the twilight of information concerning the East which Burke himself had found it so difficult to read by, a historical epitome of events from the times preceding the establishment of our factories at Surat and Cossimbuzar. Why he took so much trouble about it, he probably could hardly have told at the time. But the irritable *ennui* that beset him wanted relief; and ambition has its instincts, often salutary and wise. His memory being good, his epitome impressed on it the features and proportions of European acquisition in the East, and sooner than he could have surmised, served to facilitate his discharge of high and responsible duties.

As friends of Pitt, Addington and Wilberforce were daily brought more and more into the company of Mornington, both in town and at Holwood, and from their correspondence they would seem to have contracted a degree of intimacy which the diversity of their dispositions would hardly have led the world to suppose. A letter from Brighton, where he was detained 'by the state of his miserable nerves' dwelt with much feeling on a recent vote of the Convention denouncing the English Premier as an enemy of the human race; its author Garnier openly advocating the right of every one to assassinate him. 'This last decree of the dogs of hell against Pitt is the consummation of his glory and of their infamy. But I own I dread their venom: they are capable of encouraging any attempt, however base and inhuman, and I am afraid they might find hands to execute their projects even in this country. The very idea is enough to make one tremble, and it is the more horrid because it is impossible for any precaution to ward off such a blow. We must trust to Pitt's fortune, and to that protection which must attend him against such wickedness.'[1]

During the recess he visited the Speaker at Woodley, confessing to him the restlessness and discontent to which he was a prey. Addington saw clearly enough the ambition with which he was consumed, and said, 'You want a wider sphere; you are dying of the cramp.' His letters from this place record gratefully the solace and encouragement he found in the sympathy of his friend.[2]

The Speaker, if consulted, was not likely to have approved of a step which he now resolved on, and which though obviously dictated by motives the most generous and unworldly, brought him neither credit or satisfaction. For a considerable time he had been devoted to the society of the daughter of a French gentleman, M. Pierre Roland, sometimes mistaken for the Girondist minister of that name, whose fate, with that of his accomplished wife Manon, forms the subject of one of the most tragic scenes of the Revolution. Mademoiselle Hyacinthe Gabrielle had not been particularly well brought up; her associations were unlike those of her lover;

---

[1] 26th August, 1793.   [2] November 1793.

but she possessed charms of beauty and of wit that held him long in willing bondage. After the birth of several children she persuaded him to make her his wife; and they were married November 29, 1794, in the presence of a few of his political friends, at St. George's, Hanover Square.

On the meeting of Parliament, Mornington was put forward to defend the continuance of the war against revolutionary France. 'Regardless of the unaggressive declarations of the Constituent Assembly, her armies had overrun Piedmont and the Low Countries, and under the pretence of diffusing the blessings of social and political liberty, these countries had been made the prey of democratic ambition. France itself was become the scene of every species of tyranny and atrocity: many sections of the community were described to be in such distress that they were unable to pay the taxes requisite for the support of the State; the consequence was the emission of paper money to an amount that had totally ruined public credit. Taxation, though oppressive, failed to yield sufficient to maintain a wasteful expenditure, and the sudden confiscation of estates reduced the selling value of land to a degree that rendered spoliation unprofitable. The people had been sneered out of their religion, and the Church bereft of its possessions, without making any class wealthier or better.

'Could the inhabitants of Britain compare the situation of the French with their own and not feel a determination to guard their country from the causes that had produced so much misery, whatever might be the cost, and how great soever the hazards they might encounter?

'Did the history of Europe afford the precedent of any war since her civilisation, wherein the victor was allowed to retain all he had taken and to recover all he had lost? Such a treaty was yet to be discovered, and such demands could only proceed from a spirit of vanity, insolence, and rapacity that ought to be manfully resisted. But were Great Britain in conjunction with her allies to condescend to such meanness, would it secure her from further insult? A prostrate enemy was proverbially an object of contempt, and would always be trod upon sooner than a resolute foe that stood his ground to the last.

'Our choice must now be made between the vigorous prosecution of our present exertions, and an ambiguous state neither of open hostility or of real repose; a state in which we should suffer most of the inconveniences of war, in which we should enjoy none of the solid advantages of peace; in which, if we could purchase even at the expense of our honour and our faith a short respite from the direct attack of the enemy, we should never for a moment feel the genuine sense of permanent security, unless we could contemplate without emotion the rapid progress of the arms and principles of France in the territories of our allies, unless we could behold without anxiety the rapid approaches of the same danger threatening the British dominions, unless we could sit at ease with the axe suspended over our heads, and wait with tranquillity of mind the moment when these formidable enemies, after the extinction of every element of order and regular government in their own country, after the subjugation of every foreign power whose allegiance might assist us in our last struggles, strengthened by additional sources, animated by the prospect of new plunder, and flushed with the triumphant success of their prosperous crimes, should turn their whole force against the British monarchy, and complete their victory over the interests of civil society by the final destruction of that fair fabric of government under which these happy kingdoms have so long enjoyed the inseparable advantages of substantial liberty, settled order, and established law. We cannot have forgotten that before the

French had declared war against us, we had seen in their conduct views of aggrandisement, projects of ambition, and principles of fixed hostility against all established government, and we had been convinced that, unless the foundation of our complaints should be removed by a total alteration in their system with respect to foreign nations, war on our part would become at length inevitable. Before we can be justified in relinquishing the principles by which our proceedings have hitherto been governed, we shall require satisfactory proof, either that the impressions which we had originally conceived of the views of France were erroneous, or that by the course of subsequent events the success of the war is become desperate and impracticable. A variety of occurrences since the commencement of the war, and many new and striking proofs, have concurred to confirm the wisdom and justice of our decision, not merely on general grounds, but precisely on the very grounds on which it was originally founded. In a letter to his constituents in defence of his measures after he had fallen into disgrace, Brissot reveals the whole secret and mystery of the French Revolution, and makes an open confession of the principles by which France was directed in her intercourse with other powers, of the means which she employed and of the ends which she pursued. The views which are attributed to France previous to the war were views of aggrandisement and ambition connected with propagandism and aggression, principles incompatible with the existence of any regular Government. The particular acts by which those views were manifested were, First, the decree of November 19,[1] in which France made, according to her own language, a grant of universal fraternity and assistance; and ordered her generals everywhere to aid and abet those citizens who had suffered, or might suffer hereafter, in the cause of what she called liberty.

[1] 1792.

Her sense of liberty as applied to England was shown by the reception of seditious and treasonable addresses, and by the speeches of the President of the National Convention, expressing his wish for the auspicious institution of a British Convention, founded, as such an institution must have been, upon the destruction of every branch of our happy constitution. Secondly, the conduct of France in incorporating the territories of other powers with her own, under colour of voluntary acts of union pretended to have been freely voted by the people; particularly in the cases of Savoy and the Netherlands, of both which countries France had assumed the sovereignty. Thirdly, the opening of the Scheldt in direct violation of the most solemn treaties guaranteed by France herself. And lastly, by her general designs of hostility against Holland. We were told by Robespierre that a part of the general scheme of Brissot and his associates was to free and arm all the negroes in the French colonies in the West Indies. The Girondin, instead of attempting to refute this charge, takes merit to himself for the ingenuity and simplicity of the invention; that by the simple operation of purifying the colonial system of the French islands, he would have accomplished the destruction of all the British colonies in the West Indies.

'A Revolutionary Government! a Government which, for the ordinary administration of affairs, resorts to those means of violence and outrage which had hitherto been considered, even in France, as being exclusively appropriated to the laudable and sacred purpose of subverting all lawful and regular authority. The sense of the epithet Revolutionary, which was so lavishly applied by the Convention to every part of this new system, required some explanation. An extract from the proceedings of the National Convention will serve to exemplify the manner in which that singular phrase is understood and admired by the most unquestionable authority in the series of revolutions. M. Barrère makes a report respecting the situation of the Republic in the month of December; he reads a variety of despatches from the national commissioners in various parts of the Republic, and at length he produces a letter from Carrier, one of the commissioners of the Convention, dated Nantes, December 10. This letter, after giving an account of a successful attack upon the Royalists, concludes with the following remarkable words: "This event has been followed by another, which has however nothing new in its nature. Fifty-eight individuals, known by the names of refractory priests, arrived at Nantes from Angers. They were shut up in a barge on the river Loire, and last night they were all sunk to the bottom of that river. What a revolutionary torrent is the Loire!" You expect to hear, perhaps, that the disgusting relation of this inhuman action raised some emotions of horror, if not of compassion, in the audience; you expect to hear that the Convention manifested its resentment at this abuse of the revolutionary language; but does any symptom of such sentiments appear? No! after having listened to this interesting report, the Convention votes the following resolution: "The National Convention, highly satisfied with the report of Barrère, orders it to be printed, inserted in the votes, and sent to all the armies." Here you learn the full force and energy of their new phraseology. The Loire is a revolutionary torrent because it has been found a useful and expeditious instrument of massacre; because it has destroyed by a sudden and violent death fifty-eight men, against whom no crime was alleged but the venerable character of their sacred functions and the faithful adherence to the principles of their religion. But this event is truly said to have nothing new in its nature; I dwell upon it for the application of the phrase, not for the singularity of the fact. Every proceeding since the commencement of the troubles in France which has been dignified by the title of revolutionary is marked with similar characters of violence or blood.

'Equally anomalous and irrational was their system of finance. A letter is read in the Convention from Fouché, in which you may perceive the first symptoms of a growing indignation against gold and silver, which he says, "has been the cause of all the calamities of the Republic. I know not by what weak compliance those metals are still suffered to remain in the hands of suspected persons; let us degrade and vilify gold and silver; let us fling these deities of monarchy in the dirt, and establish the worship of the austere virtues of a Republic. I send you seventeen chests filled with gold, silver, and plate of all sorts, the spoil of churches and castles; you will see with peculiar pleasure two beautiful croziers and a ducal coronet of silver gilt." This ingenious idea of vilifying and degrading valuable effects by seizing them for the use of the Republic was not lost upon the French Minister of Finance. A few days after the receipt of this letter a citizen appeared at the bar, and desired to be permitted to exchange certain pieces of gold and silver bearing the image of the tyrant for Republican paper. This patriotic and disinterested offer, as one may imagine, was gladly accepted by the Convention; but upon a motion being made that honourable mention of this transaction should be inserted in the votes, the Chancellor of the Exchequer rose with the utmost indignation to oppose so monstrous a proposition; and delivered a most eloquent and vehement invective against gold and silver.

'Far worse than this folly was the frenzy against every species of religion. In the month of October the Archbishop of Paris enters the Convention, accompanied by a solemn procession of his vicars and by several curates of Paris. He makes a speech in which he renounces the priesthood in his own name and in the name of all his attendants, and declares that he does it because he is convinced that no national worship should be tolerated excepting the worship of Liberty and Equality. Julien, of Toulouse, a member of the Convention and a member of the Protestant Church, says: "For twenty years I have exercised the functions of a Protestant minister: I declare that I renounce them for ever. In every religion there is more or less quackery. It is glorious to be able to make this declaration under the auspices of reason, of philosophy, and of that sublime constitution which has already overturned the errors of superstition and monarchy in France, and which now prepares a similar fate for all foreign tyrannies. I declare that I will no longer enter into any other temple than the sanctuary of the laws; that I will acknowledge no other God than Liberty, no other worship than that of my country, no other gospel than the Republican Constitution. Such is my profession of moral and political faith. Dumont, one of the national commissioners, announces to the Convention that, in order to destroy fanaticism, he arrests all priests who celebrate religious ceremonies on Sundays, and that he has made several captures of these infamous bigots. The municipality of Paris decreed that all churches and temples of religious worship of whatever denomination, should be instantly shut. The cathedral church of Notre-Dame, and all the parish churches were shut up for some time until they could be regenerated and purified from every taint of Christianity.' He thus concluded: 'All the circumstances of your situation are now before you. You are now to make your option; you are now to decide whether it best becomes the dignity, the wisdom, and the spirit of a great nation to rely for existence on the arbitrary will of a restless and implacable enemy or on her own sword; you are now to decide whether you will entrust to the valour and skill of British fleets and British armies—to the approved faith an l united strength of your numerous and powerful allies—the defence of the limited monarchy of these realms, of the constitution of Parliament, of all the established ranks and orders of society among us, of the sacred rights of property, and of this whole frame of our laws, our liberty, and our religion ; or whether you will deliver over the guardianship of all these blessings to the justice of Cambon the plunderer of the Netherlands, to the moderation of Danton, to the religion of Robespierre, to the friendship of Barrère, or finally, to whatever may be the accidental caprice of any new band of malefactors, who in the last convulsions of their exhausted country, may be destined to drag the present tyrants to their own scaffolds, to seize their lawless power, to emulate the depravity of their example, and to rival the enormity of their crimes.'

A strange episode in the family history illustrates the perils and perplexities of the time. Lady Anne Wesley who married the Hon. Henry Fitzroy in 1790, had accompanied him to Portugal, whither he had been ordered by his physicians. On hearing of his death in March 1794, her youngest brother Henry, who was much attached to her, repaired to Lisbon. When returning home the vessel was seized by a French privateer and taken into Brest. On the disclosure of their rank Mr. Wesley and his sister were consigned to more than ordinarily strict surveillance in the interior with other *détenues*. A worse fate had nearly overtaken them. The Committee of Public Safety, then at the height of its sanguinary power, was reminded of the recent denunciation of its principles and practices by Mornington in the House of Commons. So rare an opportunity of vengeance was too tempting to be neglected, and without trial or inquiry Mr. Wesley and his sister were consigned to the scaffold. Their names actually stood upon the list for the next holocaust in July, when happily for them, on the eve of their impending doom, Robespierre fell, and with many others they partook of the unexpected reprieve. One may easily imagine the misery of suspense in which their family in England lay during their imprisonment. Months rolled away without their liberation. From her captivity Lady Anne wrote to her brother in July, saying they were well treated and in good health; but he saw no prospect at the time of their being set at liberty.[1] It was not until the end of autumn that means were found of effecting their exchange; and Lady Mornington who now resided permanently in London, had the happiness of again embracing the beloved daughter who had been lost and was found. By her subsequent marriage with Sir Culling Smith she became the mother of the Duchess of Beaufort and Lady Westmoreland.

The Premier did not, however, see his way as yet to give him the promotion he coveted, and he imparted once more his chagrin to his friend in the Chair. 'I am very much afraid, from a variety of circumstances, that Pitt has no idea of altering my situation this year. I cannot tell you how much I am mortified at that and other symptoms, not of unkindness but of (what perhaps I deserve) decided preference for others. I have serious thoughts of relinquishing the whole pursuit and becoming a spectator (not a very indifferent one, as you may believe, either to the success of the war or to Pitt's interest or honour), but I cannot bear to creep on in my present position.' Soon after he wrote in a different spirit. 'Before leaving town Pitt sent for me, and told me that in settling the treaty (of Coalition) he had positively stipulated that I should have the next office (to be held with the Privy Council) which should become vacant; and he further informed me that the Duke of Portland entered very readily into this arrangement, and said it was

[1] Mornington to the Speaker, July, 1794.

but reasonable that I should stand first for such a situation. This is, I own, more than I expected, seeing myself wholly passed over in the late changes, and having received no explanation on the subject. I am now satisfied that I was not entirely out of Pitt's mind, which was my principal apprehension.'[1]

Under a chief like Dundas, who was a cormorant of work, and an ever-ready debater, there was indeed little chance of distinction. Meetings of the Board were infrequent; and for the most part so entirely limited to giving formal sanction to measures previously decided on, that there was little inducement to attend: and when a Junior Commissioner was absent, he was hardly missed. In 1794 Mornington's name is recorded in the minutes as having attended but five times; the next year on as few occasions; and in 1796 but once.

[1] To the Speaker, 27th July, 1794.

CHAPTER VII.

HOLWOOD AND WALMER.

1795–7.

OUTBREAKS of the black population in the West Indies, incited by French agents from St. Domingo, scared timid friends of emancipation; but Wilberforce gave notice that early in the session of 1796 he would renew his motion for the abolition of the African trade. That year had been agreed to, even by its defenders in Parliament four years before, as the last of its duration; and to rekindle the hopes excited by the promise, 'Mornington agreed to write a pamphlet without his name, Pitt being friendly just then.'[1]

On November 4, 1795, a Royal Proclamation appeared warning the peaceable against attending seditious meetings; and a few days after Pitt brought in a Bill to suppress assemblies tending to endanger the public peace. On the second reading, November 17, a long and animated debate arose. Mornington began his speech by asking three questions:—

1. Did there exist an evil of magnitude sufficient to call for some remedy?

2. Was there power in the law as it stood, adequate to meet the evil?

3. Was the Bill competent to meet the evil, or did it exceed the degree of power necessary for that purpose?

[1] *Wilberforce's Diary*, 19th December, 1795.

At the close of the previous session the suspension of the Habeas Corpus Act was repealed, whereupon the Corresponding Society and Friends of Liberty renewed their dissemination of revolutionary pamphlets, and a monster meeting was held at Copenhagen Fields to denounce the Throne, the Church, and the Aristocracy: to petition for universal suffrage, annual elections, and equal division of landed property. Tyrannicide as the speediest means of ridding the world of evil kings, bishops, and ministers was a favourite theme of the revolutionary propaganda, and the scarcity of bread was logically shown to be ascribable not to bad weather, but to parliamentary corruption. In a cheap tract, meant for popular instruction in the wrongs and duties of the time, and sold at the printer's at which the petitions for Reform lay for signature, the guillotine was defined as 'an instrument of rare invention; for as it is the custom to decapitate and not hang kings, it is proper to have this instrument ready to make death easy to them, supposing a necessity of cutting them off.' Ankerstroem and Damien were held up to the reverence of mankind. 'The publisher was one of those named to the public by the societies in a list of patriotic printers. ("Name, name," from all parts of the House.) Citizen Lee, of Copenhagen Street,' said the Earl. 'This is not even English treason, it is all French. Does it not sound more like a bloody page of Marat, or the sanguinary code of Robespierre, than the production of an Englishman? Two other publications, he happened to know, were likewise sold by the same bookseller, entitled "King-killing" and the "Reign of George the Last." Could there be any doubt as to the aim and tendency of such publications, or that it was the duty of Parliament to put a stop to them? He believed the bulk of the people were loyal and attached to the constitution; but if men were healthy and strong, was that a reason we should suffer the indiscriminate sale of food that was poison?'

At the close of his speech, throughout which he seemed weak and nervous,[1] he apologised to the House for not entering into the legal necessity for exceptional legislation, with which he would leave others to deal. Sheridan followed, quizzing 'the noble lord whom they had seen two years before, with the same placid countenance and sonorous voice, in the same attitude, leaning gracefully upon the table, and giving an account, from shreds and patches of Brissot, that the French Republic would last but a few months longer. Unfortunately for the credit of the noble lord, not one word of all his predictions had come to pass; and he believed he was as right in his later prophecies as he had been before. He knew not the heart and disposition of the people, or he would not have accused them of susceptibility to such foolish and mischievous suggestions. But looking about for evidence of dangerous plots, and finding none, he bethought him of turning up the dirt of old bookshops and the rubbish of bookstalls to make out symptoms of treason. If the miserable scraps he had read were such, why did not the Attorney General prosecute the traitors? if not, why pass a Bill to denude the nation of its most valued privilege?'

By 213 to 43 the Bill was read a second time.

How early his hopes of promotion turned towards the East is uncertain. Subordinate office, with its irksome yoke of routine, certainty of small pay, and tantalising liability to be asked every now and then for an opinion, which, put aside for the moment, was often without acknowledgment subsequently taken, had lost its charm. He had studied assiduously in his department, though a zealot in the pursuit of pleasure. He always worked perseveringly and patiently; and in acquiring knowledge or elaborating the exposition of what he had acquired, no time or toil was grudged by him. Still he

[1] *Wilberforce's Diary.* 'Poor Mornington nervous, and Sheridan brutal.'

must have had enough of apprenticeship, and must have longed for the enjoyment of self-assertion and the sense of mastery. It is easier for a man born in the purple, even though he be poor and without high connections, to let a minister know what he wishes to be offered, than it is for an outsider, who the minister thinks should be grateful for having been admitted within the outer circle of administration. Mornington was from the first peculiarly fortunate in this respect; and through the Grenvilles he had always access to the unofficial ear of power. Pitt liked him; liked him much; liked him very much; but during the war his mind became more and more absorbed with its anxieties and oppressed with its difficulties; and in the face of continued failure abroad and hardly repressible disaffection at home, he might well ponder conscientiously the specific and comparative fitness of every candidate for important employment, and put aside claims that, however fair, might wait. Meanwhile, Arthur Wellesley (for reasons which need not be dwelt on here) asked leave to exchange from his regiment in Ireland to another serving in India, and his brother who had not much else to give him, furnished him with a letter of introduction from Lord Cornwallis to his successor Sir John Shore, which might help him in that distant field to make his way. 'Colonel Wellesley,' he wrote, 'is a sensible man and a good officer, who will no doubt conduct himself in a manner to meet your Excellency's approbation.'[1] And this was the planting out of the sapling which was destined to outgrow all other trees of the forest, and to spread its arms till princes and potentates of every degree were glad to shelter underneath its shade. Sir John, who had no stomach for warfare but liked to be civil to men of consequence at home, received the new comer kindly, and found occupation for him in the Presidency of Madras. In

[1] 10th June, 1796.

compliance with his brother's request he sent him his impressions of things around him, and his early letters bear the same stamp of colourless accuracy and calm good sense which characterised the mass of his subsequent correspondence. Unlike the official and semi-official letters to the Board of Control, they noted with a quiet photographic fidelity how the system of government under the Company looked and languished. They were confirmation from a fresh and unsophisticated view of much that Mornington, from his three years' familiarity with the weakness and rottenness of the system, was already too well prepared to believe. He valued them in this respect as confirmatory evidence, whose trustworthiness so far as it went (and it went not an inch beyond the range of personal observation), there was no room to doubt. But he valued them for another and quite a different reason, of more consequence to the world's history. To his fraternal partiality they proved that the boy he had sent to school, and the ensign he had got named a viceregal aide-de-camp, and the subaltern whose thoughtless debts he had not always chosen to pay, was at five-and-twenty going to turn out no ordinary man. If he should himself go to the East it would make a difference, his being there: and a still greater difference to Arthur, his being there.

In 1796 he found it convenient to change his nominal constituency. In a tent under an old tree which marked the boundary of what had once been the site of Old Sarum, he was formally proposed with Mr. George Hardinge, as a fit and proper person to represent the former village, of which all the houses had long since disappeared. Two clergymen, three farmers, and Lord Camelford's bailiff composed the unanimous assembly; and three times a demand was made whether anyone had a rival candidate to propose. No response being made, the former member and the Earl were declared duly elected to serve in the Commons of Great Britain; and a formal letter from the returning officer was despatched, sealed with a plenitude of wax, to acquaint those favoured burgesses with a proof thus given of the popular confidence. It must not be supposed that because the voters were select and the deliberation brief, the legislative honours so coveted cost nothing. They had in point of fact, a price quoted in the member market, and it was subject to little fluctuation; and such confidence subsisted between all the parties concerned that the money was often paid to the owner of the constituency before the object of their choice had even been mentioned to them. Mornington sat for Old Sarum till October 1797, when he was created Baron Wellesley in the peerage of England, when his place was taken by Charles W. W. Wynne. Some years later Lord Caledon purchased from Lord Camelford the seats and the farms of Old Sarum for 60,000*l.*, the net proceeds being 700*l.* a year in rent; and the members of the family of Alexander occupied the seats until the storm of 1832 blew down the tent and the representation, never more to be set up again.

The condition of affairs at home and abroad in 1796 was overcast with the deepest gloom. Bonaparte drove the Austrians everywhere before him in Northern Italy; and although Jourdan and Moreau were forced to recross the Rhine, the King of Prussia, deaf to all expostulation from his allies, concluded a convention with the French Directory by which he agreed to yield the left bank of that river. The Court of Naples, terrified at the ill-fortune of Austria, sued for peace; and Spain, under the influence of Godoy, not only seceded from the grand alliance, but suddenly declared war. In the new Parliament Opposition failed to recover any of the great constituencies it had lost, and the ministerial phalanx was numerous and compact as ever. But the public heart was sore with the dismal reiteration of reverses and the unrelaxed pressure of taxation. The debt had reached 400,000,000*l.*—a sum unparalleled and appalling when measured by the yearly earnings of the nation. In January the funds were as low as sixty-seven, and in September they touched fifty-three.

Rumours of invasion, for a time disregarded, waxed louder during the summer of 1796, and Lord Camden grew alarmed for the safety of Ireland, where popular despair of reform and emancipation rendered too easy the promptings of sedition. The confederacy organised by Wolfe Tone was still immature, but it was avowed and notorious everywhere; and that irrepressible revolutionist visited Paris to concert with Clarke and Carnot the expedition eventually led by Hoche.

The remoter coasts of the west and south of Ireland, full of numerous creeks and bays, and for the most part difficult of access from the capital, offered facilities for attack more easily forgotten at Holwood or Bulstrode than at the Phœnix Park. The Viceroy wrote privately to Mornington that he thought Ireland neglected; and his correspondent thought so too, though he 'would not vex his chief at the Treasury at such a moment by telling him so;' he preferred disclosing his apprehensions to the Speaker. 'Without being prejudiced by the deep stake he had in the safety of Ireland, he thought he might say that to neglect the defence of that country was to ensure the conquest of this, with all its attendant horrors of revolution and pillage. A revolution in Ireland would be the infallible consequence of the landing of even a small French force in that country; and anyone might judge what sort of a neighbour Ireland would become. His gloomy apprehensions were the offspring of serious and deliberate reflection; and his great fear was a blow in Ireland before sufficient preparation had been made for our defence in that most vulnerable and mortal part.'[1]

Most of their mutual friends shared these fears; Pitt alone was or seemed to be, undaunted by the dangers that encompassed them. On the same day that Mornington urged so despondingly, the Premier wrote from Weymouth,[2] whither he had travelled at some inconvenience to see the King, full of elation at Lord Chatham's being raised to the Presidency of the Council, and at obtaining the reluctant assent of George III. to making overtures of peace. Lord Malmesbury was, however, able to accomplish nothing by the proposed negotiation; and a new loan at 5 per cent., of 18,000,000*l*., with additional taxes of 2,000,000*l*. a year, formed the principal items of the Budget laid before the new Parliament.[3]

Mornington did not omit however to remind his friend the Speaker of his own claims and disappointments. He thought that, as the Privy Seal must now be given away, he might have once more a chance of promotion. Tired of the perfunctory duties of a Junior Commissioner for India, he wrote to Pitt, hoping that an opportunity of advancement might soon occur; that his wish would be to go to the Upper House, but he did not press the point, thinking it did not become him to enter into any detail with him in that stage of the business. He was well persuaded that should any occasion offer he would have the assistance of Addington; but he relied so much upon Pitt as to think the application of other friends unnecessary.[4]

At the close of 1796 Malmesbury was desired by M. De la Croix to quit Paris within forty-eight hours; but was told that he might continue negotiations by letter. The Cabinet were

---

[1] Letter to the Speaker, 4th September, 1796.
[2] Stanhope's *Life of Pitt*, vol. ii. 381.   [3] October 1796.
[4] To the Speaker, 4th September, 1796.

unanimous in resenting such an affront, and the address after Christmas, in reply to a message from the Crown, adopting and approving their policy, was carried by 212 to 37 votes. Though strong in St. Stephen's, Government was weak in the country, and public credit sank from day to day. It rained incessantly petitions against the War; and many thought the end drew nigh when George III. came from Windsor to hold a Council upon Sunday, for an Order to suspend Cash Payments.

If Pitt was not the most humane of ministers he was the easiest and best of masters. He liked to make those around him happy; and to those he trusted he was never tired of bringing gifts and gold, and the frankincense of praise, exquisite and precious when conferred by him. His servants robbed him now and then because they could not resist the temptation of never being questioned, but they doated on him all the same; sat up for him night after night without grumbling, and would have fought for him in the streets had he been insulted. His confidants, with perhaps, two exceptions, never wavered in their loyalty. It was not concession to superiority of intellect; it was devotion to the man, so gentle, lenient, blind to errors, self-risking in defence, forgiving even of neglect; yet incapable of sympathy in the varied feelings and emotions that made up the fever of their lives. Love he had but one, but to that one his whole existence from boyhood, when he stood beside his father's gouty chair, and heard his tragic boast of overruling Crown and Cabinet, and of holding Christendom at bay, to the day when three great Whig peers, after ten years' hopeless opposition, had consented to take office under him; and from that day on to the end—but one passion stirred the current of his blood with hope, or hate, or joy. Consistent or inconsistent, baffled or triumphant, securing for his country the blessings of industry and peace, or exacting reluctantly from its impoverishment the resources for a war his wisdom loathed, the all-absorbing aim and purpose of his being was to rule: and for this he knew instruments pliant and attached to be indispensable. No commonplace regard for family ties can account for the number of great offices conferred on near relatives. He made his cousin Lord Buckingham Viceroy of Ireland, and on his resignation asked for him a dukedom. In a cabinet of nine there sat already his brother Chatham and his cousin William Grenville; and he now desired that Edward Eliot, an equally near relation, should be Governor General of India. Dundas, who could refuse him nothing, forwarded the recommendation to Leadenhall Street, and the Directors acquiesced. Eliot was in private a popular man, in public a man without achievements or pretensions. But he was facile, intelligent, honourable, and devoted to his overruling kinsman; and nobody seems to have questioned the appointment. Opposition had made away with most of its means of influence for good or evil; and the public were too much occupied with the suspension of cash payments,[1] threats of invasion, suits against the Press, United Irish plots, and mutiny at the Nore, to ask or care who was to go to India. Eliot unexpectedly fell ill, and was told by his physicians that he must not think of serious work or a tropical climate: whereupon Lord Cornwallis, to his surprise, was asked a second time to undertake the onerous charge. No objection was made on the part of the Company, and the question remained, who should go to Madras?

Lord Hobart, not without some persuasion, had accepted the Government of that Presidency with an understanding, if not a promise, of the reversion of Bengal. He took little trouble to conceal his impatience at being obliged to act in subordination to the son of a supercargo—a man who avowed

---

[1] 26th February, 1797.

in public and private his sense of obligation and anxious desire to repair the original sins of invasion and oppression by doing the most careful justice to the native races. His demeanour to the Rajah of Travancore and the Nawab of Arcot drew from the Governor General at first remonstrance and at last rebuke, and their official quarrel so increased in bitterness that at the beginning of 1796 he wrote home saying he wished to be relieved of his government if Sir John Shore retained the superior post for which he was tired of waiting. Dundas had as little respect for his arrogant and fretful explosions of temper as for Shore's tenderness for native feelings or his sedulous avoidance of all pretexts for war; and he referred confidentially their respective complaints to the Master General of the Ordnance, to whom likewise the offended Nawab of the Carnatic addressed a touching appeal for protection and justice. Bred a soldier and proud of his conquests in Mysore, Cornwallis had little sympathy with theories of total abstinence from warfare; but as he subsequently proved, all his tendencies were towards forbearance, leniency, and peace. He thought however, that to maintain our position in the midst of rivals so numerous and formidable as then existed in Southern Asia, it was above all things necessary to have unity in council and firmness in action: and though sincerely averse from being personally involved again in Oriental troubles, he could not recommend the retention in office of either disputant.

Shore had evinced more regard for the prejudices and claims of the Indian army than deference for the decrees of the Horse Guards; and he had taken upon himself the responsibility of suspending a brevet in June 1796 which would have put several officers of the line over the heads of their seniors in the native regiments. This, and his difference with Lord Hobart, determined Dundas to recall both, and to ask Lord

Cornwallis to undertake a second time the arduous duty of presiding over English affairs in the East. He was sworn into office February 1, 1797; and applied himself at once to arbitrate between the conflicting military claims, as represented in England by the Court of Directors, who supported the Bengal army, and the Board of Control, who sustained the pretensions of the King's troops. By his temper and judgment he led them to agree to terms of accommodation which might, he thought, reprieve him from the necessity of immediate departure on a mission, at his time of life peculiarly unwelcome. Mornington had by diligence in his office at the Board of Control, and by thoughtful study of the history of our acquisitions in the East during the forty years that had elapsed since the battle of Plassy, qualified himself in a certain degree for administrative trust. Early in March Dundas offered him the government of Madras, which his first impulse was to accept without reserve. But his pride after some reflection whispered that he ought not to take Lord Hobart's place upon terms inferior to those on which he had held it. He consulted confidentially Lord Buckingham, who was the friend of both; and some weeks elapsed before he came to any decision.[1]

He hesitated, as he declared, to take the situation until assured that Hobart should have a pension and peerage during his father's lifetime to compensate him for the disappointment of his anticipations of further advancement in the East. But on this being settled to the satisfaction of Lord Guilford and other friends, Mornington agreed to take the subordinate post when vacant, Dundas promising him the reversion of the higher Presidency. About the middle of April he finally accepted the government of Madras, with the provisional succession to that of Bengal. His appointment not

[1] To the Marquess of Buckingham, from Hertford Street, 20th April, 1797.

having been formally made by the Court of Directors he could not yet acknowledge his destination to India. The delays which had retarded the conclusion of this arrangement had rendered it impossible for him to embark with Lord Cornwallis, with whom however he was in habits of the most confidential intercourse from day to day, and with whom he wished to pass some weeks in Bengal before the termination of his government. His own departure would probably not take place before July or August. Finding that the office of Private Civil Secretary would be well worth his brother Henry's acceptance, he resolved to take him with him. His intention was to take no other person besides servants, and as a rule to avoid all engagements in Europe, in order to guard himself against any temptation to an irregular distribution of patronage. 'In this resolution, which he formed very early, on principles which a long attention to the affairs of India had enabled him to make with some degree of confidence, he was strongly confirmed by his upright and experienced friend.'[1]

Discontent at this time had become epidemic; and every class and order of men seemed to be distressed and demoralised by its influence. Towards the end of April reports reached the Admiralty of cabals among the seamen in the Home Fleet, desultory and undefined, but of an unwonted description. Officialism, always incredulous of the gravity of irregular questionings of its authority, smiled, sneered, frowned, swore profanely, wrote one or two impatient letters to Vice-Admirals in command, but upon the whole did not think it could signify, and went to dinner. Day by day gusts of—well, not exactly of mutiny, but something very like the beginning of it—were stated to prevail at Portsmouth; and Cornwallis who was resorted to continually as a friend in need ready for all work, consented to pay a visit

[1] *Ibid.*

of observation and enquiry to the malcontent squadron. So little however was the matter thought to wear a serious aspect, that Dundas continued without interruption to ply him with minute interrogatories and verbose suggestions about military reorganisation in Bengal which at last put him fairly out of temper. While at Portsmouth he wrote, impatient at being urged to hasten his departure for Calcutta or to spend time over details of Indian legislation, 'unless the business of the fleet can be speedily adjusted, a few days may place a French army in Ireland: is this a time to be occupied about speculative arrangements of the Indian army?'[1] Already Pitt began to feel reluctance to lose him at such a crisis, and to wish that instead he would accept the government of Ireland. On his declining, Lord Camden was sounded as to whether he would object to one so much his superior in service, talent, and rank being appointed to the command in chief of the army there.[2] His letter to Cornwallis was generous and patriotic in the highest sense, offering to make way for him as head of the Irish Executive, or, if he refused, to hand him over without reserve all the powers of his office relating to military affairs. He did not however choose to be placed in such a position. Continually increasing doubts and anxieties respecting Ireland, with unconfessed misgivings as to the capacity of those entrusted with the local conduct of affairs, rendered the minister more than ever unwilling to spare his veteran colleague, and for some months longer he remained Master General of the Ordnance.

The fraction who still adhered in Parliament to Fox despondingly agreed to vote once more for a motion in favour of Reform to be proposed by Grey.[3] But the spectacle of democracy run to seed, resentment against social propagandism

---

[1] To General Ross, from Culford, 9th May, 1797.
[2] 23rd May, 1797, from Dublin Castle.   [3] 26th May, 1797.

at the point of the sword, and the revulsion of feeling caused by the ribaldry of Paine and his disciples, had estranged from the cause of progress many in all grades of the community, on whom Burke's vaticinations and invectives had been spent in vain. The debate was but the strophe and antistrophe of denunciation and despair, the issue being palpable and the last scene of the drama being come. Ninety-one votes for enquiry into the state of the representation were overborne by two hundred and fifty-six; whereupon Fox and some others, contrary to every principle of consistency, dignity, and duty, announced their resolve no longer to attend the House of Commons. Sheridan's mother wit and Fitzpatrick's sense of expediency forbade their following their leader in secession; and for the next two years the disjected members of the once powerful Liberal party were to be found, some thinly studding the benches on the left hand of the chair, others clustering round Windham and Gilbert Eliot on the benches opposite, and the rest playing whist at Brooks's or sauntering at St. Anne's Hill. A like lamentable result of extravagance in the leaders and disruption among the led was exhibited in the Irish Parliament, where Grattan and Ponsonby withdrew in womanish vexation at their counsel not being heeded, and left the despairing populace to follow the mad beckonings of Lord Edward Fitzgerald, Arthur O'Connor, and Napper Tandy.

Logically it was easy for Pitt to confute such folly, and histrionically to treat it with magnanimous disdain. But at heart he deplored everything that tended to shake popular faith in existing institutions. He knew too well the rottenness of much of the rigging, and he had sincerely striven to overhaul and refit the ship, before it had come on to blow. Anxiously he had resisted putting out to sea, and wistfully he watched for opportunity to make for shore.

Cornwallis had not been easily induced again to think of

service abroad, and it was only on the understanding that he was not expected to remain longer than might be necessary to compose certain administrative differences, that he had agreed to go. It was midsummer before Mornington could, even in confidence, say that he was about to depart for Madras, upon the understanding 'that if Cornwallis did not go to Bengal, he himself was to proceed direct to Fort William.'[1] On July 26 at the levee he took leave for Madras.

Malmesbury not long before had been sent to negotiate for peace at Lille; and his confidential correspondence shows how sick the Minister was of war. When hard terms were offered, Pitt told the plenipotentiary that 'he must stifle to the utmost every feeling of pride.'[2] Grenville, with his harder nature, would have answered saucily every boast and broken off at every new pretension of the Directory, but Pitt would not be piqued or provoked, and made him leave the door ajar. He wanted peace for the country's sake and for his own, for he was too wise not to know that—

> In war itself war is no ultimate purpose.
> The vast and sudden deeds of violence,
> Adventures wild, and wonders of the moment,
> These are not they, my son, that generate
> The calm, the blissful, and the enduring mighty!

Even when the Envoy's pliancy and patience were at length worn out, and he had to return home, Pitt was willing to entertain a clandestine offer of Barras to sell him peace for a private sum of money;—so willing as actually to commit himself in writing to terms encouraging the strange expedient;[3] and with the King's assent he undertook at any risk

---

[1] From Hertford Street, to Mr. Sullivan, 3rd July, 1797.
[2] *Colchester's Diary*, i. 117.
[3] From Holwood, to M. Barras, 23rd September, 1797.

of cavil or criticism, to give secretly 400,000*l*. to stay the ruin of industry and staunch the effusion of blood. Nor was he to be warped to wrong by the recollection of splendid victories by sea or the confident hopes, soon to be justified, of fresh triumphs, notwithstanding the late outbreak of insubordination before the mast. To estimate correctly his mood at the period in question, and justly to appreciate his foreign policy, all this must be weighed and remembered; it was pending the negotiations at Lille that, after consulting Dundas, he suddenly relieved Mornington from all further doubt and tantalisation by offering him the greatest executive office under the Crown. Believing in his friend's devotion, and still more in the power of informing him with his own spirit, he delighted him with the announcement that the days of his official apprenticeship were ended, and that he was to be sent forth to do something more than play the showy part of Satrap of Hindostan. Here then at last Fortune had ceased to jilt him, and had fallen into his arms. The fair Hyacinthe was not easily made to understand 'what for' was the speechlessness of his delight. How could he explain it to her? How explain to the most matter-of-fact Englishman, and how much less to the most fanciful of Frenchwomen, that one brief flash of ministerial will seemed to light back all his chequered and oft despondent way— from early days with Newport at Dangan, or brother Arthur getting into debt as an idle aide-de-camp in Dublin,—to this golden hill-top of promise, power, and, more than all, opportunity of fame?

He spent the third week in September at Holwood, whither Dundas came from Wimbledon to talk over Company's affairs and the means of curbing the influence of French mercenaries in India. The peaceful and frugal *régime* of Shore had lulled to rest the fretful craving of Leadenhall Street for higher dividends; and it were not well to wake it up (so thought the jobbing President of the India Board), by meddling in native squabbles. If Raymond was at Hyderabad and Piron at Ougein, so much the worse for Tippoo, and the better for us. Let them fight it out among themselves by help of European *condottieri*, who after all could never take root in the country, and who would never cease to be looked on with jealousy by every home-born soldier of the Nizam or Scindiah. But the son of Chatham was a man who through the openings of Keston woods saw visions, and in the autumn sundown dreamed enduring dreams. With axe in hand as he stalked along, putting his companion often out of breath, or rested upon some fallen stem to shelter from the shower, he would paint to the excitable imagination of Mornington how England's influence must be expanded, if her sense of power was to be retrieved, or her place in competition with her rivals was to be made permanently great. For empire thrown away in the West compensation could be sought only in the East.

In company with the brother of the Minister the Proconsul Elect returned to town, and he saw Holwood no more. To his latest day he cherished the remembrance of the genial and ennobling society he was there privileged to enjoy, and the influence of which in maturing his capacity for rule and elevating his standard of statesmanship he never undervalued.

The remaining weeks of autumn were occupied with preparations for departure. We have come to think of a journey to India as little beyond a pleasure tour, and of a residence of five years with a good salary and allowances as an enviable piece of good fortune, unclouded by any substantial cause for misgiving or regret. A few days' travelling by railway and a few weeks' by sea enable us to span one continent and half another with little effort or fatigue. Eighty years ago the ocean voyage, with fine weather and without accident took five months; and the ordinary course of post between London and Calcutta was ten. To a susceptible, nervous, impetuous temperament the contemplation was more depressing than dignity and ambition would avow. The severance of domestic habits and those of long-standing intimacy tried him sore. If not constant, he was passionately fond of the beautiful and bewitching woman whom he had made his wife; and to their children he was tenderly attached. What if he should never look into her eyes or smooth their curling locks again? To take them with him was not to be thought of; to bid them good-bye, perhaps for life, perhaps for death, was hard. Inaudibly he felt with Byron on his thirty-seventh birthday—

> The hope, the fear, the jealous care,
> The exalted portion of the pain
> And power of love I cannot share;
> But wear the chain.

Wellesley was just thirty-seven, and like the poet sought to win fame in action encompassed with peril, rather than mere distinction or pre-eminence in the more commonplace competition for celebrity at home.

Negotiations for peace had been languishing for some time when they were abruptly brought to an end by the changes consequent on the *coup d'état* of the 18th Fructidor. Lord Malmesbury was summarily desired to quit Lille and seek more definite instructions at home; and Hoche, with Tone for his adjutant-general, was sent to organise an expedition, consisting of thirty sail of the line, with 20,000 men and 50,000 stand of arms on board, intended for a descent upon the coast of Ireland. While the English fleet lay in wait for them in the Downs, Admiral Duncan and his chief officers were frequently the guests of the First Minister at Walmer; and there Mornington found them when summoned to receive his final instructions from Pitt and Dundas ere setting out for India. It was an occasion never to be forgotten, and the excitement of which cannot easily be realised in ordinary times. The fate of the world might well seem to be in their hands. The old monarchies of Christendom, after a long and wasting conflict, had succumbed; and the minor States were paralysed by fear. The Jacobin party was once more ascendant and overbearing in the councils of Republican France; and England, without an ally and heavy laden with debt and taxation, stood at bay. A man of tougher frame, and nerves less finely strung, might well have sunk in spirit at the prospect of having in a few weeks to set out on a five months' voyage to undertake the government of vast and valuable dependencies recently won by the sword; and certain to become intractable at the faintest whisper of ill-fortune or defeat.

To a man like Mornington it was of more importance than he was conscious of at the time that he should in such circumstances have been brought into hourly contact and intimate counsel with the able, shrewd, experienced head of the department at home with whom confidentially he would have to correspond; with the dauntless commander on whose skill and energy might any hour depend the life of the nation; and above all with the minister but for whose indomitable persistency under difficulties and dangers, all other elements of self-preservation would have crumbled down into submission. The calm and clear forethought of Dundas, the unboastful but buoyant confidence of victory over any odds of Duncan, the fervid faith of Pitt in the destiny of the nation and in his own, wrought without deception or delusion as a spell upon the sensitive and ambitious spirit of the Pro-consul about to be. Gazing at the look and listening to the talk of three such men at such a juncture, every high and noble aspiration quickened within him; and emulation that had theretofore been but a fitful sentiment, waxed strong and resolute of purpose. To act his part in the world-drama about to be played, with men like these for colleagues and for judges generous and just, but undeceivable and inexorable, was a stimulus and incentive of rare intensity. By anticipation he began to feel that he too would be reckoned among those who should help to shape the condition of their time. They separated; and within a week all England thrilled with the news of Camperdown.

Amid preparations for departure he wrote to the Speaker, full of exultation at his appointment and satisfaction at having obtained the peerage 'which was to him an invaluable object both public and private.' He dwelt with much concern on Pitt's impaired health, but 'relied on Farquhar's prescriptions and the air of Walmer for his restoration.[1] Surely the glorious and inestimable victory over the Franco-Dutch must have been a powerful cordial.'

But scarce had the rejoicings ceased when tidings came that peace was signed at Campo Formio on October 17, between France and Austria, by which the Netherlands and Ionian Isles were ceded to the victorious Republic.

On November 3 he was presented to the Chancellor and took the oaths and his seat as a peer by the title of Baron Wellesley; yet, strange to say, nine years were destined to elapse ere he again entered the chamber whose privileges he had been so ambitious to share.

Among the emblems of idolatry he took from home was a full-length likeness of his wife and two elder boys, painted by Hoppner in his best manner,[2] and which adorned the chief reception-room at Fort William during his residence there.

Alluding to his showy outfit the 'Morning Chronicle' observed: 'To such a degree is the frigate encumbered with stores, carriages, and baggage, that should the rencontre of an enemy make it necessary to prepare for action, Lord Mornington will inevitably suffer from clearage in the course of five minutes a loss of at least 2,000l.'

---

[1] To the Speaker, 14th October, 1797.
[2] Now in the possession of Lady Houlton.

CHAPTER VIII.

THE VOYAGE OUT.

1798.

THREE months of noteless water-way, and with scarce anyone capable of affording him sympathy or sustainment in his arduous mission, his thoughts perpetually turned towards home, and he yearned to catch the echoes of familiar voices, and of occasional glances of that recognition in which his soul was wont to sun itself.

From Funchal he wrote to Lord Auckland (November 25), acknowledging his kind attention to Lady Mornington and himself 'during the hurry or rather the agony of his last moments in England,'[1] and hoping for the continuance of his care and solicitude for her whom he had left behind, which would be 'invaluable to her and to him during their separation.'

In the long days of that half-the-world-round voyage the young Pro-consul pondered the meaning of Pitt's parting words—that England might recoup in the East the empire lost in the West. In the solitude of his cabin, as the huge East Indiaman rolled in the swell of the tropic ocean, or as he paced the deck, dressed punctiliously as for dinner in Mayfair, when with fair wind the vessel sped towards the haven of Good Hope where she would be; he ruminated all the

[1] *Correspondence of Lord Auckland*, iii. 384.

instructions for his mission and tried to anticipate and weigh all the possible contingencies that might await him on his arrival at his post.

Lord Macartney, the first British Governor of the Cape, received him with due hospitality. He had himself not long before been named for the office eventually conferred upon his fellow-countryman; and being full of years and honours, he had only been induced to accept for a brief season dignified banishment to South Africa, by a salary of 10,000*l.* a year and a pension of 2,000*l.* for life. Great importance however was attached in 1797 to the acquisition of the old Dutch settlement as a half-way hostelry and harbour on the route to the East; and the experienced and accomplished diplomatist, who from personal observation had reported on all the kingdoms of the world and the glory of them, was assured by Dundas that he was of all men living the man who could do king and country a service by deciding on the spot what ought to be done with our new possession. At the Cape despatches from Sir George Barlow (acting Governor General) were brought to his supersessor which he opened and read: thereby anticipating by six weeks what was thought and said at Calcutta. There too, he met Lord Hobart on his way home, at whose instance the troops on their way to Manilla had lately been recalled; from an apprehension lest the Carnatic, left defenceless, should be suddenly invaded by the self-styled Sultan of Mysore.

From the first acquisition of territorial power on the Coromandel coast, the Moslem rulers of the table-land which comprised an important portion of the peninsula, had been at Madras the abiding cause of disquietude and fear. With the Hindoo sovereigns of the country, the trading settlers had seldom come into collision. For two centuries the princes of the house of Wadiyar had governed from their ivory throne at Bangalore; coining money, waging frontier wars, and refusing steadily to pay homage or tribute to the Mogul emperors. By degrees hereditary decrepitude tempted ambitious favourites to steal from them the substance of power, and in 1761 an Arab mercenary had the craftiness and hardihood to possess himself of the conjoint authority of General and Minister for life. Hyder Ali never ventured to depose the Rajah, who continued to live in all the pomp and circumstance of state; and who, though closely guarded, was deferentially produced at festivals to keep up in the eyes of the multitude the show of ancient sovereignty. Tippoo, less sagacious and more vain, discontinued the practice. The Rajah disappeared from public gaze and sunk unresistingly into a state of humiliation and penury. The usurper took the title of Sultan, and refused to treat with neighbouring States unless they recognised in him that dignity. His restless ambition was for ever plotting encroachments on some of his neighbours, and a week seldom passed without some mention of sinister designs, real or imaginary, being imputed to him in the despatches to the Home Government from Fort St. George. With the character of the man and the way in which he was regarded by all within eyeshot of his scowl, Mornington was consequently familiar; and he was not disposed to undervalue Lord Hobart's estimate of detriment and danger to be apprehended from Mysore.

Colonel Wesley with his regiment had formed part of the intended expedition to Manilla, and after its recall he had been invited by him to spend some weeks at Fort St. George. The account given of him by Lord Hobart to his brother served to confirm the confidence with which the latter looked forward to finding in him a sagacious and efficient auxiliary in council and in action. He had been little more than a year in India; but, unlike most of his companions in arms at that time, he had kept his blood cool and his eyes open. He had spent his leave of absence at Madras in examining carefully but quietly the outposts of the settlement, and noting the structural defects in the works relied on for defence. Thus unconsciously he was qualifying himself to take part in affairs of the utmost moment at no distant day, of which few yet foresaw a finger of the threatening hand in the horizon.

From Major Kirkpatrick, on sick leave from the Deccan, Mornington gathered much useful information regarding the foreign auxiliary corps in the native States. His first despatch to Dundas contained a lucid epitome of what he then learned. Scindiah had twenty thousand sepoys disciplined by Europeans or Americans. This was originally De Boigne's corps, and was then commanded by M. Perron, the subordinate officers being chiefly British. Holkar, the Peishwah, and the Rajah of Berar had smaller bodies of troops similarly organised; and D'Agincourt, described as a French democrat of aggressive temper, had lately enlisted for the service of Azim ul Dowlah a separate force encamped near Hyderabad. With what distinct purpose these subsidiary legions were severally embodied by the princes who watched one another with so much jealousy and emulation did not distinctly appear. They were evidently looked upon by their despotic paymasters as useful alternatives in case of domestic need; and no serious fear of the overgrowth of English power as yet troubled the dreams of musnud or durbar. Nor does the existence of these strange *condottieri* in Moslem or Mahratta pay seem to have caused any uneasiness to the Anglo-Indian Government, save in so far as they might possibly become dangerous in the contingency of a French invasion. This had become, however, the dominant misgiving of the hour, which connected itself more or less intrusively with every other consideration. Our best ally, the Nizam, had for some years a body of troops organised on the model of our Sepoy regiments under a

Frenchman named Raymond; another under an American named Boyd; and a third under an Irishman named Finglass, formerly a quartermaster in the 19th Dragoons. The two latter forces had been taken into pay at the suggestion of the British Resident, by direction of the late Governor General, to serve as a counterpoise to the formidable force under Raymond in case at any time it should prove insubordinate. But after a time Boyd and his troopers grew weary of inaction, and took themselves off to the Mahrattas, for the sake, it was supposed, of higher incentives to heroism. The battalion of Finglass, eight hundred strong, preferred remaining at Hyderabad in friendly relation with the Company's troops. These had orders to keep an observant eye on those of Raymond, whose muster-roll had lately been increased to fourteen thousand men, besides a squadron of horse and a train of thirty guns. For their pay a large tract of country bordering on the Carnatic had been assigned over, and a fortified post having regular communication with the port of Narpilly, and several important places belonging to the Nawab of Arcot. Recruits were supplied in part from his territory and in part by deserters from our service. Most of the officers were said to be fired with Jacobin zeal against English interests and principles, and by national pride in the recently unchecked triumph of French arms. Proofs, of course, could not easily be had of correspondence between Hyderabad and Paris, but the frequency of communication with compatriots at Seringapatam who occupied a similar position in the service of Tippoo Sahib was not disguised. Raymond's contingent owed its origin rather to fear inspired by the success of a similar force in the camp of Mahdajee Scindiah, the encroaching chief of the Mahratta States with whom the Mahomedans were continually at war; and at Calcutta it had been regarded for a time as rather a useful adjunct to the defensive resources of the Nizam, the integrity and independence of whose dominion were deemed essential to preserve the balance of power in Southern India. But when by degrees the auxiliary force grew to be a principal portion of the Subadah's army, his astute minister, Azim ul Omra, began to be troubled with misgivings he dared not avow; and while acquiescing in the French commander's proposal for its augmentation, he secretly strove to excite English jealousy to make countervailing efforts for the security of his master.

Incidentally, many of the facts regarding this and other foreign corps had already come under the notice of the authorities at home, as Mornington recollected. But they assumed for the first time a sinister significance when grouped together in the graphic testimony of a soldier and diplomatist who had had opportunities of closely observing and calmly reflecting upon them. Hitherto dark and motionless as the unconnected plates in the galvanic battery, they might at any moment be brought into such contact as would convulse the hand that held them. To the mind of Mornington the possibility of the magnetic current being set in motion from afar needed no proof. 'The result from all the facts stated by Kirkpatrick is that the continuance, and still more the further growth of the corps of Raymond, ought to be prevented by every means within our power consistent with the respect due to the Court of Hyderabad and with the general principles of moderation and justice which ought to form the rule of our conduct in India. The dangers to be apprehended from the existence of this corps are not to be estimated by a consideration of its actual state of discipline, or even of its actual numbers, or degree of present influence over the counsels of the Nizam. I consider it as the basis of a French party in India, on which, according to the opportunities of fortune and the variation of events, the activity of the enemy may found a strength of the most formidable kind either in peace or war. If the war should extend to India, and if we should be under the necessity of calling forth the strength of our allies to assist us in any contest with Tippoo, what assistance could we expect from the Nizam, the main body of whose army would be officered by Frenchmen or by the agents of France, and the correspondents of Tippoo himself? But I confess I carry my opinion upon this subject still further. I have no doubt that the natural effect of the unchecked and rapid growth of such a party at the court of one of our principal allies, must be in a very short period to detach that court entirely from our interests, and finally to fix it in those of our enemies, to subject its counsels to their control and its military establishment to their direction. That it has tended to encourage Tippoo I have no doubt, and his correspondence with the leaders of the corps will sufficiently show in what light he views them.'[1]

Confidentially discussing with his old official chief the various remedies suggested by Kirkpatrick for a state of things he deemed so perilous, he puts aside as maladroit any proposal to disarm the rival contingent or to detach by corruption its subaltern officers. Better wait for an application from the Nizam, soon expected, for an increase of the British subsidiary force, and for the concession of a right to employ it against internal as well as external foes—a right hitherto always refused. In another letter on the political state of India he gave at length his reasons for thinking that it would be 'wise to check by timely aid the decline of the Nizam's weight among the powers of Hindostan. This could be done in no manner so effectual and unobjectionable as by furnishing him with a large increase of Company's troops; the pay of the augmented force to be secured in the manner best calculated to prevent future discussion and

[1] To Dundas from the Cape, 23rd February, 1798.

embarrassment. The British detachment now in his pay is not only restricted from acting against the Mahrattas in any possible case, but also from acting against certain Polygars tributary both to the Mahrattas and to the Nizam. His object would of course be to obtain our guarantee of his possessions generally, with the assistance of a large force to be employed with the same extensive powers as now apply to the corps of Raymond. For this object I have little doubt that the Nizam would sacrifice the whole French party at his court, and even the *peishcush* now paid by us on account of the Northern Circars. This point perhaps might be reconciled with the interests of the Mahrattas, if it were thought prudent to enter into similar engagements with them, or in other words to guarantee their possessions against any attack from the Nizam. The effect of such an engagement with both powers would be to place us in the situation of arbitrators between them; and perhaps their mutual apprehensions of our interposition in the case of any aggression on either side might tend to restrain the resentment and ambition of both. Such a system of treaties, so far from being liable to the objection of an undue interference in the disputes of the native powers of India, or of that description of officiousness and intriguing spirit which tends to foment divisions and to occasion war, might be made the best security for the maintenance of the peace of India as well as the strongest pledge of our disposition to preserve it from disturbance. It could not be a wise policy to suffer the Nizam and the Peishwah to weaken themselves by repeated contests while Tippoo remained at rest. Some opening had been given for our arbitration in settling the disputes between the several Mahratta chiefs; but the Government of Bengal had postponed the consideration of this proposition to a period of time which he confessed he should think the most unfavourable for the examination of this difficult question, and still more unseasonable for the negotiation of a treaty with such a power as the Mahratta States; this period of time was no other than the moment when Zemaun Shah should again approach the frontiers of Hindostan. He should certainly think it his duty, upon his arrival in India, to proceed without the delay of one moment to the examination and decision of the proposal made by the Mahrattas; if it should appear expedient to engage with them in a defensive system against the threatened invasion of the Afghan chief, there could be no doubt that such a measure would tend greatly to reconcile to them any propositions which we might wish to offer with respect to the arrangements at the Court of Hyderabad. The inclination of his present opinion rather led him to think that a general defensive alliance between all the existing powers of Hindostan (Tippoo perhaps alone excepted) against the expected invasion of Zemaun Shah, would not only be the best security against the success of such an invasion if attempted, but might have the effect of deterring that prince from an undertaking which must end in his own disappointment and ruin, if our Government in India and our allies did not neglect to make seasonable preparations of defence.'[1]

Here as in pre-vision we have the ground-plan of the lofty and splendid edifice of Paramount Power which in his three months' voyage he had been elaborating. The spirit of Captain-Generalship was upon him; he felt by anticipation that, though still under authority, he was about to enter on a scene where he should have armies under him, and where he might say to prince or king go, and he goeth, and to another come, and he cometh, and to hosts of his own fellow-servants do this, and they must do it. That he burned with the ambition to set his mark indelibly on the system of

[1] First Despatch to the President of the Board of Control; from the Cape, 23rd February, 1798.

British rule in the East, every line in his voluminous correspondence shows. But his hunger was for fame that would last, not for pelf that would perish. He coveted neither for his country or for himself mere acquisitions of money, jewels, or lands. His immediate if not his sole feeling of antagonism was to Jacobinical France, and to the Sultan of Mysore as her accessory in designs for the subversion of our power. In Asia as in Europe, this was the question of the day to which all others must give place. But as yet it hardly seemed so urgent as to set aside permanent and peaceful schemes of reform and consolidation. He longed to uplift the administrative *régime* of the Company from the pettifogging practices of the factory and the grubbing ways of the warehouse, to the higher-minded ideas of enlightened rule; and he yearned even yet more passionately to establish our relations with the native chiefs and princes upon a footing of mutual good, consistent, frank, and durable, instead of suffering them to depend on the impulses of a hand-to-mouth policy, incapable of vindication, incoherent, vacillating, unstable. How he thenceforth set about the realisation of his far-reaching aims, often imperiously and impetuously but never by unworthy means, the chronicles of his septennate in India serve to show.

Reviewing the political situation, it was obvious that, since the peace of Seringapatam, Tippoo had profited by undisturbed tranquillity within his own confines, while his neighbours had been mutually weakening themselves by war. His intrigues at Poonah and Hyderabad had failed to stir up enmity against us; but he was believed to have found more congenial confidants in the durbar of Zemaun Shah, whose zest of aggression many repulses had not cooled, and who had never relinquished the hope of making Oude a tributary of Cabul. Tippoo longed for the opportunity to act in concert with him by a renewed invasion of the

Carnatic, and both relied on timely aid from France. In the despatches from the retiring Governor-General in Council these projects had been treated with incredulity; although one of the last measures of Sir John Shore was the making of a new pact with the Nawab Vizier for his defence in case of need against the Afghan. Mornington read the facts differently. The wisdom of masterly inactivity was to him foolishness. 'I know that it is the fashion to treat the projects of Zemaun Shah very lightly. The result upon my mind of an examination of the account of his force, the detail respecting his future intentions, and the causes likely to obstruct their execution, is a conviction that Zemaun Shah has not abandoned his project of invading Hindostan, and the safest means of rendering that project abortive will be to consider it as practicable, and to take the best precautions against it.'[1] The fact was that the enterprising Shah had without molestation advanced with his army as far as Lahore, the Sikhs having been dissuaded from opposing him: when he was recalled by domestic trouble at the time not thoroughly explained. It seemed very doubtful if Scindiah would just then have cared to divert his troops from other employment to withstand his progress from Lahore to Delhi, and the imminency of the danger had appeared so great at Calcutta as to call for a temporary augmentation of native infantry. The danger past, retrenchment was hastily resumed; but had the danger really passed away? 'The balance of power in India no longer exists upon the same footing on which it was placed by the peace of Seringapatam. The question therefore must arise, how it may best be brought back again to that state in which you have directed me to maintain it. The wisest course would be to strengthen the Mahrattas and the Nizam by entering into defensive alliance with the former against Zemaun Shah, and by affording to

[1] To Dundas; from the Cape, 28th February, 1798.

the latter an addition of military strength and the means of extricating himself from the control of the French party at Hyderabad. The treaty should not contain a hostile word against the Afghan, excepting only with reference to the single case of his projects of invasion; and it should be communicated to him with assurances of our determination never to molest him in his own dominions nor to suffer him to approach ours.' Then follow numerous suggestions about reinforcements of British troops, which he urged, were indispensable. The condition of Malabar could never, he thought, be rendered satisfactory till the horde of peculators and plunderers who had long made it their prey had been eradicated. Tanjore was likewise a difficulty, the Rajah having been sentenced to deposition by the Court of Directors; but he would not hesitate to respite the condemned prince till a more convenient season. Wynaad was a district whose retrocession Tippoo claimed under the terms of the last treaty, and Mornington remembering the oral injunctions of Dundas, given him at Walmer in the presence of Mr. Pitt, promises its prompt restoration without any equivalent, notwithstanding his intense feeling of distrust of the Sultan's attitude and purpose. 'My idea is that, as on the one hand we ought never to use any high language towards Tippoo, nor ever attempt to deny him the smallest point of his just rights, so on the other, where we have distinct proofs of his machinations against us, we ought to let him know that his treachery does not escape our observation, and make him feel that he is within reach of our vigilance. At present it appears to me that he is permitted to excite ill-will against us wherever he pleases, without the least attempt on our part either to reprehend him for the suggestion, or the court to whom he applies for listening to it.'[1]

At Madras, where he stayed some days, he found abundant

[1] *Idem.*

evidence of the administrative confusion and discord, political apathy and political cowardice, of which he had heard much ere quitting England. Two parties in the council railed at one another continually, and spent their energies chiefly in reciprocal schemes of out-manœuvring. The Nawab still dwelt apart in pantomimic state, surrounded by the luxury and pomp of sovereignty, but his power had long since come to an end, the Dewanee and the command of troops having been for several years engrossed by the Company's officials. Law was formally administered in his name, salutes were fired as usual on set occasions, and in official intercourse the forms of deference were still kept up as if the old voluptuary was really Subadah of Arcot. Most curious and suggestive is a short note addressed to him by Mornington the day after his arrival, which photographs the relation that continued to subsist between Moslem authority fast crumbling away and the vigorous exotic that was fain to creep gradually over the ruin :—

'May it please your Highness,—It has given me great satisfaction to learn from General Harris that your Highness enjoys a good state of health. My first inquiries upon my arrival at Fort St. George were respecting your Highness's welfare. I return your Highness many thanks for the several obliging messages which I have had the honour to receive from you. I am very anxious to take the earliest opportunity of paying you my respects in person, and of presenting to you several letters which I am charged to deliver to you from his Majesty the King of Great Britain, from his Royal Highness the Prince of Wales, his Royal Highness the Duke of York, and the Marquess Cornwallis. I will wait upon your Highness with great pleasure at any hour that you will be pleased to appoint on to-morrow, or any day that may be agreeable to you. I have the honour to be, &c.,

'MORNINGTON.

'I date this letter from one of your Highness's houses, in which General Harris has placed me.'

George III. under his own hand commended the Earl to the confidence of his Highness as one who had filled various offices in Government with eminent virtue and ability, and in whom he counselled him to repose the utmost confidence. The Heir-Apparent wrote :—

'Carlton House, October 14, 1797.'

'The nobleman who will deliver this letter to your Highness, it is with great satisfaction I inform you, is a particular friend of my own. He is justly celebrated for his great talents, and his private character being that of honour, moderation and mildness, must necessarily recommend him to the confidence and good opinion of your Highness. I could say much more upon this subject, but when I acquaint you that his Majesty had previously bestowed upon him the most eminent marks of Royal favour, I am sure it must be deemed useless to suggest any other proof how acceptable such a nomination must be to the interests of your Highness. I shall conclude with expressing a hope that your Highness may long continue to enjoy that health and prosperity to which your exalted rank and character entitles you.

I am your affectionate friend,

G. P. W.'

Cornwallis, referring to the advice he had personally given to the father of Omdut ul Omrah, and to himself, against listening to the advice of those Europeans whose flatteries were only to serve their own corrupt purposes, urged him to speak openly and freely to 'his friend the new Viceroy, who had no object in view but the interest of his Highness and that of the Company, which must ever be inseparable.'

The Nawab, released from the fears of resentment provoked by oppression, was habitually tempted by usurers to pawn the revenues of districts pledged to the Company for the payment of their subsidiary troops; whereby the monthly kist was constantly overdue and a heavy arrear had gradually accumulated. Lord Hobart had alternately tried to coax and coerce him into surrendering the collection of the assigned districts; but he had been overruled by Sir John Shore. Mornington promised to reconsider the whole facts of the disagreement, and if possible to reconcile the susceptibilities of Chepauk with the claims of Fort St. George.

Realising beforehand the duties and responsibilities of political arbiter which his ambition prompted him to assume as representative of England in the East, he boldly etched the outlines of a new order of things which might well have made his cynical old chief at the Board of Control smile incredulously. Dundas was an unromantic man who kept neither delicate scruples nor expensive aspirations. Additional provinces were in his mind merely additional investments, about which the only question worth considering was, Would they pay? If not they were hardly worth coveting.

Had Pitt remained of the same mind in 1797 that he was when framing his first India Bill in 1784, Mornington would have been left in no uncertainty on the subject. Words more explicit inhibiting all further expansion of political dominion there could not be than those which it contained. Under no pretence was the Company thenceforth to intermeddle in native quarrels, or to set up as a rival to native powers. It might overbid or undersell them in barter or contract as much as it pleased, and hold fast its gains, however gotten, at bayonet's point. That was all in the way of adventure; and the adventure being distant and perilous, Parliament would no more be nice about method and means of bargaining or bullying than in hampering those who combined the business of merchant and buccaneer in kidnapping negroes on the Gold Coast for the replenishment of their sugar-fields in Jamaica. On the stage or in the pulpit right and wrong were said to be without degrees of latitude or longitude; but in the making of laws and in the governing of dependencies, right meant little more than the greatest amount of wrong which was worth inflicting, and wrong only meant the scandal or reproach of exposure in some blundering attempt to enforce that sort of right. The India Bill of 1784 was a set of earthworks hastily thrown up to please the Court against the daring encroachment of the Whigs upon the balance of patronage, and having served that purpose it had probably no longer any peculiar merit in the eyes of him who devised it. The world had drifted a long way since then. France, from being a worn-out, corrupt, and pauperised rival, with an amateur mechanic for a King, a prodigal Court given over to heartless trifling, an unbelieving clergy, an ill-fed army, and a nettle-eating peasantry, had passed through the fire of revolution in which the elements of old forces had been molten and sent forth in lava streams through Christendom, resistless and overwhelming. Every other power of the Continent had been humiliated and discomfited by the Republic, and our victories afloat had not saved us from insolvency. The whole position of the State was turned, and Mornington knew well how little his administrative master was like to trouble himself about the literal or any other meaning of abstract resolutions embodied in a great party Act of Parliament in days gone by. Ceylon and Trinidad had very recently been taken from old allies and retained, on no other plea than that it was better we should have them than the French; and one of the secret instructions of Dundas was that the new Governor General should surprise Batavia if opportunity served, and annex it also to the possessions of his Majesty. Sir John Shore who had been bred in the counting-house school of Indian politics, was a man of humanity and peace, who from a distance conned the Roman hand of Imperial legislation; took all the fine things about forbearance, moderation, and magnanimity said in Parliament for gospel; and who would as soon have thought of making puns at his prayers, as of reading between the lines of statutes and despatches forbidding interference in native quarrels, esoteric rules for building up a paramount power by their mutual exhaustion. So little indeed, did that admirable head clerk of the Company dream of the pageant or the prowess of empire, that he took small pains to conceal the disputes between himself and other members of the Government, notably that with Lord Hobart, which led to the recall of both. His views of Indian administration were subsequently embodied by his son in a volume of great interest and value, and may still be read with advantage by all who care to know what were the sins of oppression and misrule that grieved the soul of the just man—some of them enduring unto this day. But it appears certain that he lacked the vigour of supreme authority needful to hold any executive system firmly in hand; and that after his departure and the brief locum-tenency of Sir George Barlow, a state of things arose which would have speedily brought affairs to absolute confusion had it not been for the timely arrival of the new Pro-consul.

CHAPTER IX.

FORT WILLIAM.

1798.

MORNINGTON sailed from Madras on May 9, accompanied by his brother Henry, on the 17th landed at Fort William, and on the day following entered upon the performance of his arduous duties. A greater contrast could not have been conceived than that with which everyone was struck between the brilliant and ambitious little aristocrat still in the prime of life and the worthy but weary son of the supercargo, who round by round had climbed the Company's ladder of promotion, sat down for a while to rest at the top, and then went his way.

His first despatch, written a few days after, vividly depicts the scene on which he had entered. In Council on May 31 he entered an elaborate Minute stating fully the reasons which had led the Court of Directors and the Board of Control, as arbiters of the disputed succession in Tanjore, to decide against Ameer Singh, the brother of the late Rajah, and in favour of Serfojee his youthful son. In 1786, when at the point of death, Tuljajee, one of the earliest allies of the Company, had sent for Schwarz, the well-known missionary, for whom he had always avowed warm sentiments of friendship, and confided to his care the boy, during whose minority he desired his brother to govern the Raj. If the regent failed to renovate the resources and preserve the government committed to his care, he succeeded in propitiating the leading members of the Presidency of Madras, and in winning the friendship of Colonel (afterwards Sir David) Baird, who always spoke of him as a humane and diligent man. Serfojee by his kindly nature engaged the affection, and by his singular talents the admiration, of his German guardian. He early evinced rare aptitude for European as well as Oriental knowledge; and combining with habits of study love of the chase and athletic energy, he became as he approached to man's estate an object of no ordinary solicitude and sympathy with all around him. Schwarz saw with concern that his uncle, after many years of power, had no mind to relinquish it to his ward; but the promise he had given his father, and the belief in the rightfulness of his claim, stimulated the missionary to press upon the Company the equitable duty of seeing the legitimate heir placed on the musnud. The whole of the circumstances were at his instance brought before the authorities in England in 1797; and Mornington was directed to give validity to their judgment, and to make an amended treaty with the young Rajah as soon as he had been installed. As the initiatory step in this proceeding the Governor General placed on record his desire that the authorities at Madras should see the transfer of power effected; being careful to preserve to Ameer Singh whatever he could rightfully claim as his property, and securing to him a handsome stipend for his life. It is seldom easy however to vacate a throne; the regent demurred to the legality of the decree, and his personal friends at Madras helped him to delay its execution. The transaction has been invidiously misrepresented by Mill, by whom Schwarz is made to figure as a religious hypocrite and Mornington as an aristocratic oppressor. But the decision regarding the inheritance lay with men who had certainly no spark of missionary zeal among them; and who, as they speedily proved, were far from stimulating the new pro-consul to needless intermeddling in native affairs.

But money :—what was to be done for the wherewithal of administrative reform or military reinvigoration? The broken and embarrassed plight of the finances etched by Colonel Wellesley in a memorandum framed for the vindication of his brother's conduct forcibly depicts the embarrassing condition of things.

Non-intervention had had a fair trial. From the departure of Cornwallis in 1793, not a shot had been fired in anger or a claim made to interfere in the affairs of any native State. The attitude invariably maintained by the government of the Company was not merely unaggressive and unostentatious; it was unpretentious even to meekness, and shrinking even to the look and language of fear. Shore had seen so much of the sordid abuse of power, and was so conscience-stricken by the recollection of the suffering inflicted by arbitrary and sanguinary men, that his undivided aim in his five years' rule was to atone, as he himself declared, to an injured people for miseries that were irretrievable; and to convince, as he hoped, the native princes that in future they might regard the European intruder amongst them as a peace-loving, money-making, and inoffensive neighbour. The amiability of the experiment was indisputable; but its failure and the fatuity with which it was made admitted as little of dispute. No native prince was won to confidence or softened into friendship by vague protestations of good-will. Not one of them believed in his sincerity, for not one of them could appreciate his acts or motives: and what the abject community subject to our sway thought of its casual mitigation, there existed in his time no possible means of ascertaining. The successor to a series of ruthless despots may be made melancholy and contrite by the conviction he dares not avow, that in point of abstract morality he has no business there.

But if he has the capacity and courage to do no more than recall his videttes, shorten the allowance of ammunition to his guards, and bid his envoys and subordinates be sure to take no offence if slighted, and whatever happens to quarrel about nothing, he is only likely to tempt old grudge and fresh jealousy, envy, hatred, avarice, and temerity, to try how far it is safe to pluck his authority by the beard: and certain by the exhibition of the feebleness of forbearance to pile up all round the faggots of a deferred conflagration.

Even financially the policy of peace at any price had completely failed. The revenues of the Company had steadily declined during Shore's administration by 165,748*l*.; while the actual charges in India, notwithstanding various retrenchments and cutting down of military expenditure, were 8,178,626*l*., the total receipts were only 8,059,880*l*. a year. The debt had gone on increasing till 'the Company's credit was at the lowest ebb, and money could not be borrowed in Bengal under twelve per cent.'[1] An annual deficit of 322,530*l*. could not be disguised in the balance-sheet returned to the Directors at home, while even to provide for the ordinary outgoings, the Treasury at Calcutta was not unfrequently in want of funds.

Without active vitality of intelligence or energy, like an elephant tied in a stall, Government had waxed fat and kicked, had grown unwieldy without developing even for self-assertion muscular power. The reins had been allowed to fall upon its neck, and it tramped on sluggishly and sulkily, praised by evil-doers and a terror to those that did well.

Rivalry between the Company's troops and the King's forces had from the first prevailed. They were differently recruited, differently officered, and differently paid; in patriotic toasts they acknowledged the same allegiance, but

[1] Memorandum by Sir Arthur Wellesley in 1806, on his brother's government of India.

in the details of professional duty and fealty, the dragoons and the line trusted and obeyed only the generals sent out by the Horse Guards, while the cavalry and infantry of the Company acknowledged no military obligation to any authority but that of their joint-stock paymasters. Promotions and emoluments formed an everlasting source of jealousy, dispute, and cabal. Cornwallis as a soldier was able with difficulty to quench some controversies and compromise others, but his civilian successor found his recommendations of service and merit neglected at Whitehall; and he was unable to conceal his sense of the injustice frequently done. Committees of grievance became permanent in the barrack-room of every Company's battalion, and neglected remonstrances tempted men who for years had no enemy in the field, to begin to talk of favouritism at Whitehall as the enemy at home. A new set of army regulations framed by Dundas with the assistance of Cornwallis in 1797 had not appeased the discontent, and the tone publicly indulged in at Calcutta and Madras savoured oftentimes of incipient tendencies to mutiny. Mornington resolved not to parley with a danger so serious. He insisted on the regimental committees being dissolved, but took care at the same time to let it be understood that he would personally undertake to have justice done.

Nor was the civil administration less out of gear. The council and all the chief executive posts were filled by elderly gentlemen with accumulated savings, torpid livers, and troops of dependent kinsmen for whom they wanted to provide before they went home.

To the methodical mind of the new ruler, the first thing requisite seemed to be to reduce to order the confusion, laxity, and irresponsibility that had been suffered to overgrow like smothering weeds every branch of the public service. He would set the house in order, sponge up waste and dismiss peculation, cost what it might at first, and vex whom it would. Very far however, were his notions from those of grudging and shabby retrenchment which consists in snipping and stunting the off-shoots of expenditure while the tap-root remains untouched. He wished to stimulate rather than repress the legitimate feeling of ambition in the Civil Service, persuaded that a prevalent belief in the certainty of advancement by merit proven would infuse into the whole system a vigour and vitality which nothing else could do and the lack of which would at any price be dear. His own words best describe his views. 'In urging the necessity of attempting the reduction of our expenses, I do not mean to recommend that species of improvident economy which in this country above all others would ultimately prove real profusion and the source of every abuse. I do not mean to deprive persons holding laborious and responsible stations of the liberal reward to which they are justly entitled, and which ought upon every ground both of policy and justice to furnish them with the means of acquiring a competent fortune and of returning to their native country within a moderate period of service. On the other hand it is difficult to believe that establishments of such magnitude and intricacy as those of the British Empire in India should not in the course of time require frequent revision. Without therefore pledging myself to the amount of any saving which may ultimately appear practicable, I propose immediately to commence a general revision of all public establishments of Bengal, and to direct the adoption of a similar measure at Madras and Bombay, as well as at all our subordinate settlements and in all our recent acquisitions from the enemy. Any reduction in the effective strength of the army attended with any degree of danger to the public safety would frustrate its own object. At present I propose to reduce merely two articles of our military charges. The first the regiment of Hindostanee cavalry purchased for two lacs of rupees from

M. de Boigne in February 1796; which I propose to transfer to the Nawab Vizier on the same terms. I am aware that it is desirable to reduce rather than to augment the force of the Vizier, and this regiment may be substituted in the room of any other corps that he may be induced to disband. From August 1 it will be advisable that the troops quartered at the fort of Allahabad should cease, and that in future the garrison should receive the same allowances as that of Chunar. The revision of the several branches of our revenue may very properly be referred to the committee appointed to revise our civil establishments under my inspection. The demand of Government on the landholders is fixed in perpetuity, and consequently no addition can be made to the land revenue; but the customs, the stamp duties, and the tax on spirituous liquors may admit of considerable improvements either in the mode of collection or by the variation of the ratio, and other sources of revenue may be devised without injury to the country.'[1]

But ere any steps of importance could be taken in administrative reform, tidings came of a nature fitted to divert attention altogether from internal affairs. In one of the English journals published at Calcutta appeared a proclamation by M. Malartic, Governor of the Isle of France, dated January 30, setting forth an alliance offensive and defensive between France and Mysore. Envoys from the Sultan had been publicly received by the colonial governor with every mark of honour, and negotiations were stated to have taken place with a view to the enlistment of auxiliary troops under French officers to act in concert with those of Tippoo for the expulsion of the English from Hindostan. The temerity of the project and the arrogant tone of defiance and denunciation in which it was made known suggested naturally the idea that the document was either a forgery or that it had been

[1] Financial Minute, 12th June, 1798.

put forward without any warrant from the Sultan in order to embroil him once more with his recent adversaries. To the dyspeptic politicians who loitered on the banks of the Hooghly, it seemed incredible that, in the midst of profound peace, a single Moslem chief, recently shorn of half his dominions and surrounded by distrustful if not hostile neighbours, should rashly provoke an open rupture with no better reliance than that of a far distant European State. The Viceroy himself entertained doubts of its probability until authentic copies were received from Lord Macartney and Sir Hugh Christian on June 18. But pending this confirmation notice was confidentially given to the Madras Presidency that it might be necessary to collect forces on the Malabar coast preparatory to a rupture with their old enemy.

But before midsummer General Harris had warning to collect a force in case necessity should unfortunately require it, but not to take any public step without further orders. The Proclamation ' must become a matter of serious discussion with Tippoo. How it might turn out it would be impossible to say. M. Malartic might have exaggerated or wholly misrepresented his intentions. But if Tippoo should choose to avow the objects of his embassy to have been such as were described in the Proclamation the consequences might be very serious, and might ultimately involve us in the calamity of war.' [1]

He would send him as soon as possible the largest supply in specie which he could procure. ' If you would send with your answer any intelligent officer capable of entering into all the details of your force, of the seasons, and all other circumstances connected with the object of striking a sudden blow against Tippoo before he can receive any foreign aid, you would greatly assist me in the arrangement of my measures upon this serious occasion. You may rely upon

[1] To General Harris; from Fort William, 9th June, 1798.

my unremitting attention to whatever communications you may make to me, and upon my most cordial support in all your exertions.' Harris, who had also received a copy of the Proclamation from Mauritius, felt no doubt that Tippoo had committed himself; and that the inveteracy of his resentment would end only with his life. But withal he advised that in our great want of cash he should be permitted if he would to make the *amende honorable*. Meanwhile he would follow his instructions implicitly, and quietly move a battalion or two towards the point of assembly. 'It was very pleasing to hear that his lordship had some cash to send him, but the whole amount mentioned would not more than make up the deficiency to the end of September, and their debts were so injurious to their credit at Madras, that until something was done in liquidation of them they could not expect to raise a rupee by loan.'[1]

The Government of Madras, in a fit of apprehension or over-zeal, had publicly issued orders to Admiral Rainier for the defence of the coast of Malabar, which the Governor General did not hesitate promptly and peremptorily to countermand, rebuking what he deemed an encroachment on his supreme function. 'The protection of India belongs to me, and forms one of the most material branches of my arduous responsibility. In the discharge of this duty I shall always expect to be assisted by the co-operation of the other Presidencies, but if they offer opinions to the commanders of His Majesty's squadrons with respect to the distribution of the naval force without reference to me, or any previous knowledge of my intentions, the utmost degree of confusion must be the result.' While laying down the rule thus inflexibly, he deprecated in most soothing terms the idea of any diminution of personal confidence or respect.

But the difficulties in organising and executing an

[1] From General Harris; Fort St. George, 23rd June, 1798.

invasion of Mysore daunted the General. 'The dilatoriness, indecision, and cowardice of our allies are beyond belief to those who have not been eye-witness to these qualities in them, and there is a moral assurance that not one of them will take the field or be of the least use to us until we have secured a position to cover their advance or gained a decided advantage. The difficulties which press here are insuperable. The draught and carriage cattle even for the defensive army cannot be collected to enable us to do more than merely reach Baramahal before the monsoon in October. Mr. Cockburn, the best informed man perhaps in India on this subject, fixes nearly the same period for the equipment of the defensive army. A force capable of undertaking the siege of Seringapatam could not in all probability reach the place before February 1. The difficulty in feeding the army obliged Lord Cornwallis to relinquish the idea of a siege the first time he marched against it, and but for the almost despaired of co-operation of the Mahrattas, he would hardly have made the attempt.' [1]

Mr. Webbe, who had been for many years Secretary of the Madras Council, was aghast at the orders from Calcutta to assemble an army of observation on the coast. The terrible reverses inflicted on our troops by Hyder and his son in the second Mysore war, the fate of Baillie, of Mathews, and other gallant men in the field or in the dungeon, and his own intimate knowledge of the weakness of the civil and military system he had to administer filled him with dismay. 'I can anticipate nothing,' he exclaimed, 'but shocking disasters from a premature attack upon Tippoo in our present disabled condition, and the impeachment of Lord Mornington for his temerity.' Nor was this the hasty utterance of surprise. After time for reflection Webbe

[1] From Fort St. George; 6th July, 1798.

embodied in a Memorandum his ground for remonstrance against immediate war. 'The garrisons of the Carnatic lowlands, which all lay open to raids from Mysore, were weak and far between; and reinforcements from Europe, such as they had had in 1791, were not to be hoped for. The Nizam and the Peishwah were better able then to afford substantial help, and they were not unfriendly; yet they could not be induced to move until we had fought a whole campaign alone, and they had seen battles won and cities taken. With resources far superior in stores and troops than it would be possible now to muster, it took Cornwallis two hazardous campaigns to bring the adversary to terms; and though he had been humbled for the time and shorn of some dependencies, it was vain to doubt that he had reorganised his army and that his coffers were full of treasure. The exchequer of the Presidency was empty, and in the Coromandel banks and bazaars treated as bankrupt. If war was inevitable, and the present judged the most advantageous circumstances under which it could be commenced, he feared our situation was bad beyond the hope of remedy.' The impetuous Viceroy was vexed at these unexpected thwartings, and imperiously refused to discuss details in official correspondence or to admit that he was wrong. But he took warning in time, and pulled up on the brink of a terrible and irretrievable error.

When all the hindrances came to be duly weighed and measured, prudence dictated delay in publicly mobilising the Madras army, whose unpreparedness grew palpable as the contingency of a collision drew near. Mornington wisely yielded to the representations made to him, and instead of precipitating a rupture, set about diligently the reduction of the French corps in the different native States. The pride of the man was above the commonplace vanity of official consistency; and disdaining all disguise he wrote to the Directors: 'I have no hesitation in declaring that my original intention was, if circumstances would have admitted, to have attacked the Sultan instantly, and on both sides of his dominions, for the purpose of defeating his hostile preparations and of anticipating their declared object. I was concerned however to learn, from persons most conversant in military details at Fort St. George, that the dispersed state of the army on the coast and certain radical defects in its establishments would render the assembling of a force equal to offensive movements a much more tedious and difficult operation than I had apprehended.'

From Mr. Duncan, the Governor of Bombay, further particulars came of the proceedings at the Mauritius. The Mysore envoys while there had openly enlisted one hundred and fifty recruits, making engagements for their arms and pay. In March they proceeded to the Isle of Bourbon in the French frigate 'La Preneuse,' hoping to raise additional levies, and in April they debarked at Mangalore. 'In numbers the force was never considerable; but regarded probably as an earnest of greater help to come, it was received into Tippoo's service with public marks of favour and honour. The hostile intent of such proceedings could not be overlooked on account of their incredible want of caution and reserve. The failure to enlist a force adequate to his design was no justification of so palpable a breach of amity. He had plainly violated thereby existing treaties, and committed acts equivalent to open threats of war. It justified the occupation of his maritime provinces, and an advance upon the capital in order to dictate there binding conditions of peace; to compel him to admit a permanent Resident at his court, to which he had hitherto never yet assented, and to reimburse the cost of the expedition; finally to secure the expulsion of all French officers from his service, and to exact an engagement against their return.

Every motive of justice and policy appeared to demand the adoption of this or of some similar plan for reducing the power of Tippoo to such a condition as shall render him unable to avail himself of the solicited assistance of France, or of any other collateral aid which the course of future circumstances may offer to him for the prosecution of his declared design of expelling the British nation from India.' The army was reported to be in excellent condition, but upon due consultation it was found that the state of the frontier forts, of the field artillery, and of the stores of grain, did not admit of the sudden movement of a large body of troops, although they might be rapidly brought together. Financial embarrassment made it impossible to equip an expedition with provident completeness unless a high-handed use were made of the commercial investments of the Company to supply the military chest, proportionately reducing the remittances home, suspending the payment of the dividends, and fatally damaging the credit of the Government. 'Under these circumstances he felt with the utmost degree of pain and regret that the moment was unfavourable to the adoption of the only measure which promised effectual and permanent security to the territories committed to his charge.' But while relinquishing the idea of an immediate rupture with Tippoo, he could not brook the thought of mute submission to the affront thus offered by him, persuaded that our future security and honour would be compromised by meekly condoning an indignity so unprovoked, which would greatly 'tend to elevate the credit and hopes of Tippoo and of France, and occasion a proportionate depression of our influence and consideration in the eyes of our allies, and of all the native powers of India; therefore he called on Tippoo to make a public disavowal of the proceedings of his ambassadors; and to declare distinctly the nature of his intentions towards us and our allies.'

Meanwhile his first communication with Tippoo was one of studied courtesy. Careful to avoid the entrance into quarrels, and being still in doubt what his eventual purpose might be, he frankly proffered to discuss on friendly terms the Sultan's claim to the retrocession of Wynaad. Referring to the article in the treaty of Seringapatam which provided for an amicable settlement of boundary disputes, presuming that Tippoo's disposition was to maintain faithfully his public engagements; and promising in return a religious adherence to every stipulation in the compact, he proposed 'to depute a respectable and discreet person to meet on the frontier such officers as his Highness chose to name for the purpose of conferring together and of satisfying each other on all points respecting which any doubts might be entertained. The result will be communicated by the Government of Bombay with all practicable despatch; and they might rely upon it that after regular discussion shall have taken place, according to the established law of nations, I will not suspend for one moment the full acknowledgment of whatever shall appear to be your just right; and I have no doubt that we shall have no difficulty in terminating these long depending questions to our mutual satisfaction.'[1]

And had the vengeful spirit of the despot shown itself capable of appeasement or compromise, it is possible that a rupture might even still have been averted. Mornington understood well how averse his employers were from embarking in needless war; and distrustful as he was of Tippoo's intentions, he had many inducements to defer the risk of hostilities if he could but hold him at bay.

When room for doubt was no longer left of the embassage to Mauritius and the genuineness of Malartic's proclamation, he wrote to the Board of Control for definite instructions for his guidance in the changing condition of things.

[1] To Tippoo Sultan; from Fort William, 14th June, 1798.

So long as Tippoo could without hindrance keep up his communications with the French in time of peace there could never be security against a sudden outbreak of war; and to shut him in from supplies and reinforcements by sea, the first opportunity ought to be taken to deprive him of his provinces on the Malabar coast. His intriguing and impetuous ambition would be certain to tempt him sooner or later into affording such an opportunity. It was for the authorities at home to think betimes whether such territorial insurance would be worth the sacrifice it would necessarily entail. A very able and exhaustive despatch ends with an inquiry to which he asked from Dundas a definite and an early answer. 'The orders of the Court of Directors and the opinions of this Government have uniformly concurred in declaring that the landing of any considerable French force in Tippoo's country must be the signal for an attack upon him. I wish to know exactly if the term *considerable* is to be construed as a limitation of my discretion. It appears to me that the landing of any French force in Tippoo's country is a sufficient ground of war, upon every principle both of justice and of policy; but more especially after the public declaration which he has made of his designs against our possessions. Any other construction will compel this Government to remain an inactive spectator of his preparations for war in conjunction with France; provided only that they be made gradually, and that the French force be introduced into his country in small detachments.'[1] The reply by anticipation of the Directors was already on its way.

Simultaneously offers were made to the Nizam and the Peishwah of a new system of treaty to increase the British detachments at their respective courts upon condition that the French corps should be disbanded or removed. Each

[1] To Mr. Dundas; 6th July, 1798.

power was made acquainted with terms offered to the other, and the arbitrament of the Governor General in all cases of dispute was stipulated as a means of averting future wars. The Resident at Hyderabad was instructed to support Secunder Jah the Nizam's eldest son, whose disposition was deemed friendly, as against the undermining schemes of his brothers who were supposed to be in league with Tippoo, and to rely on Piron in any future contest for succession to the musnud. A political agent dignified with the epithet of ambassador was likewise sent to the Rajah of Berar with a view of encouraging more intimate relations with us and with the Nizam whom he inclined to aid in resistance to the growing power of Scindiah. On the other hand Scindiah was specifically assured that if he would refrain from molesting his neighbours he should have cordial and effective aid in resisting the threatened inburst of the Afghans under Zemaun Shah. Mornington sanguinely counted on the Mahratta chief's acceptance of his proffered friendship in order to insure the integrity and quietude of his troubled realm. But here as elsewhere, Asiatic despotism showed little appreciation of his exotic schemes for the establishment of a general protectorate of peace. Like the twisted snakes of ancient Greece or the thorough-bred wolf-dogs of feudalism, the purpose of their lives was to wound one another; and outlandish inculcations to be quiet and to keep at home seemed to them but unmeaning mockery. At each new turn of events, indeed, the weaker combatant was always ready to profess preference for Feringhee counsel and readiness to accept the aid of British bayonets. Few opportunities were lost by Mornington of improving occasions of this kind; and by degrees he contrived to weave a network of conventions and contracts, subsidies and stipulations, which had each ally (for so in Roman fashion he was scrupulously called) recognised as a counterpart of many more, he might have less readily agreed to sign. But all other projects paled into insignificance beside the primary aim of displacing or dispersing the Nizam's French guard.

The Resident at Hyderabad was instructed to engage for a subsidiary corps of 6,000 men to be officered by us and paid for out of assigned revenues by the Nizam, with whose minister he was to confer without any disguise or reserve. The French corps would be transported to Europe in Company's ships with their arms and stores, and landed in France without any compromise or condition. But as the whole object in view was the restoration of a triple defensive alliance on a permanent footing, it was indispensable that both the Peishwah and the Nizam should respectively engage not to readmit French troops into their dominions, and to acknowledge the Government of Fort William as a court of arbitration to whose judgment future differences were to be referred.

'Pursuing no schemes of conquest or extension of dominion, and entertaining no projects of ambition or aggrandisement either for ourselves or our allies, it is both our right and our duty to give vigour and effect to our subsisting alliances and treaties by restoring to our allies the power of fulfilling their defensive engagements with us. Through the means of moderate and pacific representations, confirmed by the force of our own example, it must also be our policy to convince the several powers of India that their real interest consists in respecting the rights of their neighbours and in cultivating their own resources within the limits of their several territories. To these efforts we must add a firm resistance against the intrusion of any foreign power which shall endeavour (to the prejudice of our alliances and interests) to acquire a preponderant influence in the scale of Indian politics either by force or intrigue; but the primary object of all our vigilance and care must be the destruction of every seed of the

French party, already grown to so dangerous a height and still increasing in the armies and councils of the Nizam, of Scindiah, and of Tippoo. The exclusion of the influence of France from the dominions of the native States is not more necessary to the preservation of our own power than to the happiness and prosperity of this part of the world.'[1]

Bent on forging a machine of government after his own design, and of materials whose temper he could thoroughly rely upon, he looked round with scrutinising gaze and studied with single eye to their capability and adaptability, all the younger men in the civil or military service of whom he could learn by any means that they would if they could go far on the upper path of distinction, and 'that they had it in them.' While he stayed at Madras Captain Malcolm ventured to forward some papers he had written on the condition of the Deccan to Henry Wesley, with an expression of a hope that they might some day be brought under his brother's notice. On the voyage to Calcutta the packet was opened, and more than one sagacious and un-timeserving suggestion took the fancy of the new ruler. In September a vacancy occurred in the Residentship at Hyderabad, which Kirkpatrick was promoted to fill: and Malcolm, to his surprise and delight, was named Assistant. The letter appointing him was highly characteristic. 'I have been governed by no other motive than my knowledge of the zeal, activity, and diligence with which you have pursued the study of the native languages and the political system of India. I wish to see you previous to your proceeding to Hyderabad. There are many circumstances relative to the political system of India which it is proper you should learn from me as early as possible. It will also be advantageous to the public service that you should thoroughly understand my opinions

[1] To J. A. Kirkpatrick; 8th July, 1798.

on the various points with a degree of accuracy which cannot be conveniently stated in writing.'[1]

Before the letter reached him Malcolm was on his way to Hyderabad, whither he was sent by Lord Clive to promote the reduction of the French corps and the proportionate increase of our own. The change had been agreed to by the Nizam, and an early day named for its completion; but adverse influences in the durbar contrived excuses for delay; and with only two battalions of sepoys at his disposal the Resident could not do more than urge and expostulate. Early in October he was enabled to tell Azim ul Omrah that four additional battalions with a due complement of guns and cavalry were on their way; and that if Piron and his compatriot officers were superseded there would be no indisposition to reincorporate the rank and file under our command; but if time were given there was reason to believe that the distrusted legion would suddenly move toward the frontier and take service under the Sultan in Mysore. The minister, sustained by the native general Meer Allum, obtained at length the assent of the Nawab. A Proclamation appeared on October 22 disbanding the French auxiliaries, and calling upon them to lay down their arms and accoutrements as a preliminary to re-enlistment in a new force. Piron, described as a German adventurer intemperate in language and of uncouth bearing, was personally unpopular with the men; but they had long known and liked their regimental officers; and called on without reason to discard old military ties of long standing, they refused to obey. For some hours the cantonment was a scene of passionate disorder. The English troops had orders to take up a position near at hand; and had the mutiny lasted for a few hours longer a sanguinary collision must have ensued. Malcolm being well acquainted with the native language, gallantly offered to go alone into

[1] Fort William, 10th September, 1798.

the camp and try what could be done by reason and persuasion. He had made some way, when a counter-cry was raised that he had been sent to betray them; and he might have fallen a victim to his humane temerity had not a number of sepoys, who had formerly served under him in the Carnatic and subsequently gone for better pay into the Deccan, recognised their former captain, and making a rush, raised him on their shoulders and borne him off in safety from their angry comrades.

Some of the French officers came to terms the same night; and, mainly through the instrumentality of Malcolm, all of them the next day gave in. Kirkpatrick, relieved from an emergency most critical, did ample justice to the merit of his able and chivalrous subordinate; and when at length Malcolm made his way to Calcutta he was received by the Governor General with the warmest tokens of recognition and confidence. His Excellency could not help showing how pleased he was with his own discrimination—with having, without even seeing him, chosen the right man for the right place. Malcolm on his part was delighted to find a ruler with the capacity and courage which he had long felt were wanting at the head of Indian affairs; and he marvelled every day more and more at the variety of Mornington's knowledge of the complicated interests confided to his care, and the maturity of his views concerning them. His promotion rapidly followed. Mutual esteem by degrees grew into a friendship lasting life-long; and Malcolm, though he did not always concur in the opinions of his distinguished patron, never tired of extolling his great qualities, and battled eloquently with those who disparaged them.

In a Minute of Council an elaborate but laconic history was put on record of the incidents and measures of the first three months of the new administration. It recounted the growth of rumour quickening into belief and ripening into fact of hostility on the part of Mysore calling for defensive armaments; of weakness in the Deccan requiring sustainment and help; and of turbulence and intrigue in the Mahratta States demanding vigilance and tact, combined with a manifestation of resolve and readiness to curb all ambitious attempts at encroachment. It laid down broadly and fearlessly the principle of the new policy of empire—the assertion of the principle that the government of the Company meant to be, and meant to be recognised as being—*primus inter pares* among the States of Hindostan. Self-consciousness breathes through every line. Three months of unquestioned power, with nothing but the sense of ultimate responsibility afar off, would have beguiled a nature less ambitious and idealising into giving way to the intoxication of power. Mornington never grew bewildered or blinded by the dangerous potion. He was seldom betrayed into official haste or heat. His enjoyment was not delirium but ineffable delight. He looked as benignantly and stepped as daintily as a king in a play. 'When it is remembered that I did not take charge of this government until the 18th of May; that the Proclamation of M. Malartic did not make its first appearance at this Presidency until the 8th, and was not authenticated until the 18th of June; I trust it will appear that I have proceeded with as much expedition as was compatible with the due consideration of the various and important questions which demanded my decision. My present intention is to explain and illustrate the principles upon which that system is founded; the means by which I hope to carry it into effect, and the ends which I expect to accomplish by its ultimate success and permanent establishment. In this retrospect of my conduct, I shall disclose without hesitation or reserve the whole train of reflections which has passed in my mind during the agitation of this intricate and extensive subject; and I shall avow without disguise every successive variation of opinion, and every instance in which I have reluctantly submitted my unaltered judgment to the pressure of practical difficulties: nor shall I deny that I have ultimately pursued a course far within the limits of that to which the sense of my own duty and character, the clearest principles of justice and of policy, the unquestionable rights and interests of the Company, and the honour of the British name in India, would have directed me, if the obstacles to my progress had not appeared absolutely insurmountable.'[1] Tippoo's last communication to Sir John Shore, received at Fort William on the day that the French force from the Isle of France landed at Mangalore, had declared that 'his friendly heart was disposed to pay every regard to truth and justice, and to strengthen the foundations of harmony and concord established between the two States; and his desire that the retiring Viceroy should impress his successor with a sense of the friendship and unanimity for many years so firmly subsisting between them.'

A despatch from the Secret Committee subsequently authenticated the fact which had already reached him by various forms of rumour that a great expedition had sailed from Toulon on May 19 for the invasion of Egypt and India. Government had in consequence ordered 4,000 additional troops for the defence of the Company's possessions, a part of which they trusted would reach India not many months after the receipt of their despatch. Should the expedition not be intercepted in the Mediterranean, and be destined for India by the way of the Red Sea or by Bussora, two men-of-war and probably a sloop would be stationed in the Straits of Babelmandel and in the Gulf of Persia. 'Our empire in the East has ever been an object of jealousy to the French; and we know that their former Government entertained sanguine hopes of being able to reach India by a shorter passage than

---

[1] Minute of Governor General, Secret Department, Fort William, 12th August, 1798.

round the Cape of Good Hope ; and we have no doubt that the present Government would risk a great deal, and even adopt measures of a most enterprising and uncommon nature, for the chance of reducing if not annihilating the British power and consequence in that quarter of the world. To effect this without the aid and previous concert of one of the Indian powers seems almost impossible and would scarcely be attempted. In the present situation of India, Tippoo appears to be the fittest instrument to be employed in the furtherance of such ambitious projects. It is highly improbable that he should have entered into any league with the French without some apparent preparation on his part of a hostile nature in furtherance of their designs. If such therefore be the case, it would be neither prudent nor politic to wait for actual hostilities on his part. We therefore recommend that you should immediately take the necessary measures for bringing him to a satisfactory explanation, accompanying it with such a disposition of your force as may give effect to it ; and should you judge that he is making preparations to act hostilely against us, it will be advisable to take the most decisive measures to carry our arms into the enemy's country, not failing to make known to the powers in alliance with us the necessity of such measure, and that we have not in view a wanton attack upon our inveterate enemy with a design to augment our own power, but a necessary and justifiable defence of our own possessions, and calling upon them for the assistance they are under engagements to furnish us. We rely on your using the latitude allowed you with the utmost discretion, that we may not be involved in war without the most inevitable necessity, of which necessity the Governor and Council must be the judge.' The despatch enclosed a copy of Malartic's Proclamation.

The Porte incensed at the unprovoked invasion of Egypt, was easily induced to write, dissuading Tippoo from his meditated alliance. Without warning and in a time of profound peace, the Republic had secretly fitted out a great armament and placed at its head their most adventurous general for the partition of the Ottoman Empire. 'Conduct so audacious, wanton, and deceitfully sudden was an unquestionable proof of enmity and treachery; from intercepted letters it appeared that the design of the French was to break up Arabia into separate republics, to undermine the ascendency of Islam everywhere, and to efface the religion of the Prophet from the face of the earth. If allowed a footing in India on the plea of opposing the English there, they were certain to prove, as they had in all other lands, deceitful and rapacious. They ought therefore to be by all means opposed in their attempts to gain a footing, and discouraged in their machinations against the English in the East.'[1] Tippoo was not to be weaned from an alliance with France whose ultimate aims he little feared, or led to forgive the injury and humiliation he had suffered at the hands of Cornwallis; and the mediation of the Porte for the settlement of minor differences between him and the Company seemed to his haughty and implacable spirit but trifling with his lust of vengeance. For him there was and could be neither rest or satisfaction till he had reconquered all that Hyder had bequeathed him and he had lost. Still the French might tarry in Egypt and come not to his aid; and till they came he must temporise and send flattering messages and letters to Calcutta. In his private answer he reminds the Porte how 'in forty years the English had successfully subverted the Mahomedan powers in the Carnatic, Bengal, and Oude; and that they were now in open confederacy with the Pagan Mahrattas who had conquered Delhi, made the emperor their captive and put out his eyes. They looked to the gradual reduction of all Southern Asia to their yoke, and what respect could a nation have for the

[1] Sultan Selim to Tippoo; 20th September, 1798.

religion of the Koran who everywhere had butchers' shops open for the sale of pork?'[1]

Apprehensions of a French invasion constantly recurred; the Persian Government made no sign of interposition; and the aims and resources of Zemaun Shah were clouded in obscurity. Bonaparte made no secret of his ambition to invade Hindostan; and even after he had devolved the command on Kleber, apprehensions from time to time were kept alive at Calcutta of the appearance of a French fleet in the Indian Sea. Coast defences were thought necessary at the mouth of the Ganges; and the civil servants of the Company with the professional and mercantile English residents were embodied in militia corps for the protection of the town.[2]

The commissioners appointed to treat respecting Wynaad having made their report, the province was evacuated by the Company's troops and restored to its former possessor. Effusive professions of friendship and vows against the interruption of peace were kept up during the autumn, while all the time it was more than suspected that hostile intrigues were carrying on with the French and preparations making for war. On October 18 tidings came of Bonaparte's landing in Egypt with his army, tidings which might well quicken the pulse of responsibility at such a time. But before the end of the month one of Nelson's lieutenants presented himself at Fort William, bearing the news of the total destruction of the French fleet at the mouth of the Nile. Calcutta was illuminated, and the event communicated without delay to Seringapatam. On November 4, preparations being advanced towards completion, Mornington addressed Tippoo in terms at once frank and bold, repudiating the semblance of any longer being the dupe of

[1] Draft reply found after the fall of Seringapatam.
[2] Letter to Lord Clive, Governor of Madras, October 11, and Despatch to Secret Committee, 30th October, 1798. Quoted by Kaye, *Life of Tucker*, p. 90.

his false professions of amity, and warning him to break with our foes or abide the consequences. 'It is impossible that you should suppose me to be ignorant of the intercourse which subsists between you and the French whom you know to be the inveterate enemies of the Company, and to be now engaged in an unjust war with the British nation. You cannot imagine me to be indifferent to the transactions which have passed between you and the enemies of my country; nor does it appear necessary or proper that I should any longer conceal from you the surprise and concern with which I have perceived you disposed to involve yourself in all the ruinous consequences of a connection which threatens to introduce into the heart of your kingdom the principles of anarchy and confusion, to shake your own authority, to weaken the obedience of your subjects, and to destroy the religion which you revere. Your letters to Sir John Shore and to me have abounded in professions of friendship. It was natural for me to be extremely slow to believe the various accounts transmitted to me of your negotiations with the French and of your military preparations; but whatever my reluctance to credit such reports might be, prudence required both of me and of the Company's allies, that we should adopt certain measures of precaution and self-defence, and these have accordingly been taken, as you will no doubt have observed.' But to avoid a rupture, Major Doveton had been deputed to negotiate terms of accommodation on behalf of the Peishwah, the Company and the Nizam, calculated to insure general peace. Time and place were left to the choice of Tippoo.[1] After seven weeks the moody despot replied that he was delighted to hear of the naval victory off the coast of Egypt, in which nine French ships had been destroyed, and he hoped the Company's Bahauder, who ever adhered to the paths of sincerity, friend-

[1] 8th November, 1798.

ship, and good faith, and had the good wishes of mankind, would at all times be successful and victorious; and that the French, who were of a crooked disposition, faithless and the enemies of mankind, might be ever depressed and ruined.' A ship had been sent to the Mauritius by trading people of his Sircar which brought back a score or two of adventurers seeking employment, and this was the only ground of ill-natured rumours. But for himself the continuance of peace with all his neighbours was nearest to his heart, and he was quite surprised at the mention of preparations for war. All he could promise was to observe existing treaties whose modification he saw no reason to desire.[1] The vakeel spent a week on the road, and the evasive epistle did not reach Fort William until Christmas day.

On the same day the Governor General embarked from the water-gate at Fort William on board the Government yacht for a frigate lying in the roadstead which was to bear him to Madras, whither his zeal for the public service impelled him to proceed, that no time should be lost in correspondence where every day and hour had become of moment in warlike preparations.

[1] Received 25th December, 1798.

CHAPTER X.

SERINGAPATAM.

1799.

AFLOAT once more upon the bosom of the Indian Sea, what anxieties and aspirations stirred within him! Amid the pressure of affairs manifold and momentous, his thoughts turned oftentimes towards home, and he longed for words of recognition and remembrance by those from whom he had been far removed for the first time. Out of sight, he would fain be not out of mind. The ultimate verdict of history on his performances in the East was a fine thing to dream of in the dim future; but the appreciation and applause of living competitors for fame is as a savour of life unto life, to a spirit consumed by ambition. He found time to keep up an animated correspondence with several of his friends in England. Auckland, who loved gossip and wrote well, kept him in news of Lady Mornington and his children, and sent him the raciest articles and pamphlets on public affairs, with confidential hints of what the world was not allowed to know. How his susceptible, eager, inquisitive nature must have gorged such delicious packets-full may be gathered from replies like the following:—

'I request you to accept my acknowledgments for your kind note of April 24, and for the "Anti-Jacobin," which has amused me extremely. India cannot furnish an adequate return for your letters and packets; and if it could, you know too well what the office of Governor General is to complain of the brevity of his letters. However I have enclosed an extract from my letter to the Court of Directors, and a return of the *late* French army at Hyderabad, which will give you some idea of the state of affairs in this quarter, and of the nature of my proceedings. The picture will be filled up by such information as you will obtain from Dundas; and as the whole will only present myself in different points of view, I think I may as well leave the work to some other hand than my own.

'On October 18 we learnt the destination of the Toulon fleet and army to be towards India. Although I certainly did not expect that the French would attempt the route by Egypt, I have been convinced for a long time that their views were turned this way, and accordingly (thank God) I took my precautions as early as the month of June. We can now defy them; and I trust you will be of opinion that the blow which I have struck at Hyderabad was not unseasonable. It took place on October 22; and the intelligence reached me nearly at the same moment with the glorious news of the victory at Aboukir. Our accounts of the state of Bonaparte's army leave little doubt of its final destruction. Instead of " Delenda est Carthago " he must say now—

> " Carthagini jam non ego nuntios
> Mittam superbos." [1]

I cannot help thinking that this event will prove the signal of a general revolt in Europe, and the source of peace and security to the whole globe.

'Let me express my gratitude, my dear Lord, for your kind attentions to Lady Mornington and to my children; such acts of friendship are of redoubled value at this dreadful distance. My health is and has uniformly been much

[1] Hor. *Ode* iv. 1. 70.

better than it usually was in England; and the pressure and variety of business has been useful to my spirits; but Lady Mornington must come out to me if she can. I am happy to hear that you are *formally* in office: you have been so *efficiently* for a long time. Pray remember me most cordially to Lady Auckland and all your amiable family. I hope they are all *remaaarkably* well in every respect whatsoever.

' If any man can quiet Ireland, Lord Cornwallis will effect that great work. I trust you will now force a union. It is difficult; but in these days difficulties are our daily food, and for one I find that I thrive upon it.

' P.S.—I hope you will continue to let me know how your quarter of the globe is managed.' [1]

The irrepressible sense of Jupitership in this is curiously in contrast with the noble and tender language of the man to whose goodness and wisdom he pays the just tribute of his admiration as Viceroy of Ireland; and who both preceded and followed him in the government of India. His boast of physical vigour amid the unaccustomed perils of Asiatic temperature and treachery reminds one of similar words in a letter of his great predecessor Warren Hastings, after he had discomfited all his foes in council and in the field:—' My enemies died, sickened or fled; I remained and carried on the government.'

Would *he* remain long enough a Sovereign in all but name of Hindostan, to build a monument as lasting of extended rule? His fate and fortune trembled in the balance. He went as executive chief to supersede during the impending crisis

---

[1] The numbers of the *Anti-Jacobin* which afforded him so much amusement were those of the 16th and 23rd April, 1798, containing Canning's well-known ' Loves of the Triangles.'

the new President of Madras, and thereby to take upon himself, in the face of the watching world, the direct responsibility for all that might ensue. Lord Clive, son of the victor of Plassey, had been appointed to the second place of importance in the East soon after he had quitted England, and the correspondence that had taken place between them showed how easily the stronger will led the more malleable. Nevertheless, a man of less judgment and temper than Clive might have chafed at his virtual supersession by the presence of his official superior on the scene. Happily no symptom of jealousy appears to have marred their unity of purpose. Mornington was too fond of flattery himself to forget how agreeable it was to others; and lavish in all things, he bestowed it ungrudgingly on those he loved and trusted. From Clive he had no secrets; and relying on the ascendency of his own intellect and will, he consulted him with affectionate frankness as carefully on points where he had long made up his mind as upon those of detail where he was open to suggestion. Their friendship never flagged; and in his reports to Government at home he never omitted an opportunity of acknowledging the devotion, probity and usefulness of his friend.

Secretary Webbe had been propitiated by finding his advice taken by the Governor General with reference to delay in commencing operations. He was delighted moreover to see at last at the head of affairs a great man who could measure the greatness of difficulties, and who never wearied in wrestling with them. He gave himself heart and soul to prepare for the struggle he would have indefinitely postponed rather than embark in unpreparedly; and Mornington, who at first resented his obduracy and railed at him in private as 'head of the faction at Madras' that stood in the way of reform, learned to estimate justly his truly excellent qualities, and to treat him with confidence and respect.

A pleasant but unconspicuous house belonging to Mr. Petrie, one of the civil servants of the Presidency, was engaged for his accommodation and that of his limited staff; and under the shade of the banyan trees in the garden he was wont, ere the sun had risen too high, to walk up and down dictating official despatches and confidential letters to his brother Henry, and to a volunteer assistant from Calcutta, soon to become one of his most prized and most devoted friends. One of the birds, called by the natives Huma, was observed to rest frequently on the topmost bough above his head; and happening to look into a Persian dictionary, he was amused to find this species of eagle noted as the emblem of prosperous empire, its image being emblazoned on the flag borne before the prince in war. Few in the narrow and busy circle of Europeans in Madras were likely to recall classic auguries; and not one probably amongst them knew that an effigy in gold of the bird of presage still held in its talons the canopy over the musnud of Mysore. What would they not have given to know that ere many weeks the typical clutch of power would be relaxed, and that the spirit of rule was about to enter into a living and yet more aspiring form?

The whole tone of administration was gradually changed. The coxcombry of clerkship was snubbed into diligence, and fine-gentleman airs had to give place to civility and regularity in office hours. Bankers and merchants took courage from the spectacle of improved vigour in all branches of the administration, and lent the Government large sums of money, where a few months before they would not discount Treasury bills at less than usurious interest. The remittances from Bengal in December were quickly exhausted, and twenty lacs in addition were called for in aid of the military chest. But by the time he had to move, Harris was provided with specie sufficient to maintain his army in the field till May.[1] Associated with him as a political council with whom he should advise on all subjects of negotiation during the campaign (subject to reference for approval to Madras) were: Colonel Close, long Resident at Poonah, Arthur Wesley commanding the 33rd regiment, Major Kirkpatrick who held a position on the staff, and Henry Wesley his brother's private secretary; with Captain Malcolm fast rising into favour and influence, and Thomas Munro, as joint secretaries. It is curious to note how, amid all the labour and solicitude of the situation, the inappeasable love of pomp craved for the means of display. In all the excitement of gathering hosts and the impending peril of the life and death grapple at hand, the Governor General found time to write to Fort William for his body-guard: a request which Sir Alured Clarke had the good sense not to comply with, and the good temper to invent plausible excuses for neglecting. It would take too long to send them by land, and the showy horses would be out of condition if sent by sea;[2] so his Lordship had to do without his toy troopers.

Twelve months before Tippoo had proffered an alliance to the French Government for the extirpation of the English from India: his father had trusted kingly France, and he put faith in Republican promises. In the last war the French had forsaken him and their ambitious foe had prevailed; but let them now give their word and keep it, send him timely reinforcements, and with the 'aid of their freed negroes and their troops of the line he would purge India of these villains.' He would pay, clothe, and feed his European auxiliaries, except in the article of liquor, total abstinence being a cardinal point of his morality; but any amount of gunpowder he would purchase gladly: and for the general prin-

---

[1] To the Court of Directors, 20th March, 1799.
[2] Private letter from Fort William, 5th March, 1799.

ciples of democracy he professed profound respect. If the Portuguese should interfere they must be expelled likewise; and the Peishwah and the Nizam must lose their dominions if they gave succour to the foe.[1]

The Directory were too busy with affairs nearer home to respond with ardour to the invitation from afar; and it was not until January 30, 1798, that the Governor of the Isle of France was persuaded by envoys from Mysore to issue the Proclamation destined to become so notable, of a joint attack upon the possessions of the Company.

In a confidential letter to the Directory, Tippoo described the embassy to the Mauritius, its objects and results, notwithstanding the different colour put upon it in December when trying to gain time. He alleged no ground of complaint against us since the last war; but avowed that his aim was to recover the provinces he had then lost, and the expulsion of the English from all their possessions in Hindostan. He was waiting only for a favourable occasion to commence the attack, and he offered to make common cause with the Republic under the most solemn vows of fidelity and zeal. He proposed a descent on the Carnatic in concert with the French landing at Porto Novo, but was ready to anticipate its arrival if assured that it would come ere long. The Portuguese colonies in Coromandel were to be partitioned between him and the Republic.[2]

Conflicting rumours from Constantinople, Bagdad, and Bussorah as to the condition of the French in Egypt concurred only in attesting the presence of a large army there; what its destination might ultimately be was unknown. From a private letter to the English minister at Philadelphia we learn the strange and almost incredible fact that from

---

[1] 2nd April, 1797.
[2] Copy of documents with the sign-manual of the Sultan found in his palace after his death.

August 26 till the end of March no authentic intelligence had reached the Indian Government regarding Bonaparte's army.[1] As was natural, Bonaparte had lost no time in communicating with the ruler of Mysore. He had in point of fact, addressed to him from Cairo a characteristic adjuration to form an intimate and active alliance.

'Liberty, French Republic, Equality. Bonaparte, member of the National Convention, General-in-Chief, to the most magnificent Sultan, our greatest friend, Tippoo Saib.

> 'Headquarters at Cairo, 7th Pluviose,
> 7th year of the Republic one and indivisible.

'You have been already informed of my arrival on the borders of the Red Sea with an innumerable and invincible army, full of the desire of delivering you from the iron yoke of England. I eagerly embrace this opportunity of testifying to you the desire I have of being informed by you, by the way of Muscat and Mocha, as to your political situation. I would even wish you could send some intelligent person to Suez or Cairo possessing your confidence, with whom I may confer. May the Almighty increase your power and destroy your enemies.'

Emissaries were forthwith sent to the General, but the negotiations languished, probably from the uncertainty as to the means of naval transport to Perim or Cambay. What hopes Tippoo still cherished in January 1799 can never now be known; but his tardiness in answering the English proposals to negotiate pointed plainly to the design of wasting the season until it should be too late to open the campaign. On February 3 no answer had come from Seringapatam to the Governor General's letter of January 9, though the journey might be made in four or five days. The troops, therefore had orders to advance, and with the consent of the

[1] From Fort St. George to Mr. Liston, 1st April, 1799.

Peishwah and Nizam, war was declared. On February 7 two vakeels with M. Du Buc, an officer of the French auxiliaries from the Mauritius, sailed from Tranquebar with letters to the French Directory, and on the 13th Tippoo's evasive answer was at length received at Fort St. George.[1]

On February 19 the Nizam's contingent, commanded by Meer Allum, consisting of 6,000 infantry, including a portion of Piron's sepoys reorganised under British officers, an equal number of subsidiary troops, and a large body of cavalry, effected a junction with the corps under the English general; and on March 5 the combined armies entered Mysore.

The definite objects of the contest were declared to be the eradication of French influence in the Peninsula and 'a considerable reduction of Tippoo's resources and power.' He had long been a source of trouble and alarm to all his neighbours, and the present was the second occasion within three years that for self-protection and at heavy cost British armies had to assemble on the Coromandel coast.

Six weeks of unremitting toil had been devoted by the Governor General to superintending every ramification of the comprehensive system of measures deemed necessary for the impending struggle. Difficulties of finance, slackness in the transport of supplies, deficiencies unsuspected in the stores of ammunition for each corps, and shortcomings in the baggage train; want of appliances for medical aid and want of horses for reconnoitring service; every conceivable pretext and device of indolence and apathy for procrastination and of avidity for jobbing; the irresolution of native allies and the habitual indifference of Anglo-Indian officials,—all had in turn to be dealt with, and their multiplied evils and dangers anticipated and averted. If he could only infuse into all around him something of his own sense of the greatness of the stake, the true way of the game and the

[1] Despatch to Court of Directors, 20th March, 1799.

glory to be won, he had no doubt of winning. Nobler aids in council or in camp man never had ; but how were subalterns without a political idea or a day's experience of camping-out, of work in the trenches or the din of battle, to be made partakers of his anxiety or partners in his ambition ? With all the confidence reposed in him by the Directors of the Company and by the Ministers of State, he could not sleep for thinking how unpardonable in the eyes of both would be the sin of failure ; how vain would be all explanations, however true ; how pitiless the reproach of costly and protracted preparation if, after all, the expedition came to nought. It must not fail. Early and late, at noontide and long past midnight, he was untiringly at work, conferring, consulting, corresponding, correcting, re-examining, coaxing, caressing, and it must be added in a whisper, occasionally cursing after the manner of our troops who 'swore terribly in Flanders.' It was the way of the time even with phlegmatic natures ; and his was a nature in which it might be said that phlegm had been left out when he was made. By degrees however, and rapidly accelerating quickness of degrees, he saw the fruit, under his signal power of forcing, begin to look as if it would ripen, and then as if it had begun to ripen, and at last as if it were really ripe. With pardonable pride he could at length survey the prospect opening before the army, and congratulate its commander that nothing had been left undone to secure its success. In a private letter to Harris when bidding him go forth and anticipating that he would soon return triumphant, he enumerates the varied pains that had been devoted to needful preparation and the advantages they were calculated to afford. It has in it the ring of a silver trumpet before dawn, solitary, penetrating, and clear.

'The army of the Carnatic under his command was unquestionably the best appointed, the most completely equipped, the most amply and liberally supplied, the most perfect in point of discipline, and the most fortunate in the acknowledged experience and abilities of its officers in every department, which ever took the field in India. It comprised a more numerous and better appointed corps of cavalry than any European power in India ever brought into action. The army on the coast of Malabar appeared to be in an equally efficient state.' As if after a final review he continued :

'A powerful force destined to co-operate from the southward was an advantage not possessed in the last war; and in the Baramahl every measure had been taken for the collection of supplies and to secure the earliest benefit from the exertions made. The appearance of a large fleet upon the coast could not fail to aid the operations by intimidating the enemy and by encouraging defection among his subjects. The Nizam's force appeared in the field at a much earlier period than in the last war, and the cordial zeal of the Court of Hyderabad for our success (so questionable then) now admitted of no doubt. There was moreover no reason to apprehend that the Peishwah would not make every effort to assist with a large body of cavalry. The General was invested with full powers for the management of these extraordinary advantages, and was surrounded by a staff uniting every species of knowledge and ability. The enemy's country, the nature of his resources, the strength of his defences, and the character of his force were subjects perfectly familiar to them : nor was any contingency likely to arise against which they would not have provided. On the other hand, Tippoo's army was known to have suffered essentially both in numbers and discipline since the last war; his finances were in great disorder; he no longer possessed the confidence of his army; his counsels were distracted by contending factions ; and his spirits were dejected and broken by the disappointment of his hopes of French assistance, by the retreat of Zemaun

Shah from Lahore, by the failure of his own intrigues at the Courts of Poonah and Hyderabad, and by the unexampled vigour, alacrity, and extent of our military preparations.'[1]

After three months of fruitless offers to negotiate, further delay was deemed inexpedient, and the allies appealed to arms. In the declaration of war Tippoo's duplicity is set forth in a brief but lucid narrative of facts, but while refusing to give him further time for the foreign succour he was awaiting, they were willing still to come to terms that might reciprocally assure his dominions and theirs against encroachment and invasion. Harris was authorised as Commander-in-Chief to receive any embassy which the Sultan might despatch to headquarters of the British army, and to concert a treaty on such conditions as might appear to the allies fitted to secure an equitable and permanent peace.[2] From Poonah came the disappointing news that in the distraction wrought by contending factions there, all chance of the promised aid from that quarter must be considered at an end. Nor was it a slight aggravation of the anxieties of the hour that week after week passed without any authentic information from home regarding the disposition of the English fleet eastward of the Cape, or of the probable fortunes of the French arms in Egypt. From Constantinople rumours came that Bonaparte's army was reduced to 17,000 men, but as to whether they were moving towards Syria or remaining stationary, there was no account. In the retrospect of after years Napoleon owned that he had often dreamed of conquering the East, and measured more than once strategically the time and toil that it would take, the men and horses requisite, the troop-ships and magazines of arms and food. His letters of blandishment to the Shereef of Mecca, the Shah of Persia, and the enterprising Ruler of

---

[1] To General Harris; Fort St. George, 23rd February, 1799.
[2] From Fort St. George, 22nd February, 1799.

Afghanistan, suggesting a concerted invasion of India, did not evoke the responses he desired. But Mornington accurately divined that in the winter of 1798 he found himself caught in a trap out of which he would try to break at any hazard. The Mamelukes overthrown, and under the tricolour order reigned at Cairo; but the ships that had convoyed his transports to Alexandria were sunk or captured, and the armies of the Porte with British auxiliaries were advancing through Palestine. Sooner than remain inactive he would go forth to meet them; and as he confessed at St. Helena, he was persuaded that once 'possessed of Acre his army might have gone to Damascus and the Euphrates; the Christians of Syria, the Druses, and the Armenians would have joined him. Many provinces of the Ottoman empire were ready for a change; they were only waiting for a man. With 100,000 men on the banks of the Euphrates he might have gone to Constantinople or to India, and have changed the face of the world. He would have founded an empire in the East, and the destinies of France would have run into a different course.'

But it was not till May 4 that Mornington's prognostics were verified by the intelligence from Bombay that Bonaparte was established in Egypt, had fortified Suez, and was collecting craft at the head of the Arabian Gulf. The season being then open for coming down the gulf, and a possibility existing that some part of the French force might escape the vigilance of our cruisers, it was become necessary to look to the protection of every point which the enemy might attempt, and to take the best precautions for our security. To defend Calcutta it would be advisable to prepare gunboats and armed vessels to cruise off the Sand Heads, within sight of which French privateers not unfrequently captured our Indiamen. The French prisoners and inhabitants of Calcutta required, he thought, the most vigilant control; and he directed the acting Governor of Bengal in his absence to take immediate steps for placing them under the strictest surveillance, giving him authority to report summarily any whose conduct or language should excite suspicion. The news thus transmitted in confidence ought not to be prematurely disclosed; but he added characteristically, 'I believe nobody will now contest the policy of my measures for the early reduction of Tippoo.'[1]

Napoleon's actual schemes on quitting Egypt, and the means whereby they were destined to be foiled, were indeed hidden from the eyes of those who prepared for battle on the banks of the Cauvery. But had it been known at Madras that already the French army had passed the isthmus and occupied Gaza without a blow, another and if possible a more imperative motive would have been supplied for hastening the advance into Mysore. The mist of a trackless desert hung impenetrably between; and for many weeks, a thousand miles apart, the like contention with empire for the stake was destined to be waged eventually with the same result. In the irony of fate the Moslem found at Acre his chief ally and deliverer in an English commodore and his blue-jackets; while at Seringapatam his French allies were unable to resist the rush of English bayonets. More dramatic still were the foreshadowings of history; Napoleon being driven from his parallels against the Syrian fortress at the very moment that Arthur Wesley was aiding in the capture of the Mysorean citadel at the head of his regiment.

Amid the distractions of the time Mornington began to ruminate projects of administrative reform for the future; and philosophically in his despatches home to note the evils arising from our short-sighted system of displacing all the men of the race which till recently had been ascendant in civil and military rule, and providing for them no peaceful

[1] To Sir Alured Clarke (private and secret), 4th May, 1799.

career whose duties or advantages should draw them into the ways of order and acquiescence in our rule.[1]

When Tippoo saw that a formidable invasion of his realm was imminent he sent a letter of egregious triviality acknowledging the admonition of Sultan Selim, but saying nothing of his response thereto; ceremoniously inquiring after the Governor General's health, and notifying his own intention to go out hunting; and intimating his willingness to receive Major Doveton if he came with a slight escort. The season was too far advanced to admit of further delay, and instead of parley on the hill-side with Doveton, he was sternly told that if he wished for peace he must now communicate with Harris, who at the head of the allied army was about to cross the frontier, but with whom he might still make terms. What these terms should be were precisely defined in a packet of sealed instructions. On passing the frontier the General was to circulate widely the declaration of war, and issue a proclamation guaranteeing from molestation all who should not oppose him in arms, offering protection for life and property to all who should furnish cattle, forage, or grain. No pretence of pacific parley was to be suffered to retard the advance to the capital; but if before it was reached, or the siege formed, authentic intimation should be given by Tippoo of his readiness to accept certain specified conditions, the commander was left discretionary power to negotiate. And should he decline to send an embassage before the junction of the invading columns and the formation of the trenches round the city, 'before opening a battery or throwing a shell into the town the commander was directed to communicate to the Sultan, either through his envoys or by flag of truce, the demands of the allies. 1. He must agree to the interchange of ambassadors when so required. 2. He must dismiss from his dominions all

---

[1] To Secret Committee, 22nd April, 1799.

citizens or soldiers of foreign States at war with Great Britain. 3. He must renounce all connection with France and debar all her people access to his country. 4. He must cede to the Company the seacoast of Malabar south of the Ghauts, and the district and fort of Sacragerry, and make equal concessions of territory to the Nizam and Peishwah. 5. He must renounce his claims to certain districts in dispute between him and his neighbours. 6. One crore and a half of rupees must be paid for the cost of the war. 7. All prisoners on either side must be released. The signature must be annexed under Tippoo's seal, and the hostages delivered within twenty-four hours.

Five days before Harris crossed the frontier, Tippoo at the head of 12,000 men entered the territory of one of our allies to attack the column under General Stuart advancing from Bombay. After a sharp encounter at Seedapore he was compelled to fall back, to await the main body of his assailants in the centre of his dominions. On March 27 a general action took place at Malavelly, the first in which Arthur Wesley was engaged. His regiment threatened in flank and front by the numerous cavalry of Tippoo, reserved their fire till at close quarters, and then advancing with fixed bayonets, won and held the central position of the day. A general rout ensued. The swollen stream of the Cauvery was forded without loss, and on April 7 the convergent corps as originally planned sat down before Seringapatam. They were there joined some days later by the corps of Stuart and Floyd. On May 4, two months after the declaration of war, the Mysore Capital was taken by storm and its infatuated ruler was slain fighting sword in hand. The surviving members of his family surrendered and all further resistance ceased.

The usurping dynasty having ceased to reign, the lineal heir of the Rajahs supplanted by them was first to be considered. He was now summoned from the prison where he had been long immured, and treated by his unexpected deliverers with kindness and consideration. The right of conquest placed indeed the whole of his ancestral territories at the disposal of the allies; and the population awe-struck at the suddenness of the earthquake in which their late oppressor and his adherents had gone down into the pit, obeisantly bowed their heads to the will of the white-faced irresistibles. Before the end of May the commandants of the provincial forts signified their readiness to surrender; the superior officers were most of them prisoners of war, and it was evident that no difficulty would arise in the re-settlement of the country from the influence of the Mahomedan minority, encouraged and enriched though they had been by Hyder and his son. It had been their policy to crush Hindoo usages, traditions, privileges and hereditary rights existing immemorially before their time, in order to concentrate in one absolute and irresponsible hand the whole power of the State. The knell of their despotism might therefore be made the first note of native restoration, comfort and peace. This magnanimous purpose the Governor General conceived, and would no doubt if he could have carried to completion. The objects of the war had been declared repeatedly to be, a reasonable indemnification for its cost, and the prevention in future of the irruptive and intrusive dangers to the general tranquillity which had made it unavoidable. For these objects some annexations of territory to that of the Nizam and that of the Company seemed indispensable, but a just rule of partition was not so obvious or plain. 'A peace founded in the gratification of any ambitious or inordinate view could neither be advantageous, honourable, or secure. The approved policy, interests and honour of the British nation therefore required that the settlement of the extensive kingdom subjected to our disposal should be founded on principles acceptable to the inhabitants of the conquered territories, just and conciliatory towards the contiguous native States, and indulgent to every party in any degree affected by the consequences of our success. To have divided the whole equally between the Company and the Nizam, to the exclusion of every other State, would have afforded strong grounds of jealousy to the Mahrattas, and aggrandised the Nizam's power beyond all bounds of discretion. It would have laid the foundation of perpetual differences, not only between the Mahrattas and the Nizam, but between the Company and both those powers. The Mahrattas unquestionably had no claim to any portion of the conquered territory, and any considerable extension of their sway was objectionable, especially when accompanied by the possession of strong fortresses bordering on the line of our frontier. It was however desirable to conciliate their goodwill, and to offer to them such a portion of territory as might give them an interest in the new settlement without offence or injury to the Nizam and without danger to the Company's possessions. On the other hand it was prudent to limit the territory retained in the hands of the Company and of the Nizam within such bounds of moderation as should bear a due proportion to their respective expenses in the contest and to the necessary means of securing the public safety of their respective dominions. An attentive investigation of every comparative view of these important questions terminated in the decision that the establishment of a central and separate government in Mysore, under the protection of the Company, and the admission of the Mahrattas to a certain participation in the division of the conquered territory, were the expedients best calculated to reconcile the interests of all parties, to secure to the Company a less invidious and more efficient share of revenue, resource, commercial advantage, and military strength, than could be obtained under any other distribution of territory or power, and to afford the most favourable prospect of general and permanent tranquillity in India.'[1] Canara, Coimbatore, Daraporam, and Wynaad fell to the lot of the Company, with certain districts lying between their possessions in the Carnatic and the coast of Malabar. These completed the coast line of the Company's possessions from sea to sea, and their fertility left no room for doubt that the revenue would meet the expenditure requisite for their government. To these were added the custody not only of the mouths of the Ghauts on our side of the hills, but the entrances to the passes on the inner side. The possession of the former alone furnished no effectual barrier for the inhabitants of the lowlands against an enemy possessing the summits of the mountains; and the acquisition therefore of all the entrances of the passes situated above the Ghauts was an essential object of security against every possible approach of danger from the table-land. Lastly, the Company were to have the city and fortress of Seringapatam, by which their communications from east to west were rendered more secure. To the Nizam were assigned provinces in the aggregate quite as valuable, and to the Peishwah a lesser accession, which being yielded as of favour, was made conditionally upon the ratification of a new treaty of alliance with the Mahratta empire. Mysore reconstituted under the son of Tippoo would still have been a source of distrust and danger from without and from within. Professions of acquiescence on the part of one bred in the treacherous school which he had been, could not be relied on even in the hour of abject submission. Humiliation of his family and the diminution of his realm would never be forgotten, and whatever his vows of friendliness and content he would be constantly impelled to repair by some enterprise hatched in conspiracy and launched without warning, the losses inflicted by the recent war. His vices and even his virtues would

---

[1] To the Court of Directors; Fort St. George, 3rd August, 1799.

impel him to a secret course of enmity. 'The hostile power of Mysore would have been weakened but not destroyed; an enemy would still have remained in the centre of our possessions watching every occasion to repair the misfortunes of his family at our expense, and forming a point of union for the machinations of every discontented faction in India and for the intrigues of every emissary in France.' There remained the alternative of restoring the legitimate Hindoo sovereignty in the person of the youthful Rajah whom every feeling of gratitude ought to bind to those who had rescued him from degrading captivity. Replaced upon the throne of his ancestors, he would naturally feel the best guarantee of its stability was the friendship of the power that had called him from the depths of misery to set him on high amongst the people. 'In the place of a power that had menaced our safety, would be substituted one whose interests and resources might be absolutely identified with our own, and the kingdom of Mysore, so long a source of calamity and alarm to the Carnatic, might become a new barrier of our defence, and might supply fresh means of wealth and strength to the Company, their subjects and allies.' The mass of the population would instinctively look up with more respect to a ruler of their own faith, and the sufferings which he and his family had undergone could not but impart, wherever they were known or remembered, an aspect of generosity to an act which had at length terminated them.

The ancient Raj with the addition of Bednore was not in terms restored to the family of its Hindoo prince, but granted anew as a fief of the empire, and recognised as such by the treaty to which the Peishwah and the Nizam were signataries. The only curtailment of its old Hindoo limits was that of Coimbatore.

By a subsidiary treaty[1] to which the Peishwah and Nizam

[1] Ratified at Fort St. George 13th July, 1799.

were parties, a civil list of a lac of pagodas and one-fifth of the total revenues of the reconstituted State were settled on Rajah Kistna Raj Udiaver, such portion of the remainder as might be requisite being pledged for the payment monthly of seven lacs to the Company to defray the cost of an auxiliary force and of European officers to be permanently maintained in Mysore. In default of payment the Governor-General was authorised ' to introduce such regulations and ordinances as he should deem expedient for the internal management and collection of the revenues, or for the better ordering of any other branch and department of the Government of Mysore; or to assume and bring under the direct management of the servants of the Company such part of the territorial possessions of his Highness as shall be necessary to render the funds efficient and available either in time of peace or war.' Mysore was further bound to furnish rateably with its neighbours money and men to resist, when called upon, any foreign foe. The financial obligation thus created implied, no doubt, political subordination and dependency; but under the circumstances it would have been hard to devise any conditions less stringent that would have afforded a reasonable chance of giving the native government newly set up, time to take root and grow strong, while yielding such portion of the fruit as would repay the cost of imperial protection: and without that protection its stability could not have been secured. In magnanimous or even forbearing justice-loving hands like those of Minto or Bentinck, the discretionary power reserved to the Viceroy for the time being would not be abused; and Mornington may be forgiven for not discrediting his successors with the suspicion that the power he was thus creating in perpetuity might come one day to be scandalously abused. But even the Brahmin minister Poorneah, wise and experienced as he was, and naturally anxious to set firm the foundations of the new government, could suggest no feasible alternative; and he recommended the young Prince's Guardian to put her signet to the pact. On June 30 he was accordingly conducted to the musnud by the British Commissioners, assisted by Meer Allum as representative of the Nizam.

While desiring sincerely to identify the future welfare of Mysore with that of the Company's possessions, and discarding with statesmanlike disdain the pitiful and rapacious ideas of making the new feudatory State subservient to the selfish ease or official cupidity of empire, Mornington felt that it would be mere weakness to throw away in deference to any theory or sentiment the opportunity which fortune had placed in his hands of establishing on a firm and intelligible basis the paramount authority, without whose reservation in case of need or doubt, any general guarantee of military protection must end in quarrel or failure. The newly-constituted State might be ultimately made happy, prosperous, and safe, if its prince and its people should accept loyally the political conditions he proposed. He desired to be thought of as a deliverer rather than a conqueror; but deliverance from the plagues of domestic oppression and frontier wars could only be assured by the recognised presence of a subsidiary force, subject to the orders of a British Resident, and the public acknowledgment that the restored Raj formed henceforth a constituent portion of the Anglo-Indian Empire. The whole policy of his administration is boldly and even sternly, but withal generously and wisely, recorded in exultant despatches to the Directors.

'In framing this engagement it was my determination to establish the most unqualified community of interests between the government of Mysore and the Company, and to render the Rajah's northern frontier in effect a powerful line of our defence. With this view I have engaged to undertake the protection of this country, in consideration of an annual subsidy of seven lacs of star pagodas; but recollecting the inconveniences and embarrassments which have arisen to all parties concerned under the double governments and conflicting authorities unfortunately established in Oude, the Carnatic, and Tanjore, I resolved to reserve to the Company the most extensive and indisputable powers of interposition in the internal affairs of Mysore, as well as an unlimited right of assuming the direct management of the country (whenever such a step might appear necessary for the security of the funds destined to the subsidy), and requiring extraordinary aid beyond the amount of the fixed subsidy either in time of war or of preparations for hostility. Under this arrangement I trust that I shall be enabled to command the whole resources of the Rajah's territory, to improve its cultivation, to extend its commerce, and to secure the welfare of its inhabitants. It appeared to me a more candid and liberal, as well as a more wise policy, to apprise the Rajah distinctly at the moment of his accession of the exact nature of his dependence, than to leave any matter for future doubt or discussion. The right of the Company to establish such an arrangement, either as affecting the Rajah or the allies, has already been stated. I entertain a sanguine expectation that the Rajah and his ministers, being fully apprised of the extensive powers reserved to the Company, will cheerfully adopt such regulations as shall render the actual exercise of these powers unnecessary. Much indulgence will be required at the commencement of the new government, and it is my intention to abstain from any pressure upon the Rajah's finances which by embarrassing them might tend to the impoverishment of the country and to the distress of the people.' Soon after the enthronement of the Rajah,[1] the Brahmin Poorneah was appointed by the commissioners to be his Highness's Dewan.

[1] 3rd August, 1799.

Colonel Close, whose intimate knowledge of the habits and language of the country had enabled him to render essential service previously, was named Résident at Bangalore, the ancient capital, which was fixed upon as the seat of the restored Hindoo Government : and the Political Commission having finished its work was dissolved. Colonel Wesley was appointed Commandant of Seringapatam, thenceforth the Company's fortress. The trust was felt to be one of delicacy as well as importance, requiring undoubted skill and integrity combined with more than ordinary vigilance and care ; and it was upon these grounds that Harris recommended him for the post. He still held the rank only of Colonel, and there were in the army several officers of superior standing. With respect to the language held by people on the occasion, Mornington wrote to Harris,—' You know that I never recommended my brother to you, and of course never suggested how or where he should be employed, and you know also that you would not have pleased me by placing him in any situation in which his appointment could be injurious to the public service. But my knowledge and experience of his discretion, judgment, temper, and integrity are such that, if you had not placed him in Seringapatam, I would have done so of my own authority, because I think him in every respect the most proper for the service.'

General Baird, who led the critical assault and by his intrepidity contributed so much to the triumph, gnashed his teeth at what he deemed a slight in having a junior preferred for the honourable and lucrative reward. ' Before the sweat was dry upon my brow, I was superseded by an inferior officer.' His biographer resents the preference as a job, and the historian brands it as a blot. Harris endeavoured to console him with the assurance that the office being essentially political, the choice implied no species of disparagement of his merits as a soldier. But the case undoubtedly was hard.

For many months he had lain a prisoner in the dungeons of the fortress which now he had stormed. He was poor and growing old, compensating fortune seemed at last to beckon him; and then when he had earned her kiss, she had mocked him. The curse of caste was upon him, to have been born a farmer's son: and it must be owned that in the Irish peer the feeling of family was strong. It may frankly be confessed, moreover, that had the Lieutenant-Colonel Commandant turned out to be what Baird in his anger called an inferior officer, or had Baird himself been left to pine without distinction or reward, the judgment of history would confirm his keen reproach. But no acknowledgment of service was ever more eloquent, or claim for another's recompense more earnest, than that addressed to Dundas on his behalf by Mornington:[1] and of comparative pretensions to strategic fame it were vain to speak.

After closing the narrative of the memorable events of the campaign and subsequent settlement, the victor indulged in pæans of triumph which might have been thought florid in a eulogistic historian, but which indited by the author and finisher of the work done in the discharge of his official duty have certainly no parallel in the chronicles of self-glorification. To point the contrast between the state of danger and discredit which he found in the summer of 1798 and the triumphant position of affairs at the close of the Mysore campaign was not difficult. The topics of the heroic antithesis were sufficiently palpable, and no colouring was needed to darken the one or brighten the other by the artist's hand. Throughout the narrative of preparation, effort, self-sacrifice, struggle, victory, and healing dispensation of benefit and kindness, praises are lavishly bestowed on all concerned; and the approving recognition of the Directors at home is invoked for the agents and officers, civil and military, whose unanimity

[1] June 1799.

and energy, fertility of resource and unweariness in well-doing, might well furnish an example for all subsequent time. But the artist takes care at each turn, with infinite tact, to note that every detail from first to last was subjected to his judgment; and that without his personal suggestion or sanction, nothing in council, in action, or in negotiation was done. He sums up the net gains to the Company thus: 'By the partition treaty an augmentation of territorial revenue of 259,056*l*., and by the subsidiary treaty 280,009*l*., together yielding, after liberal provision for the families of the vanquished princes, a net addition of 459,056*l*. a year. The ceded provinces it was estimated would under improved management produce more than double what they had yielded hitherto. At the same time the subsidy payable by the Nizam for his increased contingent furnished in lieu of the disbanded French corps amounted to 225,992*l*.; and if the improved produce of Canara, Wynaad reannexed, and Coimbatore, realised what was anticipated, the annual fruits of the policy pursued in the past few months could not be set down at less than one million sterling. Additional charges would no doubt arise on account of these new accessions and engagements. But it should not be forgotten that while the Company's territories were extended, their frontiers were contracted and strengthened, their principal enemy utterly destroyed, and an ally and dependant substituted on his throne. The accumulated charges both of our preparations and of the war must be considerable; but from the moment that Tippoo's negotiations with the French transpired, it became an indispensable duty to place the Carnatic in a posture of complete defence. The only rational system of defence against him was to assemble our armies on the coast of Coromandel and Malabar in such force, in such a state of equipment, and in such a position, as should excite in his mind a just alarm for the safety of his capital; no other plan was calculated to secure the Carnatic against the ravages of his numerous cavalry; because no other plan would have compelled him to concentrate his forces within his own territories for the defence of the vital points of his empire. His capital was not only the object of his pride but the centre of his power; it was his strongest fortification, the principal granary of his army, his only arsenal, the repository of his treasure, and the prison of the legitimate claimant of his throne as well as of the families of all his great chieftains. On its preservation depended therefore the fate of his kingdom; and my judgment was always decided that he would never abandon its defence but with his life. The rapid movement of the British forces towards the scene of their certain triumph was not only the most effectual but the most economical measure which could have been adopted to frustrate the views of the enemy and to secure the tranquillity of our possessions.'

CHAPTER XI.

LEADENHALL STREET.

1799–1801.

On sick leave from Bengal, Mr. Tucker had visited Madras in the course of the spring, and frequently lent his aid as confidential supernumerary in the Viceregal bureau. When Henry Wesley was appointed one of the Political Commission to accompany the Commander-in-Chief, his place as private secretary was filled by the convalescent votary of work. This brought him more closely than before into personal communication with the head of the Government, for whom his admiration and attachment grew apace. Till his latest day he was fond of recounting characteristic traits and anecdotes of the life they led during that busy summer at Fort St. George. When alone the Earl spent little time at table, and was content with ordinary viands : but they must be served punctiliously. An egg of doubtful freshness brought upon the French servant who acted for the time as butler and valet some hasty words of rebuke. 'Milor!' was the grave reply, 'dat not your lordship's egg—dat's the aide-de-camp's egg!' and the delinquent was forgiven. The secretary's patience was indeed sometimes tried, he thought unnecessarily. He had gone to rest one night believing his day's work done, and was half asleep when he was summoned to his Excellency's room. He hastened thither in his dressing-gown, supposing that some unexpected news had arrived permitting of no delay. In reply to his anxious inquiry if anything was wrong, the Earl put an ordinary paper into his hand without making any remark; but he probably felt the silence with which his subordinate withdrew to be a respectful reproof of his inconsiderateness: and nothing of the kind occurred again.

Mornington had the satisfaction of acquainting the Home Government that an object for which he had been negotiating some time was peacefully attained. This was the occupation of Goa, a fortified port near Bombay, in former days a place of more importance to the Portuguese than it was ever likely to be to us; but nevertheless one whose position on the coast of Malabar was certain to be coveted by a foreign foe, and to be used as a convenient gate of communication by a domestic enemy. The small garrison by whom it was held could not hope to defend its old-fashioned ramparts against bombardment from the sea or the fire of a siege train; and proposals were made to the governor that a British force should be admitted by convention within the walls, of which the pay should be ultimately arranged between the Governments of London and Lisbon. Don da Viega Cabral hearkened to the offer but hesitated to accept it. In the archives of Tippoo documents however were found which left no doubt of the intention to divide all the Portuguese possessions in India with the French: and on their perusal the qualms of the Estremadura noble gave way. On September 7 a British detachment consisting of 1,100 rank and file under Sir William Clarke, were received as welcome allies, and continued to perform garrison duty at Goa with the Portuguese troops until the general peace.

The affairs of Tanjore pressed for adjudication; but, absorbed in the manifold and tangled results of the campaign, even the Earl's untiring willingness for work failed to find leisure for the investigation of new and obscure details. One evening late he handed Tucker a bundle of papers of which he requested to have a careful *précis* by breakfast time next morning. The recently appointed secretary opened the packet in dismay, but resolved not to be wanting to his exacting chief, he gave the night to his task and completed it in time. There was little more than an hour to master the narrative of contested claims to the musnud, and how negotiations were begun, broken off, compromised, and resumed again. The Council of the Presidency assembled, to whose members the facts had more or less been familiar; and each was in turn asked to state his opinion. Accustomed to leisurely writing prolix Minutes rather than to the habit of oral condensation, several hesitated, grew confused, and were unable to explain their meaning. The Governor-General summed up, briskly and brilliantly going over the ground which Tucker feared every moment would give way beneath him, knowing as he best did how thin was the planking over all sorts of pitfalls. But the little man trotted along lightly and warily: and escaped without any noticeable stumbling. Ameer Singh, whose title had been ascertained to be ill founded, was set aside on a pension, and Serfojee, a son by adoption, was recognised as the rightful Rajah.

A new subsidiary treaty was made with Serfojee on his accession to his paternal inheritance; and his character as a ruler realised fully the promise of his youth. A quarter of a century later he was pourtrayed by Bishop Heber as one of the most singularly gifted and accomplished persons he had ever known, being able to quote Lavoisier and Linnæus fluently, to appreciate fine distinctions of character in Shakespeare, to write fair English verse, and withal to hold his own with cavalry officers in judging the points of a horse or killing a tiger at long range.

The ruler of Surat in the Bombay Presidency in the following year was induced to agree to similar terms. A further treaty was negotiated with the Nizam, by which he ceded certain provinces lately acquired by conquest, to pay for the maintenance and equipment of three additional regiments of sepoys, and for the unconditional guarantee by the Company of his dominions against the encroachment of any and all of his neighbours. This complete identification of interests did not please the Mahrattas, whose normal state was that of constant alternation between recovering from one wanton war and engaging in another. But distrusts and divisions amongst themselves prevented their combining for mutual defence.

In September he returned to Calcutta. The administrative reforms designed in the preceding year were now carried into effect. The Secretary's office was reorganised, Tucker being appointed head of the revenue and judicial departments. He was originally thought of to superintend a general scheme for assimilating executive functions and duties in the Madras Presidency to those established by Lord Cornwallis in Bengal, and which in the main had worked satisfactorily. Tucker did not want to be transferred, and deprecated the jealousy his intrusion would excite among experienced and deserving officials at Fort St. George; whose energies had been quickened by the irrepressible vigour of the Viceroy during his stay amongst them. Before Christmas they forwarded through Lord Clive a report so clear and comprehensive on the subject of reconstruction, retrenchment, and redistribution of tasks that Mornington frankly owned himself satisfied that they could supply from among themselves 'knowledge and talents sufficient for the execution of the great plan he had in contemplation without the aid of any person deputed from Bengal. He would not send Mr. Tucker because he wished to leave to the Madras service the full and undivided credit of its own reform.'[1] In this as in a thousand ways, he proved him-

[1] Letter to Clive, 31st December, 1799.

self to have the rare wisdom of faith in sentiment as a governing power. Impetuous and imperious in pursuit of great and difficult aims, he would not be baulked by indolence, stupidity, or worthlessness, or befooled by whimpering complaints of hardship. If men would not move as the public interest required, he would ride over them; nor pause to inquire if they were much hurt. But when he found them ready to doff idle and slothful ways, and willing to put their shoulders to the wheel of improvement, his sympathy was prompt and outspoken; for he longed to loyalise their temper and to breathe into their hearts something of his own spirit of pride and patriotism. Mr. Webbe the chief civil servant at Madras, who at first had seemed to Mornington to be unyielding and resistant, was prominent in suggesting the means of accomplishing what was desired; and from having been an object of distrust, perhaps even of dislike, he became thenceforth a favourite of Mornington and in time of need a genuine friend.

'I have found,' said Wellesley, 'the officers of the Secretariat to possess the industry of clerks with the talents of statesmen.'[1]

In the course of this year the Governor-General called on Mr. Tucker to accept the office of Accountant-General of India. It was no small responsibility, and no slight labour. Financial embarrassment was at this time new to the Indian Government. Lord Cornwallis, on laying down the reins of office had left an overflowing treasury; and it was not until the closing years of Sir John Shore's administration that the surplus had disappeared. But Wellesley found that terrible word *deficit* ready written for him in the Indian accounts, and costly military operations were forced upon him by the hostility of Asiatic enemies and the intrigues of their European allies. At the commencement of

[1] Ibid. page 102.

the century there were two causes ever in grievous operation to aggravate the perplexities of Indian financiers. In the first place there was a twofold demand for money. Money was required for political and for commercial purposes. There were armies to be paid; and there was the investment to be provided. In the second place there was no such thing as public credit. When the revenue was exhausted, money was to be borrowed. But money was then obtained by Government only at ruinous rates of interest. Nor was the general want of confidence in Government expressed even by the necessity of paying 12 per cent. on the money which they raised by loan. In the spring of 1800 this 12 per cent. paper—Treasury notes payable in the ensuing autumn—was selling at a discount of 3 or 4 per cent. The native bankers had no faith in Government securities, and either held back their capital or employed it in their private speculations. Exorbitant rates of interest were obtainable from the landholders, who looked under the operation of the Permanent Settlement to the realisation of a still larger interest from the improvement of their lands. And the general disorder of the Company's finances abroad opened many sources of gain to the capitalist, who was made the medium of exchange between different districts and trafficked largely in the metallic currency. The revenue payer was for the most part largely indebted to the native capitalist, through whom his payments were principally made to Government. There was a scarcity of silver coin in those days. The silver was in the hands of the native capitalist, from whom it was only to be bought at a discount, sometimes of as much as 6 or 7 per cent.

To the remedy of these evils Mr. Tucker brought the experience of a practical man of business and the skill of an adroit financier. He knew that to be weak is to be miserable: to confess weakness to be miserable in the extreme. Whilst

Government were paying 12 per cent. for the money they borrowed, their securities were at a discount because their credit was bad. It was plain enough under the circumstances to the Accountant-General that if the public credit could be established on a secure basis, all the rest would soon follow.

It is permitted neither to men or to nations all at once to take large views of financial reform. The Accountant-General had not only to provide for the wants of the Presidency to which he was immediately attached, but to answer the demands of Madras and Bombay, which could not meet their own charges. No small portion of Mr. Tucker's time during the first few months of his term of office as Finance Minister was consumed by the arrangements necessary for the supply of remittances and the regulation of exchange operations between the different treasuries in the Company's dominion.

Through the cloud of incense and flattery raised around him, Mornington's heart yearned towards home, and he would have given a thousand salaams and salutes in Hindostan for one quiet word of exultant appreciation from friends at Stowe or Holwood, to whose confidence he owed all. His imagination dwelt upon this tantalising theme till the sensation almost giddied him; and made him querulous and discontented as days and weeks rolled by without bringing from England that gush of recognition for which his thirsty egotism longed.

The fall of Seringapatam was not known in England till September 1799. The delight of ministers and court was for once thoroughly participated in by all classes of the community. Pitt and Dundas wrote commending, friends and relatives exulting; everybody sympathising, whether they would or no, in triumph so unexpected and so great. A distinguished female correspondent wrote: 'At this moment my dear Lord, you are the admiration of all Europe. May you long enjoy the glorious laurels you have gained, in health,

P

happiness, and every domestic blessing. Lady Mornington was so good as to let your lovely boys come and see me when in town. I left your friend and mine, *Le Premier*, in better health and spirits than I have seen him for some years. I spent some days at Wimbledon with the *gang*, and left with regret. I hear Lord Cornwallis talks with rapture and surprise of your noble administration in India, and he is a good judge.'[1] From his earliest friend at Eton whom for years he had not met, came a tribute truly touching. 'Believe me, no man has more warmly participated in your triumphs or done more ample homage to the ability which effected them. I often glory in the exertions of the friend of my youth in defence of our common country.'[2]

The King's speech at the opening of Parliament in September, and Pitt's affectionate letter of personal praise and official pledge of honour and reward, made up for much of the vexation of delay. Preoccupation with the pressing affairs of a singularly anxious and exciting time in Europe did not account to him for the silence of some who he thought might have written. Lord Buckingham was not one of them. He was in truth ineffably proud of the success which one of his early *protégés* had so signally attained; and in which another had taken no inconsiderable part.

The Foreign Secretary was so blinded with the mass of Continental correspondence that he was utterly unable to read the Indian despatches. Eastern objects 'infinitely to his honour and to the public service wholly occupy Wellesley's mind, but for these I have hardly a pigeon-hole left in mine, except as they are connected with his merit, which all mankind does justice to.'[3]

A letter to Lord Buckingham shows how warmly he felt

---

[1] From the Duchess of Gordon. Received February 1800.
[2] From Sir John Newport; February 1800.
[3] Grenville, Cleveland Row, 17th February, 1800.

the terms of eulogy in which his old schoolfellow Grenville had moved the thanks of the Lords for the successes in Mysore. 'Your very kind and affectionate letter of September 27 gave me the greatest pleasure, and I cannot express to you my happiness at reading the account of your manner of mentioning me in moving the address to the King on the first day of the Session. My expectations of the advantages to be derived from our success in Mysore have been fully answered; its operation pervades every interest of Great Britain in India, to the remotest extremities of this part of the world. Henry I flatter myself has afforded you full satisfaction with regard to the settlement of our conquests. Pray, my dear Lord, remember me most kindly to Lady Buckingham and all your family, and believe me ever, with the most cordial sentiments of gratitude and esteem, yours most faithfully and affectionately.

'I continue in good health, and always in better spirits in proportion to the increase of my business. Pleasure, distinct from business, is not a plant of this clime.'[1]

February 6 was by proclamation appointed as a day of thanksgiving for the restoration of peace and the success of our arms. In the early morning all the troops in garrison mustered to take part in the celebration, and the curious multitude thronged every housetop and window to witness the spectacle. Ere sunrise the civil and military functionaries of every degree assembled at Government House, and in procession accompanied Lord Wellesley on foot to church, where a *Te Deum* and appropriate anthems were sung: salvoes of artillery from the ramparts concluding the ceremonies of the day.

Henry Wesley who arrived in London soon after Christmas, brought Lady Grenville a lion's head in gold and

[1] Fort William, 27th January, 1800.

a fragment of Tippoo's throne. To wife and children there was no lack of dazzling presents.

The Court of Proprietors voted unanimously on November 13, 1799, thanks to the Governor General ' for the wisdom, energy, and decision displayed by him in the discharge of his arduous duty from the period of his arrival in India until the glorious and happy termination of the late war by which the power of the Sultan of Mysore and the influence of the French in India have been crushed, events which promise to establish on a firm basis the tranquillity and security of the British dominions in India.'

George III. readily assented on the recommendation of his Minister to advance the Earl to the dignity of Marquess in the Irish peerage, believing probably that with his slender fortune he would therewith be content. For some reason unexplained his new title was not gazetted till December, but the intimation of what he might expect was contained in a letter full of kindness and laudation from the minister, who could not have imagined that it would have been received with feelings of ineffable disappointment and chagrin.

Fed with flattery to the full, and far removed from the corrective influences which at home would hardly have sufficed to keep his egotism within bounds, the Governor-General's sense of his own glory and its desert exceeded greatly the friendly appreciation even of Pitt. Instead of satisfaction at being raised to the dignity of a Marquess, his disappointment overflowed in a letter to the minister:[1]

'He could not describe his anguish of mind in feeling himself bound by every sense of duty and honour to declare his bitter disappointment at the reception which the King had given to his services, and at the ostensible mark of favour which he had conferred upon him. In England as in India the disproportion between the service and the reward would be

28th April, 1800; Fort William, Calcutta.

imputed to some opinion existing in the King's mind of his being disqualified by some personal incapacity to receive the reward of his conduct. He left him (Mr. Pitt) to judge what the effect of such an impression was likely to be on the minds of those whom he was appointed to govern; and with what spirit or hope of success he could attempt to take that lead among the allies which it must now be the policy of the British Government to assume in India. He would confess openly that as he was confident there had been nothing *Irish* or pinchbeck in his conduct or in its result, he felt an equal confidence that he should find nothing Irish or pinchbeck in his reward. His health must necessarily suffer with his spirits; and the mortifying situation in which he was placed would soon become intolerable to him. Mr. Pitt must therefore expect either to hear of some calamity happening to him or to see him in England; where he should arrive in perfectly good spirits, in the most cordial good temper with all his friends, and in the most firm resolution to pass the remainder of his life in the country, endeavouring to forget what had been inflicted upon him, and praying, " Novos consules, legionesque Britannas, ita in Asiâ bellum gerere, ut, me consule, bella gesta sunt.".

    Ever, dear Pitt,
      Yours most affectionately,
        MORNINGTON.
(Not having yet received my double-gilt potato).'

In fact the vainglorious Governor-General had made up his own mind that a Dukedom was the fitting recompense for his conquest of Mysore, and being given to prophecy he had in all likelihood announced beforehand the coming honours which from an ungrateful country never came. Pitt was not to be moved by his friend's hysterics, and subsequent ministers proved alike obdurate. To a private friend he wrote that he should never have health or happiness till this outrage, as he called it, was repaired. The irritability of temperament to which through life he was frequently a prey, and the continued strain of daily increasing responsibilities of government, led him unconsciously to exaggerate the effect upon his bodily vigour of his political disappointment. But in more than one letter during the spring of 1800 there are allusions to physical disability from gout and other maladies; and in a private note to Sir Sidney Smith in April, he apologises for not answering a confidential communication from him respecting an expedition to the Red Sea, to drive the French out of Egypt, through 'indisposition which rendered him unable at that time to write to him with his own hand.'

Henry Wesley was sent home to render a full account of the rape and rehabilitation of Mysore as the last partner admitted to the federal household of Anglo-Indian Empire; and Mornington returned to Bengal where his presence was anxiously looked for. On his first arrival from Europe he had found government out of gear, and he had set about the business of refitting and repair. But the pressure of external danger and the military and financial requirements of the time had absorbed too much of his attention to allow him leisure for departmental or other reforms; and during his absence disorganisation and even disaffection had become manifest in a variety of ways.

While awaiting at Madras the progress of the campaign, on every detail of which he corresponded frequently with Harris and with his brothers at headquarters, accounts reached Mornington from Calcutta of the premature explosion of a conspiracy to displace the Nawab Vizier of Oude and set up in his room Vizier Ali by the help from Cabul of Zemaun Shah. The pretender had fled from Benares, and at the head of a numerous band of horse threatened to make himself troublesome; but many of his accomplices had been seized, and their papers revealed such ramifications of a widely extended plot as made the Governor-General impatient to return to Bengal. He believed, however, that completion of his enterprise against Tippoo was the primary duty of the hour, and that as long as his presence might contribute to sustain or quicken the vigour of all engaged in it, he ought not to quit Fort St. George. He had identified himself in fact so thoroughly with the expedition, and the tragic scene of the impending issue was so near at hand, that his departure from whatever cause while its fate trembled in the balance, would probably have chilled the fervour if not the faith of many who had come to take fire from his exhaustless and inflaming spirit.

Among the Mahomedan population rumours of invasion in the South by Tippoo, and in the North by Zemaun Shah, might it was feared rekindle the scattered embers of resistance to the rule of the Company, not yet thirty years old. Shums ul Dowlah, a restless and presumptuous man, who had married the daughter of the Nawab Nizam, was said to hold language openly tending to foment subversive schemes, and was suspected of plotting with certain French residents at Chandernagore, and with persons of his own religion and race in Orissa. His chief confidant was the poet Mirza-Jaen Ta-Pish, whose romantic verse was recited with applause in the presence of many a zemindar, and some of which in translation found its way to English ears. But his projects would seem to have been as transparent and as frail as the gossamer webs of Dacca, where he had been sent to dwell, to keep him out of harm's way. At Moorshedabad they were uniformly disowned and disfavoured; and save that he was compelled to give his parole to remain at or near his recognised abode, no measure of severity was taken regarding him. In a private letter from Madras the Governor-General commended his deputy's caution in not answering some foolish message which had been addressed to him by Shums ul Dowlah, the characteristically jealous terms of which are of interest now that the foolish provocation had been absolutely forgotten. 'I entirely approve of your judgment in referring so delicate and important a question to my decision. Whatever temporary inconveniences may occasionally result from the delay incident to such references, the principle on which they are founded ought to be strictly observed. The mainspring of such a machine as the Government of India can never be safely touched by any other hand than the principal mover.'

He suggests however extra vigilance in observing any tendencies to excitement in the old capital of the province. No symptom of disturbance actually manifested itself, and the interchange of amenities and courtesies was never interrupted between the palace of the Nawab and Fort William.

A more difficult case was that of the ex-Nawab of Oude, whom even Sir John Shore had found it impossible to tolerate and whom he was compelled to depose. For the sake of vengeance or with some mad expectation of regaining his forfeited throne, he had become a sort of political bandit; and surrounded by outlaws as reckless as himself he threatened to become a terror wherever he roved, and to spread the sense of insecurity under his kinsman's infirm rule. On receiving an intimation that he must quit Benares and take up his abode at Calcutta, Ali suddenly proceeded to the house of the British Resident, with whom he had hitherto lived on friendly terms, and who in endeavouring to escape from his revilings was treacherously slain. Five other English gentlemen shared his fate, and but for the accidental presence of a troop of cavalry a general massacre of all Europeans in the town would have ensued.

The traditions of The Pale were not likely to make

Mornington nice about the way of dealing with such a marauder. He wrote to Sir A. Clarke: 'I am concerned to observe the slow progress made by Major-General Stewart against Vizier Ali and his banditti. I scarcely know a point of more importance to our interests in India than the capture or death of that young assassin and the dispersion of his followers.'

After some months he was captured and brought to Calcutta where he was detained in close custody in compliance with the entreaties of the Court of Lucknow, whose fears of insurrection and invasion were continually on the increase.

A treaty of friendship with Nepaul was made in October 1800, without any mention of territorial or subsidiary conditions, but solely with a view of securing to the north-east frontier the blessings of tranquillity; and after some negotiations with the semi-barbarous sovereign of Ava apprehensions of disturbance from that quarter were likewise brought to an end.

The incentives to sedition in the local newspapers caused him much uneasiness. ' I cannot describe the anxiety excited in my mind by several paragraphs which have lately appeared in the newspapers at Calcutta. I cannot but suspect the existence of a systematic design of mischief among the editors of several papers, particularly the "Asiatic Mirror," the "Telegraph," and the "Post." In these papers paragraphs continually appear tending to magnify the character and power of the French, and to expose every existing or possible weakness in our situation.' He then gave directions that one of the editors, Dr. Bryce, should be forthwith put on board ship and sent home as an example to warn others engaged in playing with political combustibles. He was determined to adopt an entirely new system of police and press control.

One aggravating source of anxiety and difficulty, which

in our days of telegraphy and steam we almost forget how to gauge, was the length of interval which frequently occurred without communication. 'In the present year I was nearly seven months without receiving one line of authentic intelligence from England. My distress and anxiety of mind were scarcely supportable. Speedy, authentic, and regular intelligence from Europe is essential to the conduct of trade and government of this empire. If the sources of information be obstructed, no conscientious man can undertake this weighty charge.'[1] Its multivariety under his expanding and comprehensive policy grew greater day by day.

For the next five years he remained to extend and solidify our empire in Asia, regardless of the misgivings of Cannon Row, which was always beseeching him to be quiet; and the protests of Leadenhall Street, whose stockholders cursed his conquests and war loans; and the carping and nagging of all the grumblers for whom he failed to find room in his ever-expanding field of official patronage and commissariat contracts. One of these was a commercial speculator, Mr. Paull, a talkative gentleman of no great talents, who early began to accumulate grievances and grudges against the Governor-General for the purpose of impeachment on his return home.

The President of the Board of Control in moving certain financial resolutions on June 12, 1801, regarding the investments and liabilities of the Company, congratulated the country on the great improvement that had taken place in the Company's affairs. Not only were the actual balances in hand better than they had formerly been, but the outlook of resources for the future had been enhanced by the increase of territorial revenues to the extent of several millions sterling. The area added since 1798 to the Company's

---

[1] To Mr. Hugh Inglis, Chairman of the Court of Directors, 6th October, 1800.

dominion in the peninsula was in fact as large as that of the United Kingdom.

The Captain-General, as he loved to consider himself, continued to ruminate during the autumn the oft-deferred plans for the acquisition of Batavia and the Isle of France. At first he offered the command of the expedition to his brother Arthur, who sagaciously preferred remaining in Mysore, where as he said himself he was 'at the top of the tree,' having rendered essential service in reorganising the country and reconciling Wynaad and Coimbatore to our rule. In November troops were collected at Trincomalee; and Colonel Wellesley was designated for the command, with the rank of Brigadier-General. Baird, incensed at being, as he thought, again passed over, hastened to Calcutta, and in a brief interview threw his Excellency into a most noble passion by his bitter complaints of neglect, and his pointed innuendoes that he had been sacrificed to fraternal preference. There was no doubt some colour for the charge, though Colonel Wellesley had been induced reluctantly to join the gathering host in Ceylon, and to take an active part in preparing it for foreign service. Baird gained his point and was finally named for the command.[1] But Marengo and the events which followed it changed his destination. Austria had made peace, and Egypt became once more the battle-ground of France and England. To co-operate with the army under Sir Ralph Abercrombie, Wellesley undertook to send all the force that could be spared to the Red Sea. Five thousand Europeans and two thousand sepoys, after a tedious voyage landed at Cosseir, and by a ten days' march across the desert reached the Nile. Cairo had capitulated,[2] but the junction with the army under Hutchinson rendered the defence of Alexandria hopeless; hastened its surrender and the final evacuation of Egypt by General Menou.

[1] 5th February, 1801.   [2] 21st August, 1801.

The threatened march of Zemaun Shah on Delhi led to the assembling of an English corps under Sir James Craig at Cawnpore to act in concert with the army of the Nawab Vizier. Instead of venturing to call out his forces Saadut Ali early represented that he could not rely upon their fidelity, and earnestly requested that a British contingent should be sent to protect him in possession of his throne. What Vizier Ali had well-nigh accomplished might be attempted by any adventurous talookdar or agnate of the reigning house. What was called the army of Oude was no better than a licentious rabble ready to become the instrument of anarchy or revolution: and when the Afghan invader was reported to have reached Lahore, there were no terms which the terror of the Nawab Vizier would not have made to obtain a strong body of British guards. Negotiations were set on foot accordingly; and the revenues of certain provinces were pledged for the maintenance of a subsidiary force. But when through the intervention of Malcolm's embassy to Persia a diversion had been created in the province of Khorassan, and Zemaun was compelled to return for the defence of his own dominions, Saadut was persuaded by his sycophants that he had made an improvident bargain; and his payments diminished with his fears. Lord Wellesley expostulated with him on the fatuity of his conduct. 'Since my arrival in India your Excellency has repeatedly complained of the ruinous condition of your internal government, and earnestly solicited my direct interference as being indispensably necessary for the purpose of effecting a complete reform in your affairs, and especially in your military establishments. After having received a plan of reform from me, you expressed in the most deliberate and unqualified terms your approbation, and your hope that it would be carried into effect; yet you have recently declared to Lieutenant-Colonel Scott, that this same plan never in any measure met with your approbation or acceptance, or was deemed expedient by you. You have attempted by various means to delay and ultimately to frustrate the execution of the plan above mentioned. The means which your Excellency has employed for this purpose are calculated to degrade your character, to destroy all confidence between your Excellency and the British Government, to produce disorder and confusion in your dominions, and to injure the most important interests of the Company to such a degree as may be deemed nearly equivalent to positive hostility on your part. In August 1798 and June 1799, you made such forcible representations of the disordered state of your government in its military as well as civil branches, as, combined with my own intimate knowledge of the actual existence of the evils so repeatedly and emphatically described by you, authorised a full confidence in the sincerity of your reiterated wishes for my active interference and for my assistance in remedying the defects of which you so justly complained. I therefore determined to adopt without delay those measures, now apparently not less requisite for the ease and satisfaction of your Excellency's mind than essential to the safety of your person and to the security and prosperity of your dominions. The conduct of different corps of your army had in several instances previously to the approach of Zemaun Shah abundantly manifested that no reliance could be placed either on their fidelity or discipline. Many of them had mutinied, and were prevented from proceeding to acts of open violence against your Excellency's person by the presence of the Company's troops. And you not only avowed to Mr. Lumsden and Sir James Craig that your military force was inadequate to contribute any assistance towards the defence of your dominions, but you required the presence of part of the British army within your capital for the express purpose of protecting your person and authority against the excesses of your own disaffected and disorderly troops at the moment when the services of the whole of the British army were most urgently demanded upon your frontier to resist Zemaun Shah. The necessity of a radical reform of your military establishment being manifest, a letter from Sir A. Clarke delivered to you such further explanations of the proposed measure as the occasion required. This was preceded within five days by repeated complaints on your part of the turbulent and disorderly state of your troops. I proposed that the greatest part of your useless and dangerous forces should be disbanded and should be replaced by a suitable number of the Company's troops. Your Excellency declared your thorough concurrence in the sentiment Sir A. Clarke's letter contained. It is certain that the resources of your Excellency are inadequate to the double burthen of the proposed additional force of the Company and of your own existing establishment. The dismission of the troops in question is not only recommended by considerations of economy, but indispensably dictated by the soundest maxims of prudential policy. In the event of invasion a large portion of the Company's force must be constantly employed to maintain the peace of the country, for the necessity of controlling your own licentious and disaffected soldiery would increase exactly in proportion to the magnitude and imminence of external danger.' He would abstain from comment on the motives which had led to the subsequent change of the Soubahdar's intentions until he himself should have explicitly declared them. But he frankly told him he believed that the threat of abdication had not been used in earnest, but only as a pretext for delay. Equally insincere had been the steps taken for reducing gradually the mutinous corps, and for provisioning those of the Company. Perseverance in so dangerous a course must leave no other alternative than that of considering all amicable engagements as dissolved. Protracted negotiations ensued. Henry Wellesley, who had returned from England to resume his former functions, was despatched to Lucknow with a treaty of ten articles for the signature of 'Saadut Ali,' and after manifold delays and evasions he reported to his brother the conclusion of an agreement on the subject. In lieu of a money payment, certain districts yielding a revenue of one crore and thirty-five lacs of rupees were ceded to the Company. The Nawab Vizier was exonerated from all claims in future for the cost of defending either his own or the ceded territories; and the Company in return guaranteed their integrity and independence for ever. A detachment of British troops with a due complement of artillery should at all times form the personal guard of his Highness. The ceded provinces were exclusively subjected to the administration of the Company's officers, and no deficiency in their revenues was to be made up out of those of the Soubahdar.

In August the Marquess set forth with much pomp and ceremony to make a progress, as it was termed, through the North-west Provinces. At Moorshedabad he received in state the Nawab Nizam of Bengal, and at Benares the Rajah of that province. There he received the news of the battle of Alexandria which was celebrated with every mark of exultation. He was met at Cawnpore by the Nawab Vizier, accompanied by several of his sons and influential talookdars. At Lucknow, where he spent several days, he was entertained with great magnificence. The treaty was signed on November 10, 1801.

CHAPTER XII.

PARAMOUNT POWER.

1800—1802.

A GENERAL order appeared in the Gazette ordaining the observance by Europeans of a day of rest. The Supreme Government was thenceforth to be recognised as that of a Christian power, and in its administrative character to be treated as identical in principle and feeling with the established system at home. Toleration the most complete and undeviating was still to be observed towards the various native creeds; but the State publicly adopted the obligations of Christianity, and confessed that its conscience ought to be guided in morals and in laws by that hallowed rule alone. Conforming to the practice long established in England, newspapers were not allowed to be printed or published on Sunday; and under the influence of apprehensions not yet wholly dispelled of foreign intrigue insidiously working on native ignorance and credulity, the supervision of political news and political writing which had been hastily and arbitrarily adopted in a season of exceptional perturbation, was continued without relaxation, and was kept up for many years. It was one of the points in the policy of Wellesley most sharply contested by his critics at home; and that he himself came eventually to doubt its wisdom hardly admits of dispute. He was influenced apparently by the confidential reports of Kirkpatrick in 1799, describing the mischievous effect upon the native Courts of Hyderabad and Poonah of false intelligence and factious articles in the English journals published at Calcutta and Bombay. In time of war the suppression of such elements of danger by methods however summary is a duty plain and clear, but it does not follow that the measures needful in a state of siege should be prolonged after that state has passed away; and that the condition of danger and of dread did pass away in his time was his noblest vaunt. But so long as war prevailed with France neither he or any of his successors ventured to restore the liberty of the press. A rigorous censorship was kept up till 1818, when all the European world being at peace it was abrogated by Lord Hastings. How he who devised and ordained the rule felt in the end respecting it will be seen by-and-by.

To build up the administrative power which they desired should be made paramount Pitt and Dundas advised that the Governor-General of the Company should be appointed Captain General of all the King's forces in India. Theretofore the Commander-in-Chief of the royal troops was named by the Horse Guards, subject to orders and liable to be removed for reasons wholly beyond and sometimes unknown to the civil Government of the Presidency. In many cases the two functionaries were independent and co-equal; and although disunion seldom was allowed to be observable by vulgar eyes, in council it occasionally manifested itself; and in executive acts affecting the public peace or personal susceptibilities, collision of authority occurred still oftener. When a man of talent or high rank filled the Viceregal chair of state, the General Commanding-in-Chief, who was usually a self-made man, yielded much from an instinct of social and political deference, and His Excellency had his way. But few men possessing the ability of Hastings or the rank of Cornwallis were preferred by the Company; and men like Barlow or Shore exercised no such ascendency over their military colleagues. They possessed in fact neither the professional knowledge or the instinctive genius for command, and veteran commanders declined to give heed to their behests when they thought them inconsiderate or unwise. Wellesley had proved himself capable not only of planning great strategic movements and inventing the means of defence and attack, but of organising victory rapid decisive and splendid. The army of all ranks was as loud in his praise as the civil community; and they had even more cause for gratitude and admiration; for his foresight and care had shortened their term of endurance within the briefest span, and had secured their triumph at the least possible cost of health and life. When therefore, on February 26, 1801, letters patent were received creating him Captain General of all the forces of the Crown serving in the East, not a murmur of dissent or disapproval anywhere was heard. It was felt to be an acknowledgment fitting and just of pre-eminent service in war, rendered to the Crown as well as to the Company; and to be another step in knitting together the reins of supreme rule capable only of being held firmly in a single hand.

The confidence of the army and their enthusiasm for him were unbounded. In the division of the Mysore prize-money 100,000l. was by general acclamation of the camp reserved for his share. With gentleness but with dignity he declined to subtract from the victors in fight any part of their reward. Even if his family had been dependent on what he might officially acquire, he could not bear that they should be enriched by depriving brave men who had risked their lives in battle of their reward: and afterwards, when the officers tendered him a gorgeous star of St. Patrick formed of the diamonds that belonged to Tippoo, he refused it likewise, until called upon to accept it by special vote of the Directors of the Company.

By virtue of his new command he did not hesitate however to take possession of the mansion at Barrackpore previously occupied by the General-in-Chief of the forces in Bengal. In Fort William he felt penned up in a manner incompatible with his previous habits and ill-suited to his notions of the way in which it was becoming an English pro-consul should live. In the comparative seclusion of Barrackpore, his eyes (weary of glare) and nerves (ever too sensitive) kept in tension by the requirements of state, found salutary rest. To one moreover whose strategic reputation consisted altogether of departmental success as his own Minister for War, and whose military rank was after all egregiously titular, it was pleasant to occupy the quarters of the veterans who had gone before him, and to hear the clank of the orderly's scabbard early and late in the courtyard below. It could not be said by the most envious of his rivals or the most captious of his critics that he had clutched at or schemed for military precedency; or that however wanting in drill-shed knowledge, experience in camping out, or familiarity with the watchwords of deploying and close order, he was less able to plan or less qualified to direct a great campaign than the professional commanders who had preceded him. He had never led a charge or stormed a redoubt, encountered a turbaned foeman hand to hand, or taken part in the sack of a rich city. But he had fairly won, notwithstanding, by deeds of arms,—for without his power of conception, combination, and constancy deeds they had never been,—the rank and dignity of Captain General freely and spontaneously conferred: and none were found to say he had not fairly earned it.

European tourists in the East were few in those days; but those who came thither in quest of adventure, information, or amusement, or in pursuit of some object of discovery, never wanted welcome. In the monotony of a limited official circle their presence was unaffectedly prized. In the

East hospitality has from the days of the patriarchs been an universal virtue; and Englishmen, though wayfarers and sojourners, easily caught the contagion, and learned to vie in prodigal kindness to travellers from afar with the princeliest of those who were born in the land: and Wellesley's ambition was to outshine them all. Had not the instinct of munificence been fostered in him from his birth? Was there a memory of Dangan still lingering silently in his heart unassociated with those of generous profusion without respect to persons? There as here, outward luxury and show stood out the more conspicuously from the vicinage of dark surroundings. Even to this day the Viceregal mansion on the esplanade at Fort William and the handsome edifices in its immediate neighbourhood contrast strikingly with the low and crowded dwellings which for the most part constitute the Black Town, and which at the beginning of the century even more signally bespoke the political distance between the indigenous and exotic occupants. Half the Hindoo quarter at Calcutta was then built of mud, and thatched, like Irish cabins. Nor was the density of the population wanting as another feature of resemblance. From out the native hive dusky swarms came forth at sunrise and sundown to gaze upon each military parade and civil pageant; and these continually grew apace in tastefulness and splendour. The garrison quarters of Fort William had contented former Governors, but they had ceased to seem befitting as the dwelling-place of the Vice-king over kings. The new Government House, constructed under his Excellency's immediate auspices, was certainly a more suitable residence under altered circumstances. Even the original estimate of the cost caused the Secret Committee to growl; but when the total charge for omissions and additions and afterthoughts, furniture and embellishments, was presented the growl grew into a groan. Why all this waste on colonnades and verandahs, marble pavements and fantastic domes? It was not to rival heathen pomps or paynim grandeur that men had been sent forth from England to barter or to fight, but simply to improve the Company's fortune, and to make their own; and then return with whatever remnant of liver they had left to live at Clapham, Cheltenham, or Bath; and now and then to attend a Court of Proprietors in Leadenhall Street. But times had changed, and the once isolated factories along the coast had come to be concatenated into a belt of mail of which the strength was steel if the blazonry was gold. Pergunnahs for gardens had grown into Circars for tribute; and ceded provinces, though severally distinct, seemed drawn and held together magnetically by paramount power. For another half-century that power was not to wear a crown; but its representative for the time being was regarded by subject myriads, and in reality was, a sovereign wielding greater authority than any out of Europe, and as great perhaps as any there. To the Oriental mind it seemed but natural that the Feringhee over-lord should be housed magnificently; that he should be with difficulty approachable through gradations of servitors and functionaries; and that when he did appear in durbar or in cavalcade his *entourage* should be suitable to his dignity. The Marquess thought so too, and entered with zest into every minutia— of what players call the 'make up'—of the imposing part he undertook to play. With him spectacle was a science, the play an epic, and the scenery and costume matters of consummate art. Even the state barge in which he floated now and then upon the Hooghly was fashioned and equipped as none had been before. 'It reminded me,'—said a fellow countryman whom it was sent to convey from an Indiaman in the roads,—'of a fairy tale. It was very long in proportion to its width, richly ornamented with green and gold; its head a spread eagle gilt; its stern a tiger's head and body; the centre would contain twenty people, and was covered with an awning and side curtains; forward were seated twenty natives dressed in scarlet habits, with rose-coloured turbans, who pulled away most energetically and speedily gained the landing-place. His Excellency much amused me by the account he gave of the manner in which my arrival was announced to him by the messenger whom he placed purposely on the road. "Lord Sahib ka bhánja, Company ka nawasa teshrif laia;" literally translated, "the Lord's sister's son and the grandson of Mrs. Company is arrived." These titles originated from a belief of the natives that the India Company was an old woman, and that the Governors General were her children.[1] It happened to be the eve of a fête given to inaugurate the completion of Government House; and he describes the scene with all its accessories of music, feasting, illuminations, fireworks, and salvoes of artillery; with a wistful multitude at a respectful distance looking on till near day-dawn.

A portrait was painted by Robert Home, a Scotch artist who had recently ventured to the far East in search of a living, and practised his vocation at Calcutta for several years. It was full length, the dress being that worn in state, and the posture uncomfortably demonstrative of the sense of authority. In the background turbaned servitors on official Providence in shorts and bedizened with an exaggerated star of St. Patrick on the right breast, look up in gaping homage to his Excellency, while they point to his foreign guard significantly as the monitor of submission. As a conception the whole is simply detestable, betraying lamentably the conscious want of moral ascendency which after all was the only thing worth asserting politically or pictorially. But the great little man could never get clear of the histrionic, whether in giving audiences or in sitting for his picture; and the limner was but too ready to

[1] Lord Valentia's *Travels*.

play up to the whim whose gratification might make his fortune. His likeness however has one remarkable proof of its fidelity. There is the identical expression which is noticeable in Hoppner's beautiful portrait, caused by a sort of contraction of the upper lip which entirely disappeared in later times. It is not a peculiarity to be invented by any artist desiring to please an influential patron; or if inadvertently ascribed by one flatterer on canvas was unlikely to be attributed by another or second painter sedulous to win the approval of a society daily observant of the countenance pourtrayed. Hoppner was an artist of established repute, Home a comparative beginner; they could hardly have both been mistaken.

There is another curious circumstance of which one is reminded by this performance of Home. He painted about the same time a full-length portrait of Colonel Arthur Wellesley which was given by him upon request to the Soubahdar of the Deccan in recollection of the military services rendered that prince in the Mysore or the Mahratta war.

Engravings of both were made at Calcutta under the direction of the painter, and when in 1809 a sudden demand arose in England for a likeness of the victor of Talavera, the print from Home's picture was the only thing to be had, and the reproduction of this unattractive production, for want of better, graced the shop-windows of London for many a day. The young commander is certainly not invested with the form or comeliness of a hero. Nothing can be less imposing classic or picturesque. The look is hard without dignity and unprepossessing without being shrewd or able.

One of the injunctions most urgently laid on the new Lord Deputy by the Directors was to convert if possible the annual tribute paid by the Nawab of Arcot for the service of their troops into a fiscal cession of territory. Lord Hobart had tried in vain to persuade him to yield; and failing, had gone such lengths in reproach and menace as to evoke bitter complaints from his Highness in letters to the Prince of Wales (to whom he frequently sent propitiatory presents) and to Cornwallis whom he called his best friend. The Company, as he truly said, 'wanted his country anyhow.' In spite of all their disclaimers, they had become smitten with earth-hunger, that craving never to be satisfied. But while Tippoo lived and reigned, and French men-of-war made prey of their galleons in the Indian Seas, they dared not tear up existing treaties with Wallajah; or openly assume the sovereignty of his dominions. All that Mornington ventured to propose when at Madras was similar to what Sir John Shore had obtained from the Nawab of Oude, an assignment of provincial revenues in lieu of so many lacs of rupees. The justification for pressing this and the still greater change which not long afterwards was compassed by means not free from question, lay in the bewildering conflict of authorities which had arisen in a long course of political dealings between the Company and the Soubahdar. The complication and confusion of central and local powers threatened to bring the industry of the whole region to ruin, and thereby to endanger the payment of the English and Sepoy garrisons which had come to be its sole defence against external foes. In the words of the most able and eloquent defender of the rights of the family: 'The actual situation was intolerable. Never was there such a provoking array of anomalies. To no prince had such deference been paid; yet no prince was kept under such strict surveillance. He resided in Madras, beyond the limits of his own government, within British jurisdiction though exempt from it, surrounded by British troops, unable to stir hand or foot without permission, and yet exercising despotic power over millions of subjects who had learned to look to us for protection. We were dependent on the revenue of the Carnatic for the support of all our establishments in the south of India; yet we were compelled to see the Nawab destroying the resources of the country for the benefit of the birds of prey of all nations who flattered and fleeced him. Advice and remonstrance were obstinately rejected; and when pressed closely by the Governor of Madras or the Governor-General, he reviled the Honourable Company, and invoked their master, his friend and constant protector, the King of Great Britain. No other prince of India was ever admitted to the honour of direct correspondence with his Majesty; and he was received everywhere with a royal salute. The first of the family had not to thank us for his elevation, though he fell in battle fighting against the French in our quarrel. The problem of a peaceful deposition was absolutely insoluble. He could neither be persuaded nor coerced by any regular process. It was a complete deadlock, and there was no hope of escaping from it by fair means.'[1]

The correspondence of Lord Hobart and many conferences with Lord Clive confirmed Mornington's impression that the administrative plight of the Carnatic had become one of insufferable weakness and scandal. The functions of government were still exercised in the name of the Nawab who continued to squander the declining revenue of the province upon inordinate luxury; and to neglect every executive duty, judicial or financial. Mahomet Ali was recently dead, and his son Omdut ul Omrah was an idler and a wastrel who lived surrounded by native sycophants and European adventurers interested in pandering to every foolish whim. Empty phrases of courtesy and consideration lavished from time to time by royalty in England upon father and son misled them both into imagining that their friendship was really deemed a thing of moment; and they were confirmed in their self-importance by the advice of Cornwallis, on taking leave of

[1] Major Evans Bell's Statement of the Arcot Claims.

them, to cultivate amicable relations with their still formidable neighbour in Mysore. Two of Tippoo's sons given as hostages resided for some time at the Presidency and were treated with ceremonious hospitality at Fort St. George and the palace of Chepauk. Through the officers appointed to wait upon them, and after their release through the vakeels of the Sultan, a correspondence was privily kept up, chiefly consisting of the idlest gossip, but occasionally spiced with fragments of conversations real or imaginary with Omdut and other members of the family of Arcot. These were discovered among other epistolary curiosities at Seringapatam; and their language in various points being enigmatical Lord Clive was led to suspect that the Soubahdar and his son, while professing friendship for the English and treated with flattering deference and consideration, had furtively kept the enemy advised of the preparations at Madras for war. Omdut as a matter of course wholly denied the imputation. But Mr. Webbe and Colonel Close, commissioners named to examine the state of the finances, and into the abuses of all kinds which were a source of perpetual complaint, were further directed to sift and weigh the circumstances of supposed bad faith on the part of the Nawab. The whole of the evidence taken by them was sent with their report to England; and it was not until the Secret Committee and the Board of Control had expressed their concurrent opinion that a thorough change of system was necessary, that Wellesley instructed the Governor of Madras peremptorily to insist on cession of Circars adequate to pay the subsidiary garrisons.[1] No proof of political perfidy seems to have been gleaned from the mass of rubbish found at Seringapatam, and the commissioners doubtless well knew that far from cherishing any desire to exalt the power of the ruthless despot of Mysore, the princes of Arcot remembered his father and regarded him

[1] 28th May, 1801.

with detestation and dread, as low-born usurpers whom no treaties could bind and whom no chivalrous feelings restrained from the cruelties of violence and rapine. Jealousy of European predominance might innocently enough have wrung from them in unguarded moments the utterance of a wish that all the followers of the Prophet were united in bonds of common sympathy and interest; but the recollection of their fields laid waste, their villages consumed by fire, and the detention in dishonour of the ladies of a kinsman's harem seized and borne off by the marauding chief of Mysore, little inclined them to exchange the mistrusted hand of the Company for the butcher-like grasp of Tippoo. Their acquittal on the charge of bad faith was in fact confessed in the recommendation that the Nawab should still retain the inland regions of the Carnatic while those along the seaboard should be assigned to the Company. It was not however until May 1801, that the Governor-General in Council authorised Lord Clive to enforce these terms of a new subsidiary treaty. Two years had thus been allowed for extenuation, if any could be given, or improvement, if any could be shown. Omdut ul Omrah thought only of procrastinating until Pondicherry should be given back on the conclusion of a general peace, and a French flag should be again seen in the offing. The rivalry of European powers was entwined with the family history, and to that unhappy tradition he inveterately clung. The Governor whose patience was exhausted warned him in more than one personal interview of the consequences impending if he persisted in delay. But the ill-advisers who throve on corrupt and prodigal misrule prevailed, and at his death a few months after, they gave his reputed heir like fatal counsel. On Ali Hussein's refusal of the proffered treaty of cession the Governor-General proceeded to act on the authority he had received from home: Ali Hussein was set aside in favour of his cousin Azim ul Dowlah, who agreed to put an end to the unsatisfactory relations hitherto subsisting with the Company, and to recognise in their stead institutions analogous to those established in Bengal. Securing him and his descendants an ample civil list and the pomp and dignity of a court, the new treaty vested the military and financial control of affairs in the Presidency of Fort St. George. Azim was content to subside into the peaceful enjoyment of a princely pension, and in July 1801 the Carnatic was added to the Company's dominions.

It was a great satisfaction to have ultimately accomplished an object long and earnestly desired by the Company, and urgently recommended by the Directors to his special attention when he received the charge of government. They knew of his solicitude for the accomplishment of this important measure upon his arrival in 1798, and the repeated attempts he made in 1799 to effect the same salutary arrangement.[1] 'The union of all local authorities and the extinction of every principle of conflicting power would preclude the operation of those causes of discord and counteraction which must ever have impeded the progress of good government in the Carnatic.'

No sooner was the Peace of Amiens signed than the First Consul sent a squadron with fourteen hundred disciplined troops, a suitable complement of distinguished officers and a military chest filled with bullion, to take possession of the old place of arms ceded by Portugal to France. Napoleon seems to have formed expectations of raising Goa to its ancient height, otherwise he would not have sent out to a little territory of five miles of sea-coast, containing only twenty-five thousand inhabitants, and yielding a revenue of only forty thousand pagodas, so splendid an establishment as arrived under Captain General de Caen, which consisted of seven generals, a due proportion of inferior officers, and

[1] To the Secret Committee, 21st October, 1801; from Patna.

fourteen hundred regular troops. The dismantled works were once more put in repair, and the tricolour again gaily challenged British predominance. But it was then too late. The whole of the Southern peninsula was consolidated under the sway of the Company, and where local government still remained in native hands resident envoys made it difficult, if not impossible, for foreign intrigue to be carried on.

Half a century had well-nigh elapsed since the adventurous *employés* of the Company had, without any regular plan or forecast, begun their advance ' from factories to forts, from forts to fortifications, from fortifications to garrisons, from garrisons to armies, and from armies to conquests : where they could not find a danger, determined to find a quarrel.'¹ Gradually and steadily British influence had undermined, without ostensibly overturning, the Mahomedan governments of Southern Asia ; and sought to establish the predominance of European methods of taxation, discipline in war, and systems of judicature. The Nizam and the Vizier of Oude still nominally exercised separate sway under the phantom authority of the Mogul, who was a captive of pagan conquerors at Delhi. He was still in the irony of fortune designated the superior of the Lord of Dangan who reigned more absolutely and magnificently at Calcutta than George III. at Windsor. Soubahdars and rajahs had one by one been reduced to mute submission ; and the administrative question which importunately demanded solution was how were the scores of millions of Hindoo, Parsee, Persian, Malay, and half-caste population to be soberly and decently governed now that the old rule of their former conquerors had been overthrown ? In many instances it was Wellesley's hope and policy to set up again the Hindoo princes, and to restore the social and juridical systems rudely crushed rather

¹ Speech of Sir Philip Francis against Warren Hastings, 1787.

than extinguished under Akbar and Aurungzebe. To be the ultimate arbiter of all disputes, the supreme protector of all interests, the pre-eminent light of remodelled and reformed Oriental life, was the master thought that animated him. High-handed and overbearing oftentimes, and not unfrequently inexorable and unsparing in working out his impetuous purpose, he was ever anxious to vindicate victory by popular improvement; and to redeem violence offered to crumbling authority by making the community conscious of their deliverance from bad masters. The Mahomedan *régime*, though existing for several generations, had wholly failed to convert ryots, jaghireders, or rajahs to its stern simplicity of rule and creed. It had done little to justify its predominance in arts or arms, still less in learning or in law; and it had never deigned to mitigate the mortifications of conquest. The Brahmin caste, in spite of many despoilings, insults, and persecutions, had kept alive the flame of their antique faith and the culture of abstruse and applied science of the highest kind. Hindoo tanks and temples, manufactures and tombs, astronomy and metaphysics struck even the utilitarian Mill with something like reverence. Superseded as generals, the Brahmins were resorted to by their subjugators as financiers, and spendthrift oppression was fain to wheedle them as bankers into help out of its embarrassments. The imagination of Wellesley was fascinated by the hoary grandeur of institutions compared with which our own are but gourds of yester-even. Vainglorious and overbearing though he was, there was in him nothing of the Vandal, nothing of the feudal robber, nothing of the levelling Jacobin. He would if he could build up rather than pull down, persuade rather than persecute, and if the vast multitudes subject to our sway would not forego their faith in Vishnu, at least he would try to christianise the morals of public administration, and by peaceable example show in the affairs of this world a more excellent way. But how to begin or how to combine and blend the elements of a new civil hierarchy which should be English enough to ensure its loyalty to Government and acclimatised enough to stand morally in lieu of an indigenous shelter against social wrong? Was it a dream? We shall never know; but assuredly it was a specious and a splendid dream, worthy of being associated with an illustrious name.

After many ponderings, inquiries, and consultations he conceived the plan of an Indian university, in which cadets from England might be enabled to acquire Eastern literature and sciences in combination with those of the West. The cost of the undertaking would be great, and the difficulties at the outset greater: both in a certain sense recommendations in his eyes, for he was begotten and bred in prodigality and pluck; and the habit of both stuck to him to his dying day. Very vexatious habits doubtless to his merchant masters and his Accountant-General: but what would British empire in India have been without him?

'I think it necessary to apprise you of my intention to adopt without delay a plan for the improvement of the civil service at Bengal in a most important point. The state of the administration of justice, and even of the collection of revenue throughout the provinces, affords a painful example of the insufficiency of the best code of laws to secure the happiness of the people unless due provision has been made to insure a proper supply of men qualified to administer those laws in their different branches and departments. This evil is felt severely, and arises principally from a defect in the education and early habits of the young gentlemen sent out in the capacity of writers. Two or three years in some collegiate institution are requisite to impart the knowledge suitable to their intended duties. But I now wish to inform you that I feel the mischief to be so pressing, that I intend without waiting for orders from home to proceed to found such an institution at Calcutta.'[1]

'It is obvious that an education exclusively European or Indian would not qualify your servants for the situation which they are destined to fill; the foundation of their education must be laid in England and completed systematically after their arrival in India by two or three years' instruction under the discipline of some collegiate institution in branches of knowledge suitable to their intended duties. The Governor-General in Council has therefore determined to found an establishment in this Presidency of the nature of a collegiate institution; the expenses of the institution to be defrayed by a small contribution from all the civil servants in India, to be deducted from salaries. It is my intention to open it in November;—lectures on languages the following winter: Arabic, Persian, Sanscrit, Hindoostanee, Bengalee, Felinga, Mahratta, Tamul, Canara; Mahomedan and Hindoo law, ethics, civil jurisprudence and the law of nations, English law, regulations and laws enacted by the Governor-General in Council or by the Governors-General at Fort St. George and Bombay respectively for the civil government of the British territories in India, political economy, and particularly the commercial institutions and interests of the East India Company; geography, mathematics, modern languages of Europe, Greek, Latin, and English classics, general history ancient and modern, the history and antiquities of Hindostan and the Deccan, natural history, botany, chemistry, and astronomy.'[2]

On July 10, 1800, it was ordained by an order in council that a college should be founded at Fort William for the training of young men sent out under the designation of writers to take part in the local administration of affairs. The spirit of monopoly in which the Company's charter had been originally framed, and from time to time renewed,

---

[1] To Dundas; 24th October, 1799.
[2] To the Court of Directors; from Fort William, 9th July, 1800.

forbade any attempt in the first instance to open a competition for political or military employments to those who were born in the land. The Company's service was emphatically styled 'the covenanted service;' and all encroachments on the vested rights of profit and promotion, were resented by the whole hierarchy of functionaries, from the youngest 'prentice hand to the sexagenarian occupant of a Director's chair. Wellesley had indeed been early impressed with the danger of superseding without absorbing into the new *régime* the energies and abilities of Islam. He saw clearly 'the radical imperfection of our system in affording no means to conciliate the goodwill or to control the disaffection of the Mahomedans, whom we found in possession of the government and whom we had excluded from all share of executive honour and authority, without providing any adequate corrective of the passions incident to the loss of dignity wealth and power.[1] Wherever it was possible to find extra employment for able and promising youths of the supplanted race he was ready to enlist them in the cause of order, and if possible to loyalise their disposition. But every step in this direction was certain to be regarded with inappeasable envy by the whole Anglo-Indian community; and to be reported home with invidious embellishment and exaggeration: all tending to create distrust of his policy and purpose. He hardly dared disclose at the beginning what that policy and purpose would have been in its mature development; and he was content to try whether enlightened and practical European culture might not be transplanted to the banks of the Hooghley, and acclimatised there, even though its fruits for a time should be exclusively gathered by Feringhee hands.

The college of Fort William was opened with much ado of philosophic pomp, and all the inevitable fuss and fawning of colonial adulation, in 1802, without previous sanction

[1] To Secret Committee, 1800, i. 535.

from the Directors at home. To them it seemed little better than a chimera, and a very expensive one. What did their nephews and cousins want to know about the Vedas, or the outlandish logic of Menu? What was the good of an East India Company except to make money out of indigo, ivory, shawls, Dacca muslin, and Trichinopoli chains? My Lord Marquess was quite forgetting himself; an ungrateful son in a far country, wasting their substance in whims and vagaries. In Leadenhall Street a cadet simply meant a younger son or dependant who wanted a living, and who, as he could not find it at home, was ready to earn it at the expense of 'the niggers out there.' Why shut him up in a school for a couple of years while he was still young and his constitution good, instead of giving him work to do in the counting-house or the tax-collector's office? What did it signify whether the black faces liked it or no? that was their affair. But with all the fine talk about victories, trophies, subsidiary treaties, and extending domains, the provoking fact could not be gainsaid that the India Debt went on increasing, that the price of the stock was low in the market, and the returns on the investment gave but a scant dividend. Where was the money wherewith to found an Oriental university? or of what possible use could it be when founded to Honourable East India Proprietors? Cynical old Dundas said less against the scheme, but at heart had as little relish for it. Cornwallis admired the design, but doubted. Pitt admired, and did not condescend to doubt: and so the little pro-consul went on with his plan, constantly muttering to himself:—

> Exegi monumentum ære perennius. . . .
> Non omnis moriar, multaque pars mei
> Vitabit Libitinam.

Professors, the best that could be found, with good salaries, were chosen to take charge of the different classes. Settling the curriculum was a matter of interminable talk;

but it was at last settled without the talk being terminated, as most important things in this world have to be. Acolytes came in readily; the young Cadets showing up well in most of the schools. After a while it came to be understood at home that youths who were lucky enough to obtain nominations for the Company's service would have to undergo a period of collegiate training on their arrival out; and a salutary awe of the unimaginable process, and a frugal care about the charge for living before they were suffered to earn mercantile, civil, or military pay, began slowly to pervade the jobbing classes of the community. At that time there was no nice distinction between fitness for soldiering and fitness for storekeeping, capacity for weighing evidence in a court up country, or weighing tea by the thousand chests for reshipment to Europe. A youth must take his chance of what he might be set to do.

To the surprise and vexation of Wellesley, the Directors signified from the first their disapproval of the scheme as entailing a new and unnecessary charge on their revenues, more than ever encumbered by establishment charges. Jealousy of his personal pre-eminence was fostered by the lofty, if not supercilious assumption of a right not only to judge in matters the least pressing what ought to be done; but the privilege of making serious and expensive changes without deigning to wait for express permission. In time of war or civil trouble he might be pardoned for taking upon him to decide what was needful to be done; but if in schemes of finance and education their income might be permanently burdened without previous consent, where would it end? It was indispensable to take some decided step for reasserting their supremacy over their audacious satrap; and instructions accordingly went forth that the new institution on which he had bestowed so much thought and care should be absolutely remodelled on a reduced scale. His anger on receipt of the unlooked-for mandate was indescribable; he regarded it as a public repudiation of his counsel, and an unpardonable affront ungratefully and unwarrantably put upon him in the face of the world. His wrath was not to be turned aside by the complimentary language in which the order was couched. To cut down the salaries and limit the classes, as it proposed to do, would render the scheme comparatively abortive, and render him, as he believed, ridiculous. He would suspend the execution of the fatal decree, and reason with his short-sighted masters, if haply he might yet persuade them to come to his way of thinking. In an elaborate despatch of one hundred and forty-one paragraphs of his best Ciceronian composition he undertook to show that he was right, and that the college in its entirety ought to be preserved.[1] Meanwhile however other points of difference had arisen, on which he was as confident of the superiority of his autocratic wisdom, and as deeply impressed with the shabbiness and unworthiness of the contrary course he was admonished to pursue. At the end of an irritating correspondence he resigned his office, and intimated that he wished to be relieved from its responsibilities as speedily as possible.

The year 1802 was one of prosperity and peace. No menace of external danger or muttering of civil commotion was to be heard. The finances were in a fair way of being restored under the thrifty and enlightened administration of Mr. Tucker. There was good ground for expecting that 'the actual result of the year 1802–3 would be more favourable than the estimate, and that 1803–4 would certainly prove a year of unexampled prosperity; every branch of the revenue promised improvement; the civil charges would not be augmented, and the military charges might possibly

---

[1] From Fort William; 5th August, 1802.

be diminished.'[1] Under these circumstances it was natural that the founder of the College of Fort William should once more deprecate the veto of the Board of Control, and pray for stay of execution. Intending to quit India at the close of the year, he could not hope to enjoy in person the satisfaction with which the respite he pleaded for would be received; but he more than ever insisted on the policy and necessity of maintaining his favourite institution, and with his wonted vehemence declared his 'determination to devote the remainder of his political life to the object of establishing it, as the greatest benefit which could be imparted to the public service in India, and as the best security which could be provided for the welfare of our native subjects. If the Court should ultimately abolish this institution, it was his fixed and unalterable resolution to propose to Parliament immediately after his return to England a law for the restoration of an establishment which he knew to be absolutely requisite for the good government of India.' He left it to the minister's discretion how far this resolve should be made known; but the imprudence of threatening beforehand to overrule the authorities whom he was still bound to obey, hardly admits of question. Lord Dartmouth may have been the most reticent of men; but as his Excellency made it a point with him to send copies of his official letter of expostulation to Pitt, Dundas, Scott, and Wellesley Pole—lest it should be 'buried by the Court in the abyss of Leadenhall Street'—he had clearly no intention of letting the light of his indignation be hid under a bushel. Lord Castlereagh sought to bring about a compromise, and a modified scheme was submitted by him to the parsimonious Directors, and to their imperious Lieutenant. It satisfied neither; but the college was reprieved for a time. Mr. Wilberforce was one of the disinterested observers of events who expressed his

[1] Private letter to Lord Dartmouth, from Fort William; 5th August, 1802.

deep regret at the parsimony unhappily displayed. 'Considering the vast extent of our Indian possessions and revenues, he would have economised anywhere rather than in the Fort William College, which could not answer the same ends if continued on a contracted scale. He greatly deplored its having been shorn of its beams, and wished it restored to its primeval splendour.'

CHAPTER XIII.

TREATY OF BASSEIN.

1802–3.

ON New Year's Day 1802, Lord Wellesley indited from Cawnpore a comprehensive circumspect of the Company's affairs, all of which then looked prosperous and secure. There was not a ripple on the high tide of acquisition. The ceded districts from Travancore to Benares were universally tranquil. Better ways of administration were gradually winning acceptance with the subject communities; improved revenues might be reasonably counted on, and diminished military charges anticipated from a continuance of peace, whose interruption was no longer to be feared from Mahrattas or Afghans. The time was therefore come when he might with honour ask leave to return home; and he hoped the Directors would acquaint him by October with the nomination of his successor, in order that he might be able to quit his onerous post by the end of the year. His desire that the formal surrender of his trust should be accompanied with the full details of the important treaty with Oude, led him to withhold the despatch for several weeks. Meanwhile, news came of the peace of Amiens which still more completely relieved him from all anxiety regarding the stability and integrity of our Indian Empire, and confirmed his wish to be allowed to resign his government in the December following.[1]

---
[1] To the Directors from Benares; 13th March, 1802.

The President of the Board of Control expressed his earnest hope that nothing would impel him to quit a post where he had rendered services to the empire so inestimable.[1]

Returning to Calcutta after his protracted tour through the Upper Provinces, his first act on taking his seat in Council was to place upon record his unqualified praise of the conduct of Mr. Barlow, who had acted as Vice-President during his absence, not only in following the orders he had given from time to time, but also in those cases where circumstances 'rendered the signification of his previous instructions impracticable, thus leaving no room for doubt that the government would be carried on with vigour and wisdom without his presence or aid.'[2]

Extreme displeasure had been repeatedly pronounced by the Company at his supposed favouritism of the private trade whereby the worship of the great goddess Monopoly was set at nought and the gains of its craftsmen menaced with ruin. He had abused it was said his discretionary power in the case of the expedition to Egypt, to enrich private shipowners with Government freights to the extent of 30,000 tons, utterly regardless of the preferential claims of his betrayed masters to the profits of the occasion. His vindication was one not of argument but of fact. Three private ships only had been chartered by his permission to carry stores at a particular juncture; and their total tonnage barely amounted to a tenth of the supposed infraction of the rule. He had indeed expressed, perhaps unguardedly, opinions favourable to relaxations in trade; and had endeavoured to bring Leadenhall Street to his economic way of thinking. He was just thirty years, in this respect, before

---

[1] Lord Dartmouth, 9th April, 1802.
[2] Minute by the Governor General in Council, 21st April, 1802.

his time. No better motive occurred to them for his insidious counsel than that of clandestine jobbing for his personal interest; and the anger which the baseless suspicion excited broke out in discussions at home, on all manner of other affairs. The haughty disdain with which he repelled the injustice was well expressed in a confidential communication to Castlereagh,[1] in which he points to the real circumstances of the case in confutation of the charge of pelfish un-patriotism. With equal scorn he justified his choice of Henry Wellesley as lieutenant governor in Oude, the outcry against which he described as 'only an additional symptom of disordered temper.'

Egypt being evacuated by the troops under Baird on the conclusion of peace with France, our ambassador at the Porte was requested by the Sultan to express his warm acknowledgments for the timely succour sent him from India; and to present the Governor General with the star and ribbon of the Order of the Crescent, in token of his gratitude and esteem.[2]

In July 1800 the Peishwah, fearing personal duress from Scindiah, gave authority to certain of his ministers to sign a subsidiary treaty with the Company on his behalf; and the Governor General instructed the Resident to sign the engagement in case of his flight or captivity, and to order British troops to occupy certain provinces of his dominions. In the following spring the Government at home were apprised of his having offered similar terms, with an undertaking to drive the turbulent intruder from Poonah by force of arms; and no exception was taken to the course then proposed.

In the autumn of 1802, the capture of Poonah by Jeswunt Rao Holkar, the flight of the Peishwah, and the

---

[1] 12th February, 1803.
[2] Lord Elgin from Constantinople; 1st May, 1802.

gathering of the Mahratta clans under their respective chiefs, menaced the Deccan and Hindustan with the plague of general war, and almost necessitated the interposition of the British power to protect their allies and secure the integrity of their own dominion.

Late in November Wellesley wrote to Close the Resident at Poonah, apprising him that troops were collecting on the frontier with a view to interposing on behalf of the Peishwah.[1]

On receipt of the Directors' reply to his proposal to resign, in which they agreed to nominate Mr. Barlow his successor *ad interim*, he wrote to them, 'that in accordance with the wish he still entertained to return home he would then be on the eve of his departure, if an important crisis had not arisen in the state of political affairs in India. The recent distractions in the Mahratta empire had occasioned a combination of circumstances of the utmost importance to the stability of British power. He could behold a conjuncture of affairs which appeared to present the most advantageous opportunity that had ever occurred, of improving the British interests in that quarter on solid and durable foundations. He entertained no apprehension of any occurrence which could involve the British power in hostilities with any of the contending parties at Poonah. His public duty, and the service of the Honourable Company, appeared to him, however, to require that he should be prepared to continue in charge of the Government until the general state of political relations in India should assume a more settled aspect. He had therefore determined not to embark for England during the present season, unless a change of circumstances should render his departure expedient or necessary.'[2] To the Secret Committee he transmitted a narrative of all the incidents in the internecine struggle between

[1] 29th November, 1802.
[2] From Fort William; 24th December, 1802.

Scindiah, Holkar, and the Rajah of Berar; and of the confusion and distraction out of which he saw his way by timely interposition with a strong and resolute hand 'comprehending the Mahratta States in the general system of defensive alliance with the Honourable Company and its allies on the basis of the treaty concluded with the Nizam, two years before.' Every document relative to the system of measures which he had deemed it necessary to adopt for the security and promotion of British interests in the existing crisis, were therewith forwarded.

The Resident at Poonah had instructions in June to offer terms of closer alliance and greater security against the machinations of internal and external foes. But the ministers of the Peishwah trusted rather to their skill in intrigue with each and all of the turbulent feudatories contending for ascendency: and the Prince, incapable of any consistent or energetic course, wavered on from day to day without either refusing or accepting the distrusted proffer of British aid, until Jeswunt Rao appeared at the head of a commanding force before the walls of the city. Parley having failed to induce him to withdraw, the protection of Scindiah's troops encamped on the other side of the town was invoked, with the consciousness that whichever side prevailed, the Peishwah would become a dependent instead of being any longer an arbiter, or supreme authority. Clandestinely, a communication was therefore made on October 25 to Colonel Close, agreeing to the conditions of an extended subsidiary force, which in case of need, should maintain or restore the authority of his Highness, who on the same day quitted his palace and took the road to the frontier. The rival aggressors then engaged, and Holkar won. He had hoped to secure under the show of friendship, possession of the Peishwah's person, and the nomination of his own kinsman Amrut Rao to the post of Dewan while the military forces of the State should be placed at his disposal. 'This crisis of affairs appeared to afford a tempting opportunity for impartial intervention. Holkar's movement, though successful, was unpopular, and Scindiah would inevitably strive to regain his predominance.' The continuance of the contest would weaken both powers, and would afford us an opportunity of interposing for the restoration of the Peishwah's just authority, upon terms calculated to secure our relations with the Mahratta empire. 'No reasonable apprehension existed that the progress of this system of policy would be obstructed either by the union of the contending parties, or by the decisive success of either chieftain.' The pact tardily agreed to was duly ratified, and the Governor General prepared without hesitation or delay to employ the whole force at his disposal, to emancipate the Peishwah from the usurping thrall of his overbearing native protectors. Orders were despatched to Madras and Bombay for the immediate assembly of a military force, and a requisition was sent to Hyderabad for the contingent that State was bound to furnish, with a view to active intervention. Scindiah was invited to co-operate in the restoration of an independent government at Poonah. Meanwhile Holkar, baffled in his original design, meditated placing the son of Amrut on the musnud, while the timorous Peishwah asked the Governor of Bombay to send a ship of war to convey him from Bancoote to the friendly shelter of the Presidency. Holkar and Amrut became alarmed at the prospect before them; and professed to desire nothing more ardently than British mediation. But Colonel Close, acting on instructions from Fort William, declined to enter upon any compromise, and quitted the Residency for Bombay. Scindiah was equally warm in his invocation of the Company's aid. Under these circumstances the Viceregal diplomatist sanguinely believed that his interposition might prove effectual for the restoration of order and tranquillity without resort to arms, and the acquisition of commanding influence for the future in the hitherto foreign affairs of the Mahratta empire.[1]

The drift of all this is plain. The Governor General was asked to mediate, and he resolved to interpose. A new and splendid game of empire unexpectedly opened before him; and as he gazed wistfully, marshalling contingencies and realising the unheard and unseen, his imagination grew excited, and he beheld new visions of greatness and power, like him of old who, from the top of the rocks, gifted with second sight, thought aloud 'as in a trance, yet having his eyes open.' To the friend he loved and trusted most he wrote—'I have derived the greatest pleasure from the accounts of your alacrity and judgment during the existing crisis. The exertions which you have made for the early assembling of the army on the frontier of Mysore were extremely seasonable and judicious; and I anticipate the greatest advantages in the course of our negotiations from this wise precaution. My views are anxiously directed to the object of avoiding hostilities, and I request your lordship to bear this principle in mind throughout every contingency. I entertain a sanguine hope of accomplishing the great arrangement of establishing a British subsidiary force at Poonah without proceeding to extremities with any party. Indeed, all the more important powers concerned in the contest have already directly solicited our mediation, or manifested a disposition to accept it. The pacific conclusion however of these extraordinary commotions may depend so essentially on the degree of despatch with which questions may be decided of a nature exclusively and necessarily reserved for the personal decision of the Governor General, that I am desirous of proceeding with all practicable expedition to some point from which I can easily reach the principal

[1] To the Secret Committee; 24th December, 1802.

scene of negotiation, and direct the daily course of measures according to the variation of circumstances and events. With this view I propose to embark for Madras towards the close of this month; whence I can proceed into Mysore or to Bombay, or to any quarter which may require my presence.' And then, careful to disarm beforehand any personal jealousy, he renewed his declaration of 'unalterable attachment, regard and esteem' for Clive, and his confidence that his 'arrival at the seat of his lordship's Government could produce no other effect than to manifest to the world additional proofs of their indissoluble union in the public service, and of their mutual contempt of the clamour of faction, and of the low arts and intrigues of disappointed corruption.'[1]

General Wellesley was ordered to march on Poonah from Seringapatam, and Lieutenant-General Stewart from Madras, to restore our fugitive ally. The distance and difficulty of the way, it was calculated, would require three months. Mysore contributed effectively to the preparations requisite for the expedition, and Purneah rendered cordial aid.[2]

To Lake, then commanding-in-chief, he imparted at the same time his wishes and designs. It was his 'belief that the army assembled at Hurryhaul (within our own confines) would never be called upon to act, either offensively or defensively; it might possibly march to Poonah, and after having established a subsidiary force, return to its stations, or it might furnish the subsidiary force without moving its main body beyond our frontier. Its presence on the frontier, in his opinion, would deter the invasion of any party, and even of any vagrant freebooter of important strength: and the general aspect of affairs led him to believe that we should be enabled to conclude our alliance with the Peishwah, under the pacific acquiescence, if not with the cordial consent, and to

---

[1] To Lord Clive from Barrackpore; 7th January, 1803.
[2] A. Wellesley to Colonel Clive; 1st January, 1803.

the general satisfaction of all parties. The power which it was most important to hold in check was Scindiah. No serious or alarming opposition was to be feared from any other quarter, and he was inclined to believe that even Scindiah would act at least a neutral, if not an amicable part.' He left it therefore, to the General's discretion without reserve, to remain in the ceded districts in Oude, or join the army in Mysore. Should Scindiah be tempted by force of arms to thwart the negotiations with the Peishwah ' the most effectual way of controlling him would be an irruption into his dominions from Oude, and in that case the main and most critical effort must be made from the quarter where Lake then was present. Indeed, his determination was so fixed to employ every effort for the purpose of avoiding hostilities, that he thought it scarcely possible that he could be disappointed in his hope of preserving peace. And his plan was therefore, rather to form such arrangements as might present the most powerful and menacing aspect to every branch of the Mahratta empire, on every point of its frontier, than to prepare any separate army with a view to one distinct operation. The General, whatever course he might personally decide on, might rely on his cordial support.' [1] A few days after, he received from Castlereagh, who had become President of the Board of Control, warm assurances of undiminished confidence in his administration on the part of Mr. Addington and himself, and their united dissuasions of his intention to quit India until all the great objects of his policy had been completely obtained.[2]

Several of the lesser chiefs sent vakeels to offer aid, hoping to make merit beforehand,[3] and anxious to escape from their overbearing superiors, by whom they were worn out as tools, or treated as counters in the game.

[1] To the Commander-in-Chief; 7th January, 1803.
[2] 10th September, 1802; received 17th January, 1803.
[3] To Colonel Clive; 21st January, 1803.

Orders were given to General Stewart to advance from Hurryghur into the Mahratta territory at the earliest prudential moment.[1]

On the last day of the year a treaty offensive and defensive had been concluded at Bassein between Rajah Rao and the Company, by which in consideration of districts yielding twenty-six lacs of rupees, a subsidiary force of 6,000 troops under English officers, with a suitable complement of artillery and engineers, who were to be stationed permanently in the neighbourhood of Poonah, or wherever else his Highness might require their presence for the maintenance of his government. When transmitting to the Directors this important document with its formal ratification six weeks later, Wellesley declared his confidence 'that it would form the basis of eventual tranquillity greater and more durable than had theretofore ever been expected. At first it was indeed possible that Holkar and Scindiah might lay aside their mutual enmities rather than allow the suzerain of their confederacy to be indebted for his independence of their loyalty to an alien power; and no threat of their junction ought to be allowed to baffle a policy so manifest as that embodied in the treaty of Bassein. But if the Peishwah should be tempted to accept a joint proffer from them of restoration to his former authority, instead of relying on the guarantee of the treaty, it was not his intention to attempt to compel the Peishwah to adhere to the faith of his engagements.'[2]

Ministers urged the Court of Directors to join with them in requesting him to defer his departure for another year, and to give some signal proof of their continued confidence. The ratification of the treaty with Azim ul Dowlah, and approval of the Carnatic Settlement seemed the most emphatic mode of attesting their desire. Castlereagh in com-

---

[1] From Fort William; 2nd February, 1803.
[2] To the Court of Directors; 10th February, 1803.

municating their assent did not attempt to disguise the jealousy of Henry Wellesley's appointment as Vice-Governor of the ceded districts of Oude entertained by the Company; nor the prejudice with which the late proceedings, both in the Carnatic and in Surat, were viewed in many influential quarters in and out of Parliament, as manifesting a settled purpose of territorial aggrandisement, at variance with the unrepealed inhibitions of the law. For himself he was ready to defend all that had been done as expedient and just; but he thought it very probable that the questions involved in these transactions would occupy a prominent place in the debates of the ensuing session.[1] Confirmed in what he had hitherto done, though warned as to what he might attempt in the future, he proceeded to mature the comprehensive preparations already noticed for intervention in the Mahratta States. His natural temper and five years' exercise of almost absolute power, the accomplishment of vast results, and finally the acquiescence of both Cabinet and Company in the face of loud and unsparing attack, rendered him perhaps too contemptuous of criticism and too indifferent to individual pique or spleen. He overlooked or forgot the wisdom of the sacred proverb, that 'the intrinsic worthlessness of the flies that make the apothecary's ointment to stink is no measure of their power to sting.' His anxiety however continued unabated, that our interference should never assume the odious aspect of imposing on the Mahrattas a ruler whom generally they distrusted or disowned. The treaty of 1800 entitled the Peishwah to claim our active support in defence of his authority; but the spirit of our engagements with him involved no obligation of such an extent. Whatever might be the success of our arms, the ultimate object of those engagements could not be attained by a course of policy so violent and extreme. If therefore it

---

[1] From Lord Castlereagh; received 29th January, 1803.

should appear that a decided opposition to the restoration of the Peishwah was to be expected from the majority of the Mahratta Jaghiredars, and from the body of his subjects, he would instantly relinquish every attempt to restore him to the musnud.[1] This, be it observed, was not language used to deprecate antagonism or to extenuate the possibly harsh consequences of armed interposition; but was written under the seal of secrecy for the guidance of the Governor of Madras before a picket had crossed the frontier or a shot had been fired. Webbe was appointed Resident at Nagpore with a view to further the drawing of the Rajah of Berar into the projected system of defensive alliance; and Malcolm was named to succeed him in Mysore. Both were chosen for the knowledge of native customs and dialects they were known to possess, and the temper and tact for which they were distinguished.

The Peishwah received the ratification of the treaty of Bassein with demonstrations of the highest satisfaction, and did not appear to entertain any disposition to accept the invitation to the camp of Scindiah. Wellesley suspected that Scindiah, notwithstanding his original application for the aid of the British Government in restoring order to the Mahratta empire, meditated an accommodation with Holkar; and a confederacy with him and the Rajah of Berar for the purpose of frustrating our arrangements with the Peishwah. This suspicion was corroborated by the artifices practised at his camp, with a view of eluding the communication of the propositions with which Colonel Collins was charged; and the evasive replies he received after he had at length obtained access to him. 'This perverse course of policy, habitual to all the States of India, was the favourite practice of the Mahratta powers; but experience proved that a direct and steady course of policy was not less advantageous to our interests

[1] Secret to Lord Clive, 2nd February, 1803.

than it was consistent with our dignity.' Scindiah then gave a positive assurance of his wish to improve the friendship subsisting between the Peishwah, the British Government, and his own State. The extreme hazard to which his power had been recently exposed by the success of the insurgents at Poonah may have opened a more distinct view of his real interests, which were entirely consistent with those of the British Government. He may however have apprehended the permanent diminution of his influence in the Peishwah's councils under the Treaty of Bassein. But his influence had been subverted previous to our mediation, and the existence of his Government had been greatly endangered. His sincerity is confirmed by his inaction at Burhampore until the season and the progress of our forces had advanced so far that no exertion on his part could have enabled him to occupy Poonah previous to the arrival of our troops in that capital. He might however, wisely and justly, withhold his assent to any new system of engagement until he had ascertained the real sentiments of the Peishwah on the subject of the late treaty. Holkar continued to manifest an anxious desire for the accommodation of his differences with the Peishwah and with Scindiah by repeated applications to Colonel Close for British arbitration. Colonel Close urged the Peishwah to make such concessions as might compromise their existing differences and admit of his returning peaceably to his capital. But he manifested an insuperable aversion to offer any concessions to Holkar, whom he considered to be a rebel against the legitimate authority of the sovereign power of the Mahratta empire. Colonel Close therefore addressed a letter to Holkar, assuring him that our influence would be exerted for the satisfactory adjustment of his claims on Scindiah or the Peishwah, and a hope that he would refrain from any opposition to the establishment of a British force within the Peishwah's dominions. Holkar continued to exercise the utmost violence and outrage upon the inhabitants of Poonah for the purpose of extorting money for the relief of his exigencies. This created the greatest disgust, and confirmed the resolution of the Jaghiredars and of the rest of the community to support the Peishwah's cause. At the beginning of April he withdrew his army in a northerly direction towards Burhampore, to accelerate probably his negotiation with Scindiah: and this movement admitted the uninterrupted march of the combined forces of the allies to Poonah. Though his forces amounted to 40,000 cavalry, 30,000 infantry, with 180 guns, he seemed thereby to have abandoned his hopes of effecting a revolution in the Government of Poonah, and of seizing a share in the administration. The Rajah of Berar was dissatisfied at the conclusion of the Treaty of Bassein. But the Peishwah rejected every overture of the ruling authority at Poonah and of the Rajah of Berar for the adjustment of his affairs through any other channel than ours.[1] The allied forces under Lieutenant-General Stuart had orders from Lord Clive to enter the Mahratta territory, and a detachment under Major-General Wellesley was specially directed to move on Poonah from Mysore.

In his progress Bajee Rao received welcome and homage from many of the great Jaghiredars who in the days of his misrule had sulked at their country seats, and refused to attend his court. The outrages and exactions of Holkar's bandit troops and the terrors of protracted civil war had brought them back to loyalty; and condoning the faults and errors of their hereditary chief, they accompanied him with their numerous retainers to the capital, where, on May 13, he was restored to the musnud amid salvoes of British artillery and demonstrations of popular joy. Holkar had withdrawn as General Wellesley approached, and his professions waxed daily more fervid of desire for a bloodless arbitrament of his

[1] To the Secret Committee from Fort William; 19th April, 1803.

claims. But ere the last of his freebooters had disappeared partizans of his more potent rival began once more to mutter audibly complaints that he had not been a party to the restoration. Were the foreigners going to remain at Poonah; and was the head of the Mahratta League about to become independent in their hands? What if Scindiah and Ragojee Bhoonslah reappear upon the scene? Their disciplined battalions, powerful ordnance, and unnumbered squadrons of horse were known to have been lately mustering near Burhampore; and who could tell whether, sooner than endure the spectacle of alien ascendency, Holkar might not be induced to join them in a general war against the infidel? The hour was critical, and on Arthur Wellesley the responsibility lay of deciding whether to abide the chances of Mahratta intrigue and cabal, or to assume a peremptory tone to bring affairs at once to issue. The danger of waiting till the effervescence of gratitude had passed away, and his small army should be girt round at Poonah by gathering hosts, was imminent. His choice was silently but quickly made. Our Resident in the camp of Scindiah, by instructions from the General, laid before him in Durbar the full text of the Treaty of Bassein, which he and his ministers owned had in it nothing of which he could complain. But when called upon to give proof of the sincerity of his acquiescence by withdrawing his army across the Nerbudda, he sought by varied ingenuity of evasion to avoid any definite pledge as to his intentions. And when at length Colonel Collins pressed for a definite reply, he haughtily broke up the conference by saying, 'that after his interview with the Rajah of Berar appointed for the morrow he would declare whether we should have war or peace.' The mask thus dropped, Colonel Collins was at first minded to depart without further parley. But the solicitude for the preservation of peace expressed in all the Governor's letters withheld him from taking an irretraceable step; and deviating from the strict tenor of his orders from the General he yielded to importunities frequently renewed from the Mahratta ministers that he would remain at the camp at Burhampore in hopes from day to day of a peaceful solution of affairs. He was not ignorant that the Bhoonslah's tendencies were hostile, and that his influence was likely to be exercised to warp his wavering ally towards desperate counsels. But the state of the country, and just then of the weather, visibly chilled Dowlut Rao's courage, and while a hope remained of averting sanguinary conflict Collins believed that he interpreted aright the desires of his Government by leaving the door of compromise ajar.

Meanwhile at Fort William the duplicity of the Mahratta professions of peace was revealed by a letter from the Rajah of Berar to Azim ul Omrah, which announced his intention of attacking the Nizam's territory, and of his concert with Holkar and Scindiah to defeat the Treaty of Bassein. Wellesley expostulated with him on the treachery of his conduct, reminding him of his recent professions of unbroken friendship, and warning him that he could not be allowed with impunity to break the peace.[1] To Scindiah himself a remonstrance was addressed against the movement of his troops on Poonah, where the Peishwah had been peacefully restored through our intervention, and from the neighbourhood of which Holkar had withdrawn. Any further advance in that direction on the pretence of defending the chief of the confederacy from molestation could only be regarded as a proof of hostile designs against the British power and its allies. His specious professions of contentment with the Treaty of Bassein when made known to him in March, could not be reconciled with his subsequent negotiations with Bhoonslah and Holkar. To clear any erroneous apprehension from his mind of the drift and purport of the treaty, Colonel Collins was instructed

[1] From Fort William; 22nd May, 1803.

to furnish him with a copy of the whole of its provisions, by which he would see that nothing indicated a desire to subvert the independence of the Mahratta States. The Resident was to 'convince him that in concluding the late alliance with the Peishwah, the objects of the Governor General were to secure the British dominions and those of our ally the Nizam from the dangers of contiguous anarchy and confusion, to fulfil the duties of friendship towards our ally the Peishwah, and to provide at the same time for the safety of the several branches of the Mahratta empire, without disturbing the constitutional form of the State, and without affecting the legitimate independence of its feudatory chieftains.'[1]

The sincerity of these professions was as little comprehended in London as at Gwalior. Castlereagh and 'The Chairs' could not be persuaded that interference meant anything but a covered project of annexation; and the semi-barbarous Mahratta courts might naturally tremble lest the fate of Tippoo and the Nawab of Arcot should be in store for them. But it is certain that neither lust of spoil or hunger for appropriation of territory animated the counsels of Wellesley. He persuaded himself that while the lawless and fitful ambition of the three great chiefs of the confederacy remained without check or curb the tranquillity of our possessions could never be secure. To hold the balance of their rival interests, and to play the resistant energies from time to time against the aggressive schemes of his neighbour, and if possible to induce all of them practically to enter into terms of subsidiary alliance with the Company, was the far-sighted and far-reaching policy which alone he contemplated. In outline it was vast, in detail sometimes vague; but on the whole it was characterized by greatness of purpose and comprehensiveness of design: and up to this period it was possible to believe that it might be realized without war. The

[1] Secretary Edmonstone to Colonel Collins; 9th June, 1803.

demonstration however of military strength was obviously indispensable for this most favourable solution, and extraordinary efforts were made to meet the contingency of a sudden rupture, whenever and wherever it should occur. He wrote warmly congratulating the Peishwah on returning to his capital, an event which was published with due honour at all the seats of British Government. The independent authority of his Highness would be scrupulously recognised by us so long as our relations of amity lasted. His Highness was lavish in acknowledgment of the services rendered him. He professed unwavering confidence in his benefactors, and a cordial disposition to be guided by their advice. It seems still uncertain whether the counter alliance spoken of between Scindiah and the Rajah of Berar was more than defensive, and the excesses committed by Holkar's troops in the Nizam's country having been brought to an end were hardly of sufficient magnitude to call for reprisal or reparation. Such was the state of affairs towards the close of June.

But Scindiah at length resolved to set at nought all his previous professions of desire for peace and for our mediation, and General Lake had orders to prepare for a collision which to the last he endeavoured to avert. 'A few days will decide positively whether war will become inevitable; from that moment we must press forward without hesitation if the alternative should leave no prospect of peace. You will at the same time enter into my extreme solicitude to avoid every proceeding which can involve expense, and which may not be indispensable to our success.'[1]

On June 8, Bhoonslah had a long conference with Scindiah at his camp at Chickley. The Resident next day asked for a final answer regarding their intentions, but was met with the usual evasion. In a memorial addressed to the Maharajah, Colonel Collins demanded categorically a reply to

[1] To Lieut.-General Lake; 28th June, 1803.

his oft-repeated question whether he meant peace or war for the purpose of defeating the Treaty of Bassein. Should he continue with his army south of the Nerbudda, and refuse to give satisfactory assurances, the Governor General must consider friendly relations at an end, and for himself the Resident must only ask for an escort to Aurungabad. General Wellesley had advanced his troops several days' march north of Poonah, and had plenary powers conferred on him to negotiate with the Mahratta chiefs or to take hostile action. Acting on instructions from him, Colonel Collins quitted Scindiah's camp, and informed the Governor General that the rupture was complete. On receipt of this intelligence Wellesley wrote forthwith to the commander on the North-west frontier :—' I have just received a letter from Colonel Collins under date June 12, which has determined me to carry into execution with all practicable speed the general outlines of the plan of war against Scindiah stated in my letter of June 28. I shall now write to you from day to day, but I would not delay this communication for a moment. Scindiah's object is to gain time. Ours must be to act between this time and the month of October. The seizure of Agra would be a great and masterly blow. I know you will attempt it if prudent.' [1]

Lake was to gain possession, if possible, of Delhi, Agra, and a chain of posts on the right bank of the Jumnah, with a view to the occupation of the Dooab, or country lying between that river and the Ganges.

There was no desire to extend the Company's territory further, but it would be his duty to deliver Shah Alum from his captivity, and induce him to fix his residence within our confines. To alienate and take over or break up the French contingent in the pay of Scindiah was an object of primary importance, the means for compassing which were left to the General's discretion. All connections which might

[1] 5th July, 1803.

be found beyond the river line of frontier were to be placed upon a footing of defensive alliance, so as to form a hedge of locally self-governing, but politically dependent States between us and the Mahrattas. It was likewise intended to take possession of Bundlecund, the proximity of which to Benares and other cities of importance made it a constant source of danger in treacherous or hostile hands. Minute instructions as to what might be done with advantage in various contingencies were sent to Lake as suggestions for his consideration; but his judgment was left free to modify them as circumstances might seem to require; always bearing in mind the possibility that General Wellesley held full powers to treat with Scindiah, with whose main army he was likely to come into collision in the Deccan. On July 18, the two Mahratta princes were formally summoned to cross the Nerbudda, and sever their armed coalition, if they desired a continuance of peace. In case of refusal, Colonel Collins was to quit the Mahratta camp without further parley. After a week's hesitation they severally replied that they were within their own borders, where they had a right to be, and that they had sent disclaimers to the Governor General of any wish to break the Treaty of Bassein or any intention of passing the Adjuntee hills that lay between them and Poonah. In his desire to avert hostilities, Colonel Collins deviated from his orders and spent another fortnight in negotiation.

Wellesley awaited the result of the Resident's prolonged parleyings, hoping against hope, that at the last moment they might prevail: sleeplessly revolving by night all the contingencies that would need providing for in case of a rupture, and by day silently pacing the halls of Government House, nervously watching for the first tidings from Burhampore. At length they came. The die was cast, and every thought and hand must forthwith be devoted to sending instructions simultaneously, and without an hour's delay, to the generals and political agents at various distant points how they might act best respectively and in combination. Lake, Kirkpatrick, Malcolm had all to be informed authentically how and why Collins had upon August 3 finally quitted Scindiah's camp, and that three days afterwards war had begun. It taxed to the utmost all the energies, mental and physical, of the Secretariat Staff to execute the requirements of the Governor General. For many hours he remained in the midst of his young guard of civil servants dictating minute instructions, copies of important documents, or transcribing despatches with modifications and alternative paragraphs framed to provide afar off for possible events. Strung to the highest pitch of excitement and ambition, his confidential scribes throughout the sultry day and late into the night, continued at their task without sign of weariness, proud of its importance, and enthusiastic, as Metcalf loved to tell, in admiration of 'their glorious little chief.' When they had done, they were summoned to the supper table in an adjoining room, and told that they were to make merry and drink deep to the success of our arms.

On August 6, General Wellesley began his memorable march, and upon the 8th war began. His statement of the cause of the rupture was couched in terms eminently characteristic. In a frank though formal communication addressed to Scindiah he said,—' Your Highness will recollect that the British Government did not threaten to commence hostilities against you; but you threatened to commence hostilities against the British Government and its allies; and when called on to explain your intentions, you declared it was doubtful whether there would be peace or war;[1] and in conformity with your threats and your declared doubts, you assembled a large army in a station contiguous to the Nizam's frontier. On this ground I called upon you to

[1] In conference with Colonel Collins on the 27th May.

withdraw that army to its usual station, if your subsequent pacific declarations were sincere; but instead of complying with this reasonable requisition, you propose that I should withdraw the troops which are intended to defend the territories of our allies against your designs; and that you and the Rajah of Berar should be suffered to remain with your troops assembled, in readiness to take advantage of their absence. This proposition is unreasonable and inadmissible, and you must stand the consequences of the measures which I find myself compelled to adopt in order to repel your aggression. I offered you peace on terms of equality, and honourable to all parties: you have chosen war, and are responsible for all consequences.'[1]

The first of these consequences was sharp and stunning. The fort of Ahmednuggur, at the mouth of the Adjuntee Pass, was attacked and taken,[2] and the young General thenceforth pursued his venturous way. It was his first campaign in separate command, and it proved equally notable in the book of his fame and in the story of empire. The country had been desolated by internal conflicts; and without a commissariat carefully prepared and amply supplied his troops must have starved. The enemy fell back as he advanced, and it was not until September 23 that he came up with them on the banks of the Kistna, where he fought and won the battle of Assye, routing his outnumbering foes and taking ninety pieces of cannon. A month later followed the sanguinary conflict at Argaum, and on December 15 the siege and capture of Gawilghur. The Rajah of Berar sued for peace. Bhoonslah agreed to relinquish several provinces westward of the river Wurdah to the Nizam: to the Company he ceded Cuttack and Bundelcund.

---

[1] To Dowlut Rao Scindia, from the Camp at Walkee; 6th August 1803.

[2] 11th August, 1803.

The Government of the Company was recognised in future to be the arbiter of all differences with the Peishwah or the Nizam, and no European or American troops were to be thenceforth admitted into the service of Berar.[1]

Meanwhile, at the opposite extremity of Scindiah's vast dominions, Lake with an army of 10,000 men pursued his equally triumphant course. With one European and four native regiments of foot (about 4,000 men), three regiments of dragoons and five of native horse, he crossed the frontier at Alyghur. The Mahratta army, 15,000 strong, consisted of picked men highly disciplined under European officers, who were full of the confidence derived from never having been beaten in the field. They had been trained by De Boigne, a Savoyard by birth, who had learned war in the Irish Brigade of France, and who had while still young become a trusted and favoured lieutenant of Scindiah. He had been succeeded by a Frenchman named Perron, of known energy, and many of whose subalterns were his compatriots, but some of other European nationalities. Lord Wellesley was too wise to undervalue the strength of such a force; and was ready to sap its stability while preparing to confront it in the open. He knew that Perron was the object of native jealousy, and daily feared supersession by intrigue. Offers were therefore circulated guaranteeing property, rank, and pay to such European officers as might betimes come over to the side of England. So bold an offer caused men hitherto faithful to the Mahratta standard to distrust for the first time its chance of victory; and the soldier, like the woman, who hesitates is lost. Within a fortnight Perron and many of his staff covertly withdrew and left their battalions on the eve of the first battle.[2] Disheartened but undismayed at being suddenly left to unrecognised leaders, these brave troops met the onslaught of the British with such constancy

[1] 17th December, 1803.   [2] 29th August, 1803.

and vigour, that Lake was obliged to fall back, and did not venture to attack again until the afternoon, when his superior cavalry succeeded in throwing his adversaries into confusion, which their inexperienced officers were unable to retrieve. The defeat cost the victors dear, but it was decisive. On September 4 the Fort of Alyghur was taken by storm; more French officers deserted, and Scindiah was never afterwards able to array so formidable an army in the field. The Governor General recorded with effusion the glory of the day and that of Ahmednuggur, the account of which had reached him just before. In his heart he could not help feeling that but for the preparations he had made betimes for the advance of both armies long ere a whiff of conflict floated in the stirless air neither victory had been won.[1]

Lake approached Delhi on September 11, where another detachment of the French Brigade under Bourquin prepared to dispute his progress. In a sharp encounter he was again successful; and on the 16th entered the ancient capital of The Mogul. Amid the rejoicings of the multitude he proceeded to deliver from his long captivity the aged sovereign who fifty years before, had granted the English, as an exceptional favour, a firman permitting them to exercise certain privileges at the mouth of the Ganges. From penury and suffering he was now with his family to be delivered, and restored to the enjoyment of luxury and state. An incident so dramatic, and one whose consequences were likely to prove historically so significant, furnished a theme of pardonable exultation to the Pro-consular pen. 'It is impossible to describe the impression which General Lake's conduct on this interesting occasion has made on the minds of the inhabitants of Delhi, and of all the Mussulmans who have had an opportunity of being made acquainted with the occurrences of September 16. In the metaphorical language of Asia, the native

[1] General orders; 8th September, 1803.

news-writers who describe this extraordinary scene have declared that his Majesty Shah Alum recovered his sight from excess of joy. In addition to many other marks of royal favour and condescension, the Emperor was graciously pleased to confer on the General the second title in the empire.'[1]

Too late to give the old man back his sight, it would not have been too late to restore the provinces or some of them of which he had been bereft by his Mahratta foes, against whom just then virtuous indignation was loud. But beyond a limited suburban circle no restitution of lands was made. The house of Timour was declared to have regained by aid of our auxiliary arms its liberty and dignity: but we kept its possessions. The coin of the Company continued to bear the effigy of the Mogul, and 150,000*l.* a year was indeed secured for the maintenance at Delhi of palaces, elephants, harems, and household troops; but the control of the police and the command of a Sepoy garrison were entrusted to English officers, who were held responsible for the safety of the imperial family, and whose instructions were positive that under no circumstances should the Sovereign or his next heir quit the precincts of the capital from which empire had crumbled away.

From a severe attack of illness the news of these victories revived the Governor General. He wrote at length from Barrackpore, congratulating Lake, and covering him with praise.[2] 'The result must be the extinction of the last vestige of French influence in India, the defeat of the ambitious and rapacious views of the Mahratta confederates, and a speedy peace with ample indemnity and security to the allies.' You are entitled to the highest honours and rewards which your country and your King can bestow. My private

---

[1] To the Directors; September, 1803.
[2] Despatch; 30th September, 1803.

gratitude cannot be expressed.' Warm as these words of appreciation were, they did not satisfy the ardour of his excitable and enthusiastic nature. 'My life however protracted cannot furnish the means of satisfying my sentiments on this occasion. But whatever can be expected from the most cordial, firm, and zealous respect, affection, and attachment, must ever be commanded by you from me and from every person connected with me.'

Agra surrendered on October 17, and Duderneg with his staff and 2,500 men came into camp on terms of taking service with the Company. The remaining battalions of their devoted but deserted force, a fortnight later, fought desperately at Laswarri and nearly cut to pieces the 76th Foot.

Lake, the day after, recorded the final dispersion of what had been Perron's force, and the rout of Scindiah's last army, though not without great fatigue, difficulty and loss. 'I never was in so severe a business in my life, or anything like it, and I pray to God I may never be in such a situation again. Their army was better appointed than ours; no expense was spared whatever. Had we been defeated the consequences must have been most fatal. Those fellows fought like devils, or rather heroes; and had they been commanded by French officers the event would have been I fear extremely doubtful. They had a numerous artillery as well armed as they could possibly be; their gunners standing to their guns until killed by the bayonet.' [1]

A favourite charger, given to Lake by the Governor General, was killed under him during the day. At the end of his elaborate dispatch of congratulation Lord Wellesley added,— 'I grieve for my poor friend Old Port; but I have received some fine horses from Arabia, one, if not two, of which I shall endeavour to send to you.' [2]

---

[1] To the Governor General; 2nd November, 1803.
[2] 18th November, 1803.

Scindiah, like his confederate, now agreed to peace, ceding numerous and valuable provinces and fortified places. He renounced all claims on the British Government and its allies, or upon the Guickwar or the Peishwah. The losses sustained by the great officers of his court and army by the alienation of territories out of whose revenues they had been paid were to be compensated by fifteen lacs of rupees guaranteed by the Company. The Treaty was signed December 30, 1803, and followed by one of defensive alliance some weeks later, by which he secured the service of six battalions of sepoys to be stationed within or without his dominions as he might choose, and to be paid out of the revenues of the districts he had relinquished. While the discomfited Rajahs retained without question their independence, their powers of molesting each other or their neighbours were materially curtailed. The prestige of their arms was effectually dissipated; and after three-quarters of a century Scindiah is still numbered among the native allies of England in the East, and his people live in a security unknown to their forefathers.

Nearly every object named by the Governor General in his original scheme of policy was attained. Berar ceded Maritime Orissa, thus giving the Company a continuous coast from Calcutta to Madras. Certain districts (now called Berar Proper) were made over to the Nizam as his share of the spoil on a pledge never to employ any Frenchmen in his service, and to make no alliance with the Mahratta States.

CHAPTER XIV.

BHURTPORE.

1804–1805.

ADDRESSES of gratulation from the Anglo-Indian communities in all the great towns vied with each other in eulogy of the past, and augury of settled peace for the future. The praise has become history; the prophecy was doomed to fail, and was soon forgotten. Flattery would listen to no doubt of England's recognition of the wisdom, firmness, and moderation in council, which had sent forth heroism to triumph, and welcomed it back with honour unstained by excess. It was impossible that deeds so great should not be appreciated as they deserved; and if the immediate cost was heavy, the price of so many and important gains must seem to all thinking and reasonable minds as well worth paying. But his experience of the querulous and grudging temper of his employers did not lead Wellesley to equally sanguine expectations. He had for three years been in controversy with them on many and weighty affairs, and he had come to the conviction that his ways of rule would never be as their ways, or his thoughts as their thoughts. They were intent on money, he on glory; they would save where he would spend; and they would clutch and keep where he would forego or give back. War for any cause or with whatever result was the one thing hateful and to be avoided, not because of its cruelty, but on account of its cost. Just or unjust, fortunate or unfortunate, cautious or reckless, it was certain to send down the price of the Company's securities in the market; and jeopardise the balance of profit on current account. On the first news of a rupture with the Mahrattas, the price of India stock had fallen from 215 to 160 : how many brass cannon, damascened swords, mud forts taken, and circars or jaghires ceded, would be required to bring it up again to that quotation? The recovery of financial confidence which had been rapid on the cessation of hostilities could not be known in London till the middle of the year; and proprietors whose equanimity was ruffled by the sudden fall were not likely to take much comfort from mere promises in half-published despatches, that all would be sure to come right in due time.

Mr. Tucker, who had rendered important service in raising the credit of the Government while Auditor-General, early in 1804 announced his intention to resign that post to become a partner in the house of Palmer, Trail & Co., much to the chagrin of his imperious patron, who at first playfully and then peevishly upbraided him with desertion. His vindication lay in his being able to point truthfully and triumphantly to the change wrought within three years in the available resources of the State. Treasury bills which in 1799 would not be taken at twelve per cent, were now eagerly bought at Calcutta and Bombay at four; though the public expenditure and funded debt were greatly increased.[1]

Wellesley knew that while the armies under his direction were achieving so many triumphs, and his diplomacy was winning so many permanent and splendid additions to the dependencies of the Company, a considerable section of its shareholders and directors were probably engaged at home not only in public disparagement of his whole policy, but in bitter vituperation of his personal character and conduct.

[1] Minute of Council, 1st May, 1804.

Individual enmities whether caused by neglect and slight, which all men engaged in arduous public duties are liable unconsciously to offer, or by the resistance to selfish schemes and projects which is unavoidable, are seldom forgiven. He had made a surprising number of vehement and active enemies. Worthy but wearied men, returned from service in the East, regarded with aversion all tendencies to territorial aggrandisement; and frugal financiers in the City, who distrusted the sanguine prospects of paying off debt, and reducing the cost of military establishments before there was a rumour of Mahratta wars, lost all patience at the sudden expansion of liabilities which the Governor General's measures of 1803 too certainly entailed. They did not believe in the profitableness of annexation, even under favourable circumstances: and in the chance of deriving revenue from the acquisition of political ascendency, won by long marches and the transport of siege trains, they did not believe at all. The quarrel with the Mahrattas, to nine out of ten holders of India stock, seemed to be no better than a romance by which its clever author might gain celebrity brief or lasting, but about which they simply wished to read and hear nothing. Reflecting and impartial politicians with imperfect information looked sceptically upon the affair, as bit by bit its incidents were disclosed; and party spirit, never scrupulous in its choice of topics of attack, had no compunction in assailing an absent statesman for acts that were easily made to look equivocal, and which the ministers of the day sometimes found it embarrassing to defend. Papers were constantly moved for in Parliament, petitions of complaint presented, and denunciatory articles written, which it was nobody's function particularly to answer, and which thousands of dyspeptic or scandal-loving people found it amusing or exciting to read. One of the most fertile themes of sarcasm and reproach was the favouritism said to be shown to his brothers by the Marquess. The real merits of the Major-General as a strategist and administrator were not yet and could not possibly be known; and Henry Wellesley's name having never been heard of in literature or legislation, in negotiation or in the field, ill-nature took for granted that the prominence given him as Lieutenant-Governor of Oude was merely a fraternal job. He had however, extinguished the calumny by declining to take any extra pay during the period of his residence at Lucknow, and he subsequently returned to Europe, where he thenceforth remained.

A serious charge preferred in the spring of 1803, in proof of dangerous autocratic tendencies, was the delegation of unlimited powers to Lieutenant-General Stuart and Major-General Wellesley to deal with political matters of the highest moment at the head of their respective armies in the field. It was strongly contended that in point of law no high act of State, especially regarding foreign princes or communities, could properly be done by the Governor General himself, except in Council; far less could he clothe another with discretionary powers to bind his employers or his sovereign, with powers which he did not himself possess. A case for the opinion of counsel was elaborately and ingeniously framed, and submitted to Mr. Ryder [1] and Mr. Adam, who were at the time eminent practitioners of the law. They concurred in thinking that none of the statutes under which the office of Governor General was constituted permitted his authority in matters of peace or war to be devolved on any single person, not even upon the Governor General himself; and that acts done by virtue of such a commission required the confirmation of an Act of Parliament in order to give them validity. Several precedents were found for the course impugned, both Hastings

[1] Afterwards Home Secretary from 1809 to 1812.

and Cornwallis having, without question at the time, or censure afterwards, been endued by the Supreme Council of Bengal in which they presided, with the sole power of directing armies and of making compacts with foreign States. But having regard to the manifest intention of Parliament and the obvious policy of the nation, that our Chief Governor in Asia should as nearly as possible occupy in the eyes of the native princes the attitude of an independent sovereign, it was not surprising that Parliament should have been ready to ratify exceptional acts of the kind rather than disown them on merely technical grounds.

The Minutes of Council, copies of which were regularly though tardily transmitted home, disclosed the frequent absence of the Governor General from its deliberations. For the first few months he had followed the practice of his predecessors; but after his return from his long sojourn at Madras, the habit of thinking and deciding alone in the weightier matters of State seems to have been too agreeable to be laid aside. No extent of inquiry, scrutiny of details, or length of personal conference in his own cabinet wearied him; but the obligation to sit for hours in a presidential chair, and listen to the prosy and sometimes inconsequential expatiations of colleagues less thoroughly informed than himself on grave or urgent questions of policy, tired and fretted him. He could not doze, and he would not indulge in undignified comment; but he grudged the waste of time, and got into the way of sending a full-dress message in the morning that, 'His Excellency the Most Noble the Governor General signifies that it is not his intention to attend the meeting of Council, and desires that the proceedings which may be held at the meeting be communicated to him for his approbation.' In the year 1801, this intimation was recorded nine times; in 1802, twenty-eight; and in 1803, twenty-four times. The Directors did not disguise their disappointment and their discontent, which they conveyed in the mild expression of their belief that, except in case of illness, the Governor General had never before been in the habit of absenting himself from Council.

Had the treaty of Bassein realised the sanguine hopes of its author, all the world would with one accord have sung its praise. While yet its actual effect was doubtful, political sagacity showed its customary skill in taciturn reserve. But when its unripe fruit was rudely shaken down, and a trying interval of rough weather had to elapse before supplementary grafts upon that stock could even begin to bear, retrospective candour waxed eloquent in doubts as to the necessity and quality of the transaction; and as to whether it might not have been more economical at all events to let it alone. It was not until more than a year had passed, and a sanguinary campaign had been waged and won, that Castlereagh by his own confession found time deliberately to look into the whole question. He then [1] elaborately explained to the man at the helm why he ought never to have quitted port, or tempted a stormy sea, or risked much harm and loss for the sake of remote or contingent gain. We had better have been content with things as they were at the close of 1802, perhaps; and on the other hand, perhaps not. This is the art and mystery of official tape; what comes of setting an uninformed man to pretend to govern the destinies of communities and realms from the other side of the globe. Wars that are palpably remunerative are invariably held to be just; but expensive, entangling, encumbering enterprises are always liable to cause qualms of contrition. Castlereagh affected to read the Pro-consul a lecture after he had begun to lose popularity in England, on the ethics of acquisition. Here is a splendid specimen of the scruples that haunt the ministerial mind about victories that are not quite certain to pay.

[1] 4th March, 1804.

'It was not a matter of choice, but of necessity, that our existence in India should pass from that of traders to that of sovereigns. If we had not, the French would long since have taken the lead in India, to our exclusion. Events have latterly accelerated our progress so much, and we have already accomplished so much in point of power and glory that we should now be studious to give to our counsels a complexion of moderation and forbearance, trusting, as we may safely do, the preservation of our Indian possessions to the resources abundantly contained within our present limits.'

But he adds, 'The eagerness with which we appeared to press our connection upon all the leading States in succession, might naturally lead them to apprehend that we meant more than we avowed, that our object was ultimately to be masters instead of allies, and that, having obtained either possession of or absolute influence over every State, except the Mahrattas, with whom we had been in connection, our object was to obtain a similar influence over their councils. Under whatever estimate of our views it may have been formed, the fact is indisputable that a general repugnance to the British connection on the terms proposed universally prevailed amongst the great Mahratta powers. It was avoided by all as long as they had any choice. It was only embraced by the Peishwah when an exile from his dominions; and the jealousy of it was such as to have since led Holkar and Scindiah to forget their animosities, and to league with the Rajah of Berar against the Company and the Peishwah. How long the Peishwah will continue faithful to engagements which were contracted from necessity, and not from choice, in opposition to the other Mahratta States, is yet to be seen. The practical question to be considered is, whether an alliance formed under such circumstances can rest upon any other foundation than mere force; and if not, whether the means by which it is to be upheld are not destructive of its professed advantages. The Mahrattas have never in any instance commenced hostilities against us; so far then as past experience goes, there seems no special ground to apprehend future danger from them. The French officers in Scindiah's army are just objects of jealousy, and their mixing themselves in the affairs of the native Powers must be watched, and be matter of alarm in proportion to the degree in which it takes place, and as those States are near to or remote from our possessions; but this alone cannot render the alliance prudent, nor is this danger at present of a magnitude to call for the adoption of a system otherwise of dubious policy. As far as the Mahratta interests are concerned, what motive can they have in acquiescing in the ostensible head of their empire being placed in our hands? Whatever we may hold out to reconcile the Peishwah to the alliance, and however we may profess to respect his independence in the management of his own affairs, we cannot deny that in fact as well as in appearance, whilst a British army is at Poonah, he can be considered in no other light than as politically dependent on us. The same motives which before opposed Scindiah and Holkar to each other now oppose them both to us, and the Rajah of Berar joins the confederacy. Nor is it to be expected that independent States, predatory and warlike, can wish to make us the arbiter of their destiny. To aim at a permanent connection with the Mahratta powers must be, to say the least of it, extremely hazardous. It must be difficult and expensive to establish, not less difficult and expensive to retain. Such a result we disavow as our object, as in principle and policy against the laws of the land; and we should avoid therefore a course of measures the tendency of which leads naturally to that result. It may be said, if the treaty had not been pushed with the Peishwah while at Bassein, he might have refused it afterwards; but it is doubtful whether a treaty so obtained is a benefit, or whether it might not have been better to let Holkar and Scindiah fight it out before proposing any permanent connection. The advantages of such a connection had always been overrated. By keeping an army of observation on the frontier, and not mixing in Mahratta politics, except upon sure grounds, if we gained no more than securing our own territory, as well as that of our ally, the Nizam, from insult, we escaped war, whilst the Mahratta powers wasted their strength.'[1]

It remained to be considered whether the Governor General had exceeded his powers, and what instructions should be given from home for the future regulation of his conduct. It was not alleged that Holkar, when this treaty was made, had either committed or meditated hostilities against us or our allies; the treaty of Bassein was therefore not within the scope of the 42nd clause of the Act of 1793, which forbade any treaty being made to bind the Company to guarantee the territories of any State; except in return for active co-operation in a war already existing or actually imminent. But manifestly he had not exceeded his instructions, regard being had to his communication from time to time of all the proceedings at the Court of Poonah which led to the making of the treaty, and which when acquiesced in might be fairly considered by him as approved of by the authorities at home. A subsidiary treaty had been distinctly recognised as politic and just, with a view to the liberation of the Peishwah from the overruling influence of his too powerful vassal. The Company's standing army in 1803 amounted to 115,000 men, and subsidiary engagements with one or more of the Mahratta States might secure us useful auxiliaries without any excessive additions to our obligations. But were the whole of their empire to be reduced to subjection, we should be brought into contact with still more trouble-

[1] Castlereagh to Wellesley, 4th March, 1804.

some and formidable neighbours, and sacrifice a tolerable barrier for one infinitely more precarious. Our great object ought to be bringing the war to a close as speedily as possible.

The Secret Committee wrote at the same time, acknowledging the brilliant successes at Broach and Ahmednuggur; but regretting the commencement of hostilities, and in no measured terms deploring results so unlooked for from the treaty of Bassein. They were willing to modify or annul any portions of the treaty which should tend to keep alive the jealousy of the military chiefs, a permanent connection with whom they did not approve. They frankly owned however, that when formerly brought under their notice in 1800, the gravity of the objections to a guarantee of the Peishwah's dominions had not been considered, and they therefore 'desired to be understood as not attaching blame to the conduct of their Government abroad with respect to the form of the treaty itself.' Though they thought the conduct of the Mahratta princes had been faithless and aggressive, entitling us to look for indemnity for the expenses of the war, the object was not one for which they wished it to be prolonged.[1]

In reply to Lord Castlereagh's strictures, Major-General Wellesley argued that the principal motive which dictated the treaty of Bassein, and the proceedings, political and military to which it led, was the prevention of the resuscitation of French influence in India. Although in the former war they had lost their territorial possessions, it could not be doubted that every French statesman sought to diminish the power and prosperity of the British Government in Asia.

Our gains with those from Oude completed our rule over the watershed of the Ganges, the finest region and containing the most civilised population of Hindustan.

[1] To the Governor General in Council, 6th March, 1804.

Scindiah moreover accepted the gracious gift of a subsidiary force. But Ahmednuggur was restored to him to enable him to sustain himself against Holkar.

Just as the treaty was signed, despatches from England forbade the war, desiring the treaty of Bassein to be cancelled, and ordering abstention from intervention in Mahratta affairs unless we were actually attacked. The whole of the promised surplus from previous conquests had been spent in the struggle, and the dividends were not incoming. A minority of the Cabinet tried hard to defend Lord Wellesley's conquests against his critics; but the Secret Committee, in a long Minute, though acquitting him of illegality, emphatically reiterated the interdict against annexation.

On his part Wellesley did not conceal from those who had his confidence his resentment at the manner in which his advice was frequently disregarded and his acts overruled in England. Men whom he had chosen for pre-eminent fitness to fill posts of importance were in more than one instance set aside; and connections or dependants of influential proprietors sent out to supersede them. Mr. Webbe was removed from the Secretaryship of Madras, where his long experience and unfaltering rectitude had won the esteem of all who had opportunities of estimating his worth. Lord Clive, after vainly remonstrating against the injustice and impolicy of the act, resigned the presidency sooner than acquiesce; and the Governor General told the Premier that Webbe's removal would be a severe blow to the Government; while the direct appointment from home to the most confidential office ' comprised every degree of personal indignity that could be offered to Lord Clive and himself, and the result had been to drive that honest, diligent, prudent, and able public servant from India. He would not separate his character from that of Lord Clive on this painful occasion.'

In his time the power of creating new appointments, and

of fixing the amount of salaries, were open questions. Both have since been definitely settled; and in our day no new office or increase of pay can be the subject of dispute between the viceregal and imperial authorities. Patronage, in its wider sense, ceased to be a matter of contention, even before the transfer of the Company's possessions to the Crown. The choice of every officer, civil and military, lies with the local executive, and each salary is determined beforehand by the India Office at Whitehall. Lord Wellesley had to exercise in difficult times a discretion without recognised limits; and in the case of his brothers Henry and Arthur, his conduct was again and again made the topic of invidious and inflamed comment. He had upon his own responsibility given a large salary to the Commandant of Seringapatam, because, as his critics said, the Commandant was his kinsman—because, as he said, the function was an important and onerous one, and his brother was a very able man. In the discharge of his duties in Mysore, Arthur Wellesley fairly earned the confidence alike of natives and Europeans; but beyond the hunting out of Dhoondia and his bands of rapparees, there was not any very signal service for him to perform; and when the spouters and vilipenders of Leadenhall Street impugned maliciously the preference shown him, nobody dreamed of Ahmednuggur or Assye. The anger and scorn which their attacks excited in the irascible mind of the Marquess was rather heightened than abated by the events of the Mahratta campaign. He would stoop to no controversy about his acts or motives with his Joint-Stock masters. He requested Castlereagh to be assured of the deep sense he entertained of his honourable conduct in preventing a tirade of aspersion being officially transmitted from the India House during the autumn of 1803 on these subjects; instead of which a comparatively temperate despatch had been agreed to and forwarded. 'It was unnecessary to repeat his utter contempt for any opinions which might be entertained by individual proprietors or by the Court of Directors, as he expected every practicable degree of injustice and baseness from the faction.'[1] And recurring to the same irritating subject, he expressed his reliance on the Minister's justice and public spirit to frustrate the vindictive profligacy of the Directors; and to expose in the most distinct and perspicuous manner the motives, principles, conduct, and result of every branch of his administration in India: nor could he or Mr. Addington by any act of friendship afford him a protection so grateful to his feelings, or so advantageous to his character, as by a full disclosure to Parliament of every act of his administration, and of every proceeding of the Directors, since he had had the misfortune to be subjected to the ignominious tyranny of Leadenhall Street. He hoped to relinquish the service of his honourable employers in January or February 1805; but as no symptoms of tardy remorse displayed by the Honourable Court in consequence of his recent success in India would vary his estimation of the faith and honour of his very worthy and approved good masters, or protract his continuance in India for one hour beyond the limits prescribed by the public interests, so no additional outrage, injury, or insult which could issue from the most loathsome den of the India House would accelerate his departure while the public safety should appear to require his aid in that arduous station.'[2]

Such was the defiant, if not domineering frame of mind in which he was unexpectedly provoked into a new war. Southern India during the Spring had sunk into repose; the Nizam and the Peishwah no longer thought of border quarrels or feared molestation from their formidable neighbours, Scindiah or Bhoonslah. Holkar alone retained without curtailment his revenues, guns, and legions of predatory horse.

[1] 1st March, 1804. [2] 19th June, 1804.

But as he had kept clear of the terrible encounter in which his rivals had been discomfited, he could afford to rest in the comparative superiority it left him, and with unabridged possessions to exult in the humiliation he had had no share in inflicting. If the Mahrattas had really been a civilised and politic confederacy they would no doubt have coalesced against the intrusion of a stranger in their affairs; and the task of their reduction might have been much prolonged if not more doubtful.

> They say 'twas fate, a wayward fate,
>   Their web of discord wove;
> For when their foemen joined in hate,
>   They never joined in love

But hardly had the British troops been dispersed into their summer cantonments, when the Rajah of Jeypore, one of the minor States whose fidelity had earned our protection, appealed for succour against Jeswunt Rao, whose bashi-bazooks were pillaging and ravaging his principality. Lake was forthwith ordered to clear the country of the marauders. Holkar retired on his approach, but with sufficient show of fight to draw the veteran commander farther and farther from his base of operations. The hot season was approaching; no fresh laurels seemed within his grasp, and the victor of Laswarri thought he could afford to take sanitary care of his brave comrades in arms. Leaving Colonel Monson with a few sepoy battalions to watch lest Holkar should return, he withdrew his army into quarters. The Mahratta chief warily encircled the two small corps of observation, whose disastrous retreat chequered the page of triumph as it had not been since the day when Baillie was left equally forlorn in the Carnatic. The remnants of the detachment reached Agra at the end of their seven weeks' march, broken and demoralised, and Lake was compelled, sore against his will, to vex the Governor General with the details of their condition. He had early foreboded failure from Lake's unwillingness to leave a certain proportion of British troops with the native regiments under Monson. But how he bore the mortifying result which for the moment threatened to shake the prestige of ascendency recently established can only be told in his own words.

'I received this morning[1] your letter of September 2. Grievous and disastrous as the events are, the extent of the calamity does not exceed my expectation; from the first hour of Colonel Monson's retreat, I have always augured the ruin of that detachment, and if any part of it be saved I deem it so much gain. I trust that the greater part of it has arrived at Agra, but I fear that my poor friend Monson is gone. Whatever may have been his fate, or whatever the result of his misfortunes to my own fame, I will endeavour to shield his character from obloquy, nor will I attempt the mean purpose of sacrificing his reputation to save mine. His former services and his zeal entitle him to indulgence; and, however I may lament and suffer for his errors, I will not reproach his memory if he be lost, or his character if he survive. Your letter manifests your usual judgment and spirit. We must endeavour rather to retrieve than to blame what is past, and under your auspices I entertain no doubt of success. Time however is the main consideration. Every hour that shall be left to this plunderer will be marked with some calamity; we must expect a general defection of the allies, and even confusion in our own territories, unless we can attack Holkar's main force immediately with decisive success. I trust that you will be enabled to assemble your army in sufficient time to prevent further mischief; I highly applaud your determination to leave nothing to fortune, and rather to risk the internal tranquillity of the provinces for a season, than to hazard any contest on unequal grounds with

[1] To Lake, Fort William, 11th September, 1804.

the enemy. Holkar defeated, all alarm and danger will instantly vanish. When I look at the date of this letter, I cannot entertain a shadow of apprehension for the result of this war. This is the anniversary of the battle of Delhi,—a victory gained under circumstances infinitely more unfavourable than the present. Your triumphs of last year proceeded chiefly from your vigorous system of attack. In every war the native States will always gain courage in proportion as we shall allow them to attack us; and I know that you will always bear this in mind, especially against such a power as Holkar. If we cannot reduce him, we have lost our ascendency in India. You will perceive that the only effect produced on my mind by this misfortune is an anxious solicitude to afford you every aid in remedying its consequences with every degree of despatch.'[1]

It was not till the middle of October that he learned how the great events of the preceding year had been received in England. Parliament was sitting when the account reached Government of the triumph of the armies under Lake and Arthur Wellesley, and of the complete discomfiture of Scindiah and the Rajah of Berar. The House of Lords, on the motion of Lord Hobart, unanimously voted thanks to the army and their high sense of the great and important services rendered to the empire by the late illustrious operations in India. They attributed the brilliant and glorious successes which had crowned our arms in that quarter of the globe to the vigorous and comprehensive system of measures pursued by the Marquess Wellesley for bringing the various armies with promptitude and effect into the field. On the same day Castlereagh moved a like resolution of thanks in the Commons. He disclaimed any wish to commit the House to a premature approval of the policy of the Mahratta war; but of its splendid

[1] To Lake, Fort William, 11th September, 1804.

success they must all be proud. After detaching a considerable force to Ceylon, and making provision for the safety of other parts of India, Lord Wellesley was able to bring into the field against Scindiah 55,000 men. Every part of the plan of attack manifested such a degree of skill and arrangement as particularly entitled him to the gratitude of the country. It was the same judgment and vigilance which had been evinced in the complete overthrow of the late sovereign of Mysore. In three months Generals Lake and Wellesley had made more extensive conquests and won more decisive victories than had ever been achieved in the same space of time in our military history. Eight fortified places had been taken, four of these by escalade. Four pitched battles had been fought and won. In that of Assye, with 4,500 troops General Wellesley defeated a force of ten times that number, formidable from discipline, familiar with tactics, and capable of varied and rapid evolution. At Lâswarri, within forty-eight hours before the engagement, our troops had marched sixty five miles, and they had to confront twice their number, under European officers and well sustained by artillery.

Francis hesitated to endorse the policy, while he extolled the prowess displayed in the field. Fox and Grey did not wish to be committed on incomplete information to all that had been done; and Wilberforce, though he hoped and believed that eventually it would appear that a collision could not have been avoided, and that a quarrel had not been provoked, felt that he was still groping in the dark for the precise motives that had led to war, and for the justification of the additions made to our territory. No one however was disposed to challenge the proposed resolution, and it passed without a division.

It was in allusion to these judgments of Parliament that Grenville, a few days afterwards, when acknowledging the pleasure he derived from the uninterrupted interchange of old sympathies and sentiments wrote,—' I have not done more for you than you would have done for me on a like occasion; and if the intrigue planned against you is totally without effect, and your measures have been approved before they were arraigned, I cannot flatter myself with having contributed to this result by my efforts; but you may in my opinion, consider the affair as terminated.' By a strange accident Grenville's letter was intercepted at sea by a French ship of war, and with many others of a confidential nature relating to the politics of the day published at Paris, and reproduced in England some months before it ought to have reached its destination. It described minutely the condition of parties in the spring of 1804; the widening severance of the writer from Addington; and his renunciation of the enmity he formerly entertained when in office to the Old Opposition. Anticipating his correspondent's early return to England, the only advice he wished to give him was, ' not to engage for anything until he returned; but to retain the liberty of acting according to such motives as he should judge proper to direct his conduct when on the spot.'

The Court of Directors, without pronouncing an opinion on the political questions involved in the late campaign, had resolved that, ' taking into consideration the despatches relative to the late brilliant successes in the war with the Mahratta chiefs, their thanks be given to Marquess Wellesley for the zeal, vigour, activity, and ability displayed in preparing the armies of the several Presidencies to take the field, to which might be attributed in a great measure, the rapid and brilliant successes which had crowned the British arms in the East Indies.' The Court of Proprietors, notwithstanding the prevalence of bitter antipathies to his person and policy avowedly cherished by not a few, felt constrained to join in the general acclamation, and recorded their thanks in identical terms. The acknowledgments, simultaneously made, of the eminent services of the generals and of the troops under their command, were duly published in the 'Calcutta Gazette' of October 26; but qualified by political reservations. With those regarding his own conduct, which the resolutions contained, he determined to abstain from giving them publicity. Months elapsed before he could bring his haughty spirit to explain the cause of his refusal to make known what he regarded as valueless and invidious praise. 'I have never been required to offer a greater or more painful sacrifice to public duty than that by which I renounced the satisfaction of publishing in India the marks of approbation and honour conferred upon me by your Honourable Court, and by the Court of Proprietors; but it appeared to me to be necessary to submit the high personal distinction, which I should have derived from such a publication, to more important considerations of the public safety, and of the interests of the Company and of the nation. The determination expressed to withhold all judgment upon the original justice, necessity, and policy of the war, could not have been published in India by a formal act of the Government without conveying an universal impression of doubt and ambiguity respecting the stability of every arrangement connected with the progress and success of our arms. The permanency of all the treaties of peace, partition, subsidy, and alliance must have been exposed to hazard by such a public declaration, proceeding from the high authority of your Honourable Court and the Court of Proprietors; and announced by your Government in India to all your subjects, dependents, and allies. It could not be supposed that either your Honourable Court, or the Court of Proprietors, would try the justice of our cause by the success of our arms; the prosperous result of the war, therefore, could not have removed the doubts of its justice arising from the reservations expressed in your resolutions; and the irresistible inference in the minds of all the native States would have been, that your Honourable Court and the Court of Proprietors might ultimately censure the whole transaction; while the general fame of your equity and magnanimity would have precluded any supposition that in condemning the justice of our cause, you would retain the fruits of our success, or enjoy the benefits of the peace while you repudiated the necessity and policy of the war. If the origin and policy of the war shall ultimately be condemned, and the treaties of peace, partition, subsidy, and alliance shall finally be abrogated by the commands of your Honourable Court, those commands will be issued in such terms, and accompanied by such arrangements, as shall render the execution of your orders an additional bulwark to the public safety, and a fresh security to the public faith. During whatever interval of time your Honourable Court may be pleased to suspend your determination, it would neither be consistent with the welfare of the Honourable Company in India, nor with the respect due to your high authority, that one of your servants, for the gratification of personal ambition, by the ostentatious display of the honours which you had been pleased to confer upon him, should pursue a course which might embarrass the free and deliberate exercise of your wisdom and justice in a matter of the utmost importance to the national interests and honour; or that, by a premature and unseasonable publication of your favourable acceptance of his services, the same servant should risk the main object of those services, and endanger the immediate security of a great political system of arrangement which it might possibly be your future pleasure to confirm.'[1]

In October he learned that Mr. Addington's Administration was at an end, and that Pitt was again in power. Dundas had become First Lord of the Admiralty, and

[1] To the Court of Directors, 23rd March, 1805.

Castlereagh, who continued at the Board of Control, apprised his friend at Fort William of all that had taken place, and of Pitt's desire that suitable honours and rewards should be bestowed in India. Lake should have a peerage and a pension; Arthur Wellesley the Order of the Bath. 'In considering what was due to others, his own strong claims upon the King's favour did not escape Mr. Pitt's notice; he conceived however, that whatever distinction the King might be graciously disposed ultimately to confer upon his lordship, such a mark of his Majesty's approbation would be bestowed in a manner more honourable to his character, and at a moment more consonant to his feelings, at the winding up of the important transactions in which he was now engaged, than while they were yet depending.'[1] Sustained and stimulated by Wellesley, Lake became the assailant, and at the head of British dragoons and Sepoy horse literally hunted Jeswunt-Rao and his predatory host from point to point in the contested Dooab, until at length he came up at night with them at Futteghur, where they were suprised and routed with great loss. Holkar thenceforth kept within his own confines, but they were wide, and the remainder of the campaign, though full of gallant deeds, was indecisive. The Rajah of Bhurtpore sided against us, and after repeated assaults, his citadel remained impregnable. Delhi, on the other hand, was successfully defended, and Deag was taken by storm. But the continuance of the struggle month after month made Scindiah and Boonslah repent their having prematurely given in; and the drain on the Exchequer began to make the most devoted believer in the Governor-General's statesmanship and strategy look grave.

The year 1804 closed in gloom; Malwa, though overrun, was not subdued; Bhurtpore, though closely invested, was not taken; the first attempt at escalade was repulsed on Christmas

[1] Received at Calcutta 14th October, 1804.

Eve, the fourth on the 21st February. Scindiah evaded the demands to give any categorical assurance that he would not break the peace; and when the Resident was about to leave his court he found himself no longer free to do so. At another time so glaring a breach of international privilege would have fired the indignation of the Governor-General, and drawn forth quick and scathing flashes of his wrath. But he began to feel that he had done enough for personal self-assertion, and enough for national honour. The Treasury was empty. His time for quitting India must be nigh at hand. Already Barlow had been named to fill provisionally the seat of supreme authority on his vacating it; and any day might bring a successor permanently to take his place. Private communication from England revealed the weakness of the Administration and prepared him for the abandonment of his policy in the East. Two or three months passed without decisive intelligence as to Mr. Pitt's intentions; and in the absorbing interest of the aggravated struggle with France, he saw that it was vain to look for additional military force from Europe. He deemed it therefore a duty to leave a final decision for terms of peace with Holkar to whoever should come after him.

In May 1805, two letters were received in Calcutta by the overland route, announcing the reappointment of Lord Cornwallis to the Governor-Generalship of India. One of these letters was received by Mr. J. Alexander, the other by Mr. Tucker. Both gentlemen determined to keep their information to themselves; but a rumour was soon in circulation to the effect that overland letters had been received in Calcutta, and Lord Wellesley sent for Mr. Tucker. After some conversation the Governor-General exclaimed: 'I hear you have received letters from England.' Mr. Tucker assented, and Lord Wellesley asked, 'Do they contain any news of importance?' 'The appointment of Lord Cornwallis,' was the reply. The accomplished actor was too much master of himself to indidicate, by look or gesture, any opinion of the choice which had been made. But he had abundant information from confidential sources of the reasons which had led to it, and he well knew that it implied the reversal, in many essential particulars, if not the general renunciation of his comprehensive policy.[1]

When the news of Monson's retreat reached England, early in 1805, the faith of Government and the patience of the Company gave way. The proprietary were in financial despair at the dissipation of all their hopes of profit from peace, so confidently promised as secured; and Pitt's second Administration was too weak and disheartened to assume the responsibility of defending the policy of fighting on till Holkar should be extinguished. What had been won was all very well, and we must hold by it; but what we had not achieved had best be let alone, at all events until a more convenient season. Cornwallis condemned in no measured terms, the renewal of a Mahratta war, and the retention of Gwalior and Gohud against the protests of Scindiah; he was asked if he would once more go as Captain-General, to retrench expenditure and make peace at any price. On the score of health he repeatedly declined; but yielding to the importunites of the City and Whitehall, he at last agreed to go, conscious that he was never likely to return.

On July 29 the arrival in the harbour was signalled of the ship of war which brought Cornwallis to Calcutta. Lord Wellesley, leaving Barrackpore, became the guest of Sir John Colebroke; and on the following day resigned the weighty trust he had held just seven years to his successor. The antagonism of their views could not be disguised, and the new *régime* was inaugurated without delay. The bodyguard, which so long had figured gaily in the pageants of the

[1] To General Ross, from Culford, 14th October, 1804.

capital, was disbanded, and the new Lieutenant preferred an ordinary carriage and pair to the stately equipage hitherto in daily use. He wished it to be understood, as his reason for these and innumerable other changes, that he had only been induced to undertake the labour and responsibilities of executive office from the necessity felt by the Company that retrenchment should be summary and sweeping. Tucker was induced by him to take charge once more of the department of finance; and instructions were sent to Lake to attempt nothing further, but to be satisfied to hold his ground pending negotiations. To conduct these in person the new Governor-General set out for the North-west Provinces, where his health soon gave way. Scindiah was conciliated by offers to relinquish more than one place of importance he had lost; and there is reason to believe that Agra and Delhi would have been given up but for the death of Cornwallis at Gazepore.[1] Ere that event occurred Wellesley was far on his voyage home.

[1] 5th October, 1805.

CHAPTER XV

PORTSMOUTH AND PUTNEY.

1806.

ON the voyage home the excitement in which he had lived during his Pro-Consulate had time to subside. He had abundant leisure to review the great transactions of the past seven years; to estimate calmly their relative proportions, and their probable bearing as a whole on the future destiny of his country. Naturally the question rose continually to his lips, but died unuttered there,—What will England think of me? Would Pharisaism, grudge, or parsimony prompt the Company to refuse him the acknowledgment he felt to be his due for the vast possessions he had won for them in spite of themselves; and this, without deigning to appropriate personally any part of a splendid spoil? Or, if their jealous and niggard spirit should continue inveterate because he had courteously disregarded their prohibitions to make war without leave from home, or to conclude treaties expanding the obligations of empire without permission beforehand though in every case they held his acquisitions fast,—would public opinion ratify their repudiation, or overrule ungrateful reproach? About the reception that awaited him from Sovereign and Minister, he had no misgiving. Pitt who had given him his high office, and sustained him in the discharge of his duties by his sympathy and approval, was again in power; and as he learned by the last letters he had received from mutual friends, was sanguine of being able to retrieve the losses incurred in the renewed war with France. By him he had been assured of cordial welcome; and if Grenville was no longer in the Cabinet, was there not all the more likelihood therefore that he himself would be pressed to enter it? Comparing the present with Pitt's earlier Administration, and with the formidable array of talents opposed to it, he could not help believing that he would be looked upon as an accession of whom they would be glad; and he was in fact warranted by the private letters of the Premier 'to reckon confidently upon the higheet honours and rewards the State had to bestow.' Shut up for months in the cabin of an Indiaman, with no other changes or vicissitudes to chequer the monotony of the voyage than those of the fluctuating ocean, his mind dwelt upon the past and future of a career which had occupied so large a space already in the world's history; and which at forty-five he might well believe had yet long years of usefulness and fame to run. Egotism, in the apt illustration of Coleridge, 'like a fish in a globe of glass, pursues its ceaseless way without making progress or quitting its vital element.' He recurred to his favourite books, and wrote letters on chance of finding his long-neglected correspondents still alive; and paced the deck when the weather was fair, and tried hard to sleep when it was foul; but the weary months of the passage round the Cape were mainly occupied with anticipations of the reception he was to meet with at its close. As the event drew near, he grew nervous and querulous to a degree painful and uncontrollable. One of his morbid apprehensions was that relatives or friends would think that he was much changed by his residence in a tropical climate. He did not want to be told that he was changed. He persuaded himself in point of fact, that he was better and stronger than ever he had been; and so was that *vis vivida* in him which our sensitive natures only learn to enjoy and to avow when we have succeeded thoroughly and greatly. He might well be pardoned the buoyant belief that his countrymen would appreciate the great things he had done—the greatest things done by any man of the time. He forgot that memory beyond yesterday, and forethought beyond tomorrow, are unknown qualities in the multitude; and that among the reflecting and forecasting few, personal ambition, rivalry, antagonism, absorption in effort, and vindication of misconceived motives preoccupy attention to an extent that leaves but scant leisure for effusive salutation. He had stared at the blaze of his own glory till he had grown blind to the dull and disenchanting truth that ninety-nine out of every hundred people in England knew nothing about him. Yet into the tepid and muddy sea of uninquisitive indifference his self-importance was about to be quietly dropped down the side of the Indiaman come to anchor in the Solent.

Lady Wellesley and her children awaited him on landing, and several private friends pressed round him with kind welcomes. The Port-Admiral was there also, and certain military officials eager to see the little man of whom they had heard so much, and of being able to say that he had shaken them by the hand, a familiarity the thought of which had never occurred to him. There was in short, no lack of fuss, and even of affection; enough to content any ordinary general or envoy returning home. But he was neither. He had been playing king until the rarefied atmosphere of kingship had become so habitual that the murk of commonplace in the best room of the best inn in a half-lighted seaport town almost stifled him. Had the successor of Aurungzebe come to this? There he was, with wife and children, and two or three friends from town, after all his impersonation of paramount power and enjoyment of Oriental magnificence, made much of by vulgar waiters, just like any other Irish marquess on his travels. He did his best to look pleased and be gracious;

but his mortification was unspeakable; and ere dinner was half over he broke out in expletives of impatience that made the circle stare. Hyacinthe, forgetting all that had changed their lot in life since the time when as a youthful and hardly-known official he had sat at her feet adoringly, said with an unlucky laugh,—'Ah! you must not think you are in India still, where everybody ran to obey you. They mind nobody here.' The disenchantment was complete. He rose early from table and withdrew, saying he was ill, and must be left alone; nor could any subsequent explanation or expostulation mend the matter. It was the foretaste of a long course of disappointment and vexation, wholly unanticipated, that was in store for him.

On his arrival in town the welcome of many cordial friends awaited him. His first visits were to Sidmouth, by whom he had been, upon the whole, well sustained during his Indian administration; and to Grenville, who also had parted company with their illustrious chief, and who was out of office.

Pitt was at Bath, where the waters had proved unavailing to renovate his health, as they had been wont to do; and as Parliament was about to reassemble, he crept by easy stages back to his residence at Putney Hill, where a letter from Wellesley awaited him. His reply was one of the last he had the strength to write.

'My dear Wellesley,—On my arrival here last night I received with inexpressible pleasure, your most friendly and affectionate letter. If I was not strongly advised to keep out of London till I have acquired a little more strength, I would have come up immediately, for the purpose of seeing you at the first possible moment. As it is, I am afraid I must trust to your goodness to give me the satisfaction of seeing you here the first hour you can spare for the purpose. If you can, without inconvenience, make it about the middle of the day (in English style, between two and four), it would suit me rather better than any other time; but none can be inconvenient. I am recovering rather slowly from stomach complaints, followed by severe attacks of gout; but I believe I am now in the real way of amendment.

'Ever most truly and affectionately yours,
'W. PITT.'

How he clung to life and power fast fading from his grasp! He would not be thought as low as he really was, many hours in the day being too prostrate to attend to any subject of importance, and gradually becoming too weak to take the requisite amount of nourishment. But the unquailing spirit struggled hard, during every respite from pain, to forget the thraldom of disease, and escape 'shades of the prison-house begun to close' on his declining days. He could not be unconscious that his second Administration had so far failed to reanimate the hope and faith of the country. The glory of Trafalgar had not sufficed to countervail the depression caused by Austerlitz; and to meet his adversaries in debate his second Cabinet had no longer the resources of experience and ability by which his Government had been distinguished in better times. It can hardly be doubted that he looked on his early favourite, now reappearing on the scene with all the prestige of administrative success about him, as an ally just come in time, to whom it was only necessary to assign a suitable position. Nor is it likely, had the opportunity been afforded, that Wellesley would have been dissuaded by the misgivings of others, or the difficulties of the situation, from accepting a seat in the Cabinet.

On Monday, the 12th, Pitt saw Castlereagh and Hawkesbury at his house at Putney. When they were gone he was much depressed, and told the Bishop of Lincoln that he knew he could not recover. Next day he felt better, and received Lord Wellesley, who was ' the last official friend he saw. Instinctively they kept clear of business ; but the conversation with an intimate so long absent overcame him, and he fainted away before his visitor left the room.' Whatever may have been the Ex-Governor's hopes on his way to Putney, they were wholly dissipated by his visit there. His own account of the interview was given in a letter to a private friend:—' I was received by Mr. Pitt with his usual kindness and good humour. His spirits appeared to be as high as I had ever seen them, and his understanding quite as vigorous and clear. Amongst other topics, he told me, with great kindness and feeling that, since he had seen me, he had been happy to become acquainted with my brother Arthur, of whom he spoke in the highest terms of commendation. " I never met with any military officer," he said, " with whom it was so satisfactory to converse; he states every difficulty before he undertakes any service, none after he has undertaken it." But notwithstanding his kindness and cheerfulness, I saw that the hand of death was fixed upon him. This melancholy truth was not known or believed by either his friends or opponents. In the number of the latter, to my deep affliction, I found my highly respected and esteemed friend, Lord Grenville ; and I collected that measures of the utmost hostility were to be proposed in both Houses at the meeting of Parliament. I warned Lord Grenville of Mr. Pitt's approaching death. He received the fatal intelligence with the utmost feeling in an agony of tears, and immediately determined that all hostility in Parliament should be suspended.' Though full of sad foreboding, Wellesley scarcely thought that he had pressed the emaciated hand for the last time, and that he should see his face no more. But the end came rapidly, and within ten days Pitt, whom he looked up to as to no other man, had ceased to be.

Brougham says that Wellesley was looked upon as the person best fitted to take his place at the head of the Tory Administration, but that from a sense of delicacy he declined being put forward while Paull's accusation in Parliament was pending.

There is not a hint of this having ever been thought of, in the diary and correspondence of Malmesbury, who knew everything from the Duke of York, with whom he discussed the possibilities from day to day, and from Bathurst, Canning, Hawkesbury, and Palmerston, with whom he lived on the most intimate terms. With his Royal Highness he argued that to attempt to patch up the concern would end only in failure and humiliation, because there was nobody to be found in public estimation who could be named as successor to Pitt. And he pressed this view until the Duke grew angry, and showed reserve for several days. From Canning, too, he differed as to the duty of the out-going party keeping together, which his lordship did not see. But with neither is there an allusion to the ex-Proconsul for Premier. Not even when, some months later, an attempt was made at rally and reorganisation against the Talents, is there a word of anyone being named as head of the party, except the Duke of Portland.

What more than all else is conclusive on the point may be read in a letter from Wellesley himself to Wilberforce:

'I know nothing of public arrangements, and all the reports in the newspapers respecting myself are utterly groundless. To you I think it my duty to declare that the memory of my ever-to-be-lamented friend will always be the primary object of my veneration and attachment in public life, but I will never lend my hand to sustain any system of administration evidently inadequate to the difficulties and danger of the crisis. I shall be most happy to labour in any way which may promise advantage to the public service; but, having no personal object or pursuit, I shall not easily be deluded from the solemn conviction of my mind, that our recent loss cannot be repaired, nor our imminent perils be averted, otherwise than by an union of the approved talents and highest characters of the nation.'[1]

In the interval of political suspense which followed, a disappointment of a very different kind came unexpectedly upon him. Relatives and intimates delayed, while they could, to acquaint him fully with the nature of the attacks which had been made upon his character and government towards the close of the preceding session; and of which he had heard only such passing notices as to excite his contempt. But as the time for their threatened renewal drew near, it became impossible to disguise their gravity, or to defer consulting him personally as to the defence to be taken of his acts and motives. Wellesley Pole and Lord Temple undertook the painful task of making him understand that, instead of being saluted as a conqueror, it was seriously proposed that he should be tried as a culprit. All the preliminaries of national impeachment in the case of Hastings had in fact, been copied or parodied with regard to him; and however he might scoff at the disparity between his assailants and the great accuser who, by force of his persistent will and matchless powers of invective, had dragged to the bar of justice the 'captain-general of iniquity,' and however proudly he might exult in his own unsullied freedom from all imputations of cupidity or corruption, the mortifying truth quickly forced itself upon him that his public reputation was overcast by a cloud which friends might call no bigger than a man's hand, but which he felt, if not dispelled, would darken the whole field of his future in life. His chagrin was so intense

[1] Letter from Lord Wellesley to William Wilberforce, Park Lane, 15th January, 1806.

that he refused to take the oaths and his seat in the House of Lords, declaring, in a transport of passion, that until his slanderers were silenced he would not exercise any privilege as a peer. And though at the funeral of Mr. Pitt he walked with Lords Grenville, Abercorn, Euston, Bathurst, and Lowther, as a special mourner, he would not be persuaded to forego his angry resolve of abstaining from attendance in Parliament. It was, as he subsequently came to see, one of the greatest errors of his life, not merely because it filled his traducers with exultation, or because it chilled his friends with a vague sense of misgiving; but because it was the desertion of duties he had no right to renounce at the questioning of men whom in private he branded with every epithet of scorn. But Wellesley was a woman in susceptibility of feeling, though in daring and endurance a man amongst men Whether, if he had taken the opposite course, and calmly defied calumny, his name would have been included in the new Administration, we can never know. Grenville would not have shrunk from naming him to the King, for he showed throughout an unfaltering faith in his integrity, and he was a man who shrunk from nothing that he thought right. On the other hand Fox, from the first betrayed no little prejudice against him; Grey not so much; but Windham and Sheridan were among the bitterest of his accusers. Whence all the mischief, and for a time all the misery flowed, we must look back a little to descry.

For some time ere he quitted India, an obscure malcontent, whose enmity he had never even suspected, was gathering the materials for defamation at home, and with singular energy preparing to compass his ruin. James Paull, a native of Wisbeach, was bred a linen-draper; but being of a venturous turn, and not without some advantages of education, he had while young sought quicker fortune in the far-off East. He traded for several years at Lucknow in English wares. But in 1802 he was, for some reason never clearly explained, banished from Oude. His affairs would thereby have been reduced to ruin but for the intervention of the Governor General. On February 9, 1803, he wrote to Major Malcolm, then secretary at Calcutta, 'that he thenceforth carried on his extensive concerns quietly and unmolested. Knowing with what satisfaction his Excellency on all occasions remedied any injuries that were made known to him, he had taken the liberty of addressing him directly, pointing out a very serious and extensive injury that he experienced from the conduct of the Government customs-master, particularly injuries to him from the magnitude of his exports from Oude. Indeed, so vexatious were the heavy and arbitrary exactions at Ghauzepore, where no rate of valuation was defined, that they almost compelled him to stop business altogether; and any direct complaint against Mr. Ryder (the local resident) would only render things worse. He seriously trusted he had not offended his Excellency in the mode of transmitting his address. His friend Sydenham told him that direct communication with his lordship was the best. If, therefore, he had offended it was most unintentional. For sensibly did he feel the obligation he was under to his Excellency, for whom he had only sentiments of gratitude and profound respect.'[1]

This obsequious acknowledgment of the kindly disposition and public merit of the Governor-General, it need hardly be observed, was long subsequent to the Treaty of Cession made by him with the Nawab Vizier; and so long as Paull found it profitable to remain in Lucknow, his noble benefactor was the best of men. But in 1804 he seems to have quarrelled with the native authorities; and not being able to induce those at Fort William again to interpose on his behalf, he transferred the good-will of his business to others, and

[1] Auber, *British Power in India*, ii. 388.

returned home, full of resentment at their neglect of what he called his commercial wrongs. Part of the profits he had managed to save he resolved to invest in a seat in Parliament, in order to set up in the business of an un-common informer. Denunciations of misrule in Asia had lost somewhat of their power to fascinate the public mind; but they had still the vague charm of gloom and grandeur about them; and the proofs of official shortcomings in Lord Melville's case had predisposed the public ear to listen with credulity to other charges against other members of the same Administration. Newtown, in the Isle of Wight, happened to be in the market. It had long been a legislative lodging-house where inferior politicians put up for the session at a somewhat exorbitant charge. In the Pension-Book of Charles II. an entry stood: 'Sir John Holmes, a cowardly, baffled sea-captain, twice boxed and once whipped with a dog-whip, was chosen in the night, without the head officer of Newtown, and but one burgess present; yet voted this last election, and was re-elected.' Its condition had not improved during the following century, having neither church, town hall, or officer of any description; a mere collection of seafarers' huts, two of which had lately been bought from Lord Mount-Edgcumbe by Sir Richard Worsley for 2,000 guineas. It paid but 3*s.* 8*d.* yearly to the land tax; and at the period in question, of its thirty-three so-called electors, one only happened to reside. Nevertheless its joint owners, the Honourable Charles Pelham and Sir John Barrington, returned two members to Parliament, or let the respective seats when they did not happen to want them.

Early in June 1805, the ambitious accuser took his place at St. Stephen's. Not to lose time, he moved next day for certain papers to prove how prodigal, vain, and corrupt had been the administration of Lord Wellesley, and how violent, oppressive, and cruel had been his treatment of native chiefs and people. Emulating the passionate vehemence of Burke, he assumed from the first a lofty tone of virtuous indignation at the sufferings and humiliations inflicted by the wanton insolence of English power; and of stern reprobation of the wasteful extravagance which had characterised the Governor-General's warlike parades and love of courtly display. In his high-flown descriptions, his hearers knew not how much was founded on fact and how much was but efflorescence of imagination. Without varied and minute acquaintance with details, it was vain to conjecture where the narrative of official facts and motives ended, and where imitation chapters of 'The Arabian Nights' began. His pictures of the pomp and luxury of Government House were, not without skill, placed in contrast with dark revelations of diplomatic treachery and grim details of tyranny and extortion. With scant preface he proceeded at once to charge the Marquess with ill-using a Prince of the highest rank and dignity, whose court exhibited every mark of splendour, and every proof of reverence and devotion on the part of an opulent nobility, whose jewels alone were estimated as worth four millions sterling; who was sometimes attended with five hundred elephants richly caparisoned, and whose retinue required several thousand horses: who had an army of thirteen thousand cavalry, thirty thousand foot, and a numerous artillery. He was described as being one of the most faithful of all the allies of the Company, paying a vast tribute annually, and who notwithstanding had, in defiance of justice, and in the face of the most solemn treaty, been dispossessed of a country containing upwards of three millions of attached subjects, and producing a net revenue of nearly two millions sterling yearly; because he shrunk from the alternative of resisting injustice and oppression by force of arms, and experiencing the fate of all those who had attempted to oppose the encroachments of the Company's Governors abroad. The case of this unhappy prince, degraded and disgraced in the eyes of all the world, exceeded in hardship, in every point of view, and in all its bearings, that of Cheyte Singh, the Rajah of Benares, for whose expulsion from his dominions Mr. Hastings was impeached by the Commons of Great Britain; with this marked and essential distinction, that Cheyte Singh resisted demands that he thought oppressive, whereas the Vizier of Oude submitted to every demand, however illegal, arbitrary, or unjust. His character had been described by Sir John Shore as not unworthy his station; his capacity, though moderate, was not mean; his habits of economy approached to parsimony; in all his dealings he was fair and just; and if moral defects were imputable to him, they were not of the kind that offended the public eye. His public conduct was without reproach; and general tranquillity prevailed within his dominions.[1] He had been punctual generally in the payment of the monthly kist for the subsidiary force agreed to be kept up by the Company under treaty; and the misgivings as to its falling into arrear, Paull averred to be mere pretences for aggression. The Act of 1784 had expressly forbidden further territorial encroachment, as 'repugnant to the wish, the honour, and policy of the nation, and it was declared unlawful for the Governor General, without the express command of the Court of Directors, or of the Secret Committee, in any case either to declare war or commence hostilities, or enter into any treaty for making war against any of the native Princes of States of India: except when unavoidable to meet actual or impending attack; or to secure the conversion of stipulated tribute into annexed territory.' Palpably these exceptions were wide enough to leave an ambitious ruler pretences for aggressive enterprises whenever he was inclined. Direct communication overland was

[1] Despatch from the Governor-General in Council to the Secret Committee, 5th March, 1798.

in those days so tardy and uncertain as generally to preclude its being attempted ; and the course of post by sailing vessels across two oceans was seven or eight months, rendering consultation in cases of emergency impossible. The question was and must continue to be—were the emergencies the result of native combinations and intrigues, or were they of the Governor General's own creation ?

To illustrate the cupidity and corruption of Viceregal rule, great stress was laid upon the appointment of Henry Wellesley, though not a covenanted servant of the Company, or directly recognised in any way by them, as Lieutenant-Governor of Oude ; an act of fraternal preference, it was urged, at variance with law, policy, and justice. Windham, Whitbread, and Sheridan sustained, with more or less acerbity, the tone of inculpation, while Fox, too glad to forget the tedium and trouble of the last pro-consular impeachment, and groaning at the thoughts of another, submitted to be drawn within the outer circles of the eddy, without calculating how he was to avoid being again sucked into the vortex. On the other side, Lord Temple, Sir J. Anstruther, Dr. Laurence, and Wellesley Pole denounced the imputations on the retiring Governor-General as ungenerous and untrue. He was known to be on his way home: why not wait till he was on the spot, to answer for himself accusations which, until the answer came, could serve no other purpose than that of exciting unfair prejudice against him ? Castlereagh, with sagacious candour, would not refuse the papers moved for, or any other papers that could shed darkness on the subject. He understood thoroughly the reading and ruminating powers of Parliament, and how little the reputation of his illustrious friend had to fear from the multiplication of blue folios. But to quench the insinuation of jobbing, which he knew was more likely to catch unthinking credulity than any other, he quietly observed, as he sniffed the rose-bud in his button-hole, that about the Deputy-

Governorship of Oude there must be some mistake. It was indeed, a confidential trust of an arduous nature, but brief in its duration and without any pay. It turned out, in point of fact, that when in critical circumstances, a special delegate to Lucknow was considered necessary, Henry Wellesley had offered to go, with no other recompense than the increased confidence and affection of his brother. There was no more to be made of the matter, and by the advice of Fox the proposed scrutiny into general extravagance and profusion was quietly dropped likewise. It would not, indeed, have very well suited censors coming fresh o' nights from Carlton House to provoke comparisons between lavish expenditure on the banks of the Ganges and on the banks of the Thames. The Prince was just then in active Opposition; and eager to enlist recruits in Parliament, he thought it worth while to send intimation to Paull of the sympathy he felt in his proceedings.

In a curious letter, subsequently addressed to Lord Folkestone, as 'the only public man that really remained untainted by corruption,' Paull recited how, on his return from India in 1804, he took measures for obtaining a seat in Parliament, 'in order to make the conduct of the late Viceroy the subject of legal investigation.'[1] He took his place in Opposition from dislike, he said, of the principles of Mr. Pitt, and admiration of those of Mr. Fox; but also because, ' before his last departure from England, he had been honoured with very particular marks of attention and kindness by the Prince of Wales, he naturally and with great pride considered himself as belonging to his party. As he could clearly prove, he had given no small degree of satisfaction to his Royal Highness, to whom all his intentions with regard to Lord Wellesley had been fully and freely disclosed, and by whom they were unreservedly approved. At a visit made at Carlton House,

[1] In Cobbett's *Register*, 25th October, 1806.

soon after moving for the first batch of papers, 'the Prince took occasion to express his entire satisfaction at his conduct, in a manner eminently calculated to add to his zeal and perseverance in the mighty task which seeing no other man willing to undertake it, he had imposed upon himself.' 'You have opened a battery against the Marquess,' said his Royal Highness; 'his conduct in Oude has been truly shocking. I have had much conversation with my young friend Treves on the subject, who gave me the poor Nawab's picture. I trust the battery will not be silenced next session, as some Indian batteries have been.' The Prince further said that he had talked to Mr. Windham a few days before at Sir John Throgmorton's, and he congratulated Paull on the success he had experienced—'on the aid of such inflexible integrity and unbounded talent on which he might confidently rely.' This conversation occurred in July 1805, just after the prorogation.

Colonel MacMahon requested Paull, in September, at the particular instance of the Prince, to tell him on what ground he should stand in case of a dissolution with regard to his seat, as it was by all means desirable to secure for the party as many seats as possible. Paull after consideration returned an unfavourable answer; and Colonel MacMahon assured him, from his Royal Highness, that at the general election, he should be so placed as to a seat as to leave him no reason to regret that he had, without adverting to personal considerations, entered Parliament at a most critical epoch. The same assurance was not only repeated in January 1806, but a borough in Cornwall was named by the private secretary, who mentioned that the Prince had with his own hand inserted his name a few evenings before, together with those of the Hon. G. Lamb, Sir John Shelley, and others, as candidates to be retained for the favoured boroughs.

Several gentlemen who had just left Brighton told Paull

that his cause had been talked over lately at the Pavilion; and that he was sure of the hearty support of the Fox party, particularly with every one connected with Carlton House. 'But men,' he adds with plaintive patriotism, 'did not then anticipate the events which the death of Mr. Pitt were preparing; or seeing his spirit prevail with increased influence after death had silenced his delusive voice, and the tomb had received his earthly remains; with the silent and submissive acquiescence of those men, and of that man in particular to whom so many had always looked up as an example of high spirit and just and humane sentiments, he had ere long to find that all the promises he had relied on had gone to the winds, and that he was left, with a few exceptions, to contend against all the influence and arrogance of unbridled power.'[1]

Though the session of 1805 had closed without anything being done, Paull had become an object of curiosity, and in a certain degree of interest, with many active politicians, amongst others with Cobbett and Sir Francis Burdett, by whom he was introduced to Horne Tooke; to whose Sunday dinners at Putney he had a general invitation, of which he was not remiss in availing himself, as his learned host did not fail to remind him, when they fell out afterwards. Cobbett was too keen a sportsman not to pat on the back, as he said, a setter that could find such excellent game; and the applause of the 'Register,' then in the freshness of its ribald power, was enough to turn the head of any man unused to notoriety and elated with a first success.

In accordance with the general feeling, that the country stood in need of all the available talent and experience its

---

[1] The exceptions he enumerates were Mr. Windham, Doctor Laurence, Lord Ossulston, the Marquis of Douglas, Lord Archibald Hamilton, Mr. Martin of Galway, Lord Folkestone, Mr. Martin of Tewkesbury, Sir John Wrottesley, Sir William Geary, and Mr. William Smith.

service could command, the King sent for Lord Grenville, and, without restriction, bade him choose his comrades in a new Administration. He had in earlier life served with Fox, and later in the Cabinet with Pitt. Without the former he told George III. that it would be impossible to go on; but if Sidmouth and his friends would join he would make the attempt. Fox became leader of the Commons, and the coalition was accepted by the King. In the preliminary conferences many questions of moment were mooted, only to be placed in abeyance: that of India amongst the rest. Paull soon became aware of the change of Parliamentary weather. On January 27, when about to move for further papers, he was summoned to Carlton House, and told by Colonel MacMahon, that the expectant Premier had spoken strongly on behalf of Lord Wellesley; and that, lest the Ministry then forming should be embarrassed, the Prince wished that he would consent, like Mr. Sheridan and Mr. Francis, 'to lie upon his oars.' To this he replied, as Cato would have done, that his character would be ruined in the eyes of all honourable men if he were to flinch at the last moment; and that 'exquisite as might be the pain of acting contrary to the wishes of the Prince,' he must do his duty. Forthwith proceeding to the House, he moved according to his notice, for further papers, and was seconded by Lord Folkestone. Next day he wrote to Fox imploring him not to swerve from the accusations which he had encouraged him to bring. In an interview, the following week, the newly appointed Minister owned that as Sheridan had dropped the Carnatic and Francis the Mahrattas, he had hoped that Paull might cease from troubling about the Nawab of Oude. If that could not be, and as Lord Grenville had resolved to stand by the Marquess, he would himself countenance a fair investigation but would pledge himself to no specific measure. It had been suggested that he and his friends might stay away; but that he would not do. He would not sound a trumpet during the preliminary stages of the investigation; but when it came on for decision he would do his duty. He acted up to his word, abstaining generally from any part in the desultory discussions that ensued. The late Ministry and their successors, though set against one another, agreed for the most part in backing Lord Wellesley.

On January 27, 1806, Mr. Paull moved for a number of papers relating to Oude, copies of which had been surreptitiously obtained by the French Government, and published in the 'Moniteur.' The Board of Control made no objection; but Sir Theophilus Metcalfe, with the irritation of an angry friend, said their production would do harm in India. Francis ridiculed his fears, and said more mischief was likely to arise from even the revelation in France of the intercepted letters of the Viceroy, which had been published in the London journals. Wallace, on the part of Government, deprecated any reservation respecting the official correspondence, and it was ordered without a division.

Paull resumed his inappeasable course of accusation in an irrelevant and rambling style to an inattentive House. Fox, as leader, made it understood that he would not interfere in the preliminary stages, but he was believed to be hostile to the policy of the ex-Governor General. Francis also professed neutrality, but he attended constantly, and always leant strongly to the accuser.

Mr. George Johnston, an intimate of Paull dissented, but Lord Folkestone supported him. Mr. Paull, in answer to what fell from the noble lord (Castlereagh), from the near relation of Lord Wellesley (Wellesley Pole), and from the Hon. and learned baronet (Sir W. Burroughs), said that the situation Mr. Henry Wellesley was appointed to was one of great trust, honour, and emolument, as would appear when the papers were laid upon the table; a situation in fact that made him second only to Marquess Wellesley, who was second to no other man in pomp and magnificence on this earth.[1]

On February 25 he moved for papers relating to the India debt, which led to a debate between Paull, Francis, Castlereagh, Fox, Morpeth, Hiley and Addington. A search for precedents regarding impeachment was ordered. On March 10 Sidmouth wrote to Grenville respecting the necessity of taking some consistent line upon the parliamentary question on the motion for India, and Grenville consulted the papers. On the same day, Johnston moved for further documents. Lord Temple, H. Addington, Wallace, and Sir T. Metcalfe took part for Lord Wellesley. Johnston, Francis, Grant (Chairman of the East India Company), Lord Folkestone and Paull blamed him ; Fox adhered to the committee's policy, but did not encourage the attack on Wellesley. On March 11, Paull moved for papers about Lord Wellesley's conduct to the Rajah of Bhurtpore, and was seconded by Folkestone. He was defended by H. Addington, and by Lord Temple in a speech of ability and spirit, that deserved the warm acknowledgments contained in a letter to his father the next day. 'I have not learnt from authority that Mr. Fox has made any satisfactory declaration of his sentiments respecting my conduct in India. But whatever may be his intentions, or the vicissitudes of public affairs, I entertain no doubt that I shall ultimately compel the public to understand the miserable delusions which have been practised upon their judgment; and that I shall obtain from the rest of the world, and from posterity, whatever portion of justice may be withheld from me in the present times. To you my dear lord, and to Lord Temple, I am indebted for a species of support, the recollection of which will ever constitute a great part of the happiness and honour of my future life.'[2]

[1] Parl. debates, v. 566.
[2] To Lord Buckingham, 12th March, 1806.

Meanwhile, Wellesley's friends in both Houses, sympathising with the invidious and mortifying position in which he was placed, invited him on March 22 to a public dinner at Almack's Rooms. The veteran General Harris, who had taken Seringapatam, occupied the chair, supported by the Duke of Montrose, Marquesses of Buckingham, Blandford, and Thomond; Earls Fortescue, Westmoreland, Winchelsea, Sandwich, Dartmouth, Chatham, Bathurst, Camden, Malmesbury, Westmeath, Carysfort, and Limerick; Lords Hawksbury, Braybrook, Auckland, Mulgrave, Carrington, Brayring, Glastonbury, Henley, Glenberbie, Clancarty, and Castlereagh; the Speaker Abbott; Sirs Evan Napean, W. Farquhar, T. Metcalfe, W. Grant, A. Wellesley, Alured Clarke, and J. Newport; Generals Phipps, Balfour, and Forbes; Messrs. Canning, Vansittart, Sullivan, Wallace, Steele, Holford, Hobhouse, H. Addington, W. Lake, Dundas, &c. The Premier wrote to say that but for illness he should certainly have been present to bear his testimony not only of affectionate regard, but of respect for the splendid services rendered to the country by his noble friend.

The first count of the indictment formally laid upon the table was entitled 'Article of charge of high crimes and misdemeanours committed by Richard Colley, Marquis Wellesley, in his transactions with respect to the Nawab Vizier of Oude.' It set forth the extent and population of the Vizierate as about the same as England and Wales.[1] Early in the year 1800 a project was sent home for approval by the Company of amicable rearrangements with Oude, for which the basis was the cession of certain contiguous districts in lieu of the annual subsidy, and the strengthening of the contingent to defend the Vizier's territory against the hostility of Zemaun Shah. A despatch from the Secret Committee[2] explicitly commended the plan 'as not less contributing to the preservation of the Nawab Vizier's dominions than to the

---

[1] Printed by order of the House of Commons, 28th May, 1806.
[2] 4th December, 1800.

relief of the Company's finances, which seemed so necessary to be made with a view to the ultimate security of our own possessions against the Afghan chief, or of any other power hostile to the British interests.' The treaty was finally concluded,[1] and the changes under it were finally approved after two years had elapsed, by the authorities in Leadenhall Street. Yet all these facts were forgotten or misrepresented in the heat of party contest, where grounds of inculpation had to be invented or assigned.

Truly appreciated for what it specifically was, and what it was not meant to be, the policy of Wellesley, though high-handed and arbitrary, was in its aim beneficent and noble. Intrusive, hazardous, costly, and sanguinary, when defied, it undoubtedly was, as have been all great revolutionary changes in the history of the world; and when it was averred that its inspiring motive was the ambition to expand the sphere of British influence and to consolidate the resources of British power in southern Asia, the allegation must be admitted to have been correct. But, compared with what preceded and followed it, the impartial annalist will say that it was elevated in purpose, frank in its negotiation, faithful to its word, magnanimous in triumph, unvindictive in defeat, in a word, anxiously and continuously bent on reconciling the reasonable pride of native local rule with the lofty over-kingship of England.

On May 10 Grenville carried the Foreign Slave Prohibition bill in the Upper House, against the King's influence, the known dislike of the Prince of Wales, and the open thwartings of two of his colleagues. It was a real vexation to Wellesley not to be present, and take part with his friend in the good work which they had begun together several years before. But nothing could induce him to enter the House of Peers during his threatened inculpation in the House of Commons.

[1] In November 1801.

Accustomed for seven years to the life of a court more luxurious than that of royalty, the ex-Governor-General was difficult to please in a residence either in town or country. The old mansion of his family, around which so many early recollections dimly hovered, was no longer available. Before he went abroad, Dangan had for several years been unoccupied, and in 1803 it was sold by his direction to the well-known Roger O'Connor for 30,000*l.*, the chief part of which was to be allowed to remain on mortgage, and to be liquidated by half-yearly instalments. These were seldom punctually met, and various attempts were made from time to time to recover possession by the Marquess, but all in vain. Roger was an adept in the wiles of the law, and inexhaustible in the artifice of cajolery and inventive falsehood. His whole life was a romance of debauchery and crime, but his honourable connections, fascinating manners, liberal professions, and versatility of resource made him the accepted lover of more than one pretty woman, the trusted friend of men like Burdett, and the idol of the populace. Had half the truth been known of him in 1803, his offer would hardly have been accepted by the agent of the Governor-General. But as the nephew of Lord Longueville and trustee of his brother Arthur O'Connor's estates in Ireland, he was deemed an eligible purchaser, though virtually little more than a tenant with the power to secure the equity of redemption. It was not long, however, before covenants against wastes were disregarded and arrears suffered to accumulate. Fine timber began to fall on the outskirts of the demesne, and valuable pastures were let for breaking up on payment of fines. Wellesley Pole authorised bills of injunction to be filed in his absent brother's name; but explicit and exhaustive affidavits in reply were after due delay put upon the file, and the work of dilapidation went steadily on. Trees and pictures were gradually made away with, never to be restored. The outer skirts of the demesne grew shrunken, and the hills towards Laracor again grew bare. The mansion still remained, until supplies being wanting to keep up the lavish style of living which the impostor claimant of regal descent indulged in, he bethought him of the device of a large fire insurance, the amount of which in a few months he contrived to realise by committing the house to the flames. The company, without dispute, paid him 7,000*l*., and he continued to reside in a portion of the ruin, which was converted into a hunting-box; dating, for many years after, his bombastic effusions from 'Dangan Castle.' Three years later, not far from the entrance gate, occurred the tragic scene with which his name was long associated. A lawless band organised by him, attacked and robbed the mail from Dublin to Galway. Considerable sums of money and other articles of value were taken, several persons were wounded, and the guard was killed. The empty mail-bags, found within the park wall, were forwarded with a few expressions of concern and horror, to the Postmaster-General, by the worthy contriver of the outrage; and, bad as his character was, no one ventured to charge him on oath with robbery any more than with arson. Some of the wretched peasants who had been accomplices in the deed were caught, endeavouring to pass a portion of the bank-notes which had been stolen; and, being unable to give a satisfactory account of how they had come by them, five of them were hanged at Trim, to appease offended justice.

CHAPTER XVI.

NOWHERE.

1806–1808.

Fox spoke for the last time on June 19, deprecating gently but earnestly the unlimited reception of unsworn evidence at the bar, the unsatisfactory nature of which, with a view to the great ends of public justice, every man of experience and discernment knew. Witnesses who chose to offer themselves might be led into desultory statements, of which the confutation might or might not be obtainable; because the House had no power to compel witnesses to answer upon oath: and unless they were prepared to prolong the session indefinitely, it was impossible to see where inquiries so conducted would end. He did not say, but it was known, that he felt averse from repeating the experiment to which he had always been a hesitating party in the case of Warren Hastings. It is a curious illustration of the tardiness with which defects in our constitutional system, even when recognised as obvious, are cured, that three score further years were suffered to elapse ere the House of Commons was induced to assert its right to enforce the examination of witnesses on oath, and thereby to put an end to one of the most manifest anomalies in Parliamentary jurisprudence.[1]

In his anxiety to bring about, if possible, the conclusion

---

[1] See report of Select Committee of 1869 recommending the change, which was carried into effect by 34 and 35 Vic. cap. 83.

of peace, Fox persisted, against the wishes of his friends and advisers, in discharging the responsible duties of his office, and inditing or correcting every detail of the negotiations. But as their frail threads snapped one by one he grew conscious that his hold of life was loosening also. Early in August, Grenville, while unwilling to anticipate the worst, felt himself bound to provide against the time when the failing powers of his colleague would no longer enable him to perform the duties, never more onerous and critical, of the Foreign Department. He turned his eyes towards Canning, who, when he held the seals in Pitt's first Administration, had been his Under Secretary, and upon the coincidence of whose views with his own regarding the war he knew he could depend. He requested Wellesley to inquire from him on what conditions he would take office; and, until Fox was convalescent (an event of which he did not yet despair), if he would undertake the general conduct of business in the Lower House, with a seat in the Cabinet. The ambassador, as Canning called him, had full power to offer Perceval any professional office he might desire; but he was not authorised to hold out any certain expectation of room being made for others of the section who adhered to them. Canning declined to sever himself from the associates with whom to the last he had acted under Mr. Pitt; but the offer was more than once renewed, and, when the recovery of Fox was declared hopeless, with many additional inducements. Wellesley paid a visit of some days to his unpersuadable friend at South Hill Park, where, during many pleasant loiterings in the open air, there was ample opportunity for discussing fully the difficulties of the situation and the perplexities of the time. Canning believed that he had succeeded in satisfying his visitor that, in honour and prudence, he was bound to consult the feelings and the claims of others, together with his own; and that if the coalition was to be modified in the sense proposed, it must be done by the express sanction of the King. Unless Chatham, Castlereagh, and Liverpool had Cabinet offices, and Eldon a seat without office (as he had 4,000*l.* a year retiring pension), he would not join. Fitz-William and Fitz-Patrick were, it was supposed, willing to make way. But the resolution to retain Windham was an almost insuperable obstacle, from the resentment felt towards him by Pitt's old friends.

It is clear that Wellesley himself was not included in any of the contemplated arrangements, and that this must have been with his own tacit acquiescence, from his consenting to act throughout as intermediary. All idea of junction was at length abandoned.

Towards the close of the session, in discussing the Indian budget, Sir Arthur Wellesley admitted that the increased expenditure in 1803 and 1804 was above 2,000,000*l.*; but he contended that, bearing in recollection the extent and efficiency of the preparations necessary for war with the Mahrattas, this was not excessive for such operations and for such exertions. At the close of Lord Wellesley's administration in 1805, the total revenues of our empire in the East were 14,279,533*l.*, the total charges 14,645,844*l.*; the interest of the debt 1,823,040*l.*, which with other items left a deficiency for the year 1805-6 of 2,655,957*l.* But this was a deficit arising entirely from war. Every branch of the revenue had improved, as he showed in detail, during the past seven years. From 8,059,880*l.* the total had risen by more than six millions a year. The discussion was prolonged for more than one sitting, until thirty-one members only being counted as present, an adjournment took place without any decision.

The Parliament called by Addington in 1802 was dissolved by Grenville,[1] in the vague, and, as it proved, vain, hope of lessening the majority pledged to religious intoler-

---
[1] 25th October, 1806.

ance; but Ministers gained no strength to compensate for the loss they had sustained by the death of their great defender in debate. Sheridan's ambition was gratified by his being named instead for Westminster, and the whole strength of the Ministerial party was brought to bear in his support. Paull, convinced during the autumn that he had been dropped by the Prince and his friends then in power, fancied that he had made sufficient name to rally round him a majority of the electors; and, supported by Sir Francis Burdett, Cobbett, Horne Tooke, and Major Cartwright, he held meetings at the 'Crown and Anchor,' in which he pledged himself to all the popular impossibilities of the day. Whitbread at the hustings deprecated his opposition rather in the tone of remonstrance than reproof, and bade those who set great store on the impeachment of Lord Wellesley believe that the proceedings need not fail though their favourite were out of Parliament. Beaten at the poll, Paull was half-stifled, half-crazed with the sympathy of the crowd, who shouted his praise more lustily than ever, and vowed that his wrongs must be set right on petition. Bribery, treating, and intimidation were averred; subscriptions to any extent in support of the petition were promised; and Sir Francis Burdett put down his name for 1,000*l*. In the new House of Commons most of the prominent Ministerialists kept their seats; but the balance of parties was not materially changed. The place of Fox was occupied, rather than filled, by Howick, whose aptitude for business and ability in debate had not yet given him anything like the personal weight which his predecessor had long possessed with his party. The Court maintained a cold and suspicious reserve; and the aspect of foreign affairs was gloomy in the extreme. As all the schemes of Pitt for resistance to Napoleon had died at Austerlitz, so those of Fox had expired at Jena; and the Berlin Decree threatened half our export trade with interdict. England was never so bereft of allies, and even the Neutrals had begun to waver. It was a time when patriotic men might well have shown themselves ready to gulp down personal jealousies and aversions, for the sake of great principles of domestic reform or great measures of foreign policy. At the opening of the session,[1] Paull was no longer to be seen among the busy and prominent members. Lords Folkestone and Archibald Hamilton were still there; but Sheridan was too busy preparing to defend the Westminster petition, and Windham too heavily laden with the cares of the War Office, to give heed to their suggestions that the Oude charge should be resumed.

Nor was Howick's accession to the leadership encouraging, though he had never lent himself to the tactics of accusation, and had no mind to multiply supernumerary foes. Government, in point of fact, never stood more in need of reinforcement. On Christmas Day Wellesley received by appointment a visit from the Speaker, to talk over the possibility of the proceedings against him being revived in the newly-chosen House of Commons. He said that he regarded Windham as his chief adversary in the Cabinet, and Howick as the best inclined to letting the affair drop. It would be highly objectionable, on grounds of public policy, to stimulate and sustain in a manner wholly unprecedented, the prosecution of a private individual before the High Court of India Judicature. This great tribunal had been specially constituted,[2] of thirteen Peers and twenty Commoners, chosen by ballot, with one judge from each of the courts of law, to try questions from India on the requisition by the Crown or the Company. Parliament, being supreme, might adjudicate instead; but should Parliament, having once taken the matter into its own hands, decline to proceed, it would be

---

[1] 19th December, 1806.
[2] By the 24 George III. chap. 25, sect. 2.

monstrous to allow any irresponsible person to take the initiative, and set such a judicial mechanism in motion. Establish this precedent, and where would such proceedings end? or how could the administration of affairs in the East be carried on? After the interview the Speaker met the First Minister, to whom he recounted what had passed, and who promised to consult with his new lieutenant as to what should be done. Dining with the Speaker two days later, Howick gave him to understand that he was not disposed to proceed any further in the business. He thought it should be left to the India Judicature, if the Board of Control or the Court of Directors invoked its judgment; but it was clear that neither one or the other would do so. Grenville confirmed this decision; and thus relieved from much anxiety on the subject, Wellesley, on the last day of the year, took the oaths and his seat in the House of Lords.

After the holidays the committee proceeded with the trial of the return for Westminster, but had not gone far when an appeal was made by Lord Folkestone on the personal petition of Paull, who invoked the direct interference of the House to prevent an alleged tampering with witnesses, and the concealment of important documents through the influence of the sitting member. If privilege were thus abused, justice could not be done. Letters of Sheridan, offering money and employment for votes, had been made away with, which, if wrung from the delinquent hands that held them, would leave no doubt that he had compassed his return by fraud, and that Westminster's true choice was the petitioner. The approvers, who could testify to the facts, were in attendance, and counsel waited to be heard. Much time was spent in desultory discussion as to the fitting mode of procedure in a case so exceptional; and some of his friends wished Sheridan to take time to consider what he should do. But with his habitual pluck, he laughed outright at his accusers, and said he would be his own counsel. Drake, who had married his natural daughter, when dismissed from the navy had hung about him in the idler's capacity of offering to be generally useful. With comrades still more disreputable, he had been busy at the election, affecting mystery where there was none, and acting in all things without authority. Of the money subscribed by the rich men of the party he counted on too large a share, and when disappointed, in a fit of drunken spite went over to the enemy. With a scoundrel named Harris he swore to having conveyed letters from Sheridan promising certain appointments as the price of votes. But on cross-examination he was forced to admit that he had written one of the letters himself and his accomplice the other; and that neither had ever been signed or seen by their patron. Discussion arose, during which witness and counsel were ordered to withdraw. But they did so only a few feet from the bar; and Paull improved the occasion to confer with Drake, and seemingly to prompt him. General Phipps called attention to the circumstance as an open disrespect to the House, on which Paull exclaimed that he was sorry he could not himself reply in his place as a member to what had been alleged regarding him, 'but when he heard an observation so gross as that which had been made by the gallant general'—the Speaker here interposed, and ordered him to withdraw. 'He wished to collect the sense of the House as to its practice, whether petitioners, having made their election to be heard by their counsel, did not relinquish their right to be heard by themselves.' Howick, as Leader of the House, was so surprised at the extraordinary conduct of the petitioner that he had only been prevented by his feelings from calling attention to the insolent and outrageous proceeding. The House was called upon to adopt some measure in vindication of its dignity; and he therefore moved that Paull should be brought to the bar, and acquainted by the Speaker with the sense entertained by the House of the impropriety of his conduct. Having been called in, the Speaker addressed him in the following terms : ' Mr. Paull, I am directed by the House to acquaint you that, in its judgment, you have been guilty of great impropriety of conduct, and committed a gross outrage upon the privileges of the House. I have further to acquaint you that, having made your election to be heard by your counsel, you are no longer entitled, according to the practice of the House, to be heard by yourself. I am also directed to inform counsel that they must confine their examination to matters of fact respecting the tampering with witnesses and suppressing of evidence.'

Harris was forced to admit that he had worn disguises, and that, when talking to Sheridan, he had passed for a chaplain. The House got thoroughly out of temper, and gave such audible signs of its anger that a third witness, Richardson, fainted in fright and was carried out for dead. Howick rose, and declared his conviction that the patience of the House had been grossly trifled with ; and moved that the conspirators should be sent to Newgate. Lord Folkestone tried to save the honour of his friend upon the plea of credulity ; but the matter had gone too far. Paull was summoned to appear next day, and having been sharply reprimanded from the Chair, was abject in apologies. Sheridan in a few scornful phrases begged him off, and he was allowed to go. Further proceedings in the election scrutiny were postponed, and ere they could be resumed the shortest of short Parliaments, with the Ministry that had summoned it, had ceased to be. George III. dismissed Lord Grenville and his colleagues for refusing a pledge in writing never to move again in the Catholic question ; and Pitt's surviving friends, recalled to power, held office for the next twenty years. Their first act was to dissolve.

Brougham, in his enthusiastic partiality, seems to have persuaded himself that, when the coalition fell, delicacy alone hindered Wellesley from taking the government while the impeachment of his administration in India was pending. There is not a trace of any such idea having entered the mind of the King, or of any of the politicians seeking office on this occasion: the competition for Pitt's mantle lay between Perceval and Canning, and it ended in the agreement to put the Duke of Portland nominally at the head, in deference to his rank and age, and because he was too easy-tempered and unmeddlesome for either to be jealous of him. The accused Pro-consul had never been in the Cabinet; his views on the Catholic question were not acceptable at Court; and he had no parliamentary connection worth considering. But he had been an especial favourite of Pitt; he was intimate with the best men of the party, and they all had the highest respect for his administrative ability, courage, versatility, and skill.

In the formation of the new Government a desire was shown that he should be included. Hawkesbury, on March 23, said he believed that there was a good chance of his taking office: all his family wished it. On the 24th Malmesbury notes in his Diary that he was wavering all day,[1] but at last decided not to accept the seals. Canning was offered the Foreign Department, but told the Duke he would give way if Wellesley or Malmesbury would accept it. When they were out of the question, he had his choice of it or the Admiralty, and asked his friend which he ought to take. Malmesbury advised the secretaryship; whereupon he went forthwith to Burlington House, and the same afternoon kissed hands.[2]

Freemantle, who gave place at the Treasury to Henry Wellesley, inveighed bitterly against the Marquess for pro-

[1] Malmesbury's Diary, iv. 376.   [2] Ibid. iv. 377.

mising general support. He was probably still angrier at the appointment of Sir Arthur as Secretary for Ireland. But the Master of Stowe did not share his resentment, and in reply to a kind letter, received one of acknowledgment and explanation, frankly defining the position. 'Your lordship is well aware of the manner in which my brother has been treated, since he came home, by those who formed the late Government, with the exception of the family and friends of Lord Grenville, Lord Sidmouth, and yourself; and you will not be surprised that he and I, and our friends, should have thought it impossible to follow those persons into Opposition, notwithstanding that it was very painful to him to separate from Lord Grenville, and to me to have any concern in politics with a Government which you should oppose. I accepted my present office on condition that it should not prevent my being employed in my profession; and considering that Lord Wellesley had determined to support the new Government,[1] and that they were likely to be placed in difficulties in Ireland, I did not think myself at liberty to decline it.'[2] The friendship of his old chief remained unbroken; but Grenville could not so easily forgive; and the old class-fellows walked no more together.

On April 30 Parliament was dissolved, Grenville, Howick, and Romilly being exceeding wroth. Sheridan and Paull stood again for Westminster: both unsuccessfully. Burdett, the newest favourite of the populace, refused to coalesce with his former *protégé*, and outran all his competitors; Lord Cochrane, as a naval hero, came in second; and Paull was in racing language, nowhere. Forgetting former kindness, and furious at this second defeat, he wrote an offensive letter to Sir Francis, upbraiding him with treacherous desertion because he would

[1] Sir G. C. Lewis errs in saying that he 'received the Garter as the pledge of his adhesion;' it was not conferred, as will be seen, until three years later.
[2] Sir A. Wellesley to the Marquess of Buckingham, 8th July, 1807.

not take the chair for him at a 'Crown and Anchor' meeting. The reply heaped only fuel on his wrath; and a challenge was the consequence. No tragi-comedy was ever more complete in all its parts. On arriving at Wimbledon, Mr. Bellenden Ker acting on behalf of Sir Francis, tried in vain to ascertain from his opponent's second who he was and where he lived; but beyond the fact that his name was Cooper, that he knew nothing of such affairs, and was very sorry to be there at all, he would tell nothing. But one pair of pistols proved available for deadly purposes; lots were drawn for these, and for who should give the word to fire. It fell upon the peaceful Mr. Cooper, who retired so far behind a tree that neither of the combatants could see the signal. Mr. Ker had at last to perform the duty. Shots were exchanged and both parties were wounded. But one carriage was within call, and in this the belligerents and their friends returned to town. The newly-elected member lay up for a week, and then came forth once more in St. James's Street to receive the congratulations of his friends. His adversary was less fortunate. His wound, though not in any vital part, proved lingering and serious. From unaccustomed notoriety he found himself fallen into ridicule and neglect. A controversy with Horne Tooke (a singularly disagreeable antagonist at the best of times) had kept him in a fever when his physicians would have kept him cool. All his spare money had been spent upon elections; returns from India were dilatory and disappointing, and the remainder of the wasted session hardly sufficed for one or two motions for supplementary papers about India. He occupied himself with writing various accounts of his past career, sometimes in pamphlet form and sometimes in that of communications to the daily papers; two or three of his parliamentary allies looked in from time to time, and tried to soothe his disappointment with assurances that they would not give up the cause until he should be again amongst them ; but he had ceased to be an object of interest or fear ; and the world at length forgot to ask what had become of him.

The result of the general election was that the Ministers had a working majority. The Court, out of the privy purse, were said to have bought every purchasable seat. Perceval's biographer contends that there is no evidence of the Portland Administration doing more in that way than the most virtuous of their predecessors.[1]

The 'No Popery Parliament' met in June. Canning chafed at the want of a comprehensive policy, and declined dining at Perceval's, where the speech from the Throne was read. The Address was carried in the Lords by 160 to 67. Wellesley's name does not appear in the division. In the Commons it was carried by 350 to 255—in the fullest house ever known. Notwithstanding this great numerical preponderance Government seemed weak and timid, and Lord Temple wrote sneeringly, 'it proved a chattering lawyer does not make a great manager of the House of Commons.' But the Grenvilles were intensely prejudiced against Perceval, and much underrated, as the sequel proved, his capacity for leadership. He had patience, readiness, and temper ; a thorough acquaintance with the everyday working of the law ; a personal reputation without blemish, and the entire confidence of the King.

Wellesley owed too much to the Grenvilles to render it easy for him to take part actively with those who had driven them from power. Bathurst, Castlereagh, Hawkesbury, and Canning were his intimates of long standing : and in the Portland Cabinet there was not one who had lent any countenance to Paull, or who would hesitate about voting against Folkestone, whom they looked on as a dangerous lunatic. There he sat, with the obdurate air of an accuser waiting for the trial to be called on, of

[1] *Life of Perceval*, i. 252.

great offences said to be committed by a great criminal, which some at least of the outgoing Cabinet had professed to believe provable, and which men like Francis, Creevey, and Hamilton still declared they would prove. The most memorable of all accusations in the history of Parliament was not abandoned when its shameless author had broken down. It was after Titus Oates had stood in the pillory and been burnt in the hand, and Shaftesbury had taken up his lying parable, that Lord Stafford and Archbishop Plunket were put to death for the sham plot. Times had grown less sanguinary; but the love of lion-hunting had not become extinct. Burke had spent five years in prosecuting Hastings, and found congenial excitement and the recompense of the widest celebrity in the performance of the task. The very difficulty and hazard of the chase are its chief allurements; it may eventually fail, and the noble prey escape the toils; but while he crouches for the spring, there is no meddling with him.

On June 29 Folkestone moved to reprint the Oude papers of the previous session, and stated his desire to bring forward the charges made in the former Parliament against the late ruler of India. Sir John Anstruther, Mr. H. Addington, and Sir A. Wellesley urged that the decision should not be indefinitely postponed. In reply, Folkestone said he must consult others before fixing a day. Nothing further was done owing to the lateness of the session, and the most susceptible and ambitious of men, in August, saw another prorogation, with an indecisive judgment suspended over his head; leaving the uninformed still in doubt whether he had proved himself to be a reckless and sanguinary oppressor, or a great statesman who had ruled an empire honourably. The fever of vexation in which indefinite postponement and constantly renewed menace keep a proud and sensitive man cannot be easily imagined; cannot be realised at all by any who have not similarly suffered. As already mentioned, his brother Arthur was made Chief Secretary for Ireland; his chief qualification being that, in the Executive there, any day there might be imminent need of military experience and discretion. How little of the arbitrary spirit or summary tone of the camp the newly appointed Minister brought to the discharge of his civil duties his confidential correspondence of the period shows strikingly enough.[1] He had not long been established in his office when Castlereagh asked Lord Wellesley to ascertain if he would take a command in the expedition secretly fitting out for Holstein, with a view of preventing Denmark becoming the open ally of France. The service was so critical, and the confidence implied on the part of the Government so rare, that there could be little room for hesitation.* Without assigning any ostensible reason for adjourning discussions upon various local questions, magisterial and ecclesiastical, he temporarily quitted his post in Ireland, and prepared again for active service abroad. In the memorable events that ensued he bore a conspicuous part, and for his reward was raised to the rank of Lieutenant-General. When the captured Danish fleet was anchored in the Downs, he quietly resumed his perusal of police reports and correspondence with bishops and judges, as if nothing particular had happened in the interim. Brother Richard was more proud of him than ever. 'He always said that Arthur had talents, and whenever there was opportunity that he would prove it.' Nor was it less gratifying that Henry, of whom he was still fonder, was appointed one of the Secretaries of the Treasury.

Perceval led the Commons plausibly and circumspectly. Howick had gone to the Lords, and Plunket gone back to the bar. Sheridan and Whitbread, Francis and Windham,

---

[1] Some of the more remarkable passages in his letters from Dublin will be noticed elsewhere.

had in varied degrees the power of worrying; and in debate they greatly over-matched all their Ministerial opponents but Canning. In the Lords the new Government were equally at a disadvantage, and their chief aim appeared to be to tide over questions of domestic policy and fix public attention on Continental affairs. All the schemes of official advancement with which the Marquess had occupied himself seemed doomed to adjournment *sine die*. His domestic relations did not improve with the tantalising strain upon his temper. Madame had grown querulous and pretentious as he grew petulant and irritable; her society no longer had for him the charm it once possessed; and he gave himself up to other associations with as little disguise as was the prevailing fashion of the day. At Court he was always received with *empressement*; and at half the great houses in England he was welcomed with honour. He could hardly be looked upon as a party man, for he had during a whole decade absolutely taken no part in home politics. Leading men on both sides desired his adhesion and sought his friendship; and the incense thus offered to his self-importance was too grateful to be dissipated by envious disparagement or ill-natured sneers. Autumn passed away in pleasures that profited nothing, and it was the spring of 1808 before any serious change seemed likely to take place in his condition.

A letter, in pamphlet form, was in January addressed anonymously to Lord Wellesley, on the perplexities of Ireland; which Speaker Abbot believed to be Grattan's, and ' in his best style and best sense, approaching nearer to the truth than anything he had seen.' It turned out to be from the pen of John Wilson Croker, a young barrister then unknown, who in the following year entered Parliament, by an unlooked-for chance, as member for Downpatrick.[1]

In the speech from the Throne, at the opening of the next

[1] *A Sketch of the State of Ireland, Past and Present.* Dublin: Mahon, 1808.

session,[1] the chief topic was the policy of taking and detaining the Danish fleet, without a previous declaration of war, which gave rise to animated debates in both Houses. The Duke of Norfolk moved for papers[2] containing the substance of all the communications that had been made to Ministers in the course of the past year with respect to the state of the Danish navy, of any apparent increase thereof, or of any steps taken to prepare the same for sea; the proclamation and correspondence of our commanders at Copenhagen, and the substance of all the recent communications respecting the secret articles of the Treaty of Tilsit. He was supported by Lords Hutchinson, Erskine, Buckinghamshire, Moira, Jersey, St. Vincent, Grey, Darnley, and Sidmouth. He was opposed by Lords Borringdon, Harrowby, Limerick, Hawkesbury, Mulgrave, and Wellesley. It was the first occasion on which the voice of the late Governor General of India was heard in the House of Peers, and there was not a little curiosity as to the tone he was likely to assume, and the place in debate he was in future to occupy. Lord Folkestone's motion of censure awaited in the Commons its long-deferred hearing. But weary of tantalisation and regardless of empty threats, the Marquess resolved to break silence, and assert his well-earned right to pronounce judgment on the greatest question of the day. As soon as the mover of the amendment sat down he rose, and though intensely nervous and anxious, with the imperturbable calm and consummate air of ease he knew so well how to assume, he entered at length upon the antecedents and strategic circumstances of the situation. In the words of Lord Hawkesbury (afterwards Premier), the cause, not so much of Ministers, as of the country, was successfully maintained by his eloquent and argumentative speech. He warmly approved of the expedition. 'If it were said that the junction of the Danish fleet with the French could not

[1] 21st January, 1808.   [2] 8th February, 1808.

create any serious danger to us, it should be remembered that there was a wide difference between the existing state of affairs and that previous to the glorious battle of Trafalgar. Now all the great Powers of Europe were in arms against France; but at the time of the Copenhagen expedition, the whole of the Continent was subdued—subdued not merely for the purpose of conquest, but for the subjugation of England, through the overthrow of her naval supremacy.' But forty-eight votes could be mustered in support of the motion for censure in the Peers, against one hundred and five; and but seventy-three against one hundred and fifty-seven in the Commons. Next to the great oratorical success of Canning, whose matchless eloquence Erskine said had far exceeded anything that had been heard in Parliament, the honours of debate were accorded to Wellesley.

Mr. Whitbread had actively supported Sheridan for Westminster against Paull, and on the hustings said that proceedings against Lord Wellesley need not terminate though he were left without a seat in Parliament. This he construed into a pledge that he and his political friends would undertake the part of prosecutors. In a public letter on February 8, 1808, he enjoined Mr. Whitbread, whose talents and whose integrity he honoured, to redeem the implied pledge. He believed that he could convince him of the deep guilt of Lord Wellesley, and he felt persuaded that he would not be silent or inactive when he saw how the country had been disgraced, and how law, and right, and humanity had been outraged by his enormities. He had seen the failure of other trials, in despite of all that talent and eloquence could urge; but though the tribunals had refused to punish, the guilt of the criminal had been established. To have had the same success in the trial of Lord Wellesley against all the art and influence of power and corruption, would have been no small victory for justice. But he was now convinced (after the debate on Copenhagen) that any attempt to bring this arch offender to justice would be worse than useless. He must henceforth look on as a spectator of any proceedings in Parliament relative to him, until the day should arrive when the Marquess Wellesley and he might meet before an unsold, an unprejudiced, and an uninfluenced tribunal, and when a different spirit might animate the people of England.

On the following day Lord Folkestone moved that the papers in the Oude case might be printed and taken into consideration. Creevey, Windham, and Dr. Lushington were for their being referred to a select committee. Sir A. Wellesley and Lord Temple besought the House to come to a decision, in justice to the person accused. But Lord Folkestone adhered to his proposal. When at length brought on, Creevey ridiculed the notion that the House was fit to judge of the rival policies of Sir John Shore and his successor, unfolded in the seven ponderous folios printed from time to time during three years. The *gravamen* of the charge lay in the treaties which divested native Princes of part of their dominions; and the justification was to be sought in the alleged perfidy of their conduct. But the Court of Directors had denounced the conduct of the noble Marquess in these affairs, as contrary to law, defiant of the Company's authority, and tending to convert the executive Government of India into a simple despotism. They had reprobated his profuse expenditure, and generally his demeanour towards native Powers. He admitted that further delay was hard upon the accused; but was it not hard upon the Company that their judgment should be overruled, and the security of their position endangered, which would be the case if the House, upon imperfect comprehension of the facts, came to a vote of acquittal?

Windham asked whether one in twenty of those present had read the papers? If not, was not the incapacity of the

House confessed? The accusations were those which were incident to the lot of every great man; they were taxes which greatness and distinction had to pay; nor was the noble Marquess so destitute of friends, or so run down in the world, that they bore upon him with any oppressive degree of weight.

Romilly argued that justice, in this as in every other instance, required that the judges should know the facts and understand their bearing. But without the intervention of a committee, to arrange and condense the voluminous evidence before them, justice he thought, could not be done. He had himself at much inconvenience, gone through a considerable portion of the documents, and if called on to vote prematurely, he must give it against the noble Marquess. But he did not thereby mean to deny that there might not be further evidence found in the mass of papers on the table which would fairly exculpate him. On the other hand, Sir Arthur Wellesley and Mr. Bathurst contended that protracted delay was palpably unjust, and that in the course of three years, most well-informed persons had had ample opportunity of acquainting themselves of the main points at issue. The authority of Mr. Fox was cited against postponement; and Lord Folkestone pressed the House to come to a division. It was ultimately agreed that the case should be taken into consideration on its merits that day s'ennight.

Writing to Malcolm soon afterwards, Sir Arthur notes the revival of his brother from the condition of discontent and despondency in which he had lain during the intermittent but protracted attacks upon him in Parliament. He has at length 'got the better of the effect which these base attacks had made upon his mind. He has lately made a most distinguished speech in the House of Lords; and I have no doubt, he will come forward frequently in the same way. I hope that we shall be able to bring the House of Commons to a vote on the Oude case in the course of next week; not I think that it signifies essentially whether we do or not, as time has had its usual effect upon the sense or folly of the public; and has convinced them that the man they have been in the habit of abusing was the best governor for India. It is desirable, however, to come to a vote on this question, as several of Lord Wellesley's Indian friends are anxious about it, as well as others who have more respect than I have for what passes in Parliament.'[1] At length, on the 15th of March, a resolution, moved by Sir J. Anstruther, of approval and thanks was carried by 189 to 29, and the imputations of bad faith and oppression in Oude were thereby extinguished.

While a last attempt was making to find some one who would engage to bring forward the charge respecting the affairs of the Carnatic, the fevered dream that had caused so much contention came to an unlooked-for end. For many months Paull had suffered much agonising pain from the wound received in his duel with Burdett, and which, by some neglect or mismanagement, had never been completely healed. Disappointment in commercial as well as in political speculation seemed to weigh him down, and in desperation he had sought to repair his losses by resort to play. Here too he seemed at odds with fortune; here too his wayward obstinacy would not suffer him to be advised or warned. His associates Butler and Sloper observed that he grew subject more and more to fits of abstraction and despondency; but at intervals the old fire of vituperation would break out afresh in private talk or in Cobbett's 'Register.' He appeared to revive, and for the hour forgot his pain, as some subordinate of the Indian Government, or some supposed accomplice of his favourite aversion, was set in the pillory of ribald scorn. Now and then his malignity snatched a mouthful of daintier prey. The veteran

---

[1] From London, 25th February, 1808.

Lake had tottered home to enjoy the evening sunshine of sympathy and homage from surviving friends, but without having put by enough to support the advancement in the peerage which Wellesley insisted on as his due. After the taking of Delhi he had been created a baron, without inquiry as to his private means, which had never been considerable. He lived but a few months to enjoy the dignity of viscount conferred on him in 1807; and Ministers proposed that Parliament should vote a pension of 2,000*l.* a year [1] for three lives, and 9,000*l.* to raise a fitting monument, as had been done in the case of heroes of one instead of many victories. But what was Alighur or Laswarri to a morbid and baffled vilipender, who, in the terrible words of Swift, was ' dying of rage like a poisoned rat in a hole ' ? He tried to persuade the crowd, ever greedy of improbable scandal, and succeeded perhaps in convincing himself, for cruelty is credulous of pretext, that between the old General and his gallant son they had made away with a quarter of a million sterling out of Madras jobbing and Mahratta spoil. The truth came out in debate, that, during his period of command in India, Lake had saved no more than enough to clear old debts in England and make a modest provision for his younger children. Whitbread was ashamed to object to the pension, but grumbled at the proposed monument; and Lord George Cavendish sneered at soldiers having peerages without landed fortune to sustain them. Michael Angelo Taylor gave utterance to worthier sentiments, which he declared were prevalent in Opposition. ' True economy did not grudge substantial marks of gratitude for great achievements, won by intrepid constancy and signal valour; and for himself he was too glad to know that England had generals who, amid golden opportunities, disdained to enrich themselves by plunder.' On a

---

[1] The title was enjoyed in succession by his two sons, and became extinct in 1848.

division but twenty-six objected to the grant, while two hundred and ten voted in its favour.[1]

The last chance of harpooning the great Pro-Consul depended on finding some new hand with hardihood and inexperience enough to make the venture. Paull cast his eyes on Sir Thomas Turton, a young Whig of some ability, who had just come into Parliament; and, as Francis said, in his own irreverent way, 'He desired to have him, that he might sift him as wheat.' The baronet was ready, and the winnowing went on till nothing was left but the chaff. Pain and vexation meanwhile did their miserable work; day by day Paull grew more dejected, uncertain, wild. Every guinea he possessed was staked at hazard, and his last night on earth was spent at a gambling house, whence he returned in the grey dawn to his desolate home. He seems to have fruitlessly sought death by opening a vein in his arm, and then in a paroxysm of impatience, with his razor to have made an end.[2]

Mr. Brodie, who had attended him, testified at the inquest to the utter wreck of reason in which his unhappy patient had thus perished, and at the clubs next day the lurid glare he had casually shed was thought of as little as the flicker of the last wax candle.

Undeterred by the ghastly omen, the few who still clung to the cause of impeachment, in the following month resolved to bring forward the alleged wrongs of the Nawab of Arcot.

Six years after the transactions had occurred which formed the subject of complaint, Sir Thomas Turton moved,[3] 'That the power entrusted to the Marquess Wellesley had been employed by him wantonly and unjustly to deprive the lawful heir to the musnud of the Carnatic of his undoubted right of succession as Nawab of Arcot, contrary

[1] 29th February, 1808.
[2] 15th April, 1808.
[3] 17th May, 1808.

to every principle of justice and equity, in violation of the sacred faith of treaties, and to the degradation of the British name and character in India.' 'That at a time when our implacable enemy was attempting to justify his atrocities in Europe by the example of our conduct in India, it was peculiarly incumbent on the House, in the name of the people of England, to declare openly to the world that the British Parliament never did or will countenance any act of oppression and injustice in its Indian government; and that a committee be appointed to inquire into the circumstances of the case, and the substitution of Azim ul Dowlah for the son of our old ally.'

Mr. Wallace, as Secretary to the Board of Control, entered at length into the history of the Company's former dealings with the house of Wallajah, from 1706 to 1801, when Omdut ul Omrah died, leaving his throne to Hussein, both of whom were charged with encouraging the intrigues with France and Mysore against us. He argued that the Nawab was not independent, but, by the terms of undisputed treaties, our vassal or feudatory; that the administration was corrupt and oppressive, to the ruin of the country and to the peril of our position.

Lord A. Hamilton accused the Company of designs to annex the Carnatic long before its rulers were accused of hostility. Colonel Allen vindicated the Governor-General. Windham moved the adjournment. The discussion was resumed on June 11 by Sheridan, who suggested the omission of several long resolutions reciting the alleged historical incidents, and recommended the issue to be simply taken on that of censure arising therefrom. He disclaimed having ever impeached the private moral character of the noble Marquess, though he always thought that he betrayed too often a mischievous ambition that might be ultimately ruinous to British interests in the East.

Sir John Anstruther supported the course of procedure

which met the historical resolutions by the previous question and the criminatory one by a direct negative.

S. R. Lushington [1] vindicated the establishment of better ways of rule under the Company, and painted in eloquent language the extortion of the Nawab, which was ruinous to the people. The treaty with Azim was justified by the law of nations, not merely because it was beneficial to the Company, but because it would dispense happiness to millions.

On the principal question the House divided, at two in the morning: For the censure, 15; against it, 124; on which Mr. Wallace said Government thought it superfluous to ask for a counter resolution, which, had the division been less decisive, it had been intended to move.

But on June 17, Sir T. Turton, persisting in moving declaratory resolutions against the policy pursued in the Carnatic, though abstaining from any words of personal condemnation of Lord Wellesley, a division was taken on a direct vote of approval, when there appeared 98 against 19 votes. With this proceeding the accusations which had originated with Paull came to an end. For three years they had been a source of incessant mortification and annoyance; and had practically seemed to place under a ban one of the ablest men of his day, as far at least as public employment was concerned. It was natural that when they were finally refuted, and his merit as a ruler under circumstances of great difficulty and danger, had been judicially recognised, a reaction should set in, and that he should thenceforth be looked to all the more as a statesman in whom the nation might confide.

---

[1] Member for Rye, who took the opposite side in the controversy to that sustained by his kinsman.

CHAPTER XVII.

SEVILLE.

1809.

THE year 1808 had closed disastrously for the credit of England in diplomacy and in the field. Napoleon, flushed with the triumph of his civil strategy at Bayonne and Erfurth, hastened to take the command in person of his armies in Spain, and to execute his threat of driving his enemies to their ships. Mr. Hookham Frere had, through the personal preference of Canning, been sent as Minister to the Supreme Junta, for dealing with whom he possessed few of the qualities indispensable for success; while the errors of the War Office, in the instructions given to Sir John Moore and Sir David Baird, led to the disastrous retreat to Corunna. Joseph was reseated on his usurped throne at Madrid, and the cause of Spanish independence seemed to be undone. But with Cadiz still held by the insurgents, and Gibraltar intact in our hands, the elements of insurrection throughout the Peninsula gradually began to stir, and in the spring of 1809 the Portland Cabinet resolved on greater efforts than before to save Portugal and rescue Spain from foreign domination. A large force was collected at Cork, of which the command was offered to the victor of Vimeira, while the Marquess was asked to go with plenary powers as ambassador to Spain. Once more, therefore, on a field of action worthy of their combined abilities, the two brothers were to be employed.

Government, indeed, stood much in need of strengthening; and Wellesley's ambition, long deferred while the wrestling with defamation lasted, naturally aimed at a seat in the Cabinet rather than employment, however honourable, abroad.

Canning would gladly have got rid of others. But how was room to be made for him? In conversation with the Speaker he called Camden and Westmoreland 'useless lumber, and Chatham perfectly unmanageable; Wellesley would be a good colleague, but not as Premier.'[1] The chief object of his professed distrust and real jealousy was Castlereagh, whose mismanagement of the War Department, in spite of his activity and attention to routine, could only be ascribed to 'incapacity for great affairs.' But the unpardonable sin of Castlereagh was the possession of an amount of Parliamentary influence infinitely greater than his own. The Viscount's shortcomings in debate were beneath his sarcasm, and his own transcendent superiority to all rivals, signally displayed in the session of 1808, inspired him with the premature hope of attaining the leadership of the party whenever his failing Grace of Portland should retire. That event, he knew (through private intimacy), could not be far distant; and for many weeks he strove to bring about two objects,—the deposition of Castlereagh from the departmental conduct of the war, and the substitution of Lord Wellesley in his room. Even this change, though he deemed it would be propitious to the gaining of his heart's desire, was not viewed in prospect without some misgiving. Who could tell for certain whether, at the critical moment, when the hand that feebly clutched the Treasurer's staff should fail, some other member of the Cabinet might not be sent for by the King? He would like, if possible, to make sure beforehand against the mischance of having brought a new competitor into the field when displacing the old one. With the air of florid

[1] Colchester's Diary, April 1809.

banter, but with a keenness of subtle purpose, in one of their conferences he said, 'I must tell you frankly that I have serious objections, Lord Wellesley, to your being Premier; because, with your reputation, talent, and activity of mind, you would reduce all the rest of us to mere cyphers.' Words of disclaimer and deprecation were matter of course; but the egregious flattery told, as it was meant to tell. Canning wanted to be thought rather afraid of overshadowing greatness; had he really been so, he would have said nothing about it; what he did distrust was the King's estimate, not his own, of—George Canning. Till things could be brought about as was to be wished, he offered to set aside Hookham Frere, and to send the Marquess as ambassador, with extraordinary powers, to Seville; as if King Ferdinand were actually in his capital, or at the head of the insurgent forces of the realm. George III. would be more easily persuaded, he well knew, to have him for his representative abroad than for one of his Cabinet councillors at home. Beside the taint of tolerant opinions in religion, he had the fault in royal eyes, of being too grand and dignified by half. Stories had reached Windsor of the courtly airs that had prevailed at Fort William, which His Majesty did not like. He spoke of the Governor General having *considerable* merit in the conduct of affairs in India, but as inflated with pride and with his own consequence, assuming to himself the exclusive merit of all that had been done in the East, and demanding ceremonious respect much beyond what was due to his station. When reminded at Calcutta that he was exacting from those about him more than the King used to do, his lordship replied, 'Then the King is wrong; but that is no reason why I should improperly relax also.' His Majesty believed that when he came back, 'his head would be quite turned, and there would be no enduring him.'[1] But

[1] Rose's Diary, 1805.

all the more he was eligible for the position of Ambassador Extraordinary; and as it was of moment to impress the Spanish people with a sense of our determination to sustain them in their uprising against France, the Cabinet resolved to send a special mission to the Central Junta, with plenary powers to direct and control the movements of our troops and the disposition of our fleets upon the coast. The post was not altogether one to be coveted under existing circumstances. The Spaniards were known to be dispirited by defeat; their treasury was empty; their army a crowd of irregulars, ill-disciplined, ill-armed, ill-paid; and the proverbial curse of half-recognised authority filled their ignorant councils with rivalries and dissensions. On the other hand, to a mind full of ambitious aims there was not a little that was tempting in the speciality of the position. He was to go forth to challenge, in the face of Europe, the arrogant pretensions of Napoleon, and to re-organise a populace and peasantry into a nation capable of expelling their invaders. That the brother whom he had brought up to arms, and step by step promoted in his earlier career, and aided unceasingly to advance in parliamentary and official life, should have been placed in chief command in the Peninsula was in itself a strong inducement for him to accept. But unless the forces destined for Spain were adequate to the difficult undertaking he must decline the responsibility. Lord Buckinghamshire complained in the House of Lords of Sir Arthur Wellesley's being appointed to supersede General Craddock,[1] who was many years his senior, and who, after the death of Sir John Moore, had done good service by rallying the allied forces in Andalusia and preparing for the defence of Gibraltar. Ministers, however, defended their choice with spirit, and Henry Wellesley, having resigned the secretaryship of the Treasury, prepared to accompany his brother in the

[1] 14th April, 1809.

same confidential capacity in which he had served him with so much devotion in the East. Canning was profuse in his promises, and sanguine in his anticipations of being able to furnish all the men and the money that might be wanted for the vigorous carrying out of the enterprise. His friend was satisfied; he allowed his acceptance to be made known, and on the 30th of April the 'Gazette' announced his appointment.

The 'Times,' not then given to indulge in editorial comment on such matters, dwelt with peculiar emphasis on the announcement: 'We consider the appointment as an unequivocal pledge given to the nation by Ministers that they are resolved to adopt no half measures, to pursue no system of cold or timid precaution, to leave no outlets for irresolution or vacillation. Lord Wellesley cannot be an instrument for such purposes; he possesses one of the cardinal virtues, fortitude, which we would at the present moment place above the others, because it is that which the necessities of the hour render indispensable.'[1] Other testimonies of approval were not wanting; but such was the rage of party that Whitbread did not scruple to inveigh against the nomination, and publicly to warn the Spaniards against the Grecian gift, which however specious without, within was full of treachery. 'At a time when the people of England were everywhere talking of the injustice of Buonaparte towards Spain, he was surprised at the national blindness to our own aggressions recently manifested in the choice and approbation of our ambassador to that country. If there were a man in the universe who, in another part of the globe, had acted as Buonaparte had done with respect to Spain, it was the Marquess Wellesley. His conduct in the East Indies was perfectly similar to that of the French Emperor. The people of Spain, if they knew anything of the affairs of this country, must

[1] 1st May, 1809.

know what the noble lord had done in India; but then, all he did there proceeded from an ardent zeal for the public service, while Buonaparte, in acting the same part, was said to have been urged on by the instigation of the devil. They were palpably the same acts, though said to be inspired by different motives. Be that however as it might, the nomination of his lordship was certainly a bad omen, as the people of Spain must know that the Marquess Wellesley would, if the opportunity should offer, treat both Spain and Portugal as Buonaparte had done, through his ardent zeal for the service of his country!' The choice of the new envoy, nevertheless, was highly satisfactory to the country. Lord Holland, who had not been bred in a school of favourable predisposition, was too fearless and free-hearted to conceal his appreciation of the foresight, comprehensiveness, and magnanimity of his views. Far from joining in the attack of Whitbread and others, he cultivated his society when in England, corresponded with him when abroad, and constantly defended his measures, saying 'that he was the person, above all the politicians he had known, who most impressed him with the idea of a great statesman.'

Many days had not elapsed when he was informed that Government thought of diverting a considerable portion of the intended armament to sustain the ill-devised expedition to Walcheren. With characteristic decision he forthwith remonstrated against the change of plans, which he saw must compromise any chance of success in the Peninsula; and, failing to obtain satisfaction on the subject, he resigned. Owing in part to chagrin at this new disappointment, he fell ill, and was for several weeks prostrated by gout, though not secluded from intercourse and sympathy with his political friends. Canning often came and went, and towards the end of June persuaded him to set forth on his important mission, with reassurances that adequate military resources should be made available without delay. On the other hand he was induced, strange as it now appears, to leave with Canning a letter requesting his recall if ever his friend should relinquish the conduct of Foreign affairs. In other words, the wily Minister thereby believed himself secured against the contingency of a reconstruction of the Cabinet unless he were at the head. On the voyage out the Plenipotentiary wrote to Mr. Rose:—

I was highly gratified by your kind invitation to Cuffields, of which I most readily should have availed myself if I had taken the route by Torbay; but as I embarked at Portsmouth, it was not in my power to wait on you. I sailed on Monday, and we are proceeding very well. I find that the sea has been rather advantageous to my health.'

The bells were ringing for the victory of Talavera when the 'Donegal' dropped anchor in Cadiz Bay. Her coming had been awaited with anxiety, and when it was known throughout the city that the English envoy was on board, there was a general outburst of joy. The chief authorities put off without delay to welcome him, and his landing was deferred till the following day.

The occasion was indeed one that might have made any ordinary man forget ceremonial in a sense of its singularity as well as gravity. But the Ambassador Extraordinary was true to himself in the performance of his part on the world's stage. Before quitting his cabin he took his accustomed care to be arrayed befittingly, and each item of personal adornment was duly considered. When all particulars were adjusted to his conception of the character he was to sustain, as the incarnation of imperial power appearing as a deliverer of an enthralled people, he asked how his staff were dressed, and on being told that both civilians and sailors wore cocked hats with white feathers, he declared that his distinctive plumage must be green, and beneath a waving profusion of that benignant hue the countenance of the Marquess shone forth on Spain.

In a frenzy of enthusiasm a French flag taken in a recent conflict with the corps of Dupont, was suddenly spread upon the ground, that as he landed, he might as an omen tread on the ensign of Napoleon's power. It is not certain that in the tumult of the moment he realised the significance of the act; but the circumstance was laid hold of as a ground of bitter reproach, being, as was contended, a manifestation of premature and paltry triumph. The populace pressed round him with their greetings, and drew his carriage from the quay to the house of the Alcalde, where addresses of welcome, and felicitations on his brother's victories awaited him.[1]

In his own words, he was 'received at Cadiz with every demonstration of public honour, and with the most cordial and enthusiastic expressions of veneration for His Majesty's person and respect for his Government, of zealous attachment to the British alliance, and of affectionate gratitude for the benefits already derived by the Spanish nation from the generosity of His Majesty's councils; and for the persevering activity, valour, and skill of his officers and troops.' The difficulty of obtaining a suitable house at Seville caused him to linger more than ten days at Cadiz, which thereby enabled him to receive 'continual and distinguished marks of attention and respect towards His Majesty's embassy from every description of the public authorities, civil, military, and ecclesiastical, and from every class of the nobility, gentry, and people.'[2]

Popular excitement kindled as he moved from Cadiz into the interior, and at Seville he was hailed with every form of welcome indicative of national joy. Royalty was in abey-

---

[1] Mr. Jacob, who was present, says nothing of the incident in his *Notes in Spain*.

[2] Despatch to Mr. Canning, from Seville, 11th August, 1809.

ance, and the order of the day was spontaneity in the most democratic fashion. Guerilla bands took up the position that to each of them seemed best, and squabbled about preference and pre-eminence on grounds unintelligible to all but themselves, with appropriate uproar of patriotic vows and profuse invocation of all the saints in the calendar. Officials of the old Court were jostled by those of provincial importance, whom the exigency of the nation tacitly, if not always blandly, acknowledged; and self-appointed deputations from distant cities swelled the numbers of the Junta, in their eagerness to be duly demonstrative of national gratitude to England's envoy. Nor had the stronger sex all the boast of patriotism to themselves. Beautiful Andalusian women, of various ranks and antecedents, gazed from balcony and housetop upon the stirring scene; and crowds of peasant girls and dames thronged the narrow streets and narrower byeways along the route appointed for the cavalcade. But there was one conspicuous above all others by virtue of self-sacrifice, and for whom discourteous men and jealous women cheerfully made way. Augustina Zaragossa was come to meet and thank the ambassador of Britain, and she thought that her fitting place and part in the ovation was upon the lower step of the entrance to the great hall in which he was to be received in state. Accordingly the dark-eyed heroine waited there, much to the satisfaction of the multitude, who sympathised in her notion of what was becoming in the bravest of women, and delighted at her characteristic retention of the Arragonese costume, and the serious vivacity of her talk and mien. Nobody had an idea of what she meditated at the critical moment of the day, and least of all did the illuminated copy of Britannic Majesty suspect what awaited him. At last the carriage stopped, and he prepared with ineffable dignity to descend; but hardly had his foot touched the second step, when the 'Girl of the Portillo Gate' approached with a cry of ecstatic joy, clasped the exquisite envoy in her arms, and carried him triumphantly into the Town Hall, amid the frenzied 'bravas' of the multitude. A more disconcerted and displeased plenipotentiary cannot be conceived than the object of her unexpected care, when with a hearty kiss, she let him down at last at the foot of the grand staircase. But his mother-wit prompted a semblance of good humour, which he did not feel, and whispered, Better seem to share the popular mood even at the cost of dignity, than by unavailing testiness provoke a jibe. He gallantly thanked the heroine, and the more decorous portions of the ceremonial proceeded without interruption. A flattering address was duly read in sonorous accents by the Alcalde of Seville, and answered suitably in words of classic brevity and beauty. So eminent a master of language was not to be found wanting on a great historical occasion. Lord Wellesley, by all accounts, acquitted himself worthily, and won the prepossession of his difficult and somewhat querulous hearers, on whom a word mis-interpretable into condescension would have fallen like an explosive spark, even amid all the remindings of national humiliation.

But when the pageant was over, and the hour of disrobing came, pent-up irritation had its way. It was indeed hard times with the personal attendants of the ambassador for some days after he had been caressed as described, by unauthorised female fervour in utter disregard of all the rules of ambassadorial etiquette. He could not complain; but he could not forget the indignity, and those about him had to pay the penalty not to be inflicted on others. His body servant, who had long attended him, and knew his ways and weaknesses, came in for something more than an allowable share of his most noble wrath. Whether the Irish love of merriment betrayed him into some ill-concealed allusion to the unpardonable liberty taken with his august master, or whether the faithful valet had in some less unpardonable manner failed in his duty, it is said that His Excellency, in a paroxysm of rage, uplifted his delicate fist, and hit his stalwart dependant a box on the ear. The man quietly said, 'It is a pity your lordship should forget yourself, and forget me, like this; for you know that if I chose I could crush you with a blow.' Then, leaving the room, he refused to reappear until next day. The better nature of his master having regained its ascendency, he made amends by sending his offended servant his watch as a present and peace-offering.

William Jacob, who had a seat in Parliament, had been with his friend Mr. Ridout for a long tour through the southern provinces, and happened to be then in Andalusia. From many opportunities of observation he evidently formed deep impressions of the moral worth, the firmness, and the perspicacity which the new envoy displayed. 'His arrival produced an extraordinary sensation, neither prepared nor fostered by the body to whom he was sent, whose narrow souls were jealous of his character, and apprehensive lest his powerful talents should detect and expose their contracted policy and futile projects.'[1] The Junta was unpopular, and incapable in all eyes save their own. A conspiracy, on the eve of explosion, was revealed to Lord Wellesley, who thought it his duty to warn them of their danger. They affected little alarm, and were above the hypocrisy of professing gratitude; while the accomplices in the baffled plot were left to bewail their communicativeness.'[2] His conversation with the travellers, to whom he was frequently accessible, discovered an accurate knowledge and comprehensive view of the state of Spain.

The sanguinary but triumphant battle of Talavera was the first-fruit of the campaign. The tragic story needs not to be told again, but the language of the calmly-judging victor

[1] *Letters from Spain,* iv. 1809. [2] Ibid.

of the morrow, descriptive of the deplorable condition of his little army, portrays more vividly than any other words could paint the difficulties which from the first beset the conduct of affairs on the eve of the new envoy's arrival at his post. While demagogues in the Junta were reiterating their sonorous vows of devotion to country, and death to the invader, the Provisional Government, who corresponded with the English General, seemed bent upon excusing their own want of power to fulfil unbounded promises of supply and aid, by invidious criticism on his strategy, and ill-disguised reproaches at his pretended want of spirit in the cause. 'It is not a difficult matter for a gentleman in the situation of Don M. de Garay to sit down in his cabinet, and write his ideas of the glory which would result from driving the French through the Pyrenees; and I believe there is no man in Spain who has risked so much or who has sacrificed so much to effect that object as I have. But I wish that Don M. de Garay, or the gentlemen of the Junta before they blame me for not doing more, or impute to me beforehand the probable consequences of the blunders or indiscretion of others, would either come or send here somebody to satisfy the wants of our half-starved army, which, although they have been engaged for two days, and have defeated twice their numbers, in the service of Spain, have not bread to eat. It is positively a fact that, during the last seven days, the British army have not received one-third of their provisions; that at this moment there are nearly 4,000 wounded soldiers dying in the hospitals in this town from want of common assistance and necessaries, which any other country in the world would have given to its enemies; and that I can get no assistance of any description from the country. I cannot prevail upon them even to bury the dead carcases in the neighbourhood, the stench of which will destroy themselves as well as us. I positively will not move, nay, more, I will disperse my army, till I am supplied with provisions and means of transport as I ought to be.'[1] His total force did not exceed 20,000 men, and all his plans for protecting Lisbon, and crossing the frontier into Galicia, depended on additional troops promised him from England, for which he still waited in vain. On the same last day of July the Marquess wrote from Cadiz announcing his arrival. In reply to which Sir Arthur sent him the florid votes of the Junta creating him a Captain-General of Spain, but reiterating in detail the state of destitution in which his troops were left, owing to the exhausted state of the country, to the inactivity of the magistrates and people, to their disinclination to take any trouble, excepting that of packing up their property and running away when they heard of the approach of a French patrol, to their habits of insubordination and disobedience, and to the want of power in the Government and its officers. Since the 3rd instant the army had had no bread till yesterday, when about 4,000 lbs. of biscuit were divided among 30,000 mouths. . . . 'You have undertaken a Herculean task; and God knows that the chances of success are infinitely against you, particularly since the unfortunate turn which affairs have taken in Austria.' A week later he wrote that he wished much he could see him, but his situation was such that he dared not leave his camp, or spare either of the persons to converse with whom would be of any use. His Excellency had better therefore send somebody to him as soon as he could, if he should be able to hold his ground in Spain: but this he believed to be fast becoming impossible. 'A starving army is actually worse than none. The soldiers lose their discipline and their spirit. They plunder even in the presence of their officers. The officers are discontented, and almost as bad as the men; and with the army which a fort-

[1] From Talavera, 31st July, 1809, Sir A. Wellesley to Mr. Frere, Minister at Seville.

night ago beat double their numbers, I should now hesitate to meet a French corps of half their strength.'[1]

The evil tidings above referred to were the crushing defeat of Wagram, and the consequent submission of Austria to the humiliating terms exacted by Napoleon.

The intelligence of the splendid achievements of Sir Arthur Wellesley and his gallant troops at Talavera was accompanied by grave alarms respecting the state of their supplies and means of movement, thus mingling a considerable degree of concern and solicitude with the sentiments naturally inspired by the extraordinary and glorious circumstances of that memorable victory. The Ambassador's anxiety had been further increased by the despatches which Mr. Frere had been careful to forward to him during his detention at Cadiz; and the letter of Sir Arthur Wellesley exhibited the most afflicting view of the condition of the British army in Spain. This letter reached him early in the morning as he drew near to Seville, and its urgency appeared to be so great that, though his audience of credence had been fixed by the Junta for the 15th, he took advantage of the visit of Don M. de Garay soon after his arrival, to press upon his Government the indispensability of immediate supplies. The verbal and written assurances of the Spanish authorities led him to hope that immediate exertion would be made by them to fulfil the promises held out to their allies: and he sanguinely expressed to the Foreign Secretary at home his anticipation that he should be permitted to superintend the completion of the several details necessary for the commencement of an improved system of supply and movement for the troops in the field. But the impoverished state of the country, the weakness of the Government, and the inveterate defects of the military department in Spain, rendered any speedy improvement impracticable, and induced him to apprehend great

[1] From Deleytosa, 8th August, 1809.

difficulty even in the ultimate success of any plan which could then be suggested. To the causes which had produced and augmented the sufferings of the army, were to be added the perverse and intractable disposition of General Cuesta, the Commander-in-Chief of the Spanish troops acting with Sir Arthur Wellesley. Innumerable proofs of this unhappily abounded.[1]

He lost no time in addressing friendly requisitions to Don Martin de Garay, then Chief Secretary of the Provisional Government, for magazines of provisions, to be formed at such places in the rear of the allied armies as he should point out, and for the supply of 1,500 mules and 100 Valencian carts, as means of transport, according to such a plan as he should suggest.[2] Everything was promised without delay; everything had, it was said, been anticipated. Orders for mules, carts, oxen, sheep, and biscuits, with plenty of money to bring them, having been sent some days before by reliable commissariat commissioners; but, to prevent mistakes, orders should be despatched forthwith a second time. It was impossible not to seem satisfied with assurances so cordial; but unfortunately no results were visible in the British camp. The General chafed in vain from day to day at the condition of his victorious troops, who were literally half-starved, and who, for want of invalid train or ammunition waggons, were hardly able to move. They had consequently to remain on the south bank of the Tagus for nearly a month, near Deleytosa, and eventually to withdraw into Portugal; the reasons and necessities being grimly photographed between the plain-spoken Commander and his eupheuistic brother at Seville. The correspondence was published when laid before Parliament, and produced a deep conviction of the inherent difficulties of the situation, and of the rare ability, patience,

---

[1] Marquess Wellesley to Mr. Canning, 15th August, 1809.
[2] 12th August, 1809.

and endurance engaged in struggling against them. Wilberforce, long after referring to these papers, said to a friend, ' I remember thinking that I had never seen anything at all equal to them in talent.'

The envoy's language was all that fraternal faithfulness and public confidence could desire. 'Immediately after my arrival at this place, and even before I had been admitted to an audience by the Supreme Junta, I employed every endeavour to induce the Government to adopt the measures and arrangements suggested in your letter of August 8. I enclose a note, presented yesterday to the Secretary of State, and his answer. The orders of the Duc del Parque were transmitted to you by an express courier this evening, and I am inclined to believe that the Government is disposed to make every effort compatible with its powers, with the state of the country, and with the inveterate defects of the military department in Spain. You are, however, sufficiently aware of the impossibility of relying upon such efforts, unless a regular system can be established under such authorities as may secure its efficiency and seasonable operation; and, although you may be assured that I will omit no endeavour to contribute to the establishment of such a system, I cannot entertain a confident expectation of success. It is evident that, in order to secure to your army the articles which you require, supplies must be drawn from remote sources to such points as may be properly calculated for the establishment of magazines; and that your means of transport and of movement cannot now be furnished from the countries in which your army is acting. I have therefore advised this Government to call forth every resource of the southern provinces of Spain, and to convey the requisite articles, in the first instance, to Santa Elalia, a plain in the rear of Monartino, where I understand a magazine might be formed with advantage. From this magazine you might draw forward your supplies to any other points which you might think fit to indicate; but the efficiency of the whole arrangement must depend in a great degree upon the proper selection and control of the agents for the collection and the conveyance of the several articles required for your use. Under a serious and painful impression of the difficulties of your situation, and of the sufferings of your army, I feel the indispensable necessity of communicating with you on the most minute details of the subject of your distress; and I therefore forward this despatch to you, under the care of Brigadier-General Doyle and Major Armstrong, to whom I request you to state all the circumstances of your situation, and every point connected with the means of relieving your wants, and of securing you against similar inconvenience, if you should think it practicable or advisable to remain in Spain. As soon as these officers shall be fully apprised of your wishes and intentions, I request that you will direct them to return to me with your despatches. In the meanwhile I shall not fail to use every exertion to accelerate the efforts of this Government for your relief. You may be assured that I shall take a proper opportunity of representing to this Government the defects of the Spanish army, which you describe in your despatch of August 8. I have received with great concern the description contained in these letters, of the distress of your army, and of the perverse conduct of General Cuesta. This Government is disposed to remove General Cuesta from his command whenever it shall have received from you, or from the British ambassador, a regular and detailed statement of his misconduct. It is my intention to present to the Secretary of State a recital of the several facts stated in your despatches respecting General Cuesta; but, in my judgment, it would not appear to me to be proper that I should directly insist upon his removal. As far as I can collect your sentiments upon this point, they appear to coincide with mine. It is not to be supposed that this Government will continue to employ General Cuesta in the chief command of the army after having received full notice of the several facts which you have stated; and I am satisfied that his removal would be made with more cheerfulness and alacrity, and with less danger of unpopularity, if it should appear to be rather the necessary consequence of his own conduct than the result of the interference of the British ambassador.'

Another fortnight passed without succour in food or means of moving the sick and wounded; and on August 21 the army withdrew into Portugal, where they were welcomed as friends and treated as guests. The tidings were received at Seville with dismay, where the corruption and perfidy of the Spanish commissariat were unknown, and the severance of the allied corps was ascribed to some sinister influence operating on the mind of the English general. A more embarrassing position for his kinsman and friend, whose confidence in his judgment and hardihood was unwavering, and who felt his credit and success inextricably bound up with his own, cannot well be conceived.

In all the published reports of encounters in the field the bravery of the Spanish troops was lauded to the skies. It was necessary to keep up the national spirit under great disheartenment; and even Sir Arthur Wellesley, matter-of-fact in all things as he was, did not blame Spanish officers for being silent as to instances of cowardice and desertion. But among the insurrectionary levies, these in the campaign of 1809 were so frequent and so glaring that they suggested serious cause for hesitation whether the two armies should in future act together or apart. On this point, with the feeling of deference long habitual to him, Sir Arthur, after submitting his ideas to his brother, 'requested the aid of his superior judgment to enable him to decide upon it in the manner which would be most beneficial to the national interests.' At the battle of Talavera, he wrote, 'in which the Spanish army was hardly engaged, whole corps threw away their arms, and ran off, in my presence, when they were neither attacked nor threatened with an attack, but frightened I believe by their own fire. When these dastardly soldiers ran away they plundered the baggage of the British army, which was at the moment bravely engaged in their cause.'[1] So deep was his despair of cordial or efficient co-operation that he thought matters would not have been bettered had the greater armament actually been sent to the Tagus instead of the Scheldt. 'You could not have equipped it in Galicia, or anywhere in the north of Spain. If we had had 60,000 men, instead of 20,000, in all probability we should not have got to Talavera for want of means and provisions; and if we had, we should probably have had to separate without a battle, or afterwards, for want of means of subsistence.' After the presentation of the ambassador's note of urgency, supplies were forwarded, in hopes that the English would be dissuaded from recrossing the Portuguese frontier.

Proofs were accumulated in subsequent letters of the suicidal jealousy which governed all the proceedings of the Spanish authorities, and led them to withhold, with almost childish perversity, the means of transport, without which their allies were often paralysed. The damning particularity of the evidence thus furnished was rendered all the more convincing by the total abstinence from imputation of motives, or indulgence in expletives of indignation. As he read despatch after despatch, full of dignified complaint of ill-usage, the irritable ambassador could not but marvel at the discipline into which the general had brought his epistolary temper, or help feeling how volcanic his own style of com-

[1] From Merida, 24th August, 1809.

position would have become under such provocation. But he recognised too clearly the nobleness and wisdom of reproachful equanimity in remonstrance not to adopt it substantially in his communications with the members of the Junta. Disclaimers and reassurances on their part were tendered him daily, fresh and fresh, till he grew deaf to their iteration. But in his confidential replies [1] he thoroughly approved of his brother's resolution to separate his troops from those of Cuesta, and encouraged his refusal to imperil their safety again as auxiliaries in the cause till the Spanish chiefs learned to keep faith and the rank and file to hold their ground. While leaving the door of diplomatic audience ever ajar, and blandly encouraging Ministerial promise to ripen into actual performance, it was necessary that he should inflexibly sustain the stern resolve to treat Portugal as a land capable of being served and saved. No artifice was spared by the alternately boastful and panic-stricken Ministers at Seville to shake his purpose. Spain, he was one day told, had the historic spirit and sublime courage adequate to emancipate herself without foreign help; and if the sense of self-interest did not prompt Great Britain to share in the struggle, neither could she expect to share in the gains of triumph. Next day, when tidings came of some farther advance or acquisition of the French, the same men were plausible in explaining away their foolhardy talk, and unbounded in their professions of readiness to be advised and guided by the representative of the only Power that could effectually aid them. It was no secret that prominent politicians at Seville kept up constant communication with leaders of Opposition in Parliament; and these had, from the outset, denounced the expedition to restore the old monarchies of the Peninsula, and had scoffed at the embassage to a sovereign who was still a prisoner in France. If in six months from his landing the

[1] 28th, 29th, and 30th August 1809.

general, though ennobled for his success in battle, should publicly abandon a cause for which he was sent forth to fight, either as unworthy or unsustainable, what would be the ridicule and blame heaped upon the enterprise? General words of sanction from Government at home would afford little consolation if discomfiture must be ultimately confessed. But, on the other hand, the statesman and commander, however widely differing in temperament, were completely one in discerning that no course less fraught with immediate peril could lead to eventual safety. The French armies, at the end of August, south of the Pyrenees, were not fewer than 125,000 men, while those under Wellesley and Beresford combined were not a fourth of that number. Honour, humanity, and prudence concurred in forbidding any step which could put in jeopardy this small but heroic force. The Portuguese, who had been true to duty, had a paramount claim to all the aid we could afford; and the best, if not the real hope of redemption for the Spaniards was to teach them, at the point of reverse bayonets, that 'bondsmen who would be free, themselves must strike the blow,' and that stedfast loyalty to allies is far more to the purpose than rhetorical vows of gratitude in time to come.

Soon afterwards the General, growing hungrier and angrier as well he might, every hour, wrote to his most noble kinsman point blank as became him. 'I have the honour to enclose an answer which I have received from General Cuesta to the letter which I addressed to him on the 11th instant, with my reply. The plan which he proposes, of dividing between the two armies, in proportion to their numbers, all the provisions received at Truxillo, however specious in appearance, would be fallacious in practice, and would probably starve the British army. It would not be difficult to forbid the convoys of provisions coming from Seville from going to Truxillo; and it is probable that the

supplies of provisions from Seville do not amount to one-fourth of the consumption of both armies, the remainder being supplied by the country, in which, of course, the Spanish army has the preference. An arrangement of this description is impracticable of execution, even if the commissaries of the two armies would act fairly by each other; but this is not to be expected; every commissary will do the best he can for the troops to which he is attached; and many articles must be procured in the country which will not be brought to account in the magazine of Truxillo. In short, my lord, it comes to this, either the British army must be fed with the necessaries which it requires, or I will march it back into Portugal, whether that kingdom is invaded or not by the French corps, which have moved within these few days towards Placentia. I beg to mention to your Excellency that the troops have received this day and yesterday only half an allowance of bread; and the cavalry have no forage, except what they can pick up in the fields. The troops suffer considerably for want of salt, and neither officers or soldiers have had any wine for the last fortnight. In case I should move, I must leave behind me two-thirds of the small quantity of ammunition I have got, having been obliged to give all the Portuguese carts (which had carried the ammunition hitherto) to move the wounded, and not having been able to procure means of transport for anything in this country. Surely, my lord, the Junta have had time since the 19th of last month to supply the wants of the army, with which they were then made acquainted.'
His enclosed rejoinder to Cuesta was equally downright. 'When the British army entered Spain, I had reason to expect, and I expected, that a great effort would be made to afford us subsistence, at least for payment, and those means of transport, and other aids, without which, your Excellency is well aware, no army can keep the field. Your Excellency

also knows how these expectations have been fulfilled. Since I joined your army the troops have not received, upon an average, half a ration, and on some days nothing at all; and the cavalry no forage or grain, excepting what they could pick up in the fields, of an unwholesome description, by the use of which hundreds of horses have died.'

Consternation seized the Junta when the resolution of Sir Arthur was blandly and regretfully conveyed to them by the serene envoy. 'The greatest alarm was excited by the proposed return of the British army into Portugal. The Government appeared, he said, not only to contemplate the probability of that event with terror and despair, but to consider it as the symptom of a disposition to abandon the cause and to relinquish the obligations of the alliance.' De Garay, and a deputation from the Junta, urged the ambassador in the most pressing manner to use his influence for detaining the army in Spain, and for averting the destructive consequences which must ensue if the French arms should be turned into Andalusia. But though deeply sensible of the urgency of the crisis, he could not attempt any other mode of averting the calamity than the active employment of the Spanish troops in the northern provinces, and the establishment of such regulations as might render the subsistence of our army in future practicable and secure.[1] In simple Saxon he meant to make the rhetoricians and jobbers at Seville see that it would not do; and that if we were to fight for Spain, Spain must share with us cattle and corn. Had he infirmly yielded to their entreaties, disunion between himself and the general would have inevitably ensued, and ruin might have been the consequence. He had been but four days among them, and a rupture so soon was not agreeable to contemplate. But insight into character—that quality which cannot be described or analysed, imparted or taught—enabled him to

[1] To Mr. Canning, 15th August, 1809.

measure correctly those with whom he had to deal. While anxious and agitated at heart he listened patiently, smiled imperturbably, and gave them unrelenting refusals wrapt in platitudes the most polite; but he frightened them into giving some carts and mules, and a good deal of beef and biscuit, and things went better afterwards.

But administrative capability does not grow like a gourd overnight. On August 21, another despatch from Jaraicejo, announced the general's determination to endure no more, and forthwith to cross the frontier. 'I can remain in Spain no longer; and I request you to give notice to the Government that I am about to withdraw into Portugal. I have no doubt that they have given orders that we should be provided as we ought to be; but orders, I have to observe, are not sufficient. In order to carry on the contest with France to any good purpose, the labour and services of every man and beast in the country should be employed in the support of the armies; and these should be so classed and arranged as not only to secure obedience to the orders of the Government, but regularity and efficiency in the performance of the services required of them. Fifty thousand men are here collected upon a spot which cannot afford subsistence for 10,000; and there are no means of sending to a distance to make good the deficiency. I hope your Excellency and the Government will believe that I have not determined to go till it has become absolutely necessary. I assure you that there is not a general officer of this army who is not convinced of the necessity of my immediate departure.'

Anticipating the crisis which had now arrived, the ambassador had carefully prepared materials for a plan, with elaborate calculations supporting its details, by which the dreaded event might at the last moment be averted. This he now submitted to the Junta, undertaking, if it were at once adopted, to endeavour to dissuade his brother from his purpose. The members, in an agony of fear lest their frail authority should go to pieces on the disclosure that they had been talking, and not governing, besought the Marquess to believe that they had done all he wanted, and that they would do anything he asked. On the 22nd he wrote, in accordance with their entreaty, for further delay, until they could decide whether his scheme of auxiliary commissariat could be realised. 'I am fully sensible, not only of the indelicacy, but of the inutility, of attempting to offer to you any opinion of mine in a situation where your own judgment must be your best guide, and where no useful suggestions could arise in my mind which must not already have been anticipated by your own experience, comprehensive knowledge, and ardent zeal for the public welfare. Viewing, however, so nearly the painful consequences of your immediate retreat into Portugal, I have deemed it to be my duty to submit to your consideration the possibility of adopting an intermediate plan, which might combine some of the advantages of your return into Portugal, without occasioning alarm in Spain, and without endangering the foundations of the alliance between this country and Great Britain.' On the 20th, however, the army had begun to fall back ; and its commander, on the 22nd, described the plight to which matters had come—' Having no provisions, no stores, no means of transport, being overloaded with sick, the horses of the cavalry being scarcely able to march, or those of the artillery to draw the guns; and the officers and soldiers being worn down by want of food and provisions of every description. Nobody feels more disappointed and hurt than I do, that so little attention has been paid to the demands which I have frequently made; and whatever may be the consequence of the steps which I have been compelled to take, I am in no manner responsible for them.' By slow marches he drew sufficiently near the frontier to obtain relief from the Portuguese magazines. At last, on the 28th, nine cart-loads of biscuit reached them at Merida. He had also some tardy supplies of linen; but those who brought them ran away with the mules, and he was therefore forced to leave them behind.[1] To the Government at home he was compelled to confess that, after ten days spent in protestations, the Provisional Government, through their dilatory and inefficient management, had destroyed the foundation of his plan for enabling the British army to continue in Spain at any distance from the frontier of Portugal.[2]

In England the news of Talavera revived the national feeling, and the King readily acceded to the desire of Ministers that a peerage should be conferred on the successful general. A despatch from Canning conveyed to the Marquess the gratifying intelligence, but the newly-created Viscount would not, as he said, 'take up his title until the "Gazette" should arrive.' This did not come until the 26th of September.

Hitherto their political tendencies had manifested no divergence, and the younger habitually deferred to the elder brother in the conduct of public affairs. But the sense of power and responsibility matured in him opinions of his own, which by degrees assumed very different form and character. The earliest manifestations of dissent worthy of note appeared about this time. An essential part of the policy the ambassador urged upon the Spaniards was the summoning of a Cortes, according to national usage, who might he thought be trusted more safely than any ephemeral body like the Junta, with the supreme control of affairs. Without such authority he saw it was impossible to raise taxes, pay troops, exact responsibility from Ministers, or deal authori-

---

[1] Despatch, 31st August, 1809.
[2] To Canning, 2nd September, 1809.

tatively with foreign Powers. The members of the Provisional Executive affected to acquiesce, but in reality strove to baffle a design which could hardly increase their importance, and which might lead to their supersession. It had, however, been agreed upon by the English Cabinet as an object of the utmost moment, forming part as it did of a comprehensive attempt to call into activity constitutionalism in the west of Europe against the military imperialism of Napoleon. It was, in short, an effort to put insurgent Spain in line with the representative States of Christendom, and so to encourage each and all of them in fidelity to a common cause. Somewhat to the surprise of his Excellency he received from the quarter whence perhaps he least anticipated it, strong expressions of misgiving as to the expediency of the measure. The general was very uneasy at the recommendation of the assembling of the Cortes; not that he doubted the satisfaction it would give in England, but that he feared it would be worse than anything they had had yet. He acknowledged that he had a great dislike to a new popular assembly. Even our own ancient one would be quite unmanageable, and in these days would ruin us, if the present generation had not before its eyes the example of the French revolution; and if there were not certain rules and orders for its guidance and government, the knowledge and use of which render it safe and successfully direct its proceedings. But how would all this work in the Cortes, in the state in which Spain was then? He declared, if he were in Buonaparte's situation, he would leave the English and the Cortes to settle Spain in the best manner they could; and he entertained very little doubt that in a short time Spain must fall into the hands of France.[1]

Canning's instructions were to stimulate by every means the Junta to a vigorous and diligent prosecution of the war,

[1] From Badajos, 22nd September, 1809.

and while abstaining from all display of a wish to dictate in domestic affairs, to encourage the hopes of a more constitutional system of government under the monarchy, whenever it should be restored. To the Cortes, duly convened, belonged alone the right to legislate for the kingdom. But if the Junta were wise, they would earn public confidence by maturing beforehand projects of liberal laws, instead of 'throwing such topics loose before that assembly without any settled plan by which their deliberations might be guided.'[1] Lord Wellesley was warned at the same time against holding out exaggerated hopes of military aid from England, while enterprises requiring great exertions on our part had to be made elsewhere.

He had now been six weeks at Seville, and was able to appreciate fully the condition of things, both civil and military, around him. All tended to disheartenment and distrust: Cuesta had been replaced by Equia at the head of the Spanish army in Estramadura, only to withdraw it farther from the scene of conflict. The French exulted loudly: the 'Moniteur' asking why as Wellington on the eve of his retreat was created a Viscount, Chatham was not created Duke of Walcheren; and Napoleon, writing to the Czar, scoffed at the fatuity which had thrown away five-and-twenty thousand men in the marshes of Holland without firing a shot, and impelled the small British force in the Peninsula to hazard an advance which they were unable to maintain. The Opposition journals at home triumphed in fulfilment of their prognostics, and called for desistance from further intermeddling in Spanish affairs, and the penitent recall of the army.

It is remarkable that, amid the prevailing gloom, the two men who seemed to have been the least disposed to give up the game as lost were the diplomatist and the general, whose personal feelings had been most severely tried by the

27th June, 1809

vanity and unveracity that marred their best endeavours; and whose firmness in resisting reckless importunity had contributed more especially to the laying bare of the position. And now, with all his love of the magnanimous, the British envoy saw that the time had come for being very plain with the Junta and their Ministers. He formally declared to M. De Garay 'that the condition of the Spanish forces, the failure of concert and co-operation, and the mismanagement of the whole system of the military department, opposed insurmountable obstacles to the ultimate success of the English army. Even if the system of supplies could have been corrected, the defects of the Spanish army alone would have formed an irresistible motive for withholding any expectation of future co-operation while the same evils should be left unremedied, and should menace the recurrence of the same misfortunes on every similar occasion.'

The details of military disaffection, as vainglorious excitement waned, and revolutionary authority loosed its hold, is vividly described in a letter to Canning.

'Many officers, even in the highest command, were notoriously disaffected to the cause. In reviewing the events of the campaign it was impossible to imagine any rational motive for the conduct of some of the generals and officers, unless their inclinations were favourable to the enemy, and that they concerted their operations with the French, instead of the British general. Whether the Government, so ill-informed, be deficient in sincerity to the cause of Spain and the allies, is certainly questionable. Whatever jealousy existed against the British Government or the allies was principally to be found in this body, its officers or adherents; in the people no such unworthy sentiment could be traced; but it was evident that the Junta did not possess any spirit of energy or activity, any degree of authority or strength; that it was unsupported by popular attachment or goodwill; while its strange and anomalous constitution united the contradictory inconveniences of every known form of government, without possessing the advantages of any. This was the true cause, at least, of the continuance of that state of weakness, confusion, and disorder of which the British army had recently experienced the consequences in the internal administration of Spain, and especially of her military affairs.' He strongly recommended that a council of Regency consisting of five members, should be named, to exercise the powers of the Executive until the Cortes met, which ought to be with the least possible delay; and that the Junta should superintend the elections, and prepare the subjects of deliberation; that, besides the redress of domestic abuses, the grievances of the Colonies should be remedied, and a share given them in the representation of the empire. But though deeply conscious of many drawbacks and defects, he should not fail to employ every effort in his power to maintain the temper of the alliance, and to cultivate a good intelligence with the existing Ministers, as far as was compatible with the interests and honour of his own country. His persistent fortitude was not shared by Canning, whose susceptibility to ridicule, and impatience of what he termed the incapacity of his colleagues, led him to remonstrate seriously with the Duke of Portland against retaining Castlereagh at the head of the War Department. The Premier, through timidity and a wish to temporise, entertained the suggestion for a considerable time, without any intimation to him or any one but Lord Camden, that his supersession was contemplated, and on its avowal the official world was scandalised by the report of a deadly encounter on Putney Heath.[1] Mr. Canning was wounded, and both combatants resigned. Mr. Perceval was authorised to propose a coalition to the Whigs; but both Grenville and Grey declined to negotiate on any

[1] 21st September, 1809.

common basis; Lord Palmerston was named to hold the seals as *locum tenens* of the War Department, and Lord Bathurst those of Foreign Affairs while they were offered for acceptance to Lord Wellesley. Mr. Sydenham, whom he had long confidentially employed, undertook to be the bearer of the important proposal, and of his answer; while a duplicate was sent by another route. A few hours before the packet was to sail, Perceval learned from the King that on taking leave, Canning, for the first time, had disclosed the fact that on setting out for Spain, his friend had left with him a letter, desiring his recall if he should for any cause quit the Foreign Office. His last official act had consequently been to bid the Marquess leave his post, and devolve his powers on Mr. Hookham Frere, who lingered still in the orange groves of Seville. Wellesley Pole, who was Secretary of the Admiralty, had orders to stay the departure of the vessel till Bathurst and other members of the Government had time to explain all the circumstances of the case. If he would not return to join the Cabinet, all urged him to retain a position which the extreme exigency of the time required. A friend known to be in his especial confidence told Lord Auckland[1] that, notwithstanding the singular engagement entered into with Canning not to hold office without him, he felt sure he would accept. It had been he said obtained from him by management, and had occasioned him no inconsiderable misgiving and regret ere quitting England. Canning probably felt embarrassed at enforcing the obligation in a condition of things so wholly unforeseen, and enclosed the original letter, with leave if he would to disregard it. The Prince of Wales, who was already showing his willingness to give up his exclusive reliance on the comrades of Fox, wrote himself, pressing fervently his adhesion to the Government; and after some days' delay the newly-made Commissioner of Excise

---

[1] 6th October, 1809.

embarked at Plymouth on his special mission. The weather was untoward, and it took him nearly three weeks to reach his destination.

Wellesley Pole, who possessed his brother's confidence, acquainted him with all that had occurred. The prevalent feeling of the astute unwisdom of Canning's conduct was not likely to be abated by his last official act, which seemed to be a desperate attempt, when beaten, to strike an indispensable piece off the board in order to baulk his rival's play. The self-asserting spirit of Wellesley would not tamely submit to be thus used. He thought he had been wrong in having ever made his individual action dependent on the personal ambition of another man, however pre-eminent in the House of Commons he might be. He could not but feel that the show of generosity in letting him break his incautious pledge to retire with his sapping and mining friend, after it was laid before the King, and thereby made known to Ministers, was of but little value, and that, if meant seriously, it amounted rather to a challenge to break off relations of confidence than an appeal to continuing in official friendship. Canning had been left to deal with the difficulties of Court and Cabinet how he thought best, and he had dealt with them so undeftly that he had driven himself, as well as Castlereagh, out of office, and thereby rendered the Marquess, in a degree he had never intended, far less desired, *l'homme inévitable.* Yet at this very moment he plainly sought to render impracticable the reconstruction of the Administration of which till yesterday he had formed a part.

On learning how he had acted towards Castlereagh, Wellesley wrote, October 7, in terms of mingled vexation and reproach, sardonically as Belial might have done had that distinguished person ever condescended to take office and expose himself to retaliation from the keenest wit of the time. Their mutual engagement at parting in July had been not to seek separate interests with regard to power; that in the energetic prosecution of the war against military despotism they would take counsel together; and if unable to compass the adoption of such a policy, that both would refuse to share official responsibility. Palpably the only alternatives contemplated were a Cabinet of which Canning should be spokesman in the Commons, and Wellesley in the Lords; or a Cabinet identical in profession, but more vigorous and able. He had never meant to bind himself to break up the only combination possible after Canning and Castlereagh had both withdrawn, and thereby to justify the public scoff of Napoleon, with whom the Opposition, if they came in, were willing to come to terms of peace, abandoning Spain as incapable of help or rescue. This would indeed be utter self-stultification. He had not gone on a sham embassy; he had not staked character, and advised his brother to hazard reputation, for a worthless cause. In spite of reverses and dissension, it was still the cause of European liberty in his view, as he had believed it to be in that of his wayward and exacting friend, whose half suicide only made him more resolved to take office until the season should return when they might again hold it together. As for his improvident pledge to throw up his embassage, if construed literally, he had kept it *au pied de la lettre*, for he was coming home; if interpreted in spirit, it beckoned him the way to Downing Street. Without waiting for his letter, Canning ill-advisedly suggested, in a subsequent one, the ridicule he imagined would attach to an acceptance of Perceval's offer, if their recent engagement were generally made known. At this the wrath of the fearless little man boiled over in a stream of scalding sarcasm, not easily to be forgotten or forgiven. His letter bore date October 30, and, being sent in copy to Wellesley Pole, was shown to intimate friends in

London. He addressed to Mr. Perceval the following reply:—

'The papers which Mr. Sydenham has fully explained to me, by reference to every circumstance of the late extraordinary events in England, combined with such information as had already reached me, leave no doubt in my mind in regard to the principles both of public and private duty which should govern my conduct in the present crisis, and in the actual situation of his Majesty's service. I therefore accept without hesitation the office of Secretary of State for Foreign Affairs; and I shall return to England with all practicable expedition, for the purpose of discharging the duties of that important station with the zeal and attention which his Majesty may justly claim from a person so deeply indebted to his Majesty's gracious favour, and which he may expect from the whole tenor of my public life and services.' [1]

Private letters had acquainted Wellington at Lisbon with what was taking place, and he hastened his return to Badajoz, in the hope that, posting hard, he might reach his brother ere he left. It was not an occasion to be missed. Both longed for a full interchange of views and feelings, retrospects and felicitations. How much had happened of intense interest to each since they parted in England scarce six months before! The Grand Lodge of Administrative Masonry, at whose door the orator and statesman had so long waited in vain, at length opened to him: nay, they had sent across the sea to compel him to come in; and the aide-de-camp of Lord Buckingham of twenty years before [2] was now a victor in European as in Asian fight, the object of thanks by both Houses of Parliament and the toast at the ceremonious board [3] of 'his

---

[1] Seville, 28th October. 1809. Walpole's *Life of Perceval*, vol. ii. p 41.

[2] See letter from Wellington to Lord Buckingham from Badajos, 16th November, 1809.

[3] 2nd November, 1809.

Excellency,' as 'My Lord Viscount Wellington.' Three days were spent at Seville by the General amid preparations for departure, gazing at fine pictures and into black eyes, and bidding members of the Junta not to lose heart, and clearing up arrears of false reports and misunderstandings, and comparing paragraphs of English and French journals in quest of a flicker of light through the all-surrounding darkness: and then to Cadiz for as brief a span.

The recalled ambassador left Spain on November 10, amid every demonstration of respect from the people, accompanied by Mr. Forbes, Colonel Armstrong, and the Hon. Mr. Clive. The same frigate that had brought him out bore him home again. Though a fine vessel, it was the sixteenth day ere she reached the Needles. He landed at Portsmouth on Sunday, November 26, and on the 28th found himself at Apsley House.

The friends and organs of Administration took courage when all remaining doubt as to the course he would pursue had disappeared. His joining, they believed, would give strength to the Government, but whether enough to carry them through remained to be seen.[1] Grenville thought he might have anything he asked for,—the Garter, and even the Treasury.

At a council on December 6 he kissed hands as Secretary of State, and in a private audience was received by George III. very cordially, as being the only one left of the old friends he had had so long about him.

As a delicate attention his presumed wishes were anticipated by the nomination of his eldest son Richard for Queenborough on the Medway; where dockyard labourers were not allowed to vote or ask questions. One thing, long desired and long withheld, would have gratified him beyond all else—the advancement in the peerage which he

[1] Rose's Diary.

was mortified at not having received ten years before from Pitt; which neither Addington nor Grenville, though well-disposed personally, had been able to obtain for him; but which it was hardly possible for Perceval to propose to the King. The Minister had in fact set his face against new peerages: he thought, as many others did, that they had of late been injudiciously multiplied; but the facility with which they had been conceded had naturally encouraged hopes and demands in so many quarters that it became easier to lay down a general rule of refusal than to attempt to discriminate between nicely balanced claims. An English Marquessate was not to be had; but there was a vacant Garter; and might not that sufficiently mark the high degree in which the new Secretary of State was appreciated by the Crown? It had been indeed already promised to the Duke of Richmond, then Viceroy of Ireland. The new Premier told the King that, previous to the arrival of Lord Wellesley, he deemed it advisable, in order to avoid every possible misunderstanding, to prevail upon Lord Bathurst to represent to his Grace 'the urgent state of the case with regard to the late Duke of Portland's Ribbon, in connection with the application which the Duke of Rutland had made to his Majesty on behalf of Lord Wellesley, and of his anxiety upon the subject.' After Bathurst had opened the subject to his Excellency, Mr. Perceval wrote to him himself, but stating that he thought it better to take no step with regard to it until the ambassador came home; and his Grace of Richmond had, in the most handsome manner, desired Mr. Perceval to understand that if it should be found at all desirable for the benefit of the King's service, under the circumstances in which the Government was now placed, that his Majesty should give the Order to Lord Wellesley, he would readily decline urging any pretension to it whatever. Mr. Perceval had found, since his arrival, that he did feel extremely anxious upon this subject. He had first introduced the subject through Mr. Arbuthnot, to whom he had expressed his feelings upon it in the strongest manner. The Premier had since seen him, and explained what the Duke of Richmond's wishes were upon the point, adding his own private opinion that he thought the Marquess would judge better for himself if he omitted to press the object at this time: that it would be open to unfavourable interpretation as connected with his accepting his present office; but if he continued really to wish it, he would certainly submit his desire to his Majesty, with an humble recommendation that it should be complied with. His lordship thought that as it was so well known by Lord Grenville and others what his pretensions were, to ask this favour; and as the fact was that he had actually signified his intention to accept office before he knew the Duke of Portland's death had made the vacancy, it would not be possible that his conduct should, among reasonable people, be open to misapprehension. No allusion was made in the correspondence to the Order of St. Patrick, his place in which he would of course resign on obtaining the higher distinction. He expressed his wish very strongly that an early occasion should be found for representing to his Majesty his anxious desire upon the subject; and the Minister accordingly submitted that it was desirable, under the circumstances, that the King should be graciously pleased to confer the honour upon him.[1] George III. conveyed his reluctant assent in the following terms:—

'Windsor Castle, December 1, 1809.

'Although the King acquiesces in Mr. Perceval's wish that the vacant Blue Ribbon should be conferred on Lord Wellesley, his Majesty considers that his previous suggestion to

[1] Draft of letter to the King, in Mr. Perceval's handwriting, 30th November, 1809.

Lord Wellesley was perfectly well founded, and that it is to be regretted that it did not receive due attention. At the present season of the year it would not be possible to collect a sufficient number of Knights of the Garter for the ceremony of investing Lord Wellesley; nor can the delay be material.

'GEORGE R.'

Mr. Perceval then wrote:—

'I have just received his Majesty's answer to my letter recommending your lordship for the vacant Blue Ribbon. His Majesty adds, that at the present season of the year it would not be possible to collect a sufficient number of Knights of the Garter for the ceremony of investing your lordship; nor could the delay be material. I am so uninformed upon this subject as not to know what is the necessary number; but this is easily learnt, and being kept in mind, I should hope the delay will not be long. I circulated some time ago a paper giving the view which, with the aid of Huskisson, I had taken of our financial situation, and explaining the necessity which appeared to me to arise out of that situation for contracting the expenditure of the country as much as possible. I have directed a copy to be made, and I trust I shall be able to send it to you to-morrow. Permit me to request your very particular attention to it when you receive it. I do not believe the statements to be exaggerated. You will see the necessity of keeping it in view in the consideration of our future plans of military operations, to which we must all see the necessity of devoting our best attention without loss of time.'

The concession to his wishes was acknowledged in the following terms:—

'I am most deeply sensible of his Majesty's gracious favour in the intention, which he has been pleased to signify, of conferring upon me the high honour of the Order of the

Garter. I request you to assure his Majesty that my zeal for his service required no incitement; and that my gratitude, for the long course of favours and goodness which I have experienced since I have had the satisfaction to serve him, could not be increased. But the distinction which his Majesty has now been pleased to grant to me is so peculiarly calculated to mark to the world his Majesty's approbation (after full knowledge) of my endeavours to serve him and my country in many arduous situations, that I cannot receive the notification of the King's pleasure on this occasion without returning a most particular expression of my humble thanks and most cordial satisfaction. With respect to the particular moment of completing the ceremony necessary for the investiture, I am too sensible of his Majesty's condescension to feel any other inclination than that of awaiting the King's pleasure. I request you to accept my sincere acknowledgments for your kindness on this occasion, and to believe that no more acceptable addition could be made to his Majesty's favour than that it should be communicated through a person so justly entitled to high respect and esteem.'

The same day he wrote:—

'I have returned a separate answer on the subject of the Garter. With regard to the proposed delay, I wish to submit entirely to his Majesty's pleasure. It is however very desirable that the honour should follow my Spanish embassy as closely as possible.

'Instances may be found of publishing the honour in the "Gazette" before (and I believe even without) formal investiture: you will find these cases by reference. But I leave the whole of that point to your discretion.

'I shall be very happy to receive the statement of our financial situation, which you have prepared. I am fully impressed with the necessity of founding all our plans of military operation on the basis of our financial means. I am also desirous of framing the whole system of our plans, of every description, in a regular and connected manner, before we commence any scheme of action; and I shall be happy, at a very early period of time, to submit to your consideration such ideas as may have occurred to me.'

The announcement was made in the usual way, but no time for the investiture was fixed, and the delay led to some further correspondence. On December 20 the Premier wrote:—

'I mentioned to the King how desirable it was that his Majesty should complete his gracious purpose of conferring the Order of the Garter upon you, and how anxious you were (from finding that the cause of the delay was misapprehended) that the purpose should be completed as soon as was convenient to his Majesty. He cordially replied that his rule was not to hold a "chapel" before the spring or the end of March; but he desired me to say that it should take place on an early day in February. I thought I could not press it further at the time, and I think you will be of the same opinion when I detail to you more at length than I can well do in my letter the particulars which passed upon the subject. If you come down to your office to-morrow I will explain them to you, or will see you here.'[1]

The investiture did not take place until some weeks later,[2] his Majesty being amused and the Ministry amazed at the fretful impatience shown about the matter.

In Grenville's candidature for the Chancellorship of Oxford his early friend took much interest, sending his private Secretary Vaughan to vote for him. On his success he wrote congratulating him warmly. 'His residence at Seville,

---

[1] For the above, and many other confidential letters in MS., I am indebted to the kindness of the Premier's grandson, Mr. Spencer Perceval.
[2] 3rd March, 1810.

and holding the tapers for two hours at the high mass performed in the cathedral for the repose of Sir John Moore's soul, had much ameliorated his sentiments on the No Popery system.' Grenville's reply was cordial as formerly, and up to this time no trace was observable of a flaw in their old friendship.

The first copy of the 'Moniteur' read by the new Foreign Secretary was that which contained Napoleon's address to the Corps Législatif, recounting the effects of the campaign of Wagram, announcing his resolve to tranquillise the Peninsula by the overwhelming power of his then undivided armies, and ending by the memorable threat,—' When I show myself beyond the Pyrenees, the English leopard will plunge into the ocean to escape from shame and death.' Nor was this said in merely idle boast. Nine corps d'armée, consisting of 366,000 men, many of them sharers of his great victories, and led by his best lieutenants, were already mustering for the final subjugation of Spain. To Massena, with 85,000 veterans, was assigned the specific duty of evicting Wellington from Portugal.

CHAPTER XVIII.

THE FOREIGN OFFICE.

1810.

NEVER in our time was the charge of Foreign affairs so heavy with danger and trouble as at the opening of the new year.[1] Napoleon had crushed nearly all his enemies, and stood at the summit of unequalled power. Spain, Italy, Holland, and Westphalia had been in turn subdued, and conferred as kingdom-fiefs of his Empire. Prussia lay gasping from her recent wounds, and Austria was only respited on condition that her daughter should supplant in marriage the faithful and fond Josephine. The Czar, no longer querulous, had come to terms; and the Pope was a pensioner and a prisoner on parole. The Turk professed fidelity to us, and perhaps meant it as far as he dared; but he had public warning not to provoke the displeasure of him whose dominion stretched from the Tagus to the Saave, and from Hamburg to Palermo. Portugal still held out, and with squadrons in the Tagus and in Cadiz Bay, and succours afforded in sufficient time, it might still be possible to belie the sanguine vaunt that before Easter the Imperial eagle should be set on the towers of Lisbon. But masses of veteran troops were pouring through the Pyrenees to reinforce the rule of King Joseph, and to complete the extirpation of the intrusive Islanders. Could reinforcements for the out-numbered

[1] Sir G. C. Lewis, *Administrations of Great Britain*, p. 318.

bost at Badajos, numerous enough and well-enough equipped, be sent forth in time? If not, there was no European question of Foreign affairs worth solving or trying to solve.

So low had the popular spirit sunk on learning the defeat of the Spanish army at Ocana, the advance of the French on Seville, and the retreat of the British to the lines round Lisbon, that petitions influentially signed implored Government to abandon the struggle; and nearly all the leaders of Opposition prepared to take the same desponding tone. Thomas Grenville wrote despondingly to his brother,—'We are treating with America, which not to do would be madness; we are reinforcing and defending Portugal, which to do is madness.'[1] Public faith in the one favourite of fortune began to fail; and Wellington became an object of distrust and disparagement. What was he about, and what could he mean? Was he going to Cintra again?

The Common Council of London addressed the King against any reward or dignity being conferred on a man 'who, by his rash advance into Spain; his useless sacrifice of life at Talavera; his flight before a beaten enemy, and the abandoning of his wounded,' had deserved ill of his country; and a petition to the same effect was presented to the House of Commons.[2]

Unmoved by the folly of such injustice, the inflexible commander held on his difficult way; from time to time keeping his younger brother, who became envoy at Cadiz, and his elder brother in England, to whom he still looked up with a deference he did not affect to conceal, informed of all his purposes and perplexities. He sometimes feared that 'Ministers were as much alarmed as the public, or as the Opposition pretended to be; and they appeared to be of opinion that he was inclined to fight a desperate battle to answer no

---

[1] To Lord Buckingham: Cleveland Square, 10th January, 1810.
[2] 26th January, 1810.

purpose, throwing upon him the whole responsibility of bringing his army away in safety, after staying in the Peninsula until it might be necessary to evacuate it.' But the newly appointed Foreign Minister did not intend that the army should come away, *re infecta*. With due deliberation and dignity he put on record the principles and purposes of his policy; which being submitted to the King and in Council adopted, ceremoniously but completely committed the Government to an energetic support of the war. Resistance was a duty, not for the sake of the house of Bourbon or the house of Braganza, but for the sake of the people of England, whose commerce and whose independence were meant to be outflanked by the annexation of the Peninsula to the Buonapartian empire.[1]

'The condition of Spain and Portugal has engaged his Majesty's most anxious attention, and I am to signify to you his determination to maintain the cause of his allies in the Peninsula by continuing to supply to them every assistance, compatible with the resources and security of his own dominions, as long as the contest shall appear to afford any reasonable prospect of advantage against the common enemy. It is intended to employ in Portugal a force of 30,000 men and an annual sum of 980,000*l*. This great and generous effort cannot fail to inspire confidence and additional regard in the Portuguese Government and nation. You will offer, and even urge advice, as to rendering available the resources of Portugal, obtaining monthly accounts of the expenditure and the state of the corps receiving British pay; and generally, of the financial condition of the country. No jealousy or suspicion must be harboured under such a pressure of common danger. The great sacrifices which we have made for our ally must not be frustrated by any considerations inferior to the main purpose of our mutual security; nor

[1] To Mr. Villiers, at Lisbon, 6th January, 1810. MS. in Foreign Office.

can we now hesitate to take the lead in any measure evidently necessary to enable Portugal to contribute a just share of efforts and resources for the accomplishment of her own safety. His Majesty has observed with deep regret the circumstances of infirmity and irresolution which you have remarked in the councils and character of the Regency, though you have never doubted their loyalty and good faith. Experience has proved that the most powerful obstacle to the success of the French armies is the determined resistance of the body of the people. This resistance will be most active in proportion to their affection for the person of their Sovereign and for the principles of their government. The great difficulty which the French have experienced in Spain has been the general spirit of the Spanish people. The British Government would look with satisfaction on any measures in Portugal calculated to unite the masses of the nation in interests and affection with the Executive power.'

Parliament met on January 23, and the speech from the Throne, delivered by commission, was the first in whose composition Wellesley had a share; and conventional as are the forms adhered to on such occasions, the Royal message in question bears the impress of a hand more like that of Pitt than of any that had recently taken part in this peculiar species of political literature. The secession of Austria and Sweden was lamented candidly but without reproach, as the result of necessity; and our failure in the Scheldt was unfalteringly avowed. A confident hope was expressed that, though the principal ends of the expedition had not been attained, advantages in the future prosecution of the war would be found to result from the demolition of the docks and arsenals of Flushing. The expulsion of the French from Portugal by the forces under Viscount Wellington, and the glorious victory obtained at Talavera, had contributed to check the progress of the French arms in the Peninsula. King Ferdinand had summoned a meeting of the Cortes, which would give fresh animation and vigour to the councils and the arms of Spain, and successfully direct the energies and spirit of the Spanish people to the maintenance of the ancient monarchy and to the ultimate deliverance of the country. 'The most important considerations of policy and of good faith required that, as long as this great cause could be maintained with a prospect of success, it should be supported, according to the nature and circumstances of the contest, by the strenuous and continued assistance of the power and resources of his Majesty's dominions; and the Regent relied on the aid of Parliament in his anxious endeavours to frustrate the attempts of France against the independence of Spain and Portugal, and against the happiness and freedom of those loyal and resolute nations.'[1]

There is no mistaking the tramp of these serried pledges and aspirations. The vanquisher of Tippoo and Scindiah would not have taken office under circumstances so critical with any half-hearted resolution. The falterings and blunders of the past, he stipulated that he must not be expected to defend; but a new leaf must be turned over, on which all who ran might read the lines of another policy; and hence the vigorous and almost vaunting tone of the royal speech regarding foreign affairs. Grenville denounced in scathing terms, the mismanagement which had led to the disasters of Corunna and Walcheren, but carefully avoided all allusion to Wellesley's diplomatic service in Spain, or more recent adhesion to what he termed a wasteful and infatuated Administration. He possibly had some inkling of the actual condition of things in the Cabinet, where grave misgivings prevailed as to the possibility of going on. Grey alluded pointedly to the absence during the debate of the newly appointed Foreign Secretary. Without his aid his

[1] *Life of Perceval,* by Mr. Spencer Walpole, ii. 65.

colleagues had a majority indeed of fifty-two, and in the Commons they were not less fortunate. But within a week they were beaten on several occasions by majorities varying from five to thirteen, and the biographer of Perceval states that 'Lord Wellesley had made up his mind that their task was impracticable, and had concluded that the reins of government were on the eve of falling into his own hands. The disappointment which he felt at the contrary result is said to have been the cause of the rupture which ultimately took place between Perceval and him.' No breach however was observable by the outer world in their relations. Wellesley Pole was Secretary for Ireland; Henry Wellesley Minister to Spain; and a pension of two thousand pounds a year for life was voted by two hundred and thirteen to one hundred and six, on the cordial recommendation of the Premier, to the victor of Talavera.

When thanks were moved to the army in Spain, more than one biting criticism of the strategy of the general was indulged in, in both Houses. The Foreign Secretary warmly defended his gallant kinsman, neither deprecating inquiry, or depreciating the motives of Earl Grey, whose language was especially severe. 'If his noble adversary had found it painful to his feelings, as he said, to impugn the value of the services rendered by Lord Wellington, how much more painful must be the situation in which he stood, who could not but be open to private feelings, while he also had a public duty to perform, who had to vindicate the character and conduct of so near and dear a relative as a brother, of an officer whose eminent qualities he had had such frequent opportunities of observing; qualities which, whatever opinion it might please the noble earl to entertain, were attested by the universal voice of the officers and soldiers of the armies he had commanded, and of the countries in whose defence they had been exerted: of Portugal, where he was almost adored, and where he was invested with power little short of royal; and of Spain, where he was equally beloved by the people and respected by the Government.' He proceeded to analyse in detail the circumstances under which the British army crossed the frontier; the capabilities of the countries through which they had to march; the strength of the Spanish army under Cuesta, and its failure to execute its part of the concerted movement against Marshal Victor. His close correspondence from Seville (already quoted) enabled him to speak with peculiar accuracy and emphasis of the deplorable lack of supplies furnished by the Junta to our troops after the victory. Although compelled eventually to withdraw within the confines of Portugal, it could not be denied that the safety of that realm, which was the primary object we had in the campaign, was substantially secured, and that for the season the outnumbering hosts of France were effectually kept at bay. Their progress was thus arrested in the south of Spain, and breathing-time given to an old and faithful ally to organise the means of future defence. 'All these advantages were fairly to be ascribed to the skill, the courage, and the activity which directed the exertions of the English general and his army; and upon the whole, he did not hesitate to say that his brother was as justly entitled to every distinction which his Sovereign had conferred on him, and to every honour and reward which it was in the power of Parliament to bestow, as any noble lord who, for personal services, had obtained the same distinctions, or who sat there by descent from illustrious ancestors.'

No division took place, and the Minister had the satisfaction of transmitting to his brother next day the unanimous thanks of the Peers. Many angry and bitter things had likewise been said in the Commons about senseless projects, want of strategy, and criminal waste of life and treasure. But Canning, though out of humour and out of place, would not lend himself to a course he knew to be at variance with the instincts of the nation; and sooner than reveal the weakness of dissension, the more vehement section of Opposition declined to divide.

Full reports of the debates in Parliament regarding foreign affairs were carefully reproduced in the 'Moniteur,' and they contributed greatly to mislead the French and other Governments as to the real feelings of our people. Napoleon was beguiled into the belief that, because orators out of office scoffed at their rivals as incapable, and denounced their policy as spendthrift and sanguinary, they seriously meant if they came into power, that the country would consent to succumb, or that they themselves would venture to make the suggestion. But the depressing effect throughout the Continent on all the friends of national freedom was for the time as palpable as the encouragement in wrongdoing given to the aggressive schemes of despotism. England, it was said, was fairly cowed; weary of unavailing efforts, and anxious for peace at any price. Did not her ablest and most eloquent statesmen say so, and in the most unmeasured terms? *Voici, Messieurs!* And month after month the columns of the official organ of Imperialism were filled with the speeches and letters of the anti-war party in England, who were supposed to sympathise with the policy of France.

Preparatory to the discussion of military affairs, papers relative to the late campaign in the Peninsula were asked for in Parliament; and the lesser instincts in office prompted some to question how far information in detail should be made public of differences in council with our Allies, and of shortcomings on their part in the field which had led to disappointment and disaster. It would seen ungenerous, and it might prove imprudent, to mark too plainly the reasons why our sacrifices on their behalf had not been more availing.

Higher and bolder views pointed to the need of taking the nation into confidence, and satisfying them that the lives and treasure they had put in hazard for the rescue of Portugal and Spain from alien despotism had not been trifled with or thrown away. To leave it dark, or even doubtful, why it was necessary for the British to fall back after a victory, and why the Spanish army had wholly failed to protect Seville, would be to quench the national hope and wound the national faith irredeemably. If the war was to be carried on to any good purpose, public opinion must be thoroughly satisfied that our statesmen and commanders had not been wanting, and that they might be relied on whoever else was to blame. With the Foreign Secretary there was no wavering about the course to be pursued. 'In every discussion,' he said, 'my judgment has inclined to the most ample and complete disclosure of all the papers which can tend to illustrate the conduct of Government at home, of our Ministers and Generals abroad, and of the Spanish Government during the late campaign. The same principle has always been applied by me to questions in Portugal. My opinion has been that the earliest moment should be seized to open to the public every branch of our transactions. In my judgment they have been highly honourable both to our councils and to our arms; and I am satisfied that the most direct course with respect to granting information would prove the most politic and secure. The moment is arrived in which no possible objection can arise on the ground of delicacy towards the Junta (if any such objection was ever solid), and if we look either to the future exertions of Spain, or to our own means of aiding her, we must satisfy both Spain and England that our conduct has been right, and that the causes of past misfortunes are not irremediable, because those causes are to be traced to errors and to faults which may be corrected, and which we are resolved to correct by the utmost efforts of our influence. If the Spanish and Portuguese papers are to be suppressed, I confess that it appears to me that we shall deprive ourselves of our main advantage in the conflict with the Opposition. They will not be able to withstand the intrinsic and honest strength of our cause, as founded on that information. We shall be subject to every kind of prejudice, misrepresentation, and calumny if we refuse to produce evidence of what we must assert. But I wish it to be understood that I think we shall derive the greatest benefit from producing them. You will excuse my solicitude in urging most earnestly the step which I recommend from a conviction that a contrary course will lead to interminable difficulty and even disgrace.'[1]

The papers were in consequence laid upon the table, with what result will presently be seen.

From his entering office the Foreign Secretary took every opportunity of having it known that he disclaimed all participation in responsibility for the Walcheren expedition. The inquiry in the Commons occupied February and March; and at its close the evidence was summed up in resolutions of censure moved by Lord Porchester, which, if carried, must compel the retirement of all who had sanctioned the ill-starred enterprise.

'The result will be, they imagine, fatal to the existing Administration, on the point of the retention of Walcheren, with the exception of Lord Wellesley and, perhaps, Lord Harrowby. A new one must therefore be formed. The Wellesleys are satisfied the Marquess will have the King's command to that effect; and what is more they are equally confident of forming one which shall be equally permanent. Of the co-operation of The Doctor they have no doubt. Already is Lord Ellenborough's powerful assistance in the House of Lords calculated upon, who however will

[1] To Mr. Perceval; Apsley House, 12th February, 1810.

not be in the Cabinet. Lord Buckinghamshire is an old friend and a most honourable man; Bathurst very respectable and useful; Vansittart an able financier. Lord Eldon is not to be touched, nor Lord Melville to be taken in. Yorke of course will come forward prominently; nor are the doors absolutely shut, by the course which Parliamentary indignation will take as it is supposed, upon Canning and Castlereagh, as they were both out of office before the retention of Walcheren became culpable. The leanings of Lord Wellesley are all towards Castlereagh. There exists between them the most perfect understanding. The great difficulty would arise in taking both these personages into the same Cabinet after what has passed. Canning only objected to the conduct of the war; but Castlereagh will not conduct it; and would not for his private resentments break up a plan in which so many of his friends will be mixed, and in which he is treated with so much consideration. Ireland will not be disturbed, the Duke of Richmond having the greatest regard for Lord Wellesley. I should not be surprised, if all this go on, should Lord Powis [1] come into the Cabinet without office. You will see in all this that the sacrifice is Perceval, who gets nothing, nor can get anything. If Lord Wellesley does not form the new Administration, The Doctor will. In the latter case I think Lord Wellesley would hold his present office.' [2]

All these conjectures proved to be illusory. Canning and Castlereagh equally considered themselves bound in honour to bear their share of blame with their former colleagues, and in debate exerted themselves with such effect that the condemnatory resolution was rejected by a majority of forty-eight.

The unexpected result was as surprising and mortifying

---

[1] Ex-Governor of Madras.

[2] The writer of these curious conjectures was believed by Sir G. C. Lewis to be Mr. Dardis, who had the confidence both of Apsley House and Stowe.

to the Wellesleys as to the public. It was not attributed so much to any peculiar exertion made by the Government as to the course of the debate. Canning particularly distinguished himself, for he had not been tempted in the proposed arrangements to quit the path of generosity and honour. That Wellesley could have seriously contemplated trying to carry on the Government without his aid as leader of the Commons seems strange; but he probably diplomatised too finely and too long with him and Castlereagh, not intending to throw over either of them, yet not choosing to make his attainment of power conditional on the adhesion of either. The lesson was a severe one, and he lost no time in endeavouring to efface the impression, if it really existed. Not many days after, the political world was surprised at the confident assurance that a complete reconciliation had been effected with Canning. The unfortunate misunderstanding of the previous autumn, it was agreed, should be buried in oblivion, and the two friends were henceforth to act together as they had bound themselves to do twelve months before. Canning who was then in office, had laboured indefatigably to bring Wellesley in. Their relative positions were now changed, and the Marquess declared that he considered Canning's re-admission to the Cabinet indispensable, if he was himself to continue in power. 'This chivalry on his part,' wrote Lord Buckingham's correspondent, 'was very little to the taste of his nearest friends, who as little approved of the proposed sacrifice as of the reconciliation with Canning.'[1]

On March 30, Grenville moved for a Secret Committee, to whom the papers relative to the campaign in Spain and Portugal should be referred to select and prepare them for the House. The mischief that must arise from the disclosures made through the strange, unaccountable, and unpardonable

[1] 2nd April, 1810.

negligence with which the correspondence had been thrown on the table, he was afraid was already done. It was now published to the world, and would he feared prove highly injurious to the interests of the country. It was a sacred duty with Ministers to take care, in negotiations with friendly States, that the public councils of their Governments should not be betrayed, and that no improper reflections should be made public upon the Governments themselves; no disclosure should be made of the quarrels or disunions of the leading persons in such Governments, or of those who were confidentially employed by them. It was, above all, a most sacred duty to take care that the safety and the lives of persons confidentially employed, or through whom information was obtained, should not be lightly compromised or wantonly put to hazard. This rule had heretofore been invariably acted on, until Ministers then in office had, on a previous occasion, published papers that ought to have been withheld. He regretted that complaint and protest had not before been made in Parliament, as it might have prevented the repetition of conduct so unworthy and disgraceful. But it was now an imperative duty to complain of Ministers having published documents tending to betray the honour of the country and to endanger the lives of individuals. The papers relating to the Spanish campaign were full of passages most improper to be published. Their whole tenor was to show the wretched weakness of the Supreme Junta, and especially to impugn the character and conduct of the commander of the Spanish armies. A foreign commander had never before been thus brought before Parliament, with whole pages of invective against him. Such shocking injustice had not before stained their proceedings. He knew nothing of General Cuesta, but if he were a man of honour and character he must feel acutely being reviled by Ministers whose attacks would be published even in the country where he was serving. How was he to defend himself to the Spaniards against our accusations? What foreign general could feel safe if the Administration under which this country had the misfortune to groan would put on paper, make official, and circulate such imputations? In one of Mr. Frere's letters it was stated to be a matter of general suspicion that General Cuesta meditated some serious plan of vengeance for the affronts experienced on the part of the Central Junta; and that General Venegas did not possess that military reputation or commanding character necessary to counterpoise a man of Cuesta's authority and decided temper. Blake and Albuquerque were said to be the only men fit for command, and neither, through no fault of his own, was at the head of an army in the field. A letter, obviously meant to be confidential, from the Duke was addressed to the Junta, asserting the desire of the whole Spanish army that Venegas, Blake, or himself should be appointed in the room of Cuesta, who was no longer trusted or obeyed. What would be thought of the noble writer of that letter when its contents were divulged at Cadiz, where he and the commander he would have deposed were together in garrison? The putting to death of several hundred French prisoners was, without a word of censure or rebuke, ascribed to another Spanish officer; and no proof was to be found in the papers laid upon the table. Could there be a more outrageous attack upon the Junta than to proclaim that they failed to employ an able general because he was a man of rank and fortune? In what a situation was the country placed by these indiscreet and criminal disclosures! Would not British Ministers be in future shunned, and all confidence withheld by foreign Governments? He did not blame Mr. Frere for collecting and communicating information and the opinions entertained regarding individuals. The blame rested altogether with Ministers for publishing such information. He did not think that any man would have the nerve to defend such disclosures. But he was mistaken. The nerveless, because half-occupied, companion of earlier days had been disciplined by heavy responsibility into a political veteran, and Grenville's ungenerous sarcasm, at what he mistook for an incorrigible susceptibility of temperament, hissed harmlessly off its object, wrought up to a white heat of scorn. Without hesitation or any symptom of emotion he rose to reply.

He professed his readiness to accept the general principle laid down by the noble lord respecting the selection of diplomatic documents for publication. He fully owned that, in answering the demand of either House of Parliament for the production of such documents, a sacred duty was imposed on the Executive power to take care that such publications should not violate the good faith subsisting between Governments, or compromise the personal safety of individuals. Admitting freely the obligation of that duty, it was also requisite to attend to the nature of communications made to Parliament, and to the peculiar circumstances of the case, which in the present instance must be acknowledged to involve matter of great delicacy and difficulty. This was a case in which Parliament and the nation were entitled to know the truth; and it was difficult, if not impracticable, to satisfy that great public and natural right, consistently with the overstrained restrictions which the noble lord would attempt to impose on the preparation of the official documents required for the information of the House. Their Lordships would not fail to recollect how general and anxious a wish had been expressed throughout the kingdom that every aid should be afforded to Spain which might enable her to assert her national independence, and to restore her ancient monarchy on the basis of the happiness, the prosperity, and the freedom of the people. It was necessary, therefore, to show how the efforts of this country in that noble cause had been frustrated. Above all, it was necessary to show why the glorious achievements of the British arms in the Peninsula had not been followed by beneficial consequences equal to their splendour and to the fair expectations which they had raised both in this country and in Spain. This could not be effected without tracing these failures to their proper cause, and without pointing out the real source of the calamities which have been accumulated on the Peninsula. The real difficulties in the Peninsula were not fully understood in this country. It was essential, therefore, to state unreservedly all the facts and circumstances to which partial failure was to be imputed. It must be the wish of Parliament and the nation at large, as it certainly was his earnest wish, and the wish of all his colleagues, to disclose all these circumstances with the least possible reserve. This, however, could not be effectually done without producing the papers as they appear on their Lordships' table, from which it must be seen that the dissensions, the intrigues, and the corruptions of the Spanish officers, and that the weakness and incapacity of the Spanish Government, had been the real sources and springs, as well as the proximate causes, of all the misfortunes which have recently afflicted the Spanish nation. The noble lord was of opinion, however, that the publication of these documents must prove highly injurious to the character of the Spanish Government; but he appeared to have forgotten that the provisional Government, to whose conduct the papers referred, was actually extinct. The Central Junta was dissolved by its own weakness, and a different form of administration had succeeded. He and his colleagues were desirous to demonstrate the nature, the progress, and the result of these events; but they could not discharge their duty if they were to be precluded from revealing the real state of a Government which no longer existed, and which had fallen amidst the confusion occasioned by its own defects.

The noble lord had complained of the publication of Mr. Frere's letter, in which that gentleman stated his opinion of the character and conduct of General Cuesta. Now he would challenge the noble lord to rise in his place, and to mark a single point in that letter respecting General Cuesta which was not of general notoriety throughout all Spain, which was not in conformity with the opinion of every officer and soldier in the Spanish army, and of every man who really felt and avowed an attachment to the Spanish cause. So thoroughly and universally was the conviction of General Cuesta's incapacity felt, that Mr. Frere, as appeared by the papers, had actually demanded his dismissal from the command of the army, a circumstance which the noble lord had omitted to notice. He (Marquess Wellesley), on his arrival at Seville, did not think it necessary to insist on that demand, being satisfied that General Cuesta could not remain in the command; and that the influence of general opinion respecting his incapacity, the infirm state of his body, and the decrepitude of his mind, must speedily occasion his removal without any interposition of British power. The noble lord seemed to suppose (a supposition, however, in which he was mistaken) that General Cuesta still held a command at Cadiz. General Cuesta had had no command in Spain since his removal, which, to the general satisfaction of the Spanish army and people, took place in the beginning of August.

The next charge made by the noble lord against His Majesty's Government (a most serious charge if founded on fact) was a violation of honour in publishing a private letter of the Duke of Albuquerque. Now he would assert in front of that noble lord, that there was not a sentiment contained in that letter which was not of perfect notoriety throughout Spain; that there was not a sentiment in it which that illustrious person had not himself publicly and loudly proclaimed. So far from complaining of the publication of that letter, the Duke of Albuquerque would heartily rejoice at it; and confident he was that he should receive the cordial thanks of that spirited officer, of whose personal friendship he boasted, for having thus publicly recorded his real opinions, and his just pretensions, to which, on every occasion he was proud to bear testimony. But the talents and merits of that gallant and illustrious commander stood in need of no testimony from him. Let the safety of Cadiz, let his rapid march for the defence of that last hold of Spanish independence, attest his zeal, his patriotism, his skill, his fortitude, his glory. If Cadiz still was safe, its safety was due to the prompt decision of that gallant and noble mind, whose conduct formed a splendid contrast to that of many others; who might, therefore, justly condemn examples which he disdained to imitate, and avow his claims to the superior command of the armies of a country whose existence he had saved. Thus far their Lordships would see how groundless were the apprehensions, how superfluous the invectives of which the noble baron was so prodigal in censuring the pretended indiscretion of His Majesty's Ministers. But the further instances adduced by the noble lord in justification of these invectives, would afford a still stronger proof of the injustice of these charges and of the ignorance which dictated them. The noble lord, as an additional proof of the thoughtless and unfeeling indiscretion of Ministers, had stated the case of three persons, who, it seemed, would be exposed to the most imminent danger, and to the most rancorous resentment of the enemy, by the publication of certain facts in the correspondence laid upon the table. The noble lord had abstained from naming them, but he could assure him that no necessity existed for such egregious caution. Their names were well known both in Spain and France; both to the Spanish and the French Governments. Indeed, he might add, that the publication of their names, when accompanied by the mention of their hardy deeds, was one of the proudest distinctions to which the Spanish patriots aspired. This was the case of the several leaders of partisan corps, whose names had already been published in the Spanish *Gazettes* for the purpose of honour and fame, as the noble lord would have known if he had been at all acquainted with the real state of that distracted country. Another case was that of M. Barrios, who was represented as having, in retaliation for some cruel and unworthy treatment inflicted on the Spanish prisoners by a French general, caused 700 French prisoners to be driven into the Minho. No man viewed such a deed with more horror, or more lamented such outrages against the law of civilised war than he did; but was this fact first revealed by the papers on the table, and what must their Lordships think of the correctness of the information upon which the noble baron rested his charges against Ministers when they came to hear the true statement of that fact? Was not the perpetration of that deed notorious throughout Spain— notorious to the French Government? Did not Barrios himself not only loudly proclaim, but proudly boast of it at Seville? Was it not published in all the Spanish and French *Gazettes?* Had not Barrios even been publicly proscribed by name by the French Government? Where, then, was the secret which the publication of these papers had disclosed? The transaction, however dreadful, was public. M. Barrios had first made a solemn remonstrance against Marshal Ney's proceedings towards the Spanish prisoners, and, failing in that remonstrance, retaliation had been ordered. The noble lord then pathetically deplored the dangers to which the Governor of Avila had been exposed by the publication of these documents. The papers would convict him of having betrayed to the Spanish General

Cuesta, letters and despatches from Joseph Buonaparte and General Jourdain, thereby exposing him to the most cruel resentment of the enemy. But what was the fact? Avila was in the hands of the French; and the Governor of Avila was in the French interest. It was not he who betrayed the letters into the hands of General Cuesta, but they were found upon a Spanish friar, to whom they had been confidentially trusted; what danger, then, could the Governor of Avila incur from the production of those papers? The Governor of Avila was still attached to the cause of the invader; and even while he (Wellesley) was in Spain the whole of these despatches, which had been delivered to General Cuesta, with all the circumstances of the case, were published at Seville. None of the persons, therefore, for whose safety the humanity of the noble lord was so alarmed, had been exposed to any danger by the publication of the papers on the table. He believed moreover that they were then out of the reach of the enemy's power; what then was the cause which had thus disturbed the noble lord's temper and perverted his judgment? The noble lord could not have read the papers, or he did not understand them. With what confidence then did he come there to charge others with neglect, when he himself was so grossly misinformed, and yet presumed to pass so severe a sentence? The noble lord had betrayed the utmost ignorance with respect to every point upon which he had touched; and he (Lord Wellesley) was justified in again asserting that the noble lord stood convicted, either of not having read the papers on the table, or, if he had read them, of not understanding them. He trusted, therefore, that their Lordships would spurn the imputation of indiscretion and neglect with which the noble lord had charged His Majesty's Ministers; and that they would reject a motion which would deprive them of that full information respecting the affairs of Spain which alone could guide their future determination with regard to the interests of that country. The papers already on the table, and those yet to be produced, would amply supply that information, and would disclose the truth in full and open day. Their Lordships would then see that the weakness, the dissensions, and the corruption of the Spanish officers and Government were the real sources and springs of many disasters and calamities which had befallen the Spanish nation. That knowledge would furnish the grounds of a better system of policy for Spain, and perhaps for England, the ally of Spain. That was a question, however, which he should have another occasion more fully to discuss. At present he should implore their Lordships not to accede to the motion intercepting the papers by a secret committee. He implored them not to obscure by their own act the lights necessary for a full and clear knowledge of those great and interesting questions. A most material part of the correspondence consisted of his own despatches during his late embassy to Spain. These were essential to illustrate the events which had preceded his arrival in that country as well as the probable course of its future fate. He, therefore, implored their Lordships that they would not permit any part of his own despatches to be suppressed; that they would not permit the noble lord to rob him of the advantage of a fuller manifestation of the conduct which he had pursued during his mission; and that at least the record of his transactions in Spain might be presented to their Lordships and the public pure and entire.

Earl Grey endeavoured to sustain some of the charges made against the Minister; but the feeling of the House was too manifest to be trifled with, and the motion was rejected without a division.

Apsley House was filled with felicitations all next day at the triumph of the Secretary of State over his assailants.

Bathurst and Harrowby were especially warm in sympathetic praise; and the faithful fetch-and-carry for his patron at Stowe, wrote that the result of the debate in the Lords was considered by the Wellesleys as another Talavera. They had been congratulated upon Lord Wellesley's speech, and its effect, in a manner sufficiently flattering to make them vain. The acerbity manifested in the discussion between Grenville and his early friend was a theme of comment and regret; their old schoolfellow, Moss, the Bishop of Oxford, doing his best to assuage the feelings of bitterness.

Of Grenville the correspondent said little to his brother, by whom his unconciliatory manner and arrogance of pretension were too well known. Even to Pitt he would not give way in the choice of measures to be pursued in 1804, and he provoked his illustrious kinsman to exclaim, 'I will teach that proud man that I can do without him.' Since then he had himself been Premier, and thenceforth could be induced to think of no secondary place. But few beside wished for him again in that capacity. Erskine in his cups made no secret that he thought him 'the damn'dest fellow in the universe.'[1] He was not wholly unconscious of his unpopularity, and sometimes owned he felt by temperament unfit for the management of men. A coolness had arisen between him and his old class-fellow, unexplained at the time, yet not difficult to explain. So long as the ex-Governor General lay under the harrow of Paull's threats of impeachment, Grenville was kind and considerate enough. But when the cloud had passed away, Wellesley chafed at what he deemed the want of due appreciation of his political value as an ally, and retrospectively grew resentful at never having been asked to join the Cabinet except by Perceval. He would show men the difference, and assert himself without

[1] Grey Bennet's Journal.

anybody's leave. With Lord Buckingham and his son he continued to live on a friendlier footing; but no one could talk to Grenville about the weakness of the Administration, or the need of a change of hands, without perceiving that in his mind there was but one possible First Minister,—the man whom nearly everyone else regarded as intolerable. And hence it came to pass that, throughout the interminable intrigues of 1810, all other combinations were in turn devised and attempted, reverted to and given up as impracticable. Sidmouth had been Premier, like Grenville, and for a much longer time. Personally he had many friends, and he was the favourite of the King. He was willing to waive his claim to priority in favour of Wellesley, but with his old assailant Canning he repeatedly refused to sit in Council; and the merciless wit could not be bound over in sufficient recognisances to keep his tongue from molesting the 'Doctor.' Then there was Castlereagh, who did not pretend to the lead, but who had a devoted following in Parliament, without whom he was resolved that no Government should go on. How to reconcile all these rivalries, or even most of them, was a problem, and a perplexing one it proved. Perceval, though resenting the tone taken by the Wellesleys on the Walcheren affair, professed his readiness to entertain any reasonable project for strengthening the Government. But he could not be expected to put Sidmouth in his shoes, and neither of them was desirous of holding office under him. There was indeed one way of determining these difficulties, to which many would accede: namely, the putting Lord Wellesley at the head of the Government, when the hunger for place, competitorship, and pretensions might, under his banner, all be adjusted and satisfied, and thus a strong, consistent, and united Government be formed. On all hands it seemed settled that the Opposition were placed at an immeasurable distance from office by the late unexpected majority, and that the King's death alone could terminate their exclusion.

The strange episode of Sir F. Burdett's committal to the Tower, for libel on the House of Commons, diverted public attention for a time from the vote on Walcheren, and the discussion regarding the Papers on Spain. On the evening of April 6, the inmates of Apsley House were alarmed at finding it surrounded by an excited crowd, by whom all the windows facing Piccadilly were speedily broken, in vengeance for the support given by Government to the authority of the Speaker. The houses of Wellesley Pole in Saville Row, Mr. Yorke in Hill Street, and Lord Westmoreland in Grosvenor Square shared the same fate. But the especial enmity of the mob was directed to the official residence of Mr. Perceval in Downing Street, and the mansion in St. James's Square of Lord Castlereagh, who, though no longer in office, held the first place in popular aversion. His servants at first persuaded those who would have broken in that he was no longer there, and to appease their incredulity admitted that he had escaped by the roof, and that Lady Castlereagh, then an invalid, would suffer much from their violent intrusion. The appearance of a party of the Coldstreams interrupted the parley, and the young officer, whose commission dated but a few days before, believed he had come in time to prevent mischief, and amused himself with listening to coarse banter interspersed with angry threats as he paced up and down. To his surprise a voice over his shoulder muttered through the folds of a huge muffler, in which his face was nearly hidden, 'Pray let me pass; I must get in.' The astonished ensign refused peremptorily to allow the door to be opened, expostulating on the madness of the risk. 'But my wife is in the house; she has not been able to follow me; and you must let me pass.' It was Castlereagh, who not without difficulty could be induced to desist and withdraw from the scene before he could be recognised. At midnight the populace dispersed, and no act of violence occurred.[1]

From Hyde Park Corner to St. James's Street was occupied for the next two days, and throughout the night, by crowds, who compelled every passenger they recognised to pay homage to the member for Westminster. The Serjeant-at-Arms was suffered to come and go more than once without the honourable baronet, who denied the validity of the Speaker's warrant, and said he would obey the King's writ alone; and he took his morning ride as usual, to the intense delight of his worshippers. The Cabinet assembled to consider what was to be done, and in their reluctance to resort to force, prolonged the state of insecurity until the morning of the 9th, when all the approaches to Stratton Street being filled with troops, the house of Sir Francis was broken open, and he was removed to the Tower. At the moment of his entering the carriage, his hand was grasped by the defaulting possessor of Dangan—Roger O'Connor, who, true to himself, was ready for any turmoil. The Serjeant-at-Arms refused to allow him to enter the carriage, but Sir Francis said to him gaily, 'They can't prevent you from following.' He did so; and Lord Moira, as Lieutenant of the Tower, having provided such comfort as was possible for his uncoveted charge, O'Connor helped, as he was peculiarly qualified to do, to make the first evening of State-prisonership pass convivially.

As the effervescence caused by the arrest subsided, Ministerial rumours and intrigues recovered their floating power, and fresh designs were said to be afoot for putting the Foreign Secretary at the head of affairs. But the Walcheren vote deterred waverers from embarking in a cause which had about it little promise of immediate success. Mutual distrust

[1] The officer was Mr. Cowell, who late in life took the name of Stepney, and sat for Carmarthen in a recent Parliament.

and bitterness thenceforth prevailed indeed between official colleagues, sooner or later certain to cause disruption. But had it been asked, Where would the ostensible cause of separation be found? the answer would hardly have been clear. Before the result of the late inquiry, and pending it, it was laid down as a principle by Lord Wellesley, and in the then state of things, acceded to by the other members of the Government, that they were too weak to go on, and that they must strengthen their hands by every possible means and in every event. Hence arose negotiations with Sidmouth, Castlereagh, and Canning, very little, it must be presumed, to the taste of Mr. Perceval, who accordingly when the very unexpected result took place, quickly found out and maintained his opinion that, with the addition of Mr. Yorke, the Government was quite strong enough; and in any case would not treat with the Doctor after the vote he gave on the Walcheren business. On the other hand, Lord Wellesley did not think it strong enough, constituted as it then was, even with Mr. Yorke (or, in other words, that no Administration that could be found would be so of which he was not the head), and he intended to make it weaker by resignation at the end of the session. Should this take place, they would see a triple alliance between Lords Wellesley and Sidmouth, and Canning, to which, if they could, they would add Castlereagh; but the temptation to take the latter in would be too great not to induce Perceval to make him offers which he would prefer to anything the malcontents could afford him. Besides that, he always preferred possession to speculation. Once more the confederacy was organising. The double-faced confidant kept Stowe informed of what he learned in Piccadilly, heightening the flavour with an occasional dash of sarcasm.

Among the minor, or rather more secret, causes of dissatisfaction on the part of Perceval was his consciousness that had he been outvoted, or nearly outvoted, his *sacré* was quite prepared, his funeral procession marshalled out, and his possessions as quietly distributed among his self-appointed executors as if he were actually dead and buried. He made some of them, however, pointedly feel his resuscitation, no longer evincing his former deference to my Lord Marquess on any point. In a matter connected with the interests of the French King and Princes, where the Foreign Secretary thought the honour and dignity of the country concerned, he met with such opposition from the Treasury that it came to a downright quarrel, which, had not a compromise taken place, would have ended in a resignation. For the rest, Wellesley complained that he had not sufficient weight in Council; that there was nothing doing there which marked energy or activity; that the affairs of the country were almost at a standstill, and were likely to remain so; and that so little was his private interest in any of the departments, that since his accession to office, he had not been able to make an exciseman. Added to all this, he hardly disguised being out of friendship, or even intimacy, with several of his colleagues. ' Such was the public condition of the statesman, and his domestic life was not more free from the trials of tantalisation. Such was the melancholy career of a man of the greatest abilities, and of a tender and sensitive heart. He expressed himself, with almost tears in his eyes, as to the reception given him in the House of Lords by Lord Buckingham. If the writer might be permitted on such a subject to speak, he thought it was a most serious misfortune to all parties, and even to the country, that he was not included in the *projet* of Lord Grenville's Administration. In his train, he was satisfied, the Marquess would have been contented to remain; an able and efficient coadjutor he would have occasionally been found, while his general indolence and habits of life would have kept far from his practice that political activity upon which he had been forced by the apparent proscription and perpetual system of exclusion he seemed doomed to meet with from all parties. The elevation he was since raised to he would struggle to maintain, and henceforward he would be either a most troublesome friend or a most formidable enemy.'[1]

In the beginning of April, Spain wanted to obtain a loan of 2,000,000*l.* from England, which Perceval was willing to grant, at the rate of 200,000*l.* per month till the whole sum was advanced. He proceeded to lay down the exact manner in which the loan should be given. Henry Wellesley, however, naturally desired to apply to the utmost extent possible the resources of this country in favour of the Spanish Government, and in the course of the summer he drew upon the Treasury from Cadiz for 400,000*l.* Lord Wellesley announced the fact to Perceval, who had thus the mortification of seeing the money which he had collected for Wellington's support diverted by his lordship's brother to another purpose. The Foreign Secretary replied officially to the despatch; but before sending it he consulted the Premier, who thought the whole proceeding so irregular and objectionable that he strengthened some of the expressions of remonstrance and rebuke, and Lord Wellesley resented these alterations, because they had the appearance of reflecting on his brother.

'Apsley House, Sunday, July 22, 1810.

'MY DEAR SIR,—I have examined the proposed alterations of my despatch to Mr. Wellesley, and I have adopted such of them as I could approve, after having thrown them into a shape more consistent with the order of my thoughts and with the general tenor of the despatch. The proposed alterations respecting Mr. Wellesley's *supposed* drafts on the Treasury, I confess, appear to me much stronger than the

[1] To the Marquess of Buckingham, from the correspondent already quoted.

occasion requires. Indeed, all the necessary suggestions of caution appear to me to be quite clearly expressed in the original draft. I now send the whole to you for transmission to the King, requesting you to forward it by the messenger who brings it to you.

'If you should wish the draft to be again altered, I request you to return it to me, as I should not wish it to go to the King without my own final corrections.

'Yours, always sincerely,

'WELLESLEY.'

The experience of the session had decisively demonstrated the critical condition of the Government. Its existence depended on the support of persons who might at any moment be driven into Opposition. The small knot of men who had allied themselves with Sidmouth, and those who had identified themselves with Canning, were able at any moment to convert the Ministerial majority into a minority. Bathurst's defection at the beginning of the session had led to the defeat of the Government on the Walcheren committee; Canning's desertion towards the close had contributed to Bankes' successive victories on the Sinecure resolutions. Wellesley and Liverpool offered to resign their offices in favour of Canning and Castlereagh, in the event of their being secured. But the Cabinet interposed, as they desired that other offices should be found for them than those which had been the scene of their quarrel. The negotiations were fruitless, the offers being declined. The following is some correspondence relating to these transactions,

'Private and confidential.   'Apsley House, June 14, 1810.

'MY DEAR SIR,—The events of the session of Parliament appear to me to have proved the necessity of augmenting the strength of the Government, especially in the House of

Commons. Your information and mine leads to the certainty that it would not be practicable to unite the friends of Lords Sidmouth and Castlereagh, and of Mr. Canning; because it has been ascertained that Lord Sidmouth and his friends cannot consent to act with Mr. Canning. Although the grounds of this defection are entitled to great respect, I confess that I cannot admit the justice and reason of such an exclusion, particularly in the present crisis, when Lord Grey has opened such an attack upon all those leading principles which constituted the basis of Mr. Pitt's Government. Under these circumstances I wish to urge a serious consideration of the necessity of making an immediate effort for the purpose of obtaining the aid of Mr. Canning and his friends. For this purpose I am desirous of vacating the office which I now hold, in order to admit Mr. Canning; and I am willing either to accept any other suitable office in the Cabinet, or to remain in the Cabinet without office, until a vacancy can be conveniently made for me. You may be assured that I shall most cheerfully act under either arrangement, provided the great advantage of Mr. Canning's assistance can be obtained by it. I have already repeatedly stated this idea to you, but it has not been regularly considered by the Cabinet; I wish you would have the goodness to take their opinion upon it as soon as possible. Although I cannot positively answer for Mr. Canning's acceptance of a proposal to act in the present Government, I would not suggest such a plan if I were not convinced that he could not decline an arrangement founded on the basis which I have stated.

'Believe me, &c.,

'S. Perceval, Esq.'   'WELLESLEY.

'Private and confidential.   'Dorking, July 23, 1810.

'MY DEAR SIR,—Some time since I took the liberty of stating to you my opinion that, unless some steps were immediately taken to favour Mr. Canning's admission into the

Cabinet, that advantage would be entirely lost to the present Government; at the same time, I renewed my former offer respecting my present office, and I stated a desire that the subject should again be considered by the Cabinet. The great pressure of indispensable matter of practical detail has prevented you, and the Cabinet, and myself, from touching this very delicate but (in my judgment) indispensable discussion. I do not know whether you have had any means of consulting others on the point. When I spoke to you, you seemed still to consider the difficulties with regard to Lord Castlereagh to be insuperable. My information leads me to hope that Lord Castlereagh would be found reasonable and practicable on every part of the question. At all events, it is very desirable to bring the matter to a final and positive determination, and (if it is determined to be either useless or dangerous to accept my offer) to apprise Canning distinctly of his situation. I understand that he is to see you to-morrow on some ordinary business, and I think great advantage might result from your conversing freely with him on the whole subject, and stating your sense of the difficulties which exist, and hearing his ideas with regard to their removal. For my own part, I desire you to consider me to be entirely at your disposal, with the most anxious wish, however, that you would employ me and my office for the purpose of obtaining the benefit of Canning's assistance, connected with the accession of Lord Castlereagh.

'Yours, &c.,

'WELLESLEY.'

Lord Lansdowne, who had lately been called to the Upper House by the death of his brother, was bent on confuting the prognostic of Palmerston [1] that the Opposition would seriously lose by the change. He had mastered the complicated details of the unsuccessful policy and strategy which, in the three

[1] Then Secretary at War.

preceding years, had ended in the Convention of Cintra, the embarkation at Corunna, and the retreat after Talavera. And he gave notice of his intention to bring the whole question under the consideration of the Peers. His motion was deferred from week to week in consequence of the illness of Grenville; but it took place eventually on June 8, when he distinguished himself greatly by the comprehensive and temperate nature of his views. In youth as little as in age he was incapable of injustice to serve a party turn; and though, by training and by habit, essentially a party man who enjoyed hard hitting, and took good-humouredly his share of exclusion and reproach for the sake of his opinions, he never was betrayed into personal acrimony or invidious exaggeration of errors or of faults. In him there was no spice of faction, and no taint of guile. No man more consistently and efficiently throughout life leaned against the policy of aggressive war. He hated strife at home, and did his best to quench international enmities abroad. But he was no more of a Quaker than a Quixote; and with him the sole question regarding the Peninsula seems to have been, Were we justified in meddling at all, if we were not reasonably certain of success? He pointed to many blots and blunders in former negotiations and campaigns; but said not a word disparaging of the army or its general; not a syllable disrespectful of the new Foreign Minister. He had in truth no little sympathy with him, especially with regard to Irish affairs; and in his reply Wellesley took care to repay with interest the consideration shown him. After summing up ably the advantages we still possessed, and our resources yet unexhausted, he asked, Why, then, should we depart from that salutary line of policy? What is there to dissuade or discourage us from adhering to it? For his part, he could discover nothing in the aspect of Spanish affairs that wore anything like the hue or complexion of despair. If, indeed, it appeared that the spirit of resistance had begun to languish in the breasts of patriotic

Spaniards; if miscarriages, disasters, and defeats had been observed to damp the ardour and break down the energies of the Spanish mind, it might be believed that further assistance to the cause would prove unavailing. But, fortunately for this country, not only was there life still in Spain, but her patriotic heart still continued to beat high. The generous and exalted sentiment which first prompted us to lend our aid to her cause, should therefore still inspirit us to continue that aid to the last moment. The struggle was not merely a Spanish struggle. Assuredly, in that struggle were committed the vital interests of England. With the fate of Spain the fate of England was inseparably blended. Should we not, therefore, stand by her to the last? For his part, as an adviser of the Crown, he should not cease to recommend to his Sovereign to continue to assist her. It should not dishearten us that Spain appeared to be at the very crisis of her fate; we should on the contrary extend a more anxious care over her at a moment so critical. For, in nature, how often have the apparent symptoms of dissolution been the presages of new life and of renovated vigour? Therefore he would cling to Spain in her last struggle; therefore he would watch her last agonies; he would wash and heal her wounds; he would receive her parting breath; he would catch and cherish the last vital spark of her expiring patriotism; yes,—

> Date, vulnera lymphis,
> Abluam, et extremus si quis super halitus errat,
> Ore legam.

Nor let it be deemed a mere office of pious charity; an exaggerated representation of his feelings, an overcharged picture of the circumstances that called them forth. In the cause of Spain, the cause of honour and of interest were equally involved and inseparably allied. It was a cause in favour of which the finest feelings of the heart united with the soundest dictates of the understanding. Under that conviction it was impossible for him to accede to the resolutions moved by the noble marquess, one of which tended to censure transactions which, in his humble opinion, were entitled to praise, and the other purposed to impute blame to those on whom their approbation might be more fitly conferred.[1] The motion was rejected by a large majority.

A few days after there was a Council at Windsor, to settle the speech on the prorogation, to which all the royal dukes were summoned except the Prince of Wales. Why he was omitted is not easily explained, as he happened to be at the Castle on the day in question; but the Foreign Secretary had to bear the brunt of his ill-humour. After an audience to communicate the details of the victory of Busaco, which the King naturally received with satisfaction, he hastened to acquaint the Prince with the good news, full of his brother's prowess, the moral effects of the victory, and so forth. His Royal Highness on seeing him exclaimed, 'I condole with you heartily, my dear lord, upon poor Arthur's retreat after his battle. Massena has quite out-generalled him.' Neither the place or the presence could restrain the little man's wrath, which broke forth in terms that Lords of the Bedchamber deemed highly unbecoming and Under-Secretaries, when they heard of it, lamented as imprudent. But he knew better than they with whom he had to deal; and he manfully did his duty in telling the selfish and frivolous Heir-Apparent the true value of a battle won in great part by native levies under English generalship. What he foretold, in quivering accents of indignation at the Prince's folly, has since become matter of history. Busaco taught the Portuguese troops to meet the onslaught of the French legions without fear. Its moral effect was incalculable. Truly, said Napoleon, looking back over the field of his chequered fortune, 'the difference between a battle won and a battle lost is immense.'

[1] Parl. Deb. vol. xvii. pp. 495-6.

CHAPTER XIX

TORRES VEDRAS.

1810.

HE had not been long at Downing Street when an officer of one of the Irish regiments in the service of France presented an introduction from Lord Yarmouth, who said he knew him well, and believed that he had something of importance to communicate. Captain Fagan said he came from Fouché to inquire if England were disposed towards peace, and to give assurances that France was so inclined. He brought, however, no proposals of a definite kind, nor any credentials investing him with a diplomatic character. The new Minister smiled graciously, listened attentively, and answered blandly; said he was under no vow to make everlasting war, and that the Government would give cheerfully their best consideration to any terms of pacification that would restore freedom to the seas and repose to so many wearied lands. But all must depend on the nature of the stipulations made, and the recognition, as a basis, that any settlement of disputes must comprehend the interests of our Peninsular and other allies. The only scrap of his handwriting which the unaccredited envoy was able to show consisted of an epitome of six lines of these preliminaries. Secret correspondence with his employer at Paris was circuitous and slow, and the spring wore away without his being able to furnish any proof of his having any authority to treat. Meanwhile a very different personage presented himself on a like errand, commanding much more attention; but as it proved to no better purpose. M. Pierre Labouchère, a leading partner in the house of Hope, at Amsterdam, had married the daughter of Sir F. Baring, whose great commercial eminence and ability gave him the ear of every Minister when he came. Wellesley made a point of consulting the great merchants on vexed questions of embargo, right of search, and blockade, with whose complicated details they were best acquainted. M. Labouchère had come to England at the instance of M. Ouverard, a well-known army contractor in France, with whom he had extensive dealings, and who, strange to say, without the knowledge of Napoleon, had been commissioned to ascertain if possible through some safe hand, if England would make peace. He had much to say, and was thoroughly skilled in the art of unofficial diplomacy, and his accurate and varied knowledge of financial and trading interests enabled him to make an impressive case for the expediency of putting an end to the war. Napoleon's marriage with an arch-duchess was a pledge that he no longer sought the overthrow of old dynasties. His open quarrel with the Vatican proved equally that he did not mean to tamper with religion as an element of disturbance. If the east and north of Spain were left to Joseph, Ferdinand might keep Andalusia and Valentia; and the Royalists of the Faubourg St. Germain, who were beginning to attorn to the irresistible Empire, would like to see the head of the exiled Bourbons offered a throne in Spanish America. But if the Dutch continued to wink hard at English goods being imported in spite of the Berlin Decree, Napoleon would enforce his will by the annexation of Holland, providing for King Louis elsewhere. And if the Continent were once hermetically sealed, England would be unable to prolong the struggle. In reply, the Foreign Secretary made very little of the threatened absorption of the Dutch, which he treated as practically accomplished. He valued as little the power of coastguards to interdict British produce or manufactures; and he pointed triumphantly to the vast increase of our shipping and exports every year since the Imperial ban had been laid upon them,—a fact which his visitor understood even better than himself.

Owing to our ascendency at sea, the exports of the United Kingdom had risen from 30,387,490*l.* to 46,292,632*l.* in the year just concluded. The Americans continued to take their full share of the Mediterranean trade by putting into Malta for part cargoes of English goods, as the Russians did for the like purpose at Heligoland. Their being forced to sail under a neutral flag was more a point of honour than a downright loss of trade. Nevertheless, if propositions duly authorised were intended, they should certainly have a candid and unprejudiced consideration. M. Labouchère went back to Antwerp, and conferred once more with M. Ouverard; and made a second voyage to Yarmouth and a second visit to Apsley House, in hopes of being instrumental in bringing about an accommodation. Napoleon hesitated about superseding his brother, and was not disinclined to rest for a while from his martial labours. Unluckily his suspicions were aroused by accidental circumstances that his Minister of Police was acting in various matters without consulting him. Ouverard was arrested, and, to save himself, disclosed all. Fouché was disgraced. The desultory warfare in the southern provinces of Spain went on, and Holland was incorporated with the Empire.

Negotiations with Sidmouth, Castlereagh, and Canning were continued during the autumn, at the instance of Wellesley, who ceased not to urge upon the Premier the necessity of strengthening by some means the Administration. Without Canning, he reiterated his personal unwillingness to retain office, and to gain him as a colleague in the Secretariat, he was willing to give up the Foreign Office, and take that of War and Colonies, then, and for many years afterwards, united. But Castlereagh, while repudiating personal resentment, told his uncle, Lord Camden, that the public would not bear with temper or treat with respect two men re-entering together the Cabinet they had quitted to take each other's lives scarce a twelvemonth before; and the Premier thought that the weight of unpopularity was against Castlereagh. Sidmouth was still more obdurate; he was not unwilling to support Government or to share their responsibility; but men ought not to sit together in the Cabinet especially in times so critical, who could neither feel or show confidence; and never, therefore, would he consent to act with Canning. To make room for him, the Foreign Minister again professed his readiness to resign. This all his colleagues felt to be inadmissible, and they agreed to go on as they were. Ere parting for the holidays, late in August, Perceval is said to have pressed him to say whether, as every suggestion of his had been tried to reinforce the Government, they had not a right to claim his cordial and unreserved co-operation? To this in general terms he assented, but he is said to have added, that as they had no longer any hopes of that efficient strength and aid he had sought for, so a greater weight of labour and responsibility would be thrown upon him. 'You, Mr. Perceval, are going out of town; so am I; but when we again meet, you must have your mind made up to give me a greater share of patronage and influence in the conduct of the war than I have hitherto had, and which, in every event, I think myself entitled to.' Without any definite reply they parted.[1]

Two objects mainly occupied the thoughts of the Foreign Secretary—the war in the Peninsula and peace with the United States. He had made the adequate sustainment of

[1] Mr. D. to Lord Buckingham, 1st October, 1810.

our armies engaged in the great struggle against French encroachment the sole condition of his taking office, whether as Minister abroad or Minister at home. All he had seen and learned during his sojourn in Spain intensified his conviction that, without vigorous and comprehensive measures by sea and land, Spain could not be delivered from the yoke of Napoleon; and that parsimony and peddling in military administration were, under the circumstances, mere fatuous schemes for overreaching ourselves. Lisbon had indeed been saved by the self-reliant and indomitable energy displayed in the formation of the lines of Torres Vedras; and he had faith in his brother's calm forecast that, if duly supported from home, he could hold his ground in Portugal, and compel the invaders to fall back to sustain the unstable fabric of their system in Spain: a promise destined to be literally and definitively fulfilled. But beyond the confines of the lesser kingdom the tide of conquest swept unbroken almost to the gates of Cadiz; and it needed the high courage and confidence of one who had himself planned and executed successfully great campaigns to persuade a Cabinet of second-rate politicians to look their duty in the face, and risk their collective existence as a Government, day after day, on measures indispensable for making any serious attempt at restoring national independence. It were worse than useless for England to serve as a mere auxiliary in a war of emancipation if the direction of affairs was to remain with the feeble and distracted Executive beleaguered in the only great city still recognising Ferdinand as king. He had personally weighed the moral and intellectual capacity of nearly all the soldiers and statesmen who spouted in the Cortes or squabbled for command, and he knew that unless we were prepared to undertake the responsibility in chief, and to direct the conduct of movements in the field, nothing but discomfiture could come of further conflict. It was infinitely to his credit that, under all the disheartening circumstances of the case, he was able, rather by the weight of his character than by any arts of suasion, to obtain the supplies requisite for what seemed then a daring, if not a desperate purpose. It was a purpose condemned from first to last as impracticable, and therefore impolitic, prodigal, and quixotic, by most of the leaders of Opposition; and agreed to with a shudder and a sigh as perilous in the extreme by many whose hearts were not big enough to hope for its success. But he had one advantage, and a great one, the loyal and consistent, though frugal support of the First Minister, who certainly owed him neither confidence or affection. They wrangled about other matters continually, and sometimes about the application of particular sums to objects of pressing moment. But Perceval never swerved from his pledge to carry on the war with all the resources of the country, and seldom grudged the outlay that the English commander on the Tagus, or the English ambassador at Cadiz, reported to be necessary. To keep the peace with America was indeed his anxious desire; and he omitted nothing to confirm as far as in him lay the personal goodwill subsisting between the Foreign Secretary and the Republican Envoy at our Court. Wellington's urgent demands for money to feed his own and the Portuguese troops were met by the Treasury as fast as possible, and at the beginning of May, 'money was sent in profusion to him; soldiers he wanted none.'[1]

The financial difficulties of the Government are succinctly but lucidly stated in the biography of the Minister. 'It was true that our credit was still firm; that money could be borrowed on the most advantageous terms; and that increased taxation had not interfered with the growth of the revenue. But our prosperity was in part fictitious; the supply of money was large, but the money circulated only within the United

[1] Mr. D. to Lord Buckingham, 1st May, 1810.

Kingdom. The suspension of cash payments had drawn gold away, and inconvertible paper was useless in the Peninsula. There every payment had to be made in gold or silver. The Treasury had less difficulty in obtaining the ways and means than in the purchase of specie. At the close of 1809 it had been calculated that the war in the Peninsula would involve a gross charge of 3,000,000*l.* a year. In the course of the autumn it became apparent that a sum of at least 5,000,000*l.* would be necessary; and the means had to be provided in the face of a hostile Opposition and a doubting country.'[1]

Wellington wrote: 'Seeing, as I do, more than a chance of final success, if we can maintain our position in this country (Portugal), although none by our departure from our cautious defensive system, I should not do my duty by the Government if I did not urge them with importunity even to greater exertion.'

Massena, sent by Napoleon to drive the presumptuous Islanders out of Portugal, found to his surprise, the great earthworks formed round the capital by Wellington impenetrable. Timely supplies from England enabled him to assemble and maintain 130,000 men within the lines, a force of whose collective strength past experience of the war in the Peninsula did not lead the French Marshal to dream. Surprised at the extent and strength of works, the existence of which had only become known to him five days before he came upon them, Massena spent more than a week in examining their nature, without discovering any point weak enough to tempt him to an attack. The war was in fact reduced to one of blockade—the French commander's object being to keep his army in food until reinforcements could reach him; the English general's to starve the French ere succour could arrive. Irregular corps of native militia were encouraged to act upon their flanks, avoiding serious encounters in the field, but

[1] Mr. S. Walpole's *Life of Perceval*, ii. 112.

harassing their convoys and destroying local magazines. The struggle throughout October was a wager of endurance rather than of hardihood; multitudes from the ravaged provinces sought refuge in the city and its environs. The means of subsistence rose to famine prices, and corn was sent for to Ireland and Algiers. The Portuguese Ministers lost heart at the appalling misery around them, and even British officers and envoys wrote home in despair. Their letters, sent confidentially by the Secretary for War, reached Wellington at the critical moment of his defence of his great strategic masterpiece, when, had he wavered or yielded, all would have been lost. Beset on every side, the English general rose like a giant. Without noticing either the arguments or the forebodings of Stewart's and Spencer's letters, he took a calm, historical review of the grounds upon which he had undertaken the defence of Portugal. And were all other records of his genius lost, says Napier, those in which he demonstrated his own prudence and foresight, and traced the probable course of future events both as regarded his own and the enemy's designs, would vindicate his great reputation to posterity.[1] In a tone firm, almost fierce, he rebuked the pusillanimous conduct of the authorities at Lisbon for pandering to the ill-humour of the ignorant populace, when their duty was to keep order in the city and to provide food for their compatriots in the trenches. But he had been entrusted with the safety of Portugal by the Regent of that country and his own Sovereign, and he would not suffer any person to interfere with his measures. Of their eventual success he had no doubt. To Henry Wellesley, at Cadiz, he wrote[2] while the strain was most intense:

'I have no idea what the French will, or rather what they can, do. I think it is certain that they can do us no mischief,

---

[1] *History of the Peninsular War*, iii. 365.
[2] 21st October, 1810.

and that they will lose the greatest part of their army if they attack us. They will starve if they stay much longer, and they will experience great difficulty in their retreat.

'Ever yours most affectionately.'

Within a fortnight Massena gave orders to fall back, sending General Foy to tell Napoleon the hopelessness of his undertaking, without great reinforcements. For these he lingered long, disputing every step with consummate skill and intrepid tenacity. But week by week of winter passed in vain looking for succour which came not, while his ranks were thinned by disease and hunger. He had entered Portugal at the head of 65,000 men, and recrossed the frontier with less than two thirds of that number.[1] Portugal was thus delivered, and to that deliverance there can be no doubt that the diplomacy directed by the British Foreign Office contributed in no unimportant degree.

During the long interval of peace which followed the recognition of Independence, the commerce of America throve apace; and except the occasional exercise of the old claim to search on board her ships for seamen who had deserted or eluded impressment, no cause of controversy arose between the two Governments. But on the outbreak of war with France in 1793, the rule of 1756 which had long remained dormant was revived, whereby neutrals were forbidden, under pain of capture and forfeiture, to carry produce of French colonies to the mother country, or to bear her manufactures to them. In a treaty, negotiated by Mr. Jay the following year, indemnity was secured in certain cases to the shipowners of the United States, while the rule was maintained against other neutrals. And when doubts arose as to the efficacy of the exemption, a formal note from Lord Hawkesbury[2] declared that they might import anything save contraband of

---

[1] 5th April, 1811.   [2] 11th April, 1801.

war from Guadaloupe, Martinique, or Mauritius, and reexport it to Havre or Marseilles. Subsequently the English Court of Admiralty refused to admit proof of the payment of duties at New York as sufficient evidence of re-export *bonâ fide*, and the cargoes were, under this decision, confiscated. Indignant protests thereupon rang throughout the United States. Public meetings held up the conduct of the British Government to obloquy as faithless and overreaching; and President Jefferson indited more than one expatiation on the natural principles that free ships made free goods, and that no people had a right to govern by their laws the ships of another nation navigating the ocean. By what law then could they board a ship while in peaceable and orderly use of the common element? He recognised no natural precept for submission to such a right. The doctrine hat the rights of nations remaining quietly in the exercise of moral and social duties, were to give way to the convenience of those who preferred plundering and murdering one another, was a monstrous doctrine. Could two nations turning tigers break up in one instant the peaceable relations of the whole world? But although these principles were of great importance to the interests of peaceable nations, yet in the actual state of things he thought they were not worth a war.[1] While Louisiana was still held by France, and Florida was still possessed by Spain, and Canada remained loyal to England, war with either of the belligerents was not to be rashly ventured on by a Commonwealth scarcely emerging from the period of national adolescence. But in the following decade its rapid growth in strength and opulence grew manifest in nothing more remarkably than the increasing muscularity of its resistance to the old country's claim to lay down the law of the sea. In 1806, Jefferson felt strong enough to take a more decided tone regarding neutrality. The French had

[1] To Mr. Livingston, Minister at Paris, 9th September, 1801.

ceded Louisiana, and negotiations were proceeding with the Spaniards for the annexation of Florida. That done, the Government of Washington might take a more self-asserting position towards European Powers. 'With England,' wrote the President, 'I think we shall cut off the resource of impressing our seamen to fight her battles, and establish the inviolability of our flag in our commerce with her enemies. We shall thus become what we sincerely wish to be, honestly neutral, and truly useful to both belligerents: to the one, by keeping open a market for the consumption of her manufactures, while they are excluded from all the countries under the power of her enemy; to the other, by securing for her a safe carriage of all her productions, metropolitan or colonial, while her own means are restrained by her enemy, and may therefore be employed in other useful pursuits.'[1] Neither of the combatants, however, were in any mood to tolerate abstract professions of American goodwill; and each rivalled the other in passionate resort to inflamed menace and undiscriminating desire to inflict injury.

Mr. Pinkney was sent in April 1806 to act jointly with Mr. Monroe in negotiating a settlement of differences, and Lords Auckland and Holland were named by Mr. Fox to confer with them. But such was the temper of the time that ere they met, an Order in Council was issued declaring the entire coast from Brest to the mouths of the Elbe to be in a state of blockade. In the November following, Napoleon retaliated by his celebrated Decree[2] from Berlin, imposing a like interdict on all the shores of England and her dependencies. The Commissioners tried hard to accommodate the dispute, and after months of friendly conference, imagined that they had hit upon terms that would have accomplished their pacific purpose.[3] But they were deemed as little

[1] To Mr. Bowdoin, 10th July, 1806. [2] 21st November, 1806.
[3] 31st December, 1806

acceptable by President Madison as by the Grenville Cabinet; and on January 7, 1807, another step in mutual exasperation was taken under the advice of Lord Howick, Orders in Council being issued which professed to treat as in a state of blockade the French Empire and all its dependencies, whether colonial or allied. The Milan decrees followed on the 27th December, and the pitiless warfare against industry and civilisation continued without let or hindrance during the next seven years. The new Foreign Secretary hated and despised such methods of warfare; but Madison's confidential letters show that he had little hope of Wellesley being able, though well-disposed, to drag his anti-American colleagues into a change of policy, supported as they would be by the speeches and proceedings of Congress. From these the inference would be that one party preferred the submission of their trade to British regulation, and that the other confessed the impossibility of resisting it; a voluntary embargo being proclaimed by a glutted market in England, and the apprehension of British blockades and French confiscations.[1] Supercilious talk on the part of an envoy sent by Canning had wounded American susceptibilities, and he was in consequence recalled; still Madison expressed surprise how little Wellesley's views corresponded with theirs about Jackson's conduct; and the manner in which the vacancy caused in the Legation by his recall was to be supplied by an agent of subordinate rank, showed that 'a sacrifice was meant of the respect belonging to their Government, either to the pride of Great Britain, or to the feelings of those in America who had taken sides with it against their own. On either supposition, it would be necessary to counteract the ignoble purpose. On finding the substitution of a *chargé* to be an intentional degradation of diplomatic intercourse on the part of Great Britain, it would be deemed

[1] To Jefferson, 23rd April, 1810.

proper that no higher functionary should represent the United States at London.'[1] But Pinkney was not to lose sight of the expediency of 'mingling moderation and even conciliation' with expressions of offended dignity.

American shipowners complained loudly of search being made by British cruisers for contraband of war, and of the delay and loss incurred in consequence, when any article of questionable character was found on board these vessels. Representations of hardship thus inflicted were made through the Ministers resident in London and Paris, and claims in certain cases were made for compensation; but with small results in pecuniary or diplomatic satisfaction. All jurists of authority, from Grotius to Kent, recognised the right of belligerents to shut out supplies from enemies' ports under due notice to blockade. What constituted actual blockade, and what supplies were to be considered contraband of war, remained, as they must always remain, topics of contention in the Admiralty Courts in each particular case; but about the general principle of international law there could be no dispute. Though strong things might be said in Congress, exciting articles circulated by the press, and plausible reproaches made by implication in despatches and minutes of conversation, no general cause of quarrel lay against this country, any more than against France, because in the rage of internecine war both had egregiously expanded the circle of commercial interdict at the expense, and to the detriment, of the rest of the world. The Cabinet of Washington tried hard indeed to persuade both Governments to relax, if not to renounce, their decrees against trade. Mr. Pinkney was instructed to assure Mr. Canning and his successor at the Foreign Office that if our Orders in Council were allowed to lapse, the French Emperor might be relied on practically to forego the rigorous execution of the Milan decrees. Wellesley seems to have en-

[1] To Mr. Pinkney, 23rd May, 1810.

couraged the idea of mutual relaxation, though he dared not give any definite pledge, or hold out the expectation that in the exasperated temper of the nation it would be possible beforehand to make any formal renunciation of the rights of blockade or search. The French Government in its turn, was equally evasive, and the American Envoy could only build up, again and again, a house of cards inscribed with friendly, regretful, and humane sentiments, which, by ingenuous implication, were made to signify an intention to concede the matters in dispute, but which whenever leaned upon tumbled to the ground. It suited France to contend that the mouths of rivers undefended by forts or flotillas were not legitimately subject to blockade; for with this exemption, merchantmen under neutral flags would have been able to unload their cargoes safely, and set sail with their relading, at the inland wharves of the Elbe, the Scheldt, and the Seine. This, of course, was inadmissible by English statesmen like Fox, Grenville, Hawkesbury, Grey, Perceval, and Canning; each and all of whom had asserted our right to blockade the whole western coast of the hostile Empire; and whatever Wellesley's individual predilections may have been in favour of freer trade he knew that it would have been merely suicidal on his part to assert that they had all been in the wrong. There was nothing for it but to temporise, wait for events, and in honeyed words deprecate the imprudence of driving him to endorse anew anti-commercial threats that had not been of his devising. Left to himself, Mr. Pinkney was well inclined to listen, half believingly at all events, to the earnest, gentle, and complimentary phrases of the Marquess: but he was urged continually from Washington to press for a definite answer respecting the Orders in Council. The French Minister of Foreign Affairs assured the Plenipotentiary of the Republic at Paris[1] that the only condition required for the

[1] 30th April, 1810.

revocation of the Decree of Berlin would be the previous revocation by the British Government of her blockades of France of anterior date. But this previous step was deemed impossible.

In January 1807 an Order in Council was framed by Lord Grey, allowing American ships to trade in security with France, provided on their way they touched at some port of the United Kingdom; and the privilege was made use of to a considerable extent. But as a political affront the pretension to levy toll in this fashion on the traffic of the seas was resented vehemently; and there can be no doubt that the strange contrivance, too clever by half, tended eventually to embitter the unhappy quarrel. Congress passed, in retaliation, a Non-intercourse Act, which forbade any French or English vessel from entering their harbours, and compelled such as lay there to quit immediately, with or without lading.

Yet it was not without difficulty that the Senate had been induced, in the spring of 1809, to adopt this further step of legislative retaliation. Many commercial interests in the Union shrunk from the additional losses thus self-imposed; still popular resentment enabled Government to obtain a legislative sanction for a measure which it was hoped would bring one, if not both, the overbearing belligerents to terms. Napoleon, furious at the injury inflicted on his subjects by a Republican Government, which he at heart detested, as keeping up the bad example of institutions he hoped to obliterate throughout Christendom, and persuading himself that whatever injured the Americans would, by reflex action, damage the incorrigible English likewise, issued a decree[1] confiscating all American ships and cargoes which had entered, or should in future enter, any port of the Empire since May 20, 1808, and devoted the value, without appeal, to the Sinking Fund. He soon found cause to repent of a proceeding which

[1] From Rambouillet, 14th May, 1810.

threatened to fix the undivided animosity of America upon himself and his system; for his reckless impatience to compel the Americans to fall in with his designs had impelled him to adopt measures, compared with which those resorted to by our Government seemed forbearing. Even Madison owned that his 'confiscations comprised robbery, theft, and breach of trust, exceeding in turpitude any of his enormities not wasting human blood.' There was a possibility, however, that negotiations at Paris might take a favourable turn when it was seen that the Non-intercourse Act opened a way for free trade with either of the belligerents that might come to terms. On the publication of the diplomatic correspondence 'so strong a feeling was produced in the States by General Armstrong's picture of French robbery, that the attitude in which England was placed by the correspondence between Pinkney and Wellesley was overlooked. Nevertheless, public attention began to fix itself on the proof afforded that the original sin against neutrals lay with Great Britain.'[1] The temper of the American Executive, under Madison, became every day more hostile. Whenever party feeling seemed disposed to extenuate the reserve or resistance of England, the President reverted to grievances and grudges of old standing, Jackson's saucy demeanour while envoy, the continued impressment of seamen, and above all, the leaving only a *chargé d'affairs* at Washington, which, it was broadly hinted more than once, would fully justify Pinkney in appointing a like substitute in his stead, and forthwith returning home.[2]

Ere these incentives to quarrel reached Europe, General Armstrong had persuaded M. Champagny to offer a suspension of the Imperial decrees to America and England, if the latter would acknowledge herself in the wrong, and revoke her Orders

---

[1] To Jefferson, 25th May, and 22nd June, 1810.
[2] Madison to Pinkney 30th October, 1810.

in Council; or to the former alone, if she would withdraw the embargo and break the blockade. Pinkney thereupon resolved to lie upon his oars a little longer, and on August 9 the 'Moniteur' contained the announcement that upon the understanding (come to without our privity) that Great Britain was ready penitentially to forego all she had theretofore been asserting triumphantly and profitably on the high seas, France would magnanimously restore universal freedom to commerce. With ineffable disdain the Foreign Secretary observed absolute silence on the occasion, and made no allusion whatever to the arrogant proposition in his intercourse with the diplomatists resident at our Court.

Blandishment had suddenly become the order of the day at Paris, where Republican interests were concerned. 'The Emperor loved the Americans; their prosperity and their commerce were within the scope of his policy. The independence of the States was one of the principal titles to glory valued by France, and his Majesty had always taken pleasure in aggrandizing the Union, and whatever could contribute to its welfare and greatness he would deem conformable to the interests of his Empire.' Months elapsed without any corresponding act of revocation on the part of our Government. The American Envoy grew impatient, and pressed for an explanation of the delay in more than one personal interview. A brief though courteous communication from the Foreign Office of December 4 averred that, 'after the most accurate inquiry, we had not been able to obtain any authentic intelligence of the actual repeal of the French decrees, or of the restoration of the commerce of neutral nations to the condition in which it stood previous to their promulgation. If Mr. Pinkney was in possession of any such information, we should be happy to receive it.' The doubt thus cast on the value of M. Champagny's pledge drew forth an elaborate reply, full of the bitterest reproach and sarcasm at our unreadiness to meet the offer of the French with equivalent concession, and ending with a renewed protest against the pretensions of Great Britain to postpone the justice which she owed to America. If it could even be admitted that France was more emphatically bound to repeal her almost nominal decrees than Great Britain to repeal her substantial orders, what more could reasonably be required by the latter than had been done by the former? If there were room to apprehend that the repealed decrees might have some operation in case the Orders in Council were withdrawn, as there was no sudden and formidable peril to which Great Britain could be exposed by that operation, there could be no reason for declining to act at once upon the declaration of France, and leave it to the future to try its sincerity, if that sincerity were suspected.[1] Wellesley, in reply, expressed his regret that it should have been thought necessary to introduce any topics which might tend to interrupt the conciliatory spirit in which it was the sincere disposition of our Government to conduct every negotiation with that of the United States. The letter of the French Minister for Foreign Affairs did not appear to contain such a notification of the repeal of the decrees of Berlin and Milan as could justify us in repealing the Orders in Council. It stated that these decrees, from November 1, would cease to be in force, it being understood that in consequence the English should revoke their Orders in Council, and renounce the new principles of blockade which they had attempted to establish. The purport of this appeared to be that the repeal would take effect provided that Great Britain, before November 1, in consequence of this declaration, should renounce those principles of blockade which France alleged to be new. America might further understand that the decrees would be repealed as far as regards her, provided she resented any refusal of our Government to renounce the new principles.

[1] 10th December, 1810.

of blockade, and revoke the Orders in Council; but that the repeal would not continue in force unless, within a reasonable time, we should fulfil the two conditions stated distinctly in the letter of the French Minister. If nothing more had been required than the repeal of our orders, we should not have hesitated to declare the perfect readiness of the Government to fulfil that condition. It appeared, however, not only by the letter of M. Champagny, but by Mr. Pinkney's explanation, that the repeal of the orders would not satisfy either the French or American Governments. Our Government was required to renounce those principles of blockade which the French Government alleged to be new. The Berlin Decree asserts that we had extended the right of blockade to commercial unfortified towns, and to ports, harbours, mouths of rivers, which, according to the principles and practices of all civilised nations, is only applicable to fortified places. The American Government was understood to require us expressly to revoke the order of May 1806, as a practical instance of our renunciation of those principles of blockade which Great Britain had asserted to be ancient, established by the laws of maritime war, and acknowledged by all civilised nations, and on which depended our most valuable rights and interests. If the French decrees were to be considered as still in force, unless we should renounce those established foundations of our maritime rights and interests, the time had not arrived when the repeal of our Orders in Council could be claimed from us with reference to the safety and honour of the nation. He concluded by reiterating the assurance that the British Government retained an anxious solicitude to revoke the orders complained of, as soon as the French decrees should be effectually repealed without conditions injurious to the maritime rights and honour of the United Kingdom.[1]

The calmness and firmness thus manifested provoked a

[1] 29th December, 1810.

still angrier recapitulation of complaints, and some of the expressions of the American Envoy would doubtless have provoked the severity of Grenville, or the mockery of Canning had he held the pen. But pride and ambition alike whispered prudence to him who, at the beginning of 1811, believed that the day was not distant when he would be called by the Regent to the head of affairs. In the existing condition of parties and of external circumstances he could not be unconscious how much his perplexities would be increased by a rupture with America, and how much confidence would be lessened, justly or unjustly, in the Minister who happened unluckily to break off amicable relations. He felt nevertheless that it was impossible to submit to be browbeaten into admitting that all that had been done, and said, and written, for the last five years was in utter disregard of public right and law. Having submitted Mr. Pinkney's communication [1] to the Regent he was commanded, he said, to abstain from any course of argument, and from any expression which (however justified by the general tenor of his observations) might tend to interrupt the good understanding which it was the wish of his Royal Highness to maintain with the Government of the United States. No statement in reply to his former letter appeared to affect the general principles which he had the honour to communicate on December 29. Great Britain had always insisted upon her right of self-defence against the system of commercial warfare pursued by France, and the British Orders in Council were founded upon a just principle of retaliation against the French decrees. The incidental operations of the Orders in Council upon the commerce of the United States (although deeply to be lamented) must be ascribed exclusively to the violence and injustice of the enemy, which compelled this country to resort to adequate means of defence. It could not even be

[1] 14th January, 1811.

admitted that the foundation of the original question should be changed, and that the measures of retaliation adopted against France should now be relinquished at the desire of the United States, without any reference to the actual conduct of the enemy. We could not accede to the conditions demanded by France, or to blend the questions which had arisen upon the Orders in Council with any discussion of the general principles of blockade. This declaration did not preclude an amicable discussion upon the subject of any particular blockade of which the circumstances might appear to the Government of the United States to be exceptional, or to require explanation.[1]

Mr. Pinkney asked an audience to take leave, which was forthwith granted, with an intimation that Mr. Augustus Foster, till then Minister at Stockholm, had been appointed to Washington. The interval of several months which had elapsed since the recall of Mr. Jackson, because he was unacceptable to the American President, was unofficially explained ' by the earnest desire of rendering the appointment satisfactory to the United States, and conducive to the effectual establishment of harmony between the two Governments.' The Foreign Secretary was therefore ' concerned to find that the Government of the United States should suppose that any indisposition could exist on the part of his Majesty's Government to place our mission on the most acceptable footing. Under these circumstances Mr. Pinkney would exercise his own judgment respecting the propriety of requiring an audience of leave.'[2] This cheap sacrifice of a ram caught in a thicket appeased for the moment impending wrath. The American waived his audience of leave; but, not to be too condescending, wrote to say that he ' concluded it was the intention of the British Government to seek immediately those adjustments with America without which the new appoint-

[1] 11th February, 1811. [2] 15th February, 1811.

ment could produce no beneficial effect. He presumed that, for the restoration of harmony between the two countries, the Orders in Council would be relinquished without delay; the blockades of 1806 annulled; the case of the *Chesapeake* arranged; and, in general, that all such just and reasonable acts would be done as were necessary to make us friends. His motives, he trusted, would not be misinterpreted if, anxious so to regulate his conduct as that the best results might be accomplished, he took the liberty of requesting such explanations on these heads as his lordship might think fit to give him.'[1] From Apsley House a private letter repeated in terms nearly identical the general expression of willingness to discuss details of any matter of complaint or grievance, and referred to previous correspondence for the explanation of English views and purposes. 'But it would be neither candid or just to countenance any interpretation which might favour a supposition that it was intended by our Government to relinquish any of the principles which they had so often endeavoured to explain to him.[2] Upon this the Minister, in compliance with his instructions from President Madison, took his departure, and diplomatic relations were suspended, though not actually broken off, for some time.

Meanwhile a change of person in the Executive power of the State had taken place, which men of opposite parties, who agreed in nothing else, concurred in regarding as of paramount importance, and in which they were destined all to be completely mistaken. After fifty years the reign of George III. had come to an end, and while life and the use of his bodily faculties were still left him, the feeble powers of understanding he had hitherto possessed were taken away; and the son who, for a quarter of a century, he had regarded with distrust, aversion, and contempt, was in everything except the name substituted for him on the throne. On

[1] 17th February, 1811.   [2] 23rd February, 1811.

October 25, while surrounded by his usual domestic circle, his Majesty, without any premonitory symptoms of illness, suddenly appeared to be suffering from mental alienation, in a form so painful that the Queen peremptorily dismissed her children and the household, and with rare presence of mind assumed the charge of her afflicted lord. The Court physicians were speedily in attendance, and the Ministers and Princes of the blood summoned to Windsor. But among many men there were many minds as to the cause, nature, degree, and probable duration of the malady. The King had been at intervals similarly afflicted before, and it was therefore natural to anticipate that the delirium might again subside without leaving any palpable effects. Every motive which could influence men inspired to sway their judgments, and to sever their courses on the occasion. Few were indeed allowed access to the apartments in which the aged monarch was secluded, and those who were, did not always agree in their estimate of appearances or the expectations they expressed with regard to the future. The Premier and the Chancellor were officially bound to see the King, in order that they might judge for themselves, and advise their colleagues what should be done in the painful emergency.

Lord Eldon, on more than one occasion, spent some time with him alone, by the advice of Sir H. Halford, because, as he told the Privy Council, 'the King showed such respect for the Chancellor, and awe of him,' that he would be rendered thereby more amenable to advice. Whitbread pressed for the meaning of the words 'respect' and 'awe,' and asked if the King did not feel the same for Mr. Perceval. Sir Henry was puzzled; but the questions and answers did not appear in the examination, as they were expunged by twelve to six.[1] A good deal more of the medical evidence was likewise suppressed. When questioned as to the exciting

[1] MS. Journal of H. Grey Bennet, M.P. for Shrewsbury.

causes of previous aberration, the Court physicians, agreeing with those of 1801, ascribed it to the controversy on the Catholic question with Mr. Pitt, which led to his resignation, and with those of 1804 to the publication of his Majesty's correspondence with his eldest son. In fact it appeared that in all cases of opposition or irritation, George III. was, and had been, subject to what the physicians thought fit to call *hurries* and *flurries* (explained afterwards as 'temporary deliriums).' In other words, he had been unable to bring a cool judgment to the discussion of any proposition of his Ministers against which he entertained a prepossession. Hence his aversion to particular men, his vehemence upon particular subjects, his resolution upon the Catholic question, and his explanation of the Coronation oath.[1]

Lords Camden and Wellesley visited Windsor, and by permission of the Queen, had a prolonged interview with the physicians, whose hopes and misgivings, sufficiently perplexing, they reported fully to the Cabinet. Speaking to one of his confidants of the uncertainties of the future, the Foreign Secretary said 'that he would not act in the matter in any sneaking or mean way; that if the King was not well enough to sign the commission before the 29th, the physicians should be publicly examined, and that upon their evidence he would be guided as a juror. If it were favourable towards a speedy recovery, he would then support the present order of things to the last. If he thought it a question of doubtful or distant recovery, he would not hesitate a moment in giving the country an efficient Government, the want of which had already begun to be most seriously felt.'[2]

The Chancellor and the Foreign Secretary visited Windsor again on November 1, to ascertain the opinion of the physicians. They concurred in stating that his Majesty was incapable of signing any document of State; secondly, his malady was

---

[1] MS. Journal of H. Grey Bennet, M.P. for Shrewsbury.
[2] To Lord Buckingham, 1st November, 1810.

referable to distress of mind regarding the Princess Amelia; thirdly, that they had known many instances of recovery in like cases. The two Ministers saw the King: when they came out, Lord Eldon threw up his hands despondingly.[1] After two adjournments of a fortnight each, it was at length thought necessary that Parliament should deliberate, and determine on the best means of supplying the want of supreme authority in the State. As a first step the physicians were examined before committees of the two Houses; but, excepting Willis, none of them could pronounce any decided opinion as to the exact nature of the King's infirmity.

Public sympathy for the sad condition of the sufferer, and commiseration for its immediate cause, naturally disarmed political animosities for the time, and enabled Ministers without difficulty to take their measures of preparation for establishing a Regency. Warned by previous experience the Prince remained in comparative seclusion at Windsor, leaving all parties free to conjecture what he would do if called to power. A Bill, founded on the three resolutions of 1788, appointing the Prince of Wales Regent of the kingdom, but limiting the exercise for a year of certain prerogatives, was opposed in the Commons by his political friends, but carried by a large majority. On December 27 it was appointed to be read a first time in the Lords; and although it was known that the Grenvilles felt bound in honour and consistency to adhere to the course they had taken twenty years before, the opposite opinion, strongly expressed by all the Princes of the blood, was understood to be sufficiently indicative of the personal feelings of the Heir Apparent, who was at last about to assume the rank and power of sovereignty. The Cabinet were indeed unanimous as to the proposed measure, but it was felt that it behoved them to make their unanimity apparent to the world. It was agreed that Lord

[1] From W. H. Freemantle, Englefield Green, 1st November, 1810.

Liverpool should make the introductory statement, and that the Chancellor and the Foreign Secretary should be prepared to reply. The prevalent belief that the Ministry would be changed, and the expectation of many that Wellesley would form part of a new combination, if he were not placed at the head, rendered his position not a little embarrassing; but he accepted the obligation frankly, and as was his wont, shut himself up for a day or two before, in order to prepare himself for the onerous duty circumstances imposed upon him. The day came, and a crowded House waited with unusual interest the renewal of the contention in which all the greatest men of their time had been formerly engaged. Grey was absent, and the amendment on the resolutions was moved by Holland and supported by the Duke of Norfolk, Lord Erskine, the Duke of York, Lord Lansdowne, and Lord Grenville, who expressed his astonishment at the dead silence which some of the most responsible individuals in the committee observed upon the occasion. The Chancellor accepted the challenge, and, in his ponderous way, summed up the legal arguments for limitation; but for the rest, the defence of Government was left to secondary men; and, although on a division they prevailed by 100 to 74, one who watched the scene with searching eye thought he 'never saw a set of men look so crestfallen and beaten to the ground.'[1] For the signal opportunity had come and gone, and Wellesley had failed to grasp it. There he sat from hour to hour, conscious that men's gaze was fixed upon him as one who was qualified, nay, called upon to speak with authority, and whose silence would be inexplicable. Canning, who waited restlessly to hear him with that solicitude and sympathy which a great actor alone can feel in a comrade whose success is linked with his own, could not contain his vexation as he came out: 'You entered the House the most expected man in England; you leave

[1] Journal of . G. Bennet.

it self-undone.' He made no remonstrance, for explanation he had none to give that by Canning would have been credible. It was in fact one of those strange caprices of fortune by which the career of an eminent man having in him too much of nervous sensibility is liable to be chequered. He knew too well how much his colleagues had naturally looked to him as specially charged with the function of vindicating their policy. In Council he had cited the words of Pitt again and again; and his intimates knew that he had for days been absorbed in preparation for a great oratorical effort. But when he should have risen to answer Holland or Erskine, some unaccountable irresolution came upon him, and he let the occasion pass without uttering a word. Nothing could exceed the mortification of his friends, except his own. Ill-nature quickly ascribed the cause to be a visit he had paid a few hours previously to Carlton House; and the whisper everywhere went round that he had 'ratted' at the last moment for the sake of power. Even his warm admirers shrank from defending his unpardonable silence; they began to speak of his being gone by as a public man, wanting the moral courage that can alone sustain character for consistency. The crowd talked of him next day as a deserter, and his own chagrin was such that he himself confessed in private, should the King recover, his conduct must seem wholly inexcusable. And yet there existed no substantial reason for the obloquy he had brought upon himself. 'No being living was, to my knowledge, more anxious to play his part upon this occasion as an inheritor of Mr. Pitt's system and as a personal friend to the King. His visit to the Prince was unofficial, and marked by harshness and ill-humour on both sides. His preparation was ample and complete, and his views of the whole Regency question squared to a tittle with those of his brother Ministers. To those who were most interested about him, it was a species of *défaillance* more alarming than even the verification of the worst suggestions of his enemies. It augured *un homme passé*: and the most dangerous symptom of the whole was that he entirely agreed in the opinion. All this was to be retrieved, if it could be retrieved, in the progress of the Bill, when he could, if he would, in reply to Lord Grey, take an opportunity of going over the whole question in the fullest detail, and unequivocally declaring his opinions thereon. Such were at least his pledges to his friends.'[1]

[1] Mr. D. to Marquis of Buckingham, undated letter, written probably early in January.

CHAPTER XX.

OATLANDS AND DORKING.

1811–12.

JANUARY was spent by Parliament in discussing the details of restriction on the powers of the Regency. The chiefs of Opposition were in daily communication with the Prince, and but for their jealousies among themselves he would probably have been ruled by them. His impatience at the restrictions Ministers sought to impose on him beguiled them into reiterated objections and protests; and parties were so nearly balanced that, with Grenville's help, an amendment of Lord Lansdowne's was carried by a majority of three. But the old colleague of Pitt, who had republished his speech on limited Regency as a masterpiece of constitutional wisdom, suddenly revoked, and as one of his ardent Whig allies exclaimed, 'thereby lost the game.' He hoped indeed, to make amends by moving to reduce the terms of limitation from twelve to six months. This did not satisfy the Prince, though he desired him and Lord Grey to frame his answer to the Address of the two Houses. Over-secure of their supposed ascendency, they tried to reconcile the opposing views held upon the theory of executive sovereignty at Carlton House and at Dropmore, declining the aid of the more pliant Moira as a coadjutor in their task. Sheridan, who had his own slights to resent, adroitly fixed the attention of his revelling Highness on certain turns of phrase, which he condemned as 'flimsy attempts to cover Grenville's consistency at the expense of the Prince,' and readily framed another draft, which being approved in preference, he handed to Lord Grey at Holland House, with comments and explanations ill-suited to appease the Earl's wounded dignity. A stately admonition on the princely error of not being guided solely by the counsel of responsible advisers, gave Sheridan ample opportunity for casting ridicule on the dictatorial pretensions of the Ministers about to be. The inherited jealousy of Ministerial mentorship thus kindled was for a time indeed repressed, but thenceforth, every now and then, it threatened to break out, to Moira's worldly-wise regret and disapproval. In the first scheme for the distribution of offices he agreed to go to Ireland as Viceroy, with Sheridan as chief Secretary; but the Prince did not want to lose the company of either, to which he had grown accustomed, and instead, suggested Lansdowne as a better Lord-Lieutenant. Grey, Whitbread, and Ponsonby were to be Secretaries of State, and Grenville, though he would not resign his incompatible post of Auditor of the Exchequer, took it as a matter of course that he should be First Lord of the Treasury. Erskine, it was felt, could not again be forced upon the Court of Chancery, and he was content to be Speaker only of the Upper House; but Piggott and Romilly were unexceptionable law officers; the Great Seal might be put in commission; and a better Secretary of the Treasury than Horner there could not be. Meanwhile Perceval kept his friends together, and though nearly single-handed in debate, made so good a fight that even his adversaries acknowledged the temper and talent he had shown. Yet all the world agreed that however gallantly he might prolong the struggle it could only end in his discomfiture and displacement, as soon as the Act was passed which should clothe the Heir Apparent with the Chief Magistracy of the realm. In the prolonged discussions, Wellesley took no part, and his name only appears as voting in divisions and as one of the managers for the Peers in conferences upon certain minor amendments in the Painted Chamber.

A last and as it proved an ill-advised attempt to modify the limitations was made by Ponsonby, contrary to his better judgment, to please the Prince, giving Ministers an increased majority. When it was over, Mr. Brand told Plummer Ward how much he admired Perceval's bearing in the struggle, and said laughingly, that perhaps after all, the Regent might retain him for three months, on the chance of the King's recovery, and then fall in love with him and keep him on. This was on January 21, and within a week his Royal Highness had begun to listen to suggestions from the Queen, which led to the renunciation of all his previous counsels. Up to January 31, Rose still believed a Ministerial change was certain as soon as the Bill should pass. 'By ——! they shall not remain one hour!' had been the exclamation of the Prince only a few days before; and Sheridan, blinding or blinded, maintained that it was their own fault if the Tories had to go; for if they had not been so punctilious about the precedent of 1789 they might hold on. Yet few had more contributed than he to keep alive the feelings of impatience and dislike with which the Prince regarded the unyielding tone and reprehending look of Grey.

On February 12 the Regent, to the surprise of all parties, wrote to Mr. Perceval that he had no intention of making any immediate change in the Administration; and his first speech to Parliament was indistinguishable in sentiment and purport from those of his father. Filial duty and consideration for the afflicted condition of his sovereign alone prompted him, he said, to put in abeyance the principles he had hitherto professed, and to set aside the claims and expectations he had encouraged to the last moment. Lords Grenville and Grey were actually engaged in forming a new Administration when the confidential Adam came in and told them 'all was over.' Their anger could not be concealed; but when they had slept on it, they thought it more politic as well as more dignified to say they believed the inconsistency of the Prince attributable to the restrictions which in other matters fettered his choice; and that, when the statutable limitation of his power should expire, they would naturally and inevitably come into possession of their long-deferred inheritance. Grenville and Grey took leave of the Prince on February 3: 'they parted good friends, with many protestations on each side.' There was a Council at Carlton House, at which there was a numerous attendance, almost every Privy Councillor in town being present. The Prince kept the Council waiting two hours; the King never detained anybody a minute. He was very civil to some and very rude to others, particularly to the Speaker Abbot and to Perceval, turning his head away while they kissed his hand. He had brought into the Council room that morning the busts of Mr. Fox and the Duke of Bedford; and they were placed at the head of the table. The situation of the Ministers was most distressing. Upon some one wishing Lord Harrowby joy, he replied, 'Joy! how can I feel it? we have to do business with a man who hates us, and only wishes power to turn us out.' He was much advised to do so by Moira, Hutchinson, and Sheridan; but Yarmouth and Lady Hertford laboured the other way. The country seemed against limitations, and being heartily tired of the state of things, looked to a change of any sort. All the world forgot what the Prince had done or not done during his previous life. People thought more was said than was true. Cobbett took the lead in this tone, and was of much service to his cause.[1]

The Foreign Secretary thus found himself unexpectedly retained in his position, and the direction of Foreign Affairs

[1] Grey Bennet's Journal, February 1811.

was the function which of all others he preferred if he could not be First Minister. In ordinary times it involved an extent and degree of individual sway in the affairs of the world greater than that which was exercised by the head of any other department; in times like those in which the country was engaged in life-and-death wrestle with the power of Napoleon, it was one of boundless responsibility, and to a man of egotistic temperament daily stimulative of the sense of personal ascendency. It was a period, to use the words of Canning, 'when one hour of office was worth a year of ordinary dignity and pay;' and few men were more capable of enjoying the intoxicating pleasures of the position than Wellesley. So keen indeed was his zest for the exercise of far-seeing and far-reaching control in great affairs, that he could not brook the idea of consulting or conferring with those he deemed ineffably his inferiors, though bound up with them in the bundle of official life. For weeks together he abstained from attending the Cabinet, leaving to the head of the Treasury and the Secretary for War the duty of explaining the details of the measures he had concerted with them. He was, besides, too impatient of contradiction and too disdainful of the commonplace doubts and objections which less daring and ambitious associates in office were apt to suggest. Mr. Perceval, while he kept his temper, chafed at the want of consideration, and indeed breach of conventional rule of mutual confidence and intercommunication, on which the Executive in a constitutional State can alone securely rest. Wellesley frequently acted and no doubt felt as if he, and not Perceval, were head of the Administration.

The Address in the Commons at the opening of the first session of Regency was moved by Mr. M. Milnes,[1] and seconded, in a maiden speech, by Richard Wellesley, who chiefly dwelt upon the constancy and courage of the troops

[1] Father of Lord Houghton.

in Portugal, under his distinguished relative, which had insured the deliverance of that kingdom from the miseries of invasion.

Notwithstanding all we had done and were ready to risk for Portugal, jealousy of Wellington's peremptory tone as Commander-in-Chief of the allied forces, and of the equally wise interposition of our envoy at Lisbon, troubled the Brazilian Court, whose dreamy idleness was haunted with misgivings of our ultimate purpose. From Rio, Strangford wrote that symptoms of recurring 'discontent and suspicion were unequivocally exhibited by the Regent at the interference at Lisbon of Mr. Stuart and Admiral Berkley' on behalf of persons who had incurred the resentment of the local government there.[1] Could nothing be said to appease these groundless feelings of mistrust? or nothing done to back the Count Linhares, who, because he was our friend in council, intrigue was busily endeavouring to undermine?

Wellesley did not deign to resent the petulance and folly that imputed furtive aims to England, or think of bidding his inflexible brother palter for a moment with the demagogues in office, whose fatuity, had he even seemed to yield to them, would have ruined all. Months before he had anticipated the distant mischief, and prepared to circumvent the folly in his own Oriental way. As he read the anxious plenipotentiary's despatch on March 25, he felt serenely confident that already the wayward mood had changed, for reasons he had not thought it necessary to disclose; and on April 19 an account reached him of the delight and gratitude of the Brazilian Court on the receipt of costly presents sent in the King's name; and above all, for the restoration of the *Minerva*, a ship of war re-captured from the enemy, at sight of which, as she entered the beautiful harbour of Rio de

---

[1] From the English Minister to Brazil, 20th January, 1811. MS. in Foreign Office.

Janeiro, the whole population went fairly mad with joy.[1] It was one of the fine strokes in the world-game he loved to play, which by prosaic colleagues would have been deemed fantastical, and by economic critics indefensible; but which history, that does not find the fate of nations governed merely by huxter interest or hard logic, deems not unworthy of record. Already the danger of disunion in Portugal had passed away, and the French had re-crossed the frontier to return no more. Greater efforts than previously ought to be made if we were to secure the fruit of this success. At the instance of the Foreign Secretary[2] Parliament was asked for two millions for the maintenance of the Portuguese army, which, notwithstanding the admitted symptoms of decline in the export trade, and in spite of the forebodings of Grenville and Ponsonby, who argued that all our sacrifices would prove vain, were granted by decisive majorities.

Lord Temple thought that Canning seemed determined to abide by Wellesley, but looked for a junction with Grenville and Grey. There had for some time been a coolness between himself and the Foreign Secretary; but the latter made an advance towards reconciliation which was accepted; he expressed his readiness to meet Grenville, and an interview between the two old friends was arranged for an early day. But Thomas Grenville disliked Canning so bitterly that he objected to his brother making any confidence with Wellesley, and laboured to keep them apart. The friends of Gloucester Lodge, meanwhile, were as outspoken about the necessity of a change as those of Apsley House. The progress of the war, though overhung with the darkness of uncertainty, was lighted up from time to time with lurid gleams of triumph that stirred the popular heart. Men had not ceased to recount the dangers

[1] From Lord Strangford, 20th February, 1811, idem.
[2] See his speech on address to the Regent pledging the Peers to support Portugal, 21st March, 1811.

of Barossa when they were gladdened by the success of Fuentes D'Onore and fevered with excitement by the tragic tale of Albuera.[1] But more and more as the strain on the national resources was prolonged, the need of unifying and consolidating them grew urgent in the minds of liberal and enlightened statesmen; and the infatuation grew more obvious of keeping in a state of political outlawry millions of the hardiest and bravest subjects of the Crown. Wellesley never disguised his sentiments on the subject. In the debate on the Catholic Petition on June 18 he did not speak, but in the division he voted with the Whigs against Liverpool and Eldon. The fact is worth noticing in reference to the ultimate breach between him and them in the ensuing year.

A first draft of the Regent's speech closing the session did not satisfy him, and he was asked by the Premier to 'let him have the benefit of his emendatory elisions.' On the back of his brief note he replied, 'Happening to be out of town until the hour of going to the House of Lords to-day, I have scarcely had time to read the draft of the speech with due attention, and you require that it should be returned to-morrow morning. As you wish for free observation upon it, you will not be offended when I tell you that I object to the whole plan of it, which in my opinion, is totally inadequate to the occasion. The great feature of the present session (with respect to the very existence of this empire) is the effort which Parliament has made to support the war in the Peninsula; and the principles from which that effort proceeded are, in my judgment, essentially necessary to be stated in the opening of the speech, quite distinctly from the success of our operations. I have many other objections to the draft, both in point of substance and style; but as I really think that the general plan of the speech is far below the magnitude of the occasion, I state this sentiment to you

---

[1] 16th May, 1811.

without delay; I am satisfied that on reconsideration of the draft you will approve very few words which are now on the paper.'[1]

As delivered by commission, on July 24, it particularly expressed the Regent's approbation of the wisdom and firmness manifested in continuing the exertions of the country in the cause of our allies, to prosecute the war with increased activity and vigour. The determined perseverance in a system of liberal aid to the brave and loyal nations of the Peninsula had progressively augmented their means and spirit of resistance, while the humane attentions to the sufferings of the inhabitants, under the unexampled cruelty of the enemy, had confirmed the alliance by new ties of affection, and could not fail to inspire additional zeal and animation in the maintenance of the common cause. This was his part of the speech, and Perceval was welcome to formulate the residue as he pleased.

Russia having given indications that she was weary of the war at sea, instructions were to be sent to Sir James Saumarez (then commanding the Fleet in the Baltic) to conclude a suspension of hostilities, and if opportunity served, to sign preliminaries of peace. Perceval had nothing to object to the draft sent to him for approval, which met his ideas exactly. He enclosed, however, on a separate paper, as a suggestion for consideration, another mode of turning the passage, introducing the mention of the resolutions on trade which would equally convey the meaning and was less capable of being construed into an implied conditional promise of direct aid to Russia. He saw no objection to giving the admiral power to sign preliminary articles, except that he doubted whether it might not, by betraying too great an eagerness and forwardness on our part, rather tend to defeat our object. But upon this point particularly he

[1] Endorsed in Mr. Perceval's handwriting, 15th July, 1811.

lamented that they had not had a Cabinet; he thought their colleagues would be a little surprised to find such a measure taken without any previous communication with them; and indeed, he would feel that if it would occasion too much delay to have a Cabinet upon the paper before it was despatched, it was very desirable that it should be circulated as soon as possible. Though he did not conceive that there was any point on which any of their colleagues could differ from them; it was not impossible, especially with those who were every week in town, that they might not feel hurt at the appearance of not having been consulted upon such important subjects. This last observation applied to the despatch respecting the mediation with the South American colonies of Spain and the instructions sent to Mr. Smith. They would be sure to have a pretty full Cabinet on Wednesday, if the Marquess would summon it for that day, and he might then read to them his instructions to Mr. H. Wellesley and the first forms of his letter to Mr. Smith.[1] This was exactly the sort of appeal from his own confident judgment which the Secretary chafed at as superfluous and even absurd, and which on all possible occasions, he endeavoured to elude. The Cabinet was not called by him; and when it met, he was obliged to be out of town.

In September advices were received from the Northern Powers indicating the revival of a spirit of resistance to Napoleon's overbearing ascendency. Alexander's pride was wounded by the preference unceremoniously shown for Marie Louisa's hand to that of his sister; and his country was suffering severely from the operation of the Continental system. He had put his army in Poland once more upon an active footing, and its efficiency, under the reforming influence of Barclay de Tolly, had been greatly improved since the Treaty of Tilsit. If called on, as he expected to

[1] From Downing Street, 9th August, 1811.

be, to repay the war loan of ten millions due to Holland, he must consider it an act of hostility, and he was ready to combine with England and Prussia, if the latter could be induced to move and the former to hold on her intrepid way. From all quarters came the acknowledgment that the dauntless stand made in the Peninsula had rekindled hope and faith that previously seemed dead. The enthusiasm of the Foreign Secretary on beginning to perceive the result of his policy took the form once more it had taken in India. His indolence vanished, and his love of pleasure was forgotten in his zest for work. Week after week he postponed leaving town, and devoted hours continuously every day to the expanding business of his office, whose records still preserve the traces of his energetic and comprehensive labour. One who saw him frequently, describes the constancy of his application, and the intense satisfaction at the recognition from afar of the spirit he had infused. 'It was his sanguine belief that the face of Europe was about to undergo the most material change for the better, and all brought about by his counsels.'[1]

At Oatlands, where the Prince stayed often late in the autumn, the Foreign Secretary was a frequent visitor; and his friends believed that the influence of the Duke of York was exerted actively in support of his views. At Carlton House the Duke of Cumberland, who leaned rather to those of the Chancellor and Mr. Perceval, seems to have subsequently gained the ear of his indolent and irresolute brother, who shrunk from the trouble of any immediate change of hands. He was heard for the first time to complain of the conduct of the Catholics in agitating in Ireland, thereby weakening his Government, and perversely casting doubt upon the sincerity of his intentions towards them. He would not be intimidated into premature concession, and he

[1] Mr. D. to Lord Buckingham, 17th September, 1811.

would make no alteration in the Ministry, which would have the appearance of yielding to menace.

But again the humour changed, and subjects of renewed dissatisfaction arose with the First Minister, which led him to resume his former professions of preference for Apsley House.

The Regent was compelled by a sprained ankle to keep his room for several weeks at the country residence of his brother, and he was glad of the society of one whose intelligence was the newest, and whose resources in conversation were the best. Foreign affairs at the time had the interest and variety of romance; and compared with the business of other departments, had the supreme merit of being amusing: and Wellesley knew well how to amuse. A man with whom Grattan, Pitt, Canning, and Pozzo di Borgo loved to talk, and whom half the women of fashion loved to call 'dear Marquess,' was sure of welcome beside the sofa of the invalid voluptuary. During sultry afternoons he was often constrained to stay on till dinner-time, and sometimes till too late for driving into town. An opportunity thus afforded for sowing the waste brain of idle royalty with martial thoughts was not to be neglected; and putting aside many claims of business and pleasure that would otherwise have occupied him, the Secretary held himself ready to be commanded to Oatlands whenever princely idleness was in a European humour. Might it not still be possible to work his vanity into a species of ambition to rescue the western States of the Continent from military domination? If enthusiasm for mere right had never existed, and early lessons of public duty had all been scoffed away or drowned in wassail, might not something be made of egotism languishing for a new emotion? Could it not be coaxed and wheedled into good— the good of the public? Even though but for a season, would it not be better than high play, foppery, broad jests, and midnight bowls? The Royal *ennuyé* listened, and daily liked to listen more, to Wellesley's ever-fresh and always graphic details of war in Spain, and combinations for renewed resistance at Berlin, Stockholm, and St. Petersburg. The Regent listened with interest to the splendid visions continually presented to him of concerted action abroad, organised by our intelligence and through our instrumentality. Russia no longer asked for subsidies, and only urged that the war in the South should be pressed with unremitting vigour. For this an additional effort ought to be made in Galicia, to divide the attention of the French armies, and to enable Wellington once more to advance towards Madrid. Fresh armaments and provision for additional expenditure of 3,000,000*l.* would be indispensable; but the country was eager for the liberation of Spain, and if we succeeded in allaying the irritation of America, the elasticity of our commerce would, without serious hurt, sustain the increased burthen. Information on this and a variety of other points connected with foreign trade was sought daily from bankers and merchants, to whom Wellesley gave long interviews at Downing Street, and sent away impressed with the conviction that there was not another Minister like him for sympathy in their interest or comprehension of their affairs. But while Perceval remained at the Treasury, it was doubtful how far his policy could be carried into effect. The Prince and his brothers, as far as they were consulted, were said to desire a change, and the rumour ran that the Dukes of Norfolk, Devonshire, and Northumberland, with Lords Holland and Lansdowne, were ready to take part in an Administration of which the Marquess should be the head, and Canning spokesman in the Commons.

Pozzo di Borgo was at this time in England. He was already known as a man of singular talents and attainments, full of varied information and original suggestion; a great linguist, a rare political strategist, and above all, a good hater. Napoleon had in vain tried to appease his aversion; but he was a Corsican, and his life was devoted to the undoing of his hitherto invincible fellow-countryman. Compelled to quit the service of the Czar, he had agreed to meet Stein, the Ex-Chancellor of Prussia, at Troppau, in the autumn of 1809,[1] to interchange longings for vengeance, and to concert the re-organisation of a conspiracy against Napoleon by matter-of-fact politicians deemed chimerical, but which before long was felt in the quickened pulse of every prostrate community. Wellesley invited him to visit England, and he had to make his way by Smyrna, Malta, and Cadiz. They had many communings and conferences while he stayed. Few men, indeed, could comprehend one another more thoroughly; and in the eventful period which ensued, Pozzo di Borgo justified amply the high estimate formed of his sagacity and versatility by the English Secretary of State. With his colleagues it seldom occurred to Wellesley to talk, still less to confer, on ground-plans of a re-modelled Europe or the intricate details of various designs and elevations. He thought it enough to engage when he could the attention, or touch the listless ambition of the Royal Sybarite, without whose sanction he could not venture to act, and whose self-love led him to prefer the anti-constitutional way of dealing with each Minister about the business of his department, instead of with a dozen Ministers bound together by the solidarity of a Cabinet. Had there been in high office in 1811 any second man possessing knowledge and versatility in Foreign Affairs, the practice could not have arisen imperceptibly of which, when it threatened to become habitual, his colleagues vaguely and moodily complained.

The inconvenience of the head of a department acting upon his own responsibility in important matters without

[1] *Stein and Pozzo di Borgo*, by Count Ouvaroff, 1847.

communication with his colleagues was exemplified by the autocratic resolve of the Most Noble Secretary to appoint commissioners who were to mediate between Spain and her revolted colonies. Rose, surprised at the announcement in the newspapers, was still more amazed to find that his friends in the Cabinet knew as little about the matter until a day or two before the appointment appeared in the *Gazette*. The true reason of the hurry was, he insinuates, an impatience to provide for Mr. Sydenham; but the alleged reason was that the Duke of Infantado pressed it with so much importunity as a measure necessary to strengthen the feeble hands of the governing Junta, that the English Foreign Office found it difficult not to yield. The fact was, says the astute party manager, that my Lord Marquess had exercised absolute power so long in India that he had no great relish for consultation with others in the Cabinet. But if it be true that the Spanish Minister's importunities drew him into that doubtful position, it will account in some degree for the vexation and discontent which he betrayed in a letter to the Secretary of the Treasury on the subject.[1]

'Private.

'I return the draft which you have been so kind as to send to me, with a few suggestions on the margin. The conduct of Portugal, or rather the Portuguese Government, is a good exercise of political patience for a young Minister. I have been engaged in one continued squabble with that Government and our other ally of Spain since I held the seals; and if any statesman can point out to me the means of inducing either to attend to reason, truth, or justice, I shall be much obliged to him.'

Another illustration of the want of administrative intimacy, for it would be ironical to talk of consultative unity,

[1] From Dorking, 7th November, 1811.

in the Government, is to be found in a note of the scrupulous and well-tempered, but sometimes sorely tried, First Lord to the intractable Secretary. Beginning with a few lines about a rough draft enclosed of the speech from the Throne at the opening of Parliament, on which he invites the 'amplest criticism,' he proceeds: 'A warrant has been brought from the Treasury this morning for my signature for 1,000*l.* for Sir Robert Wilson, to enable him to prepare for some mission, and your letter to the Lords of the Treasury, I perceive, is dated 29th of November, and the warrant was ordered under your instructions by the Lords of the Treasury. I do not think you ever mentioned the subject of the mission to me; if you have, it is so long ago that I have entirely forgotten it; and as I know not whither he is going—whether Egypt, Constantinople, Palestine, or elsewhere—nor what the object of his mission is, I am sure you will not be surprised at my requesting to know something concerning it. I remember hearing, but I think it was only from common rumour, some time ago that there was a mention of sending him with Mr. Liston; but I thought it had been with some view to his attending on the Turkish army, and the way of conducting the campaign against the Russians. However, as he cannot possibly reach that destination till the conclusion of the campaign, or rather, to judge by the late news, till the war itself be over, I think notwithstanding, if that were the original intention, that it may have been changed. At all events, I should be glad to see his instructions; and if you have prepared them, I will be obliged to you to send them to me.' [1]

The Marquess replied the next day: 'To the best of my recollection I communicated to you some time ago the intention of employing Sir Robert Wilson. I have desired Mr. Hamilton to state the object of that appointment in a

[1] 25th December, 1811.

note which I now enclose to you. I should certainly have conversed more fully on the subject with you if I had thought it deserving of your attention.'

In November we have the following :—

'I send you a private letter from Mr. Thornton, to which I shall pay immediate attention. Be so good as to return it to me. I also send an interesting interception.

'With the Swedish papers (which I sent to the Regent this morning) I have received an order to attend at Oatlands to-morrow, for the purpose of meeting Count Münster, and of discussing the affairs of the North, on which his Royal Highness is very anxious. I am afraid that I shall not be able to return in time for Lord Westmoreland's dinner.'

Late on the 27th he wrote to say: 'Just as I reached Oatlands, this morning at half-past twelve, the Princesses arrived from Windsor, which event prevented me from seeing the Prince until a very late hour. I am but this moment arrived in town, and have had no dinner, and am so much tired (partly from the extreme heat of the room at Oatlands) that I should have no power of rendering justice to any subject of public business to-night, even if I could reach you in any reasonable time.

'The subject of my audience to-day was Sweden; but the Prince generally stated to me the same ideas which I have already mentioned to you, with much increased earnestness, and indeed on some points with considerable force. He informed me that he had seen the Queen yesterday, and that her Majesty entirely approved all his views respecting the King, the Household, and the settlement for the Queen and the Princesses.

'He continues to think that the dignity of the King and the comfort of his situation will be best provided for by a separate establishment, under a new office of the highest rank. That the Regent should have the whole Civil List, and the full state, as well as power, of the Crown, and should resign his allowances as Prince of Wales. That the Queen should have an independent allowance, and the Princesses the same. He considers this part of the arrangement to be inseparable from the settlement of the Regency on a permanent basis. He will state many very strong considerations in favour of his plan, and appears intent on carrying it into execution. He said to-day that, after the discussion with you shall have taken place (unless you agreed), he should wait to receive your propositions in writing, in order that he might answer them. I rather understood this to be a proof of his determination to abide by his own ideas than a symptom of any intention to depart from them in consequence of what he might receive in writing from you.

'As, I suppose, you will pass the greater part of to-morrow at Oatlands, I would fix Friday, at two, for the Cabinet on the other points in my department, if that day should be convenient.'[1]

The majority of the Cabinet fell in reluctantly with the ideas of Carlton House. There was real need for economy in the permanent charges which the Exchequer had to bear; and there was no temptation in a party sense to provide for the endowment of opponents who were counting audibly the days till they should come into power. Parsimony, in public or in private, was not among the foibles of the Marquess, but he seems to have concurred in nearly all the views propounded by the Treasury.

'The Prince Regent sent an order to me, which reached me at this place last night, directing me to attend his Royal Highness at Oatlands, at twelve to-day. He began by asking me whether I had seen the paper which he had received from you respecting the new settlement of the Regency. I said (as you know I must have said) that I had not seen the

[1] To Perceval, 27th November, 1811

paper, but that I was acquainted with the substance of its contents. He then communicated your paper to me, and said that he intended to state his ideas in writing on the whole subject; that he was aware of the impropriety of desiring me to offer any advice in the present state of the question, but that he wished to declare his sentiments freely to me. I thought it was my duty to inform his Royal Highness that I could not, in this stage of the discussion, offer any opinion on the subject, either of your paper or of his intended answer; and as this sentiment agreed with his own feeling he did not ask any opinion from me; but he proceeded to express nearly the same views of the subject which he had stated to you and to me on former occasions. I collected from his Royal Highness's conversation that your paper had produced no change in his opinion, and that he entertained a strong persuasion that his statement would have great weight, and would satisfy you that you had taken an erroneous view of the question.

'He informed me that he would send a copy to the Lord Chancellor, and that he would send me another copy. I should be glad to know when you propose to assemble a Cabinet for the consideration of your paper and of his Royal Highness's statement? I conclude that it cannot be sooner than Wednesday. I shall not be in town to-morrow.'[1]

A serious difference arose about the sum requisite to clear the debts contracted by the Prince during the year of Limitation. It was specially to this point in dispute that the foregoing note referred.

Perceval at once replied:—

'I thank you for your letter, and regret extremely that his Royal Highness continues so attached to his former opinion respecting the new settlement of the Regency. I had called a Cabinet meeting for this day, at two o'clock;

[1] MS. Dorking, 2nd December, 1811.

but I did so under the impression that I should previously have received the Prince's observations upon my paper. I heard from Mr. Adam last night that I was not to expect them till to-morrow, and have therefore determined to postpone the Cabinet till *two* to-morrow. I trust you will be able to attend it, and also to take a Cabinet dinner with me on the same day.'[1]

A seat at the Board of Treasury for his son would, Perceval thought, propitiate a discontented colleague; and a private note acknowledged the offer in friendly terms.[2] Unspoken scruples would not let him accept it without explanation; he requested therefore that the Premier ' would not write to the Prince Regent respecting his son until he had had an opportunity of speaking to him.' Read by the incidents of the following days it is plainer to us than it was then to Perceval why he did not wish the nomination of Richard Wellesley to be submitted for approval to the Prince, with whom he was in constant communication. But the appointment was gazetted on the last day of the year, and Richard Wellesley was returned for East Grinstead, a close borough belonging to the Dorset family, which Lord Whitworth (the husband of the last Duchess) had placed at the disposal of the Government.

The unfortunate dispute about the claim on the Treasury to liquidate the debts of Carlton House had in point of fact become a cause of disagreement in the Cabinet.

Early in December the Prince had sent, through Mr. Adam, a paper containing an account of the excess of expenditure during the first year of Regency, then drawing to a close; with an expression of his desire that a supplementary vote of 150,000*l*. should be proposed when Parliament met. The First Lord thought he could hardly ask with propriety for so

---

[1] Draft letter from Mr. Perceval.
[2] MS. Apsley House, 14th December.

large a sum, and he was authorised by his colleagues to submit their strong impression that it would not be without difficulty 100,000*l.* could be obtained; that the attempt to obtain 150,000*l.* would be extremely hazardous, very likely to fail in Parliament, and even if it were obtained, certain to be injurious in its impression on the public. He could not represent them as unanimous upon the point, for Lord Wellesley continued to think that it would be preferable to ask for 150,000*l.*, not conceiving that there would be that difference in public impression between the two sums, and feeling that less than 150,000*l.* would not adequately meet the expenses of the former year, and of the necessary establishment for the permanent Regency. On this representation of the matter Wellesley observed :—

'I return you the papers respecting the plan for the settlement of the Royal Household under the unrestricted Regency, which I have examined with as much care as the time would admit. Many of the objections which occurred to me during the discussion are now removed, and it is not my wish to record any formal dissent against such parts of the arrangement as still appear to me to be imperfect, nor shall I at any time hereafter express my disapprobation of a plan which has been finally approved by so many persons whom I respect and esteem. It would, however, be uncandid to suppress from you the knowledge of my sentiments, even in this stage of the transaction, and I wish this note to be privately communicated by you to the Prince Regent.

'I am of opinion that the Groom of the Stole, who is to preside over the King's establishment, must be invested with some new title designating his new powers; and the precedence which it is essential to give him must be annexed to that new title. It will not be proper to give the Groom of the Stole *eo nomine* precedence over the great officers of the Household. This point, I should imagine, might be easily arranged. But I entertain great apprehension that a sum of less than one hundred-and-fifty thousand pounds will not be adequate to the relief of the Prince Regent's incumbrances, and I should certainly have wished that a sum to that amount should have been proposed to Parliament. I will not dispute against your knowledge of the temper of the House of Commons; nor will I ever censure the grant as inadequate hereafter. I confess, however, that I think a considerable effort should be made on this point, and even some risk incurred, rather than expose the Prince Regent to the difficulties which I apprehend. Upon inferior matters of detail, and some parts of the principle of the general plan, I will not repeat the observations which I have already made, and of which the foundation still remains unaltered, because I am anxious to acquiesce in the sentiments of others to the utmost possible extent; and I shall not hereafter disturb the unanimity which seems to prevail on these arrangements: but it would neither be just to you nor to the Prince Regent that the actual state of my opinions, as expressed in this form, should be suppressed.'

Some delay occurred in the formal communication he desired, and he thus reiterated his view.

'I did not understand clearly from you in what manner you intended to signify the decision of the Cabinet to the Prince Regent respecting the amount of the sum to be proposed to Parliament for his Royal Highness's service; but I request that, in signifying it, you will communicate my opinion that the sum of one hundred-and-fifty thousand pounds would have been preferable to that which is now fixed. The reference seems to be of a more formal nature than any document yet received from the Prince Regent during this discussion. You will use your discretion as to the mode of stating my sentiments; but I conceive that, after such a reference, it would not be candid on my part to allow my opinion to be suppressed. It is indifferent to me whether a regular minute of Cabinet be drawn or not; but I wish substantially that my sentiments should be stated distinctly.'

Wellesley Pole, then Secretary for Ireland, differed in opinion from his brother, and disapproved of the course he had taken. Acquainted confidentially, by Perceval's desire, with what had occurred, and the views entertained by the Cabinet, he expressed his concurrence with theirs, and his regret that it should have been thought necessary to make the Regent aware that one of them had been dissentient. The Duke of Richmond pronounced a like judgment, though neither of them, confessedly, was aware what Lord Wellesley had to say about the matter; and neither had had the experience of Cabinet office which would have warranted him in determining how far a Secretary of State is bound, or is at liberty, to keep the secrets of his fellow Ministers from the Head of the State. For weeks the subject had been under discussion, and during that time he was, and was known to be, in constant personal communication with the Prince, whose pecuniary necessities were notorious. However foolishly incurred, they could not be left unrelieved without serious damage to the credit and influence of Government. Was it strange that a Minister in his confidence should think 50,000*l.* an extra weight of little moment in the trembling balance of the time? Or was it conceivable that he should have kept up the farce from day to day of duping a man like the Regent by pretending that he thought so, or that he could retain his influence with him, if he stooped to so transparent a part? The question was not whether 100,000*l.* was not enough to grant, or whether the Cabinet were not justifiable in stickling for that sum, on the eve as they supposed of their political opponents succeeding to power. Wellesley never affected to share their sectarian jealousy or party prejudice. He had always avowed his belief in Catholic Emancipation as the wisest measure for the internal government of the country and the best way of supporting the war. Bred a Whig, he was avowedly desirous of coalition with Holland and Grey; trained in administration under Pitt, he was the inheritor, with Grenville and Canning, of his tolerant principles. The Prince had up to this time professed the same opinions, and now that he was about to become the Executive head of the State, was it unnatural that Wellesley should expect to be especially trusted by him, and that he should have shown, and pretended to show, little sympathy with the grudging temper of a Ministerial *régime* supposed to be near its end; that he looked forward sanguinely to a new combination of ability and experience—without regard to party antecedents, or that he should have thought himself well fitted to be its chief? That he assented easily at least to this particular demand of the Prince for more money we may assume without proof; and if so, is it imaginable that he should have submitted to be misrepresented to him as one of an unanimous Cabinet who made it a point of financial honour to decline recommending it to Parliament? His acquiescence in the curtailment of the grant did not satisfy his colleagues, who wanted its sincere adoption; and this he refused as humiliating.

Perceval and Liverpool proposed a draft speech for the Regent at the opening of the session, of which their critical colleague as usual disapproved. He drafted another, to which they in turn demurred. They discussed it point by point at Apsley House, and in the end he had his way. As ultimately agreed upon, there were many touches of pathos concerning the situation of the King, a just tribute to Wellington's indomitable fortitude, and fervid vows of resolution to maintain the cause of Spanish independence till the last hour. His prosaic colleagues would have been more reticent and matter-of-fact; but finding him resolved to put nobler words into the lips of the Heir Apparent at the opening of his virtual reign, they gulped them all. No direct communication passed between the Premier and the Regent on the subject. Wellesley was with his Royal Highness on January 2 for five hours. He complained of Perceval's silence, but added, 'I knew the affair would ultimately be in your hands, and I did not care about it,' upon which the Secretary repeated his part of it, word for word, from memory, with which the Prince was delighted. He had just then named physician in ordinary, Knighton, whom the Marquess had taken with him to Seville. Lady Melbourne wanted the place for her favourite physician, but Knighton was an adept in the arts of pleasing, and was supposed to be familiar with the habits and peculiarities of many in the great world, a man well calculated to acquire influence and, as the event proved, to keep it. Colonel MacMahon read aloud to him his patron's letter of acknowledgment, which he said was admirable. 'You may be as sure of it as of your existence, that Lord Wellesley will be at the head of the Government as soon as the restrictions are removed.' Did he talk without knowing, or did anybody know? At Holland House they were full of misgivings as to what was really intended; and in Downing Street they were, or professed to be, as utterly in the dark. Only at Hyde Park Corner was there a placid sunshine of expectation, overcast by no cloud of uncertainty. The Regent had talked so much and so often and so long of his desire, and what he called his determination, to have a man of superior mind for his Minister, and he had lavished in turn so many epithets of antipathy on Perceval, Sidmouth, and Grey, that no one else seemed possible. A few days before Parliament met the Prince suddenly asked him if he would have any objection to shake hands with Lord Grenville. 'Certainly not,' he replied; 'public measures had separated them, but he ever had, and ever would have, the greatest private regard for him.' But Grenville's speech on the Address, which criticised the conduct of the war and the negotiations with America, irritated him greatly. The Duke of Cumberland, true to his rôle of mischief-making, said, 'I always knew you had a hankering after your old friend Grenville—what do you say to him now?' There was no division on the Address in the Upper House; but the Opposition were resolved to bring the Catholic question to issue without further delay.

An apprehended rupture with America rendered the distracted condition of Ireland a cause for public alarm; and Lord Fitzwilliam gave notice of motion for the removal of religious disabilities. Lord Liverpool, on the other hand, accepted the challenge on the part of Ministers, declaring that 'by the existing system of ascendency Government would stand or fall.'

Wellesley's position, already sufficiently embarrassing, was rendered thus no longer tenable; and on January 16 he waited on the Regent, and tendered his resignation. Lord Bathurst was charged by him to communicate the fact to Mr. Perceval; but, for some cause unexplained, the first intimation he received of the circumstance was in audience next day at Carlton House. He wrote at once:—

'It is with great regret that I have just received from Lord Bathurst the communication which you desired him to make to me; it would have taken me completely by surprise had it not been for what his Royal Highness the Prince Regent told me this morning, which prepared me to expect such a communication. I understand that your determination is too completely fixed to give me any hopes of a change in it, and, consequently, I have nothing to do except, in expressing my thanks for your desire to arrange the time, both for acting upon this determination and for making it known in the way least likely to embarrass His Royal Highness's Government, to express my deep regret that you should have found it necessary to adopt such a determination at all.

'Your disposition, which Bathurst also informed me of, to leave your son to act entirely as he may choose upon this occasion, I receive most gladly as a mark of kindness to myself, for which I am very grateful. I shall, therefore, unless I should hear from you to the contrary, feel myself at liberty in due time to endeavour to prevail upon Mr. Wellesley to continue to hold his present situation at the Treasury, in which I am persuaded he may at once be very usefully occupied in introducing himself into a general knowledge of the course of public business, and also be affording me the most useful assistance.'[1]

The rejoinder was as follows: 'I request you to accept my thanks for your letter, which has afforded me the satisfaction of knowing that you have received my communication, through our common friend Bathurst, in the spirit in which it was intended; and I assure you that my sentiments and my determination are entirely unconnected with any feelings of unkindness or disrespect.

'Your disposition towards Richard is justly entitled to my sincere acknowledgments; I have not had an opportunity of conversing with him since I received your letter; but I am satisfied that he will be inclined to act in whatever manner may be thought by you most convenient for the Government, and that he will be ready to resign both his seat at the Treasury and in Parliament whenever you may wish it.

'I intended to have mentioned my wishes to Lord Bathurst sooner, but by an accident was prevented from fixing an earlier hour for meeting him; this circumstance delayed the direct communication to you—my intention had been to state my feelings to the Prince Regent and to you as nearly as possible at the same time.'[2]

In a paper confidentially shown to his friends he stated

[1] From Downing Street, 17th January, 1812.
[2] Apsley House, 18th January, 1812.

his reason for resigning to be, that 'for a long time past his general opinions on various important questions had not sufficient weight to justify him towards the public, or towards his own character, in continuing in office; and because he had no hope of obtaining from the Cabinet, as then constituted, a greater portion of attention than he had already experienced. His objections arose in a great degree from the narrow and imperfect scale on which the efforts in the Peninsula were conducted: it was always stated to him that it was impracticable to enlarge that system. The Cabinet followed Mr. Perceval implicitly; while he thought it perfectly practicable, and that it was neither safe nor honest towards this country or the allies to continue the present contracted scheme. No hope existed of converting Mr. Perceval or any of his colleagues; no alternative therefore remained but to resign, or to submit to be the instrument of a system which he never advised, and which he never could approve. He had frequently with great reluctance yielded his opinions to the Cabinet on many other important points, and in doing so was convinced that he had submitted to opinions more incorrect than his own; and had sacrificed to temporary harmony more than he could justify in point of strict public duty. He was convinced by experience that the Cabinet neither possessed ability or knowledge to devise a good plan, nor temper and discernment to adopt what he thought necessary. To Mr. Perceval's judgment or attainments he could not pay any deference without injury to the public service. With these views and sentiments he had desired permission to withdraw from the Cabinet, not requiring any change in his own situation, and imploring no other favour than the facility of resignation.'

Doubts have been suggested as to the Catholic question having been a cause of his quitting office, because it is not one of the topics dwelt upon in his correspondence with

Perceval. To what purpose would it have been introduced? The Foreign Secretary had consented to join men pledged to exclusion, as Fox and Grey had done in 1806. George III. still reigned, and so far he had gone to the furthermost length of compromise compatible with conventional ideas of self-respect. Mr. Perceval could not expect to talk him out of the leading principles of his life, and he was too discreet and well-conditioned to try. On his part Wellesley could not suppose that one whose main reliance in the Cabinet was Eldon, and whose chief confidant in private was Sidmouth, was open to conversion to Liberal policy in Church and State. The regal necessity in 1809 for postponing the vital question of the day seemed to render its discussion in the Cabinet useless waste of time; the less said about it therefore the better. Both he and Canning relied, as well they might, on Carlton House being favourable to a policy of sectarian equality; but it is as certainly true that they did not wait for a signal there, or bate the breath of their advocacy when the neutral flag was unfurled.

There was a Cabinet on January 20, at which Wellesley stated his intention of declaring his views in debate on the impending motion by Lord Fitzwilliam in favour of Emancipation. Mr. Perceval said, good-humouredly, that Canning had, on the same point, differed with most of them, and yet they contrived to get on very well together. The difference need not, therefore, break up the Administration. When this was communicated to the Prince he summoned the Chancellor, Mr. Perceval, and Lord Liverpool, to confer upon the matter with the Foreign Secretary in his presence, and a long discussion, in which he sided with the latter, led to no actual decision. But at an audience soon after, the Premier was said to have yielded so far that his Royal Highness declared himself satisfied, but upon what conditions he did not think it necessary to divulge. Wellesley then informed him that as the Household question was settled, he felt that he could no longer serve under Mr. Perceval, but would regulate his retirement in accordance with the convenience of his Royal Highness. His son Richard would give up his seat and office whenever it was desirable, but he was at liberty to hold them, if he pleased. The Premier, with the usual courtesies of regret, acknowledged the perfect fairness which had marked the whole transaction, but he used no remonstrance or solicitation to remain. Castlereagh was forthwith recommended as his successor. The Prince demurred to anyone being named, saying that he regarded the resignation as prospective only, and not positive or complete. But Perceval refused to allow matters to remain in abeyance, and Mr. Peel was sent with the offer of the seals to Castlereagh, for whatever interval the existing Cabinet might remain in power. Instead of accepting, he said, haughtily, he would not be made a stop-gap for anyone, but that should the Regent subsequently call upon him to take office, as part of a permanent arrangement, he should be willing to serve. The inclusion of Lord Sidmouth and his friends was then proposed, which made the Prince very angry ; and words went so high that he at last, exclaimed, ' You cannot be ignorant of my sentiments towards that person, in whom I will never have confidence, or in anyone who forces him upon me.' No immediate change consequently took place in the Foreign Office ; the whole of the abortive negotiation with Castlereagh and Sidmouth being repeated by the Regent to the person whom it most concerned.[1]

He continued to discharge the duties of his department with unremitting care. American affairs, however, became a source of daily increasing anxiety, and the Premier urged, somewhat peevishly, that there should be no delay in sending instructions to our Minister at Washington.

[1] Mr. D. to Lord Buckingham, 1st February, 1812

'Understanding that the *Gleaner* is still waiting for your despatches to Foster, which I had hoped had been completely settled on last Wednesday se'nnight, I am sure you will not be surprised that, with the feeling I had that Foster's last despatches required the most immediate answer, I should express the most anxious wish that no further delay should prevent you sending them.'[1]

With equanimity unruffled he put aside the untimely suggestion of supervision.

'My despatches to Mr. Foster have been signed for some time past, but were detained by me from considerations which I will state to you hereafter. They are now sent away. The delay is not great, as the wind has been contrary.

'Last night I received despatches from Mr. Foster, which require most serious attention. I shall be able to send them to you this day, with my opinion upon them for circulation. In the meanwhile I wish to suggest that it would be proper *now* to grant the fullest information on the American question. I think you will be of my opinion as soon as you have read Mr. Foster's despatches. I am confined to-day by illness, and I shall not be able to attend the Cabinet.'[2]

Perceval had good reasons for believing that he should be retained in his position. In a letter to Wellington, assuring him of undiminished support notwithstanding his brother's secession, he stated unreservedly that 'the Regent had no intention of looking to any other person than himself to form his permanent Administration.'[3] The very day before this was written, Wellesley had a lengthened audience, in the course of which he said, 'The difference between Perceval and me is that he thinks the existing disabilities are beneficial to the State, and necessary to be maintained as so many safeguards to its well-being. On the contrary, I have always

[1] Perceval to Lord Wellesley, 28th January, 1812.
[2] Apsley House, 29th January, 1812.   [3] 22nd January, 1812.

considered these as evils in themselves, which, sooner or later, must endanger it if persisted in. He of course wishes their continuance; I think their abolition essential; but the mode of getting rid of a system which has obtained for such a length of time is, I confess, a difficulty of no common weight and magnitude.'[1] This was said to the Regent in a long audience, in the course of which his Royal Highness said more than once, ' Admirable! this will do, my dear lord; my own sentiments exactly.' And they parted well pleased with the assurance that in debate these sentiments would be avowed.

He kept his word; and on Lord Fitzwilliam's motion filled with signal courage and temper the difficult part he had assigned himself, of advocating on the broadest grounds Catholic enfranchisement, while keeping his word to the Regent and his late colleagues that he would never surrender to the threat of violence, or humiliate authority by yielding to sedition. This was his maxim and principle throughout. He loved religious freedom much,. but he loved public order more. He had a firm faith that equity would in the end prevail; but even equity demanded by the voice of tumult he would stoutly refuse. He saw too plainly the vacillation and worthlessness of him whose reign was about to begin, and whose first Minister he had for months been assured that he should be; and he knew that by the course he was pursuing he was satisfying neither of the two great parties in the State that contended for the mastery. He had broken with the Tories without being adopted by the Whigs; and at the moment in question it would have been hard to say whether he was viewed with more repugnance by Grenville or by Eldon. But this consideration gave him small concern. His solicitude for the cause of the Roman Catholics could not be surpassed. From the first dawn of his reason to the present hour, his anxiety for their effectual relief had been the

[1] Mr. D. to Lord Buckingham, 21st January, 1812.

warm sentiment of his heart; confirmed and animated by experience and reflection, and by the deliberate exercise of his judgment, not unaccustomed to the practical consideration of great affairs of State; he had been bred and educated in the principles of rational liberality, equally remote from intolerant bigotry and from licentious disregard of established order. He had always supported every former proposal for the relief of the Roman Catholics; but the heat of the contention had exaggerated and distorted the true character of this question on both sides. The claim had been urged in accents of violence and terror, spurning all accompanying conditions, all provident or amicable delay. The demand issued forth in the array of war, and no alternative appeared but submission or battle. On the other side every delay was a peremptory sentence of eternal exclusion, representing concession as perilous to the State and sacrilegious to the Church. All conditions were ridiculed as nugatory or impossible; while all the restraints of penal laws were said to be a positive good—a venerable and sacred institution, consecrated as an essential article of faith, not a safeguard to be respected and preserved, for the temporary security of the altar, but as the very ark of our religion. The path of discretion must be sought between these extremes. The Catholics had formerly been outlawed, not as erring sectaries, but as dangerous partisans of despotism which sought to subvert Constitutional rule. But when that danger had passed away, they had been gradually admitted to hold land, to exercise the franchise, to practise at the bar, to serve in the army. It ought to be the policy of every wise State to collect all descriptions of persons possessing political power within the general frame of the community; to mix and blend their individual pursuits with the common interests of the State, and to attach them by the powerful ties of honourable ambition and honest gain to the established order of rule. It was no longer a question whether political power should be given to the Catholics, but whether they should now be refused those appendages to their power which would identify its exercise with the interests of the State, and would constitute bonds and pledges of attachment to the Government and ties of union with the Commonwealth. The restraints which still existed, cemented and embodied discontent, without impairing the force or activity of political power. Remove these restraints, and you dissolve the ties of discontent, you disperse the sentiment of disaffection, and you inspire the powerful motives of individual interest in an Establishment which offered so many immediate advantages of emolument and honour.'

Lansdowne, though differing from his vote, praised in unmeasured terms the sentiments and principles enunciated; marvelling only how they could have failed to dissuade his colleagues in the Cabinet from the unyielding policy of intolerance they avowed.

His speech occupied an hour and a half in delivery, and the debate was prolonged throughout the night. At daybreak the numbers told were seventy-nine for going into committee on the state of Ireland, one hundred and sixty-two against it.

The first exercise of sovereign power advised by Perceval was the advance of Wellington to the dignity of an Earl, to be accompanied by a message from the Regent recommending the Commons to reward his services with a pension of 2,000*l.* a year, in recognition of the capture of Ciudad Rodrigo.

To a private note informing him of what was intended, the outgoing Minister replied: 'I assure you that I am very sensible of your kindness in communicating to me the advice which you have given to the Regent, and his Royal Highness's gracious reception of it, on the subject of Lord Wellington's deserved honours. Better advice was never given, and advice so good has seldom been so well received. I cannot (perhaps I ought not) attempt to conceal the personal interest which I take in these honours; but I know you will do me the justice to believe that my sense of their value rests entirely on the great public principle that my brother merits what you have most justly and honourably recommended; and that the Regent, in acceding to your advice, has discharged the highest duty which he owes to the military character of the country. I shall carefully observe your injunction of secrecy, and I will not mention the subject to any person whatever until I shall have received your permission.'[1]

It did not escape wistful notice at the time, or fade from bitter recollection afterwards, that his formal act of resignation took place on the very day when Parliament was engaged in according its meed of acknowledgment of gallant deeds. The General could not but lament the severance that had taken place, on public as on private grounds. He had no time to waste in the expression of vain regrets; but he made no secret of his vexation, at what he justly looked on as a great mistake.

To Henry Wellesley, Perceval wrote announcing his brother's resolution: 'I believe the ground to be that he did not think the Government, as at present arranged, what it ought to be, and that particularly he did not think his own situation, as it were under me as Prime Minister, was what it should be.

'I am certainly anxious to know what effect this determination of your brother's will have upon you. I hope, when I assure you that it is the full determination of the Government and of his Royal Highness to persevere in their exertions in the cause of Spain, and his concurrence in our anxious wish, that we may have the benefit of your services in forwarding that cause; that you will not feel any reason from this event for wishing to retire from the mission in which we have been all so well pleased and satisfied with your exertions. The seals

[1] Apsley House, 7th February, 1812. MS. in the Perceval Papers.

will, till a successor can be appointed, be placed in Lord Liverpool's hands.'[1]

A strange letter from the Secretary for War is of the same date:—

'I am not aware of the existence of any distinct difference of opinion in the Cabinet on any political question of importance which has led to your brother's determination. He says generally that he has not the weight in the Government which he expected when he accepted office. I have never seen any want of attention to his opinion, nor do I recollect a single question (except one of comparatively little moment, lately, respecting the King's and Regent's establishments) to which he entered a dissent. The Government through a Cabinet is necessarily a Government *inter pares*, in which every man must expect to have his opinion and his despatches canvassed; and this previous canvass of opinion and measures appears to be absolutely necessary under a Constitution where the public acts of Government will be ultimately hostilely debated in Parliament. I have always regretted that Lord Wellesley's habits of late have prevented his seeing as much of his colleagues and mixing as much in general business as is usual with persons in public office. I do not believe he has attended more than half the Cabinet meetings which have taken place since he has been in Government; and this circumstance, combined with others, unavoidably prevented him from having the same common feelings with his colleagues as exist among those who not only act but live together. Lord Wellesley declares it is not his intention to go into Opposition, and he does not even wish his son to resign his seat at the Treasury.

'The event is as yet a secret, but it must be known in a few days. If you wish to know my opinion as to the effect of it, I am persuaded it will not, under present circumstances,

[1] To Henry Wellesley, 19th February, 1812.

materially prejudice the Government. The Prince takes it very quietly, and appears now determined to support the present Government with all his influence. Indeed, he says he has no alternative: this may appear to you to be strange, after all that has passed; but so it is. It is Perceval's intention immediately to sound Castlereagh about his return to office.'[1]

Before he had given up the seals, Ministers in the Lower House were pressed to produce the correspondence with America regarding the blockade and right of search, and unwisely, as he thought, they hesitated to do so.

'I am very much concerned to find from your note that my opinion in favour of the production of a portion of the American papers to Parliament is not likely to meet with the concurrence of the Cabinet. Further consideration of the subject has certainly confirmed my judgment of the advantage which would be derived to our cause by producing at least such of the instructions as contain the explanation of the principles on which the Orders in Council were founded, and are still continued in force. It is extremely disagreeable to me, in the very peculiar situation in which I am now placed, to urge any difference of opinion against the sentiments of the Cabinet, and I therefore wish to leave the decision to them, without giving any further trouble than the statement of my sentiments as described in this note.

'It does not appear that any notice of a motion for any of these papers in the House of Lords has yet been announced. I certainly should feel great difficulty in refusing that part of the papers which relates to the general principle of the question at issue with America. But it seems probable that I may not be involved in this difficulty. The Duke of Infantado has not yet furnished me with the Spanish communications which he had promised.

[1] Liverpool to Lord Wellington, February 1812.

'I have not received the despatches from Mr. Foster which were sent in circulation until this moment. I shall not be able to prepare an answer to them to be submitted to a Cabinet at two to-morrow; but perhaps it might be proper to meet. I must attend the Prince Regent between twelve and one. You will of course use your discretion respecting the calling a Cabinet. Perhaps Monday, at two, might answer better. I confess that my opinion is entirely different from that which you state respecting the production of the American papers. I think we ought to lay *all* of them before Parliament. I most anxiously hope that you will not prevent me from the discharge of this duty, which, in my opinion, affords the best chance of avoiding a war with America. Our case is yet imperfectly known—I think it is solid and clear. I must therefore (excuse the phrase) most seriously remonstrate against the notion of withholding the documents in my office, which will (in my judgment) fully explain to the public the true nature of our dispute with America.'[1]

His expostulation had its effect, and the papers were eventually produced.

[1] Apsley House, 12th February, 1812.

CHAPTER XXI

THRESHOLD OF THE TREASURY.

1812.

THE Queen still reigned at Windsor, and the Princess of Wales kept open house at Blackheath; but the Court and Cabinet of the Prince was governed from Manchester Square. Years and fading looks had not yet diminished the ascendency of Lady Hertford,[1] who made her son Lord in Waiting, and her husband Lord Chamberlain.

Lord Yarmouth had been recalled from Paris for his incompetency by Grenville, whom he hated accordingly, but he never after filled any political post. He had been sent by the Regent to discuss the details of the new Civil List at Apsley House, where the personal demands of his Royal Highness were deemed unattainably large. Wellesley declared that, 'either from stupidity or want of common manners Yarmouth had not one solitary qualification for the office he was put upon.' In fact no Minister could comply with the Prince's extravagant claims. The Marquess told his brother-in-law, Culling Smith, to tell the Duke of York that if the Prince persisted in his demands in too high a tone he would talk to him in a way he had not yet experienced. On the other hand, Perceval was said

---

[1] Isabella, Marchioness of Hertford, daughter of Lord Irwin, married 1776, died 12th April 1836; Lord Yarmouth was born in 1777.

to have discussed the matter with too much warmth; but was criticised, and to some extent confuted, by the Foreign Secretary. Indiscreet friends might chuckle at the idea that he was taking part with the Prince against a parsimonious rival; but, in truth, he rather strove to compromise the affair in a reasonable way, and his interposition went for little with the Royal prodigal, who, finding he could not gain all he wished, suddenly changed his course, waived for the time certain points in dispute, and secretly began to listen to suggestions for retaining some of the Ministers. Adam and MacMahon said that at the last moment the Prince had given up three-fourths of the demands on his own account, and that all the rest would be carried through without difficulty. It was supposed that the part taken by Wellesley in the recent controversy had not been fully made known at Carlton House, and that in a fit of despair a surrender had been made at discretion.

The Restrictions expired in February 1812. On the 13th a letter to the Duke of York proposed to Grey a union of some of his friends with Ministers, suggesting thereby the omission of Grenville. Grey asked leave to confer with him. The step was regarded by Grenville as the same by which George III. tried to separate Shelburne and Rockingham, by sending for the former when the latter was the recognised head of Opposition. 'But the trick would entirely fail, he confidently believed. He had been betrayed once by the King, and he had no taste for affording to his son the same opportunity. As to coalescing with Perceval or Wellesley, he believed Grey quite as determined against it as himself. The whole would end in the continuance of Perceval, with Castlereagh and Sidmouth to help him. This was what Lord Yarmouth meant, whose intentions alone were of any consequence.'[1] We have thus

[1] To Lord Buckingham, from Camelford House, 13th February 1812.

confessed the foregone conclusion which stood in the way of all the proposals for Ministerial union made by Wellesley; a sunken rock, of which he was not, or would not, be aware, and over which the smooth waters of punctiliousness ebbed and flowed for weeks and months to come. Grey, after conference with Grenville, told the Duke that they felt themselves in honour bound to decline any combination which was not prepared to settle forthwith the Catholic question; in other words, they would enter an exclusively Whig Cabinet, or none.

On receipt of this reply the Prince repaired to Manchester Square for feminine counsel. During his absence Wellesley saw MacMahon at Carlton House, who told him that on that morning his master had said to Moira that, 'let Perceval and his myrmidons do what they would, no earthly consideration should induce him to part with Wellesley, whom he could not go on without.' But just as he was going to dinner he received a message to the effect that, in consequence of what had occurred, his Royal Highness had no choice but to retain the existing Ministry. The same evening Wellesley requested an audience to deliver up the seals, which he took with him for the purpose. In the ante-room he asked Colonel MacMahon if he had been aware when they met that afternoon of the contents of the Regent's note, or of his resolve to retain Perceval. With much embarrassment the private secretary assured him of his utter ignorance till then of the change of views. The Prince entreated him to suspend his resignation for a few days; the Chancellor would call upon him and explain that the arrangement was but temporary; and that, being his own master, he was quite untrammelled in the choice of a First Minister. Once more he was duped by his ambition into relying on the most unreliable of men.

He told Lord Eldon, when he called next day, that he

retained the seals upon the understanding that the first place at the Treasury was only held *ad interim*. The Chancellor said there must be some strange misapprehension, as his Royal Highness assured him distinctly that Perceval's reappointment was permanent. Under these circumstances there was nothing to discuss, and the Chancellor withdrew. On the 18th Tyrwhitt brought an offer from the Prince, in flattering terms, of the Lord-Lieutenancy of Ireland. 'What!' he exclaimed, 'with Perceval in the front? No no.' And on the following day he finally gave up the seals. The Prince as usual was full of emotion, and trusted their separation would not be for long. The retiring Minister adjured him 'not to make a Government upon the principle of religious exclusion.' He might still bring about a union of parties through Moira or Holland, if he would; but 'the wretched people who refused to listen to the claims and wishes of such a portion of his subjects as the Irish Catholics, ought as politicians to be driven into the ranks of private life.' Liverpool was in attendance, to take temporary charge of the Foreign Portfolio, which soon afterwards was confided to Castlereagh. Moira, tired of the trifling and tergiversation he had witnessed, had an audience to take leave, saying he could be no longer useful. He was offered the Garter, Ireland, India, anything he would name; but he declined with equal dignity and feeling. Lords Albemarle, Darlington, Scarborough, Guilford, Saye and Sele, were in turn offered places in the Household, and the Dukes of Norfolk and Bedford refused the Blue Riband. The House of Commons showed its ill-humour by refusing, on a division of 115 to 112, the salary of a sinecure office conferred on Colonel MacMahon.

Richard Wellesley continued to sit for East Grinstead, but he felt that his position daily became more embarrassing. While retaining his office he was honourably bound to give

Ministers the benefit of his vote. But the questions raised by Sir Thomas Turton's motion on the state of the nation caused him such distress of mind that, without consulting his father, he wrote to the Premier, putting an end to obligations hopelessly conflicting.

'I cannot reconcile it to my sense of propriety and of honour, in conformity with the sentiments of Lord Wellesley, which are known to me, and with my own feelings and opinions, to continue to hold the seat in Parliament of which you had the kindness to decline the surrender when I resigned my seat at the Treasury. I was anxious not to inform you of my intention before the decision of the question of last night, on which I had heard that all the strength of Opposition would be exerted against you, and I most sincerely hope that I have not chosen a moment at which you may feel any inconvenience in giving me the Chiltern Hundreds, for which I would request you to move as soon as it may suit with your arrangements. In making this request I am unwilling to omit the expression of the gratitude which I can in no circumstances cease to entertain for the many instances of personal and of political favour which you have conferred upon me.'[1]

The Minister advised him to consult his father before he insisted on vacating his seat. Having done so, he wrote again:—

'I have lost no time in learning the sentiments of Lord Wellesley, and in communicating them to you, in consequence of the desire you expressed to me last night that I should be present at the division of to-morrow. I find that, consistently with those sentiments as they have been detailed to me, I must request you to move for a new writ for East Grinstead to-morrow, or as soon as it may be convenient to

[1] 25th February, 1812.

you, as it would not be possible for me to vote with you on the question, and I should not have felt it proper to have absented myself without repeating to you, as soon as I had a distinct knowledge of my father's opinions and decision, my wish to have the Chiltern Hundreds.'[1]

The impending motion alluded to was avowedly meant to censure the policy of the Administration, on which it was expected a warm debate would arise, and a strict party vote be given. The Premier's reply was polite and kind.

'I received your letter late last night. Nothing remains for me to do but comply, though most reluctantly, with your request; and I have accordingly executed your appointment to the Chiltern Hundreds, which I will direct the proper officer to deliver to you, and I will take care that the new writ shall be moved for East Grinstead before the debate takes place this day, unless upon communication with Lord Whitworth I shall find it his lordship's desire that it might be delayed; in which event, I am sure you will feel it due to his lordship's kindness, and possibly to his interest, to suffer the motion to be delayed for a day or two.

'I cannot send this letter without taking the opportunity it affords me of repeating the very sincere regret that I feel at being compelled to be instrumental in removing you from Parliament. I am sure you will not do me the injustice to believe that the wish which I expressed that you might be contented to retain your seat at East Grinstead on whichever side of the House you might place yourself, proceeded from undervaluing the weight and effect of your exertions in Parliament, and I therefore repeat the assurance that that wish was most sincere, and that your feelings of delicacy and honour could not reconcile you to retain your seat only increases my regret at losing you. As I cannot refer our

[1] From Grosvenor Square, 26th February, 1812.

political separation to any cause which should deprive me of a share of your good opinion, which I may hitherto have hoped that I possessed, I shall indulge in the pleasing belief that you will permit me still to consider and subscribe myself, with every good wish for your prosperity, your very affectionate and faithful friend and servant.'[1]

As one reason for supporting the motion for a committee of the whole House, William Lamb dwelt upon the recent withdrawal of Lord Wellesley from the Government. 'No one would deny to him the reputation of an enlarged and statesmanlike capacity. He thought Ministers had lost much of their strength by his secession, and were besides rather weakened by the accession of Lord Castlereagh.' Tierney dwelt upon the same topic, and challenged the Chancellor of the Exchequer to state why, at the moment when support to our General in Spain was declared to be of paramount importance, his brother had quitted the Cabinet. No response was made by Perceval, and Canning feared that in losing the noble Marquess the Administration had lost the stimulus of those successes which had graced the last two years; he would still hope that some of his spirit might linger, and that such an impetus had already been given that more would be achieved in future. The general system of our foreign relations he highly approved, and should any other set of men be placed at the helm, who would think it expedient to abandon the war in the Peninsula, by which the country had been raised to its present glorious height of character, he would give them his determined opposition. It was proposed about the same time to bring Wellesley Pole into the Cabinet. The Prince refused, saying 'he would have had no objection had his brother been at the head of it, but he would not reward the one by abandoning the other.' The

[1] Downing Street, 27th February, 1812.

Courier of March 4 announced that Richard Wellesley had resigned his place at the Board of Treasury and vacated his seat in Parliament.

Although both Canning and Wellesley were thought to have lost influence, they continued to be regarded by men of judgment, like Lords Lansdowne and Temple, as indispensable elements in any party aspiring to power; and their own bearing in public and private gradually identified them more and more with the leaders of the Whigs.[1]

On March 12 a letter, dated from York, and bearing the signature of 'Vetus,' appeared in the *Times*, defending with signal ability Wellesley's conduct and character. The outlines of his policy at home and abroad were traced as if by his own hand; and the subtlest distinctions of sentiment and purpose were explained, as if he were thinking aloud, with a certain redundancy of phrase. The style was distinguished by polished sarcasm and keen invective, not unworthy of Junius; but the writer emphatically disclaimed even personal acquaintance with him whom he designated the first statesman of the age; and the editor subsequently declared that not a sentence of the series of which this was the beginning had been suggested or even been seen by him until it appeared in print. The contrary was indeed freely asserted, and peculiarities of manner and opinion were fastened on as proofs of imputed origin. They were in fact from the pen of Major Sterling, and attracted much attention, not only from their intrinsic merit, but from the unusual space afforded them from time to time in a journal winning its way rapidly to political and literary pre-eminence.

On March 19 Lord Boringdon sought to unite all shades of Opposition in the Upper House in support of an Address praying for the formation of a strong Government, founded on the principles of unsectarian enfranchisement. Wellesley

[1] Lord Temple to his father, 25th April, 1812.

voted for the motion, but did not speak, and it was defeated by a large majority. Popular irritation daily increased in Ireland as the abandonment by the Prince of all his promises and professions became generally understood. The bitterness of disappointment broke forth in fierce upbraidings; while in England the acuteness of distress found utterance in prolonged complaint.

On April 21 Lord Donoughmore moved in the Peers for a committee on the penal laws remaining unrepealed. He denounced with unreserved warmth the abandonment of former principles and promises by the Regent under the spell of some evil genius who might add to the allurements of Calypso's court the charms of that matured enchantress. In support of the motion Wellesley spoke at length : ' In answer to those who would keep up civil exclusion for the sake of maintaining the Anglican Establishment, he presented a picture of the weakness of the Church as it then existed, which certainly a wise Government would not have failed to take into consideration. I do not wish to speak with disrespect of the Protestant Establishment, whose security is too readily believed in this country, nor to cast any reflection upon those who preside over that Establishment; yet I know that the true state of the Church of Ireland, in a very great degree, consists of bishops without clergy, churches without ministers, and ministers without churches; parishes of considerable extent without clergymen, church, or glebe; many parishes frequently consolidated into one, with a common church too remote for the parishioners to resort to. Can an Institution so circumstanced possess internal strength for its own defence against the mass of opposition excited against it? And is not that strength less likely to be increased by arming itself with violence against the mass of discontent set in array by the intolerance of the laws enacted for its support?'

Earlier in the debate Byron's youthful voice was heard

pleading, in treble but articulate tones, the cause of justice. On May 11, as Mr. Perceval was entering the House of Commons he was shot through the chest by Bellingham, and in a few moments expired. While Court and Parliament were filled with horror at the dreadful deed, the mob evinced unmistakable signs of satisfaction. At Nottingham, when the news arrived, destitute crowds paraded the streets with flags and drums, and in other towns there were manifestations of a similar spirit. In the Cabinet no one but the Chancellor for some days avowed the belief that they might still hold together. The Regent bade him ask his colleagues individually if they thought they could go on under one of their number whom he might name, and the curious record is preserved of their doubtings and their fears. Castlereagh alone was looked upon as capable of leading the Commons, and Liverpool the Lords; but which should be Premier was the question. The funds rose two per cent., on the general supposition that a Government was about to be formed on a more comprehensive basis. The Prince railed constantly at 'Grey and his other early friends, who he said had behaved to him like scoundrels;' of Grenville he had nothing to complain, though he did not like him; but he wished Canning and Wellesley should be asked to join. Liverpool was authorised accordingly to invite them. In an interview at Gloucester Lodge [1] he explained that the general policy of administration was to be unchanged; that he himself was to have the Treasury, and Castlereagh was to lead the Commons. In a subsequent visit to Apsley House he intimated that he had seen Mr. Canning, who deferred giving a reply till he had consulted his friends. 'Then am I,' said the Marquess, ' to be considered one of his suite?' The *gaucherie* was readily excused; but the whole tenor of the communication palpably bespoke foregone conclusions. Liverpool could as

---

[1] Sunday, 17th May, 1812.

little expect that Wellesley would act under him as a 'No Popery' chief, as that the greatest orator in the Commons would play second to the least expert or effective of debaters. He and Eldon saw power within their grasp, and intrepidly strove for its attainment by the reconstitution of a Cabinet as nearly as possible identified with the principles of sectarian ascendency. With their former colleagues in prominent office this would have been impossible, and upon such a basis neither of them would come in. Wellesley gave his answer in writing the following day. Over-rigged as usual with flapping sail of compliment, it was laden as usual with well-chosen articles of wisdom and of weight.

'If the highest offices in the State are to be filled by persons who still conceive themselves to be bound by duty, honour, and conscience not only to resist any mitigation of the present condition of the Roman Catholics, but even to prevent the consideration of the laws affecting them, I cannot concur in the principle on which the Administration is to conduct this important branch of public affairs. The declaration of Lord Liverpool precludes the hope of any such change in the policy of the Administration as could satisfy my judgment. Without any other obstacle, this alone compels me to decline the proposition made to me. The Cabinet might, in my opinion, be formed on an intermediary principle, equally exempt from the dangers of instant unqualified concession, and from those of inconsiderate peremptory exclusion; the entire resources of the empire might be applied to the great objects of the war with general consent, upon a full understanding of the real exigency of the present crisis; and concord and union at home might secure ultimate and permanent success abroad.'

The Prince shrank from being identified with a system of rule utterly at variance with all the professions of his past life, nd Liverpool indited accordingly a rejoinder attenuating in phraseology the intolerant rigour of his previous declarations. But he made no offer of re-opening the door, and merely flung certain pleasing platitudes out of the window. The letters, by agreement, appeared in the *Times* and *Chronicle* of May 20; but a note was appended, that further correspondence would appear. 'That is impossible,' exclaimed the new Premier, 'as there is no other letter.' There was, however, one, of rare ability and eloquence, which he received at a late hour in the evening, and which the public read next day. It vindicated completely the consistency of Wellesley and the construction he had placed on the designs and declarations of his rival for power. Liverpool was so angry at its publication without his consent, at a juncture so critical, that he led most of his colleagues to regard it as a final breach; and speaking of Wellesley's use of his admissions, said, 'It was not safe to be in the same room with him.'[1]

On any other day the letter, which is a masterpiece of courtly sarcasm and pitiless logic, terse, bland, searching, and severe, would have riveted general attention. But every eye was fixed on the morning of May 22 on the announcement in another column that the House of Commons had, upon the previous night, voted want of confidence in the old Ministry by a majority of four. Mr. Stuart Wortley, a firm friend of Pitt, and staunch supporter of Perceval, had, with the approval of many like himself, moved an address to the Regent, imploring him, in the perilous condition of the country, to take immediate steps for the formation of a strong and efficient Government. And it was presented at the levée the same afternoon by him and Lord Milton.

Wortley's success was wholly unexpected, and crazed the Opposition with delight. He had been a faithful supporter

[1] Grey Bennet, who had the story from Lord Holland, MS. journal.

of Ministers through many difficulties; they were scared by his uplifted hand against them, and prostrated by the blow.

So hopeless did it seem to carry on the Government, and so dangerous the attempt, that most of the Cabinet were ready to resign. Eldon, Liverpool, and Westmoreland thought they might still go on, if they were suffered to do so; the majority, however, felt bound to advise the Regent to reply that the desire of the Commons should be taken into immediate consideration. Apsley House might well believe the hour at length was come, when its master was, by force of circumstances no one had foreseen,—*l'homme inévitable*.

In an audience on May 22 he was directed to inquire from the heads of the two great parties in Parliament whether any obstacles existed to such a fusion as would meet the wishes of the House of Commons. He asked permission to communicate simultaneously with the leaders on both sides the principles on which alone he could undertake the duty, and frankly to invite their co-operation. These were, the relief of Catholics from civil disability, and a more vigorous prosecution of the Spanish war. The distribution of offices was left entirely open. At his request, Canning called on Lord Liverpool to inquire if he or any of his colleagues were disposed to take part in a new combination from which there should be no exclusion on account of past differences, and which Grey and Grenville would be invited to join. A reply stated curtly that all the members of the late Cabinet felt bound, particularly after what had recently passed, to decline the proposal of becoming members of an Administration to be founded by Lord Wellesley.[1] Bathurst did not believe the Opposition would imitate their example, for they were sick of being out of office, and would take Wellesley at his word.[2] Canning expostulated in vain at the narrow and

[1] Liverpool to Canning Fife House, 23rd May, 1812.
[2] To Rose, 24th May.

invidious character of the reply, which Lady Bathurst owned was an angry and intemperate movement all of them regretted when it had been sent.

Meanwhile Wellesley addressed himself directly to Lord Grey, at whose house Grenville came to meet him. The Prince had warned him in the outset against resorting to the chiefs of Opposition. 'He could forgive Grenville, but he would rather abdicate the Regency than see Lord Grey or Tierney in his service. He would have nothing to do with him if he embarked with them.' Wellesley observed he was sorry for it, as he 'thought the Prince's honour and the country's interest required it.'[1] He knew how valueless were vows of aversion or attachment, and forthwith tendered office to the Whig chiefs. He told them that he 'considered himself merely as the instrument of executing his Royal Highness's commands, to lay before him the plan of a new Administration that he neither claimed or desired for himself any Cabinet station. His pride would have exulted in the historic fact that he had been Premier of England; but love of ease, love of pleasure, love of magnificence his means could ill afford, made him at heart desire the Lieutenantcy of Ireland: and for this he would have been willing to stand out of Grenville's way.[2] On the 24th they answered that 'they had derived very high gratification from his Lordship's powerful exertions in support of the claims of the Roman Catholics, as well as from the manner in which that subject was adverted to in his minute; and they did not hesitate to assure him that they would warmly support any proposals made by any Ministers for the immediate consideration of those claims, without which they had no hope of rendering their services useful. But they were of opinion that the direction of the

---

[1] T. Grenville to his brother, 28th May.
[2] Temple to his father, 12th November.

military operations in an extensive war, and the more or less vigorous prosecution of those operations, were questions not of principle but of policy, to be regulated by circumstances, in their nature temporary and fluctuating, and in many cases known only to persons in official stations; and they could not conceal that in the existing state of the finances they entertained the strongest doubts of the practicability of an increase in any branch of the public expenditure.' They presented their reply in person, and were in conversation told the result of Canning's fruitless attempt to negotiate with members of the old Cabinet. Lansdowne, Holland, and Moira signified their cordial good wishes and general concurrence in the note of Grenville and Grey; but none of them considered that any definite offer had been made to them by the authority of the Prince; and the day wore on in apparent indecision. In the evening Wellesley had an audience to present the written answers he had received. His Royal Highness thought he would dine and sleep before making up his mind, and said the Marquess should hear from him. The political world spent Monday likewise in going to and fro and wondering how it would end.

Grenville from the first disbelieved in the sincerity of the Regent's profession of willingness to take a united Administration; for he was at heart as adverse to Wellesley as to himself and Grey, and meant only to make a case against them which might enable him to go to the House of Commons and say, 'You see I cannot make persons unite who refuse to do so: I must take one or other of the parties, and of the two I prefer the present to their opponents.'[1] He was in such a state of irritation at this time that he could not be spoken to; and Liverpool, in the greatest consternation, sent an express for the Duke of York at Oatlands,[2]—his in-

---

[1] To Lord Buckingham, 24th May.   [2] Grey to Grenville, 26th May.

fluence being alone capable of moderating such irascibility. Sheridan and Canning were frequently at Apsley House, and both were regarded as judicious friends. On the 26th, Brougham, who had taken in hand the troublesome and threatening controversy about Orders in Council, asked if it were possible that the fallen Cabinet was to be set up again. Grenville's confidential letters to his brother describe the pitiable inconsistency and irresolution of the Regent, who sometimes affected to treat Wellesley's commission as at an end, and sometimes as only suspended. 'Never was such a state of things seen. The money in the Treasury cannot be made to hold out beyond this day se'nnight. The violence and contempt expressed for the Prince are beyond all imagination, and are truly shocking to hear.' The air was loud with questionings as to what was to be done; but day after day passed and the whispering galleries of Carlton House gave forth no intelligible sound. By Saturday the City was out of patience and Parliament out of temper at the unexplained prolongation of suspense; and before the Commons rose Mr. Martin gave notice of an Address, calling for a redemption of the pledge already given, that a Government would be forthwith formed, able and strong enough to conduct the affairs of the country. It was not, however, till June 1 that the bitter pill was swallowed, and full powers given to form an Administration. Canning announced the circumstance in Parliament with the air of one who believed he had overcome all hindrances and outrun all rivals for the long-coveted leadership of the Commons. Wellesley was named First Lord of the Treasury; Erskine, Privy Seal; Canning and Moira to have leading offices; the Opposition chiefs were to name four, if the Cabinet consisted of twelve, and five if it contained thirteen members. A Whig preponderance was thus suggested, not only in principles of legislation but in those involved in the distribution of patronage, as afterwards explained by Moira, with the approval of the Duke of Bedford.[1] The reply approved by forty peers, assembled on the 3rd at Camelford House, and by seventy Commoners, consulted the same day by Mr. Ponsonby, declined the proposal. 'It is to the principles of disunion and jealousy that we object; to the supposed balance of contending interests in a Cabinet so measured out by preliminary stipulation. It tends, as we think, to establish within the Cabinet itself a system of counteraction inconsistent with the prosecution of any uniform and beneficial course of policy. We must, therefore, request permission to decline all participation in a Government constituted on such principles.'

Had authority been given to explain what was meant when suffering the proposition to be encumbered by unusual conditions, and had it been possible to place reliance on the sincerity or steadfastness of the Prince, the attempt would not even then have been abandoned. But his Royal Highness was only too eager to seize the opportunity to exonerate himself from his oft-repeated promises to Wellesley; and, pointing in a rage to the palpable distrust betrayed in every line of the reply, he peremptorily declared the commission of the Marquess at an end, and said the task of forming a Government must be committed to other hands. Moira was, in fact, chosen for his next dupe: a man who, with many estimable and chivalrous qualities, had no intellectual power or practical experience fitting him to be Prime Minister in the easiest times: and the times were exceptionally difficult. Yet for some days he was ostensibly employed, with Sheridan's and Erskine's help, to try what could be done. Private letters testified the uneasiness felt lest he should be empowered to make such offers as patriotic men could not well refuse, and which, notwithstanding, they felt it unsafe

---

[1] Minute of conversation between Wellesley and Grey at Portman Square, 1st June.

to accept. But on his declaring that no right would be conceded to change the great officers of the Household, Grey and Grenville intimated haughtily that they would entertain the matter no further. As a last resource he was given leave to try whether it might not be possible to get together a sufficient number of men, comparatively independent of party ties, who might command public confidence and fill the great offices of State. One or two territorial magnates were supposed to be willing to join, and Canning, Erskine, and Sheridan were counted on; but when Wellesley was asked to embark in the 'phantom ship' his personal goodwill to Moira hardly kept his indignation within bounds.

More than one sharp altercation arose in Parliament regarding what had taken place. In the House of Lords, on June 3, Wellesley stated that, in obedience to the commands of the Regent, he had with due deference, but with the freedom which the duty of a Privy Councillor owes to the sovereign and the country, stated his opinion with a view to the forming of an Administration. He had that day tendered his resignation of the authority vested in him. He deeply lamented that the most dreadful personal animosities, that the most terrible difficulties arising out of complicated questions, should have interposed obstacles to prevent that arrangement which it was so highly desirable and so essential to the interests and welfare of the country should be made. That such personal feelings and obstacles should have stood in the way of fusion at so arduous and perilous a crisis was indeed deeply to be deplored. He had solicited and obtained permission to tell the House, if they desired it, all the circumstances attending the progress of the transaction in which he had any share. But, if permitted, he would advise the Peers not to call for such disclosure, being convinced that in the present situation of affairs it would be highly mischievous to the public interests. Still if commanded he was ready to make it. Lord Grenville concurred in the advice, but disclaimed for himself and his friends any share in the animosities adverted to. The Secretary for War made a similar disclaimer, and concurred in deprecating a disclosure of circumstances which would be neither proper or decent. Moira said it had been his lot to be the humble instrument of conciliation, and it had been his endeavour to smooth the difficulties which unhappily existed. He deeply lamented that differences and estrangements had rendered his endeavours unavailing, and that points of form should stand in the way of conciliation, and of an arrangement essential to the welfare of the country. Grey thought that Moira's zeal for the service of the Prince and the public had led him to overstep the line of forbearance others had observed. He and Grenville had not been actuated by any consideration of points of form, but by essential principles of government. In whatever share he had had in these transactions, the noble Marquess would, he trusted, admit that he had not been influenced in any respect by personal animosities. (Lord Wellesley bowed assent, and called, 'Hear! hear!') No further observation was made and the House adjourned.

On Friday, June 5, Moira recurred to the phrase 'dreadful personal animosities,' which Wellesley had used on the former occasion. It had been construed as applying to the highest quarter, and as such, was calculated to have the worst effect on the public mind. From long personal experience he could unequivocally contradict any such insinuation, as he was sure the noble Marquess would do if he were present. He had to state positively that, in the commission to form a Government, Wellesley was entirely unshackled: no individual being named by the Prince, or any seat reserved. Grenville and Grey confuted this assertion by quoting the terms of the proposition in writing made to them on June 1, in which four of the intended Cabinet were expressly named.

Moira declared that, in his judgment, it was impossible that any man placed in a situation of such difficulty could have conducted himself with more high honour or more delicate uprightness; but there had been some misapprehension, which when removed, negotiations would, he trusted, be resumed successfully.

On the following Monday, Liverpool having announced his appointment as First Lord of the Treasury, Wellesley said he had authority to explain every part of the course he had pursued. He wished that three great principles should form the basis of the Administration: a conciliatory adjustment of Catholic claims; a vigorous support of the war in Spain; and that office should combine men of various politics. He had used the phrase 'dreadful personal animosities' advisedly, and meant it to apply to the noble Earl now placed at the head of affairs and his colleagues; for it was from their conduct that obstacles arose to the arrangement he had hoped to make. He did not charge their animosity to himself as a crime; he merely stated the fact.

Lord Harrowby asked was it fitting such a charge should be insinuated without the production of proof. If the noble Marquess was prepared to state there what he had said elsewhere of Ministers, let him not postpone the discussion till a future day, but take the earliest opportunity of explaining fully all he meant by the charge.

Wellesley had no motive for deferring the explanation challenged, and his reply was among the most effective of his utterances in Parliament.

'One would really think from the lofty tone and manner of the noble Earl—a tone and manner to which I can bend only in common politeness, but to which I by no means submit—that I could not bring proofs of what I have asserted, or that I would insinuate a charge without having ground on which to support it. My noble friend Lord Grenville had said that the words had dropped from me incidentally; but he was too accurate to have said that I had spoken inadvertently or unadvisedly. I forbore to enter into details on a former occasion lest I should excite irritation; and that I had rightly judged upon that point, the speech of the noble Earl clearly proves. But if the noble lords disclaim any personal animosity, I am bound, in a Parliamentary sense, to suppose that I was mistaken.'

After reading the propositions for a united Cabinet laid before the leading members of parties hitherto opposed, and the replies respectively made by them, he proceeded: 'The House must judge whether I was not justified in believing that the refusal on the one side to enter into such a combination was founded on personal animosities. Allusion has been made to a statement of my reasons for resigning as Secretary of State, which appeared in print after the death of Mr. Perceval. Does the noble lord mean to insinuate that I was a party to the publication of the statement to which he alludes? and yet, if he does not mean that, how does he make out that its publication rendered it impossible for him and his colleagues to unite with me in Administration? He ought not to have presumed to state—I use the word in its strongest sense—that the publication was by my authority. I expressly deny it. The facts are simply these. When I resigned my office, his Royal Highness, with a benignity peculiar to him, requested me to retain it until the expiration of the restrictions upon the Regency. I obeyed his commands, but finding that, previous to the expiration of the restrictions, Mr. Perceval had recommended two or three times my immediate supersession, I did, in conversation with the Lord Chancellor, say that it was unmannerly to have done so. There were many other reasons for my wishing to resign. The vilest calumnies were circulated on the subject. I was charged with extravagant ambition, and with bargaining for power. This was all calumny. I simply asked leave to resign. There are many expressions in the statement manifestly not mine. Some of my friends who were anxious about the cause of my retirement took down in writing expressions dropped in private conversation, some of which I would now recall, but which I would not substantially retract. A publication was uniformly refused. I was horror-struck at seeing it published at the time; and I would have given any sum to have it recalled. The paper was not mine. It may be a trifling thing to talk of language, but it was not couched in language which I should have used in a document intended for the public eye at a moment when the country had lost a man of the most irreproachable character, of the most perfect integrity, and full of every private virtue. But all this does not make it necessary that I should acknowledge him to be possessed of that power and frame of mind which marks out a man for the conduct of great public concerns. It can be no insult to any man to say that he is not qualified for the highest office in the State. I highly respect and esteem my noble friend opposite—for so I must still call him—but it does not follow from that that I am bound to consider him as a fit man to be placed at the head of the Government. In the Cabinet I endeavoured to act as far as I could with cordiality; but I did imagine until now that I had shown sufficient ill-humour to convince my coadjutors of the different opinions which I entertained. I may perhaps be thought blamable in allowing the publication of the correspondence regarding the late Ministerial negotiation. If I have erred, I have erred from habit, for it is a very ordinary practice with me to satisfy the public by authentic information upon subjects they regard with painful anxiety. But I am not aware that in the letters on either side there was one word that ought to be withheld.'

The summary supersession of Wellesley, without affording

him an opportunity to explain away the difficulties of the tri-partite scheme of a Cabinet to the Opposition lords, and the peremptory transfer of his commission to Moira, told the political world plainly that the supposed preference of the Regent for him as First Minister need be thought of no more. His rivals exulted at the dissipation of what they had always believed to be a myth woven out of idle compliment and hollow flatteries, as they said, by his overweening egotism ; while friends, like Canning and Moira, Sheridan and Holland, reluctantly came to the conclusion that it was only another instance of the utter faithlessness of the Prince, who had either egregiously deceived him throughout, or had recklessly flung overboard at the bidding of a mistress one of the ablest and most devoted servants of the Crown. He could not, indeed, realise suddenly the fact in the light in which others regarded it. Premier for a day he had failed, as he was obliged to own, in inducing either Whigs or Tories to accept him for chief; and the chance was not given him of attempting to form a combination out of the men who hung loosely by party obligation ; yet he clung to the belief, shared by most of the eminent politicians of the period, that the Perceval Cabinet patched up, as the phrase went, under Lord Liverpool could not stand.

The exigency of national affairs became daily more critical. Castlereagh was still untried in the Foreign Department ; the outcry against the Orders in Council was at its height, the tables of both Houses were laden with petitions for their revocation, and the Commons were occupied day after day in hearing evidence against their disastrous effect from merchants and manufacturers examined at the bar. It was no secret that Wellesley's last effort before quitting Downing Street was towards conciliation with America ; and his successor, on April 23, had advised a proclamation withdrawing the blockade conditionally upon a corresponding annulment by Congress of all interdictory acts of retaliation; but the offer was not made in time. Party feeling in the States ran too high to be restrained by pacific counsels, and on June 18 the House of Representatives, in secret session, by a majority of seventy-nine against forty-nine, passed a resolution declaring the two countries to be at war. The actual rupture was unknown in England until some weeks later, and the rest of the session was signalised by debates in every way calculated to confirm a belief in the instability of the Cabinet reconstituted upon the principle of sectarian ascendency. Canning, on June 22, moved a resolution pledging the House to take the subject of Catholic Disabilities into consideration early in the following session, and notwithstanding Castlereagh's propitiatory assurance that he was ready to fulfil the expectations raised at the Union, a majority of 235 against 106 agreed to the motion. More signal still seemed to be the proffers of opinion made in the Peers. On July 1 Wellesley proposed the same pledge in identical terms. His speech was the best he ever made, comprehensive, eloquent, touching the very quick of popular disappointment, and free from all taint of personal chagrin. The Dukes of Kent and Sussex and most of the great territorial nobles, English as well as Irish, gave him their support. Ministers ventured only to move the previous question, and were able to muster but 126 votes to 125, escaping thus by a bare majority of one. Court and Cabinet were humbled in the dust, and their friends might well tell him and Canning that they would not have to wait for long. Conflicting rumours were in circulation regarding the British advance into Spain. Wellington was known to have crossed the Portuguese frontier on June 13, and Marmont, it was said, had fallen back in order to protect Madrid. He was known to have a numerous and well-appointed *corps d'armée* under his command, and the recollection of what had happened three years before damped the courage of

Ministerial augury and dipped in gall the pen of Whig criticism. Wellesley refused to entertain any misgivings; he could not bring himself to believe in the failure of the great policy for which he had so long contended, and for the sake of which he had risked and lost the highest prize of personal ambition. To all who asked his opinion he answered feverishly but firmly, 'Arthur will not fail.' Still he was anxious; and after Court and Fashion had gone on their autumn rambles he lingered near town eager to catch the first whisper of the triumph he had toiled for and foretold, and which he felt was near. At length the tidings came, greater even than he had mutely ventured to imagine. Assaye, Talavera, and Ciudad Rodrigo were eclipsed by the glory of Salamanca, not merely for the trophies won in fight, but because it opened to the victors the gates of the Capital. The importance of the event at the moment Napoleon was about to open his long-meditated campaign against Russia, could hardly be exaggerated; and for Wellesley the sense of pride, satisfaction, and delight was ineffable. For days he was overwhelmed with inquiries and congratulations. He could afford to forgive all his enemies and forget all his disappointments now. Liverpool wrote to acquaint him that an early *Gazette* would notify his brother's advancement to a Marquisate, a fact which he at once communicated to Lady Mornington, then in her seventieth year. London vied with Madrid in ebullitions of popular joy: for three nights the town was illuminated. Curious to observe the characteristics of the scene, upon the second night Wellesley, accompanied by his son and his private secretary, drove in an open carriage to Whitehall, where he was recognised and cheered vociferously. In the excitement of the moment he addressed a few words of cordial thanks to the crowd. The horses were taken, in spite of his remonstrances, from the carriage, and he was drawn in vicarious triumph to St. Paul's, on to the Mansion House, and then back to his own residence in Piccadilly: the populace insisting more than once on his addressing them.

As he watched the glare over the wearied town die out the fear stole over him that the part of pre-eminence in great affairs he had aspired to play had come to an end. The younger brother to whose advancement he had so much contributed already outstripped him in the race of fame, and would to-morrow take precedence of him in rank as a Peer. The greatness of the man would fain have waived back the approach of jealousy, but the weakness of the man rendered him unable at times to still its whisperings. He wrote felicitating the victor affectionately and in his grandest manner: and on learning how ill supplied was the commissariat and military chest, watched anxiously for news of further movements in Castile.

Having given to his country an empire in the East, he would fain have perfected at home the design of Union left incomplete by Pitt. But his counsel was discarded. Thenceforth his place in politics became of less and less importance, and several years rolled by ere he was called upon again to fill any responsible situation.

END OF THE FIRST VOLUME.

LONDON: PRINTED BY
SPOTTISWOODE AND CO., NEW-STREET SQUARE
AND PARLIAMENT STREET

October, 1879.

CHATTO & WINDUS'S
LIST OF BOOKS.

Imperial 8vo, with 147 fine Engravings, half-morocco, 36s.
THE EARLY TEUTONIC, ITALIAN,
AND FRENCH MASTERS.
Translated and Edited from the Dohme Series by A. H. KEANE, M.A.I. With numerous Illustrations. [*Just ready.*

Crown 8vo, 1,200 pages, cloth extra, 12s. 6d.
THE READER'S HANDBOOK
OF ALLUSIONS, REFERENCES, PLOTS, AND STORIES.
By the Rev. E. COBHAM BREWER, LL.D. [*In the press.*

ABSTRACT OF CONTENTS.—*Authors and Dates of Dramas, Operas, and Oratorios—Curiosities connected with Dates, Dynasties, Names, and Letters—Dates of Poems, Novels, Tales—Dying Words of Historic Characters—Errors of References and Illustrations—Anachronisms—Historical, Legendary, Dramatic, and other Parallels—Lists of Bogie Names, of noted Diamonds and Nuggets, Dwarfs and Giants, Fools and Jesters, Favourites of Great Men, Improvisators, Kings with Character Names, Knights, Literary Impostors, of Lives exceeding 100 years, of Medical Quacks, of the Oaths of Great Men, Relics, Revolutionary Songs, Ring Posies, the Sagas, &c.—Names and Characters of Dramas, Novels, Tales, Romances, Epic Poems, &c.—Characteristics of Noted Artists—Plots of Plays, the Stories of Epic Poems, Ballads, and other Tales—Pseudonyms, Eponyms, Nicknames, titular Surnames, names of Similitude—Saints who are Patrons of Diseases, Places, and Trades—Sovereigns of England: their titles and superscriptions, the Days of their Death—Stimulants used by Public Actors and Orators—Striking lines of noted Authors, and Sayings of Great Men—Superstitions and Traditions about Animals; &c. &c.*

Crown 8vo, Coloured Frontispiece and Illustrations, cloth gilt, 7s. 6d.
Advertising, A History of.
From the Earliest Times. Illustrated by Anecdotes, Curious Specimens, and Notes of Successful Advertisers. By HENRY SAMPSON.

"*We have here a book to be thankful for. We recommend the present volume, which takes us through antiquity, the middle ages, and the present time, illustrating all in turn by advertisements—serious, comic, roguish, or downright rascally. The volume is full of entertainment from the first page to the last.*"—ATHENÆUM.

Crown 8vo, cloth extra, with 639 Illustrations, 7s. 6d.
Architectural Styles, A Handbook of.
Translated from the German of A. ROSENGARTEN by W. COLLETT-SANDARS. With 639 Illustrations.

Crown 8vo, with Portrait and Facsimile, cloth extra, 7s. 6d.
Artemus Ward's Works:
The Works of CHARLES FARRER BROWNE, better known as ARTEMUS WARD. With Portrait, Facsimile of Handwriting, &c.

AFGHANISTAN AND THE RUSSIAN ADVANCE ON MERV.
Second Edition, demy 8vo, cloth extra, with Map and Illustrations, 18s.
Baker's Clouds in the East:
Travels and Adventures on the Perso-Turcoman Frontier. By VALENTINE BAKER. Second Edition, revised and corrected.

Crown 8vo, cloth extra, 6s.
Balzac.—The Comédie Humaine and its
Author. With Translations from Balzac. By H. H. WALKER.
"*Deserves the highest praise. The best compliment we can pay him is to hope that we may soon see his translation of the 'Comédie Humaine' followed by another work. Good taste, good style, and conscientious work.*"—EXAMINER.

Crown 8vo, cloth extra, 7s. 6d.
Bankers, A Handbook of London;
With some Account of their Predecessors, the Early Goldsmiths: together with Lists of Bankers from 1677 to 1876. By F. G. HILTON PRICE.

Crown 8vo, cloth extra, 7s. 6d.
Bardsley's Our English Surnames:
Their Sources and Significations. By CHARLES WAREING BARDSLEY, M.A. Second Edition, revised throughout, and considerably enlarged.
"*Mr. Bardsley has faithfully consulted the original mediæval documents and works from which the origin and development of surnames can alone be satisfactorily traced. He has furnished a valuable contribution to the literature of surnames, and we hope to hear more of him in this field.*"—TIMES.

Small 4to, green and gold, 6s. 6d.; gilt edges, 7s. 6d.
Bechstein's As Pretty as Seven,
And other German Stories. Collected by LUDWIG BECHSTEIN. Additional Tales by Brothers GRIMM, and 100 Illustrations by RICHTER.

Demy 8vo, cloth extra, with Map and Illustrations, 12s.
Beerbohm's Wanderings in Patagonia;
Or, Life among the Ostrich-Hunters. By JULIUS BEERBOHM.
"*Full of well-told and exciting incident. . . . . A ride, which at all times would have had a wild and savage attraction, was destined by the merest chance to prove unexpectedly perilous and adventurous. . . . These stirring scenes, throughout which Mr. Beerbohm shows no slight degree of bravery and coolness, are described in a manner which is both spirited and modest. . . . A thoroughly readable story, which well fills up a not unmanageable volume.*"—GRAPHIC.

Imperial 4to, cloth extra, gilt and gilt edges, 21s. per volume.

Beautiful Pictures by British Artists:

A Gathering of Favourites from our Picture Galleries. In Two Series.

The FIRST SERIES including Examples by WILKIE, CONSTABLE, TURNER, MULREADY, LANDSEER, MACLISE, E. M. WARD, FRITH, Sir JOHN GILBERT, LESLIE, ANSDELL, MARCUS STONE, Sir NOEL PATON, FAED, EYRE CROWE, GAVIN O'NEIL, and MADOX BROWN.

The SECOND SERIES containing Pictures by ARMITAGE, FAED, GOODALL, HEMSLEY, HORSLEY, MARKS, NICHOLLS, Sir NOEL PATON, PICKERSGILL, G. SMITH, MARCUS STONE, SOLOMON, STRAIGHT, E. M. WARD, and WARREN.

All engraved on Steel in the highest style of Art. Edited, with Notices of the Artists, by SYDNEY ARMYTAGE, M.A.

"*This book is well got up, and good engravings by Jeens, Lumb Stocks, and others, bring back to us Royal Academy Exhibitions of past years.*"—TIMES.

One Shilling Monthly, Illustrated by ARTHUR HOPKINS.

Belgravia

For January, 1879, will contain the First Chapters of Two New Novels (each to be continued throughout the year):—I. THE CONFIDENTIAL AGENT. By JAMES PAYN, Author of "By Proxy," &c.—II. THE LEADEN CASKET. By Mrs. A. W. HUNT, Author of "Thornicroft's Model," &c. This number will also contain the First of a Series of Twelve Articles on "Our Old Country Towns," with Five Illustrations by ALFRED RIMMER.

*** *The THIRTY-NINTH Volume of BELGRAVIA, elegantly bound in crimson cloth, full gilt side and back, gilt edges, price 7s. 6d., is now ready.—Handsome Cases for binding volumes can be had at 2s. each.*

One Shilling, with numerous Illustrations.

Belgravia Annual, The,

For Christmas, 1879. With Contributions from F. W. ROBINSON, JAMES PAYN, DUTTON COOK, J. ARBUTHNOT WILSON, CUTHBERT BEDE, JEAN MIDDLEMASS, PERCY FITZGERALD, and others. [*Nov.*

Demy 8vo, Illustrated, uniform in size for binding.

Blackburn's Art Handbooks:

Academy Notes, 1875. With 40 Illustrations. 1s.
Academy Notes, 1876. With 107 Illustrations. 1s.
Academy Notes, 1877. With 143 Illustrations. 1s.
Academy Notes, 1878. With 150 Illustrations. 1s.
Academy Notes, 1879. With 146 Illustrations. 1s.
Grosvenor Notes, 1878. With 68 Illustrations. 1s.
Grosvenor Notes, 1879. With 60 Illustrations. 1s.
Dudley Notes, 1878. With 64 Illustrations. 1s.
Pictures at the Paris Exhibition, 1878. 80 Illustrations. 1s.
Pictures at South Kensington. (The Raphael Cartoons, Sheepshanks Collection, &c.) With 70 Illustrations. 1s.
The English Pictures at the National Gallery. With 114 Illustrations. 1s.

ART HANDBOOKS—*continued.*

The Old Masters at the National Gallery. 128 Illusts. 1s. 6d.

Academy Notes, 1875–79. Complete in One Volume, with nearly 600 Illustrations, in Facsimile. Demy 8vo, cloth limp, 6s.

A Complete Illustrated Catalogue to the National Gallery. With Notes by HENRY BLACKBURN, and 242 Illustrations. Demy 8vo, cloth limp, 3s.

UNIFORM WITH "ACADEMY NOTES."

Royal Scottish Academy Notes, 1878. 117 Illustrations. 1s.
Royal Scottish Academy Notes, 1879. 125 Illustrations. 1s.
Glasgow Institute of Fine Arts Notes, 1878. 95 Illustrations. 1s.
Glasgow Institute of Fine Arts Notes, 1879. 100 Illusts. 1s.
Walker Art Gallery Notes, Liverpool, 1878. 112 Illusts. 1s.
Walker Art Gallery Notes, Liverpool, 1879. 100 Illusts. 1s.
Royal Manchester Institution Notes, 1878. 88 Illustrations. 1s.
Royal Society of Artists Notes, Birmingham, 1878. 95 Illustrations, 1s.

Children of the Great City. By F. W. LAWSON. With Facsimile Sketches by the Artist. Demy 8vo, 1s.

Folio, half-bound boards, India Proofs, 21s.

Blake (William).
Etchings from his Works. By W. B. SCOTT. With descriptive Text.

"*The best side of Blake's work is given here, and makes a really attractive volume, which all can enjoy. . . . The etching is of the best kind, more refined and delicate than the original work.*"—SATURDAY REVIEW.

Crown 8vo, cloth extra, gilt, with Illustrations, 7s. 6d.

Boccaccio's Decameron;
or, Ten Days' Entertainment. Translated into English, with an Introduction by THOMAS WRIGHT, Esq., M.A., F.S.A. With Portrait, and STOTHARD'S beautiful Copperplates.

Crown 8vo, cloth extra, gilt, 7s. 6d.

Brand's Observations on Popular Antiquities,
chiefly Illustrating the Origin of our Vulgar Customs, Ceremonies, and Superstitions. With the Additions of Sir HENRY ELLIS. An entirely New and Revised Edition, with fine full-page Illustrations.

Bret Harte, Works by:
The Select Works of Bret Harte, in Prose and Poetry. With Introductory Essay by J. M. BELLEW, Portrait of the Author, and 50 Illustrations. Crown 8vo, cloth extra, 7s. 6d.

"*Not many months before my friend's death, he had sent me two sketches of a young American writer (Bret Harte), far away in California ('The Outcasts of Poker Flat,' and another), in which he had found such subtle strokes of character as he had not anywhere else in late years discovered; the manner resembling himself, but the matter fresh to a degree that had surprised him; the painting in all respects masterly, and the wild rude thing painted a quite wonderful reality. I have rarely known him more honestly moved.*"—FORSTER'S LIFE OF DICKENS.

BRET HARTE'S WORKS—*continued.*

An Heiress of Red Dog, and other Stories. By BRET HARTE.
Post 8vo, illustrated boards, 2s.; cloth limp, 2s. 6d.

"*Few modern English-writing humourists have achieved the popularity of Mr. Bret Harte. He has passed, so to speak, beyond book-fame into talk-fame. People who may never perhaps have held one of his little volumes in their hands, are perfectly familiar with some at least of their contents . . . . Pictures of Californian camp-life, unapproached in their quaint picturesqueness and deep human interest.*"—DAILY NEWS.

The Twins of Table Mountain. By BRET HARTE. Fcap. 8vo, picture cover, 1s.; crown 8vo, cloth extra, 3s. 6d.

The Luck of Roaring Camp, and other Sketches. By BRET HARTE. Post 8vo, illustrated boards, 2s.

Small crown 8vo, cloth extra, gilt, with full-page Portraits, 4s. 6d.
Brewster's (Sir David) Martyrs of Science.

Small crown 8vo, cloth extra, gilt, with Astronomical Plates, 4s. 6d.
Brewster's (Sir D.) More Worlds than One,
the Creed of the Philosopher and the Hope of the Christian.

Demy 8vo, profusely Illustrated in Colours, 30s.
British Flora Medica:
A History of the Medicinal Plants of Great Britain. Illustrated by a Figure of each Plant, COLOURED BY HAND. By BENJAMIN H. BARTON, F.L.S., and THOMAS CASTLE, M.D., F.R.S. A New Edition, revised and partly re-written by JOHN R. JACKSON, A.L.S., Curator of the Museums of Economic Botany, Royal Gardens, Kew.

THE STOTHARD BUNYAN.—Crown 8vo, cloth extra, gilt, 7s. 6d.
Bunyan's Pilgrim's Progress.
Edited by Rev. T. SCOTT. With 17 beautiful Steel Plates by STOTHARD, engraved by GOODALL; and numerous Woodcuts.

Crown 8vo, cloth extra, gilt, with Illustrations, 7s. 6d.
Byron's Letters and Journals.
With Notices of his Life. By THOMAS MOORE. A Reprint of the Original Edition newly revised, with Twelve full-page Plates.

Demy 8vo, cloth extra, 14s.
Campbell's (Sir G.) White and Black:
The Outcome of a Visit to the United States. By Sir GEORGE CAMPBELL, M.P.
"*Few persons are likely to take it up without finishing it.*"—NONCONFORMIST.

Oblong 4to, half-bound boards, 21s.
Canters in Crampshire.
By G. BOWERS. I. Gallops from Gorseborough. II. Scrambles with Scratch Packs. III. Studies with Stag Hounds.

Also, in the press, oblong 4to, beautifully Coloured, price 21s.
A New Volume of Hunting Sketches. By G. BOWERS. Coloured in facsimile of the originals.

Crown 8vo. cloth extra, 1s. 6d.
Carlyle (Thomas) On the Choice of Books.
With Portrait and Memoir.

Small 4to, cloth gilt, with Coloured Illustrations, 10s. 6d.
Chaucer for Children:
A Golden Key. By Mrs. H. R. HAWEIS. With Eight Coloured Pictures and numerous Woodcuts by the Author.

"*It must not only take a high place among the Christmas and New Year books of this season, but is also of permanent value as an introduction to the study of Chaucer, whose works, in selections of some kind or other, are now text-books in every school that aspires to give sound instruction in English.*"—ACADEMY.

Crown 8vo, cloth limp, with Map and Illustrations, 2s. 6d.
Cleopatra's Needle:
Its Acquisition and Removal to England Described. By Sir J. E. ALEXANDER.

Crown 8vo, cloth extra, gilt, 7s. 6d.
Colman's Humorous Works:
"Broad Grins," "My Nightgown and Slippers," and other Humorous Works, Prose and Poetical, of GEORGE COLMAN. With Life by G. B. BUCKSTONE, and Frontispiece by HOGARTH.

Two Vols. royal 8vo, with Sixty-five Illustrations, 28s.
Conway's Demonology and Devil-Lore.
By MONCURE DANIEL CONWAY, M.A., B.D. of Divinity College, Harvard University; Member of the Anthropological Inst., London.

"*A valuable contribution to mythological literature. . . . There is much good writing among these disquisitions, a vast fund of humanity, undeniable earnestness, and a delicate sense of humour, all set forth in pure English.*"—CONTEMPORARY REVIEW.

Square 8vo, cloth extra, profusely Illustrated, 6s.
Conway's A Necklace of Stories for the
Young. By MONCURE D. CONWAY. Illustrated by W. J. HENNESSY

Demy 8vo, cloth extra, with Coloured Illustrations and Maps, 24s.
Cope's History of the Rifle Brigade
(The Prince Consort's Own), formerly the 95th. By Sir WILLIAM H. COPE, formerly Lieutenant, Rifle Brigade.

Crown 8vo, cloth extra, gilt, with 13 Portraits, 7s. 6d.
Creasy's Memoirs of Eminent Etonians;
with Notices of the Early History of Eton College. By Sir EDWARD CREASY, Author of "The Fifteen Decisive Battles of the World."

"*A new edition of 'Creasy's Etonians' will be welcome. The book was a favourite a quarter of a century ago, and it has maintained its reputation. The value of this new edition is enhanced by the fact that Sir Edward Creasy has added to it several memoirs of Etonians who have died since the first edition appeared. The work is eminently interesting.*"—SCOTSMAN.

Crown 8vo, cloth gilt, Two very thick Volumes, 7s. 6d. each.
Cruikshank's Comic Almanack.
Complete in TWO SERIES: The FIRST from 1835 to 1843; the SECOND from 1844 to 1853. A Gathering of the BEST HUMOUR of THACKERAY, HOOD, MAYHEW, ALBERT SMITH, A'BECKETT, ROBERT BROUGH, &c. With 2,000 Woodcuts and Steel Engravings by CRUIKSHANK, HINE, LANDELLS, &c.

Parts I. to XIV. now ready, 21s. each.
Cussans' History of Hertfordshire.
By JOHN E. CUSSANS. Illustrated with full-page Plates on Copper and Stone, and a profusion of small Woodcuts.

"*Mr. Cussans has, from sources not accessible to Clutterbuck, made most valuable additions to the manorial history of the county from the earliest period downwards, cleared up many doubtful points, and given original details concerning various subjects untouched or imperfectly treated by that writer. The pedigrees seem to have been constructed with great care, and are a valuable addition to the genealogical history of the county. Mr. Cussans appears to have done his work conscientiously, and to have spared neither time, labour, nor expense to render his volumes worthy of ranking in the highest class of County Histories.*"
—ACADEMY.

COMPLETION OF PLANCHÉ'S CYCLOPÆDIA OF COSTUME.
Now ready, in Two Volumes, demy 4to, handsomely bound in half-morocco, gilt, profusely Illustrated with Coloured and Plain Plates and Woodcuts, price £7 7s.

Cyclopædia of Costume;
or, A Dictionary of Dress—Regal, Ecclesiastical, Civil, and Military—from the Earliest Period in England to the reign of George the Third. Including Notices of Contemporaneous Fashions on the Continent, and a General History of the Costumes of the Principal Countries of Europe. By J. R. PLANCHÉ, Somerset Herald.

The Volumes may also be had separately (each Complete in itself) at £3 13s. 6d. each:
Vol. I. THE DICTIONARY.
Vol. II. A GENERAL HISTORY OF COSTUME IN EUROPE.
Also in 25 Parts, at 5s. each. Cases for binding, 5s. each.

"*A comprehensive and highly valuable book of reference. . . . We have rarely failed to find in this book an account of an article of dress, while in most of the entries curious and instructive details are given. . . . Mr. Planché's enormous labour of love, the production of a text which, whether in its dictionary form or in that of the 'General History,' is within its intended scope immeasurably the best and richest work on Costume in English. . . . This book is not only one of the most readable works of the kind, but intrinsically attractive and amusing.*"—ATHENÆUM.

"*A most readable and interesting work—and it can scarcely be consulted in vain, whether the reader is in search for information as to military, court, ecclesiastical, legal, or professional costume. . . . All the chromo-lithographs, and most of the woodcut illustrations—the latter amounting to several thousands—are very elaborately executed; and the work forms a livre de luxe which renders it equally suited to the library and the ladies' drawing-room.*"—TIMES.

"*One of the most perfect works ever published upon the subject. The illustrations are numerous and excellent, and would, even without the letterpress, render the work an invaluable book of reference for information as to costumes for fancy balls and character quadrilles. . . . Beautifully printed and superbly illustrated.*"—STANDARD.

Demy 8vo, cloth extra, with Illustrations, 24s.

Dodge's (Colonel) The Hunting Grounds of

the Great West: A Description of the Plains, Game, and Indians of the Great North American Desert. By RICHARD IRVING DODGE, Lieutenant-Colonel of the United States Army. With an Introduction by WILLIAM BLACKMORE; Map, and numerous Illustrations drawn by ERNEST GRISET.

"*This magnificent volume is one of the most able and most interesting works which has ever proceeded from an American pen, while its freshness is equal to that of any similar book. Col. Dodge has chosen a subject of which he is master, and treated it with a fulness that leaves nothing to be desired, and in a style which charming equally for its picturesqueness and purity.*"—NONCONFORMIST.

Demy 8vo, cloth extra, 12s. 6d.

Doran's Memories of our Great Towns.

With Anecdotic Gleanings concerning their Worthies and their Oddities. By Dr. JOHN DORAN, F.S.A.

"*A greater genius for writing of the anecdotic kind few men have had. As to giving any idea of the contents of the book, it is quite impossible. Those who know how Dr. Doran used to write—it is sad to have to use the past tense of one of the most cheerful of men—will understand what we mean; and those who do not must take it on trust from us that this is a remarkably entertaining volume.*"—SPECTATOR.

Second Edition, demy 8vo, cloth gilt, with Illustrations, 18s.

Dunraven's The Great Divide:

A Narrative of Travels in the Upper Yellowstone in the Summer of 1874. By the EARL of DUNRAVEN. With Maps and numerous striking full-page Illustrations by VALENTINE W. BROMLEY.

"*There has not for a long time appeared a better book of travel than Lord Dunraven's 'The Great Divide.' . . . The book is full of clever observation, and both narrative and illustrations are thoroughly good.*"—ATHENÆUM.

Crown 8vo, cloth boards, 6s. per Volume.

Early English Poets.

Edited, with Introductions and Annotations, by Rev. A. B. GROSART.

"*Mr. Grosart has spent the most laborious and the most enthusiastic care on the perfect restoration and preservation of the text; and it is very unlikely that any other edition of the poet can ever be called for. . . . From Mr. Grosart we always expect and always receive the final results of most patient and competent scholarship.*"—EXAMINER.

1. **Fletcher's (Giles, B.D.) Complete Poems:** Christ's Victorie in Heaven, Christ's Victorie on Earth, Christ's Triumph over Death, and Minor Poems. With Memorial-Introduction and Notes. One Vol.

2. **Davies' (Sir John) Complete** Poetical Works, including Psalms I. to L. in Verse, and other hitherto Unpublished MSS., for the first time Collected and Edited. Memorial-Introduction and Notes. Two Vols.

3. **Herrick's (Robert) Hesperides,** Noble Numbers, and Complete Collected Poems. With Memorial-Introduction and Notes, Steel Portrait, Index of First Lines, and Glossarial Index, &c. Three Vols.

4. **Sidney's (Sir Philip) Complete** Poetical Works, including all those in "Arcadia." With Portrait, Memorial-Introduction, Essay on the Poetry of Sidney, and Notes. Three Vols.

Crown 8vo, cloth extra, gilt, with Illustrations, 6s.

Emanuel On Diamonds and Precious
Stones ; their History, Value, and Properties ; with Simple Tests for ascertaining their Reality. By HARRY EMANUEL, F.R.G.S. With numerous Illustrations, Tinted and Plain.

Crown 8vo, cloth extra, with Illustrations, 7s. 6d.

Englishman's House, The:
A Practical Guide to all interested in Selecting or Building a House, with full Estimates of Cost, Quantities, &c. By C. J. RICHARDSON. Third Edition. With nearly 600 Illustrations.

Folio, cloth extra, £1 11s. 6d.

Examples of Contemporary Art.
Etchings from Representative Works by living English and Foreign Artists. Edited, with Critical Notes, by J. COMYNS CARR.

"*It would not be easy to meet with a more sumptuous, and at the same time a more tasteful and instructive drawing-room book.*"—NONCONFORMIST.

Crown 8vo, cloth extra, with Illustrations, 6s.

Fairholt's Tobacco:
Its History and Associations ; with an Account of the Plant and its Manufacture, and its Modes of Use in all Ages and Countries. By F. W. FAIRHOLT, F.S.A. With Coloured Frontispiece and upwards of 100 Illustrations by the Author.

"*A very pleasant and instructive history of tobacco and its associations, which we cordially recommend alike to the votaries and to the enemies of the much-maligned but certainly not neglected weed. . . . Full of interest and information.*"—DAILY NEWS.

Crown 8vo, cloth extra, with Illustrations, 4s. 6d.

Faraday's Chemical History of a Candle.
Lectures delivered to a Juvenile Audience. A New Edition. Edited by W. CROOKES, F.C.S. With numerous Illustrations.

Crown 8vo, cloth extra, with Illustrations, 4s. 6d.

Faraday's Various Forces of Nature.
A New Edition. Edited by W. CROOKES, F.C.S. With numerous Illustrations.

Crown 8vo, cloth extra, with Illustrations, 7s. 6d.

Finger-Ring Lore:
Historical, Legendary, and Anecdotal. By WILLIAM JONES, F.S.A. With Hundreds of Illustrations of Curious Rings of all Ages and Countries.

"*One of those gossiping books which are as full of amusement as of instruction.*"—ATHENÆUM.

One Shilling Monthly, Illustrated.

Gentleman's Magazine, The,
 For January, 1879, will contain the First Chapters of a New Novel by R. E. FRANCILLON.

 ⁎ *Now ready, the Volume for* JANUARY *to* JUNE, 1879, *cloth extra, price* 8s. 6d.; *and Cases for binding, price* 2s. *each.*

Demy 8vo, pictorial cover, price 1s.

Gentleman's Annual, The,
 for Christmas, 1879. Containing Two Complete Stories: ESTHER'S GLOVE, by R. E. FRANCILLON; and THE ROMANCE OF GIOVANNI CALVOTTI, by D. CHRISTIE MURRAY. [*November.*

THE RUSKIN GRIMM.—Square 8vo, cloth extra, 6s. 6d.; gilt edges, 7s. 6d.

German Popular Stories.
 Collected by the Brothers GRIMM, and Translated by EDGAR TAYLOR. Edited with an Introduction by JOHN RUSKIN. With 22 Illustrations after the inimitable designs of GEORGE CRUIKSHANK. Both Series Complete.

 "The illustrations of this volume . . . are of quite sterling and admirable art, of a class precisely parallel in elevation to the character of the tales which they illustrate; and the original etchings, as I have before said in the Appendix to my 'Elements of Drawing,' were unrivalled in masterfulness of touch since Rembrandt (in some qualities of delineation, unrivalled even by him). . . . To make somewhat enlarged copies of them, looking at them through a magnifying glass, and never putting two lines where Cruikshank has put only one, would be an exercise in decision and severe drawing which would leave afterwards little to be learnt in schools."—Extract from Introduction by JOHN RUSKIN.

Post 8vo, cloth limp, 2s. 6d.

Glenny's A Year's Work in Garden and
 Greenhouse: Practical Advice to Amateur Gardeners. By GEORGE GLENNY. [*In the press.*

A New Edition, demy 8vo, cloth extra, with Illustrations, 15s.

Greeks and Romans, The Life of the,
 Described from Antique Monuments. By ERNST GUHL and W. KONER. Translated from the Third German Edition, and Edited by Dr. F. HUEFFER. With 545 Illustrations.

Crown 8vo, cloth extra, gilt, with Illustrations, 7s. 6d.

Greenwood's Low-Life Deeps:
 An Account of the Strange Fish to be found there; including "The Man and Dog Fight," with much additional and confirmatory evidence; "With a Tally-Man," "A Fallen Star," "The Betting Barber," "A Coal Marriage," &c. By JAMES GREENWOOD. With Illustrations in tint by ALFRED CONCANEN.

Crown 8vo, cloth extra, gilt, with Illustrations, 7s. 6d.

Greenwood's Wilds of London:
 Descriptive Sketches, from Personal Observations and Experience, of Remarkable Scenes, People, and Places in London. By JAMES GREENWOOD. With 12 Tinted Illustrations by ALFRED CONCANEN.

Square 16mo (Tauchnitz size), cloth extra, 2s. per volume.

Golden Library, The:

Ballad History of England. By W. C. BENNETT.

Bayard Taylor's Diversions of the Echo Club.

Byron's Don Juan.

Emerson's Letters and Social Aims.

Godwin's (William) Lives of the Necromancers.

Holmes's Autocrat of the Breakfast Table. With an Introduction by G. A. SALA.

Holmes's Professor at the Breakfast Table.

Hood's Whims and Oddities. Complete. With all the original Illustrations.

Irving's (Washington) Tales of a Traveller.

Irving's (Washington) Tales of the Alhambra.

Jesse's (Edward) Scenes and Occupations of Country Life.

Lamb's Essays of Elia. Both Series Complete in One Vol.

Leigh Hunt's Essays: A Tale for a Chimney Corner, and other Pieces. With Portrait, and Introduction by EDMUND OLLIER.

Mallory's (Sir Thomas) Mort d'Arthur: The Stories of King Arthur and of the Knights of the Round Table. Edited by B. MONTGOMERIE RANKING.

Pascal's Provincial Letters. A New Translation, with Historical Introduction and Notes, by T. M'CRIE, D.D.

Pope's Poetical Works. Complete.

Rochefoucauld's Maxims and Moral Reflections. With Notes, and an Introductory Essay by SAINTE-BEUVE.

St. Pierre's Paul and Virginia, and The Indian Cottage. Edited, with Life, by the Rev. E. CLARKE.

Shelley's Early Poems, and Queen Mab, with Essay by LEIGH HUNT.

Shelley's Later Poems: Laon and Cythna, &c.

Shelley's Posthumous Poems, the Shelley Papers, &c.

Shelley's Prose Works, including A Refutation of Deism, Zastrozzi, St. Irvyne, &c.

White's Natural History of Selborne. Edited, with additions, by THOMAS BROWN, F.L.S.

Crown 8vo, cloth gilt and gilt edges, 7s. 6d.

Golden Treasury of Thought, The:

An ENCYCLOPÆDIA OF QUOTATIONS from Writers of all Times and Countries. Selected and Edited by THEODORE TAYLOR.

Large 4to, with 14 facsimile Plates, price ONE GUINEA.

Grosvenor Gallery Illustrated Catalogue.

Winter Exhibition (1877-78) of Drawings by the Old Masters and Water-Colour Drawings by Deceased Artists of the British School. With a Critical Introduction by J. COMYNS CARR.

Crown 8vo, cloth extra, gilt, with Illustrations, 4s. 6d.

Guyot's Earth and Man;

or, Physical Geography in its Relation to the History of Mankind. With Additions by Professors AGASSIZ, PIERCE, and GRAY; 12 Maps and Engravings on Steel, some Coloured, and copious Index.

Medium 8vo, cloth extra, gilt, with Illustrations, 7s. 6d.
Hall's (Mrs. S. C.) Sketches of Irish Character.
With numerous Illustrations on Steel and Wood by MACLISE, GILBERT, HARVEY, and G. CRUIKSHANK.

"*The Irish Sketches of this lady resemble Miss Mitford's beautiful English sketches in 'Our Village,' but they are far more vigorous and picturesque and bright.*"—BLACKWOOD'S MAGAZINE.

Post 8vo, cloth extra, 4s. 6d.; a few large-paper copies, half-Roxb., 10s. 6d.
Handwriting, The Philosophy of.
By Don FELIX DE SALAMANCA. With 134 Facsimiles of Signatures.
[*In the press.*

Small 8vo, cloth limp, with numerous Illustrations, 1s. 6d.;
or illustrated cover, 1s.
Haweis's (Mrs.) The Art of Dress.
By Mrs. H. R. HAWEIS, Author of "The Art of Beauty," &c. Illustrated by the Author.

"*A well-considered attempt to apply canons of good taste to the costumes of ladies of our time. . . . Mrs. Haweis writes frankly and to the point, she does not mince matters, but boldly remonstrates with her own sex on the follies they indulge in. . . . We may recommend the book to the ladies whom it concerns.*"—ATHENÆUM.

Square 8vo, cloth extra, gilt, gilt edges, with Coloured Frontispiece
and numerous Illustrations, 10s. 6d.
Haweis's (Mrs.) The Art of Beauty.
By Mrs. H. R. HAWEIS, Author of "Chaucer for Children." With nearly One Hundred Illustrations by the Author.

"*A most interesting book, full of valuable hints and suggestions. . . . . If young ladies would but lend their ears for a little to Mrs. Haweis, we are quite sure that it would result in their being at once more tasteful, more happy, and more healthy than they now often are, with their false hair, high heels, tight corsets, and ever so much else of the same sort.*"—NONCONFORMIST.

Fcap. 8vo, picture cover, 1s.; cloth extra, 2s. 6d.
Hawthorne. — Mrs. Gainsborough's Diamonds: A Romance. By JULIAN HAWTHORNE.

ELEVENTH EDITION. Vols. I. and II., demy 8vo, 12s. each.
History of Our Own Times, from the Accession
of Queen Victoria to the Berlin Congress. By JUSTIN MCCARTHY.

"*Criticism is disarmed before a composition which provokes little but approval. This is a really good book on a really interesting subject, and words piled on words could say no more for it. . . . Such is the effect of its general justice, its breadth of view, and its sparkling buoyancy, that very few of its readers will close these volumes without looking forward with interest to the two that are to follow.*"— SATURDAY REVIEW.

*** Vols. III. and IV., completing the work, are now in the press

Crown 8vo, cloth extra, gilt, 7s. 6d.
Hood's (Thomas) Choice Works,
In Prose and Verse. Including the CREAM OF THE COMIC ANNUALS. With Life of the Author, Portrait, and over Two Hundred Original Illustrations.

Square crown 8vo, cloth extra, gilt edges, 6s.
Hood's (Tom) From Nowhere to the North
Pole: A Noah's Arkæological Narrative. With 25 Illustrations by W. BRUNTON and E. C. BARNES.

"*The amusing letterpress is profusely interspersed with the jingling rhymes which children love and learn so easily. Messrs. Brunton and Barnes do full justice to the writer's meaning, and a pleasanter result of the harmonious co-operation of author and artist could not be desired.*" —TIMES.

Crown 8vo, cloth extra, gilt, 7s. 6d.
Hook's (Theodore) Choice Humorous Works,
including his Ludicrous Adventures, Bons-mots, Puns, and Hoaxes. With a new Life of the Author, Portraits, Facsimiles, and Illustrations.

Small 8vo, cloth limp, with Illustrations, 2s. 6d.
House of Life (The):
HUMAN PHYSIOLOGY, with its Applications to the Preservation of Health. For use in Classes and Popular Reading. With numerous Illustrations. By Mrs. F. FENWICK MILLER.

"*A clear and convenient little book.*"—SATURDAY REVIEW.
"*An admirable introduction to a subject which all who value health and enjoy life should have at their fingers' ends.*"—ECHO.

Crown 8vo, cloth extra, 7s. 6d.
Howell's Conflicts of Capital and Labour
Historically and Economically considered. Being a History and Review of the Trade Unions of Great Britain, showing their Origin, Progress, Constitution, and Objects, in their Political, Social, Economical, and Industrial Aspects. By GEORGE HOWELL.

"*This book is an attempt, and on the whole a successful attempt, to place the work of trade unions in the past, and their objects in the future, fairly before the public from the working man's point of view.*"—PALL MALL GAZETTE.

Demy 8vo, cloth extra, 12s. 6d.
Hueffer's The Troubadours:
A History of Provencal Life and Literature in the Middle Ages. By FRANCIS HUEFFER.

"*This very pleasant volume, in which a very difficult subject is handled in a light and lively manner, but at the same time with an erudition and amount of information which show him to be thoroughly master of the language and literature of Provence.*"—TIMES.

A NEW EDITION, Revised and partly Re-written, with several New Chapters and Illustrations, crown 8vo, cloth extra, 7s. 6d.

Jennings' The Rosicrucians:

Their Rites and Mysteries. With Chapters on the Ancient Fire and Serpent Worshippers, and Explanations of the Mystic Symbols represented in the Monuments and Talismans of the Primæval Philosophers. By HARGRAVE JENNINGS. With Five full-page Plates and upwards of 300 Illustrations.

"*Mr. Hargrave Jennings is well known for his research in matters of antiquity and folk-lore, and his claims for his work that it is the first impartially written explanatory history of the alchemical philosophers since the days of James I. and Charles I. . . . The book has been compiled in a very interesting manner, is well illustrated with the majestic symbols of the order, and may be described as one of those volumes which may be taken up and dipped into at random for half-an-hour's reading, or, on the other hand, appealed to by the student as a source of valuable information on a system which has not only exercised for hundreds of years an extraordinary influence on the mental development of so shrewd a people as the Jews, but has captivated the minds of some of the greatest thinkers of Christendom in the sixteenth and seventeenth centuries*"—LEEDS MERCURY.

Two Vols. 8vo, with 52 Illustrations and Maps, cloth extra, gilt, 14s.

Josephus' Complete Works.

Translated by WHISTON. Containing both "The Antiquities of the Jews" and "The Wars of the Jews."

Small 8vo, cloth, full gilt, gilt edges, with Illustrations, 6s.

Kavanaghs' Pearl Fountain,

And other Fairy Stories. By BRIDGET and JULIA KAVANAGH. With Thirty Illustrations by J. MOYR SMITH.

"*Genuine new fairy stories of the old type, some of them as delightful as the best of Grimm's 'German Popular Stories.' . . . . For the most part the stories are downright, thorough-going fairy stories of the most admirable kind. . . . . Mr. Moyr Smith's illustrations, too, are admirable.*"—SPECTATOR.

Crown 8vo, illustrated boards, with numerous Plates, 2s. 6d.

Lace (Old Point), and How to Copy and

Imitate it. By DAISY WATERHOUSE HAWKINS. With 17 Illustrations by the Author.

Crown 8vo, cloth extra, with numerous Illustrations, 10s. 6d.

Lamb (Mary and Charles):

Their Poems, Letters, and Remains. With Reminiscences and Notes by W. CAREW HAZLITT. With HANCOCK's Portrait of the Essayist, Facsimiles of the Title-pages of the rare First Editions of Lamb's and Coleridge's Works, and numerous Illustrations.

"*Very many passages will delight those fond of literary trifles; hardly any portion will fail in interest for lovers of Charles Lamb and his sister.*"—STANDARD.

Small 8vo, cloth extra, 5s.

Lamb's Poetry for Children, and Prince

Dorus. Carefully Reprinted from unique copies.

"*The quaint and delightful little book, over the recovery of which all the hearts of his lovers are yet warm with rejoicing.*"—A. C. SWINBURNE.

Crown 8vo, cloth extra, gilt, with Portraits, 7s. 6d.
Lamb's Complete Works,
In Prose and Verse, reprinted from the Original Editions, with many Pieces hitherto unpublished. Edited, with Notes and Introduction, by R. H. SHEPHERD. With Two Portraits and Facsimile of a Page of the "Essay on Roast Pig."

"*A complete edition of Lamb's writings, in prose and verse, has long been wanted, and is now supplied. The editor appears to have taken great pains to bring together Lamb's scattered contributions, and his collection contains a number of pieces which are now reproduced for the first time since their original appearance in various old periodicals.*"—SATURDAY REVIEW.

Demy 8vo, cloth extra, with Maps and Illustrations, 18s.
Lamont's Yachting in the Arctic Seas;
or, Notes of Five Voyages of Sport and Discovery in the Neighbourhood of Spitzbergen and Novaya Zemlya. By JAMES LAMONT, F.R.G.S. With numerous full-page Illustrations by Dr. LIVESAY.

"*After wading through numberless volumes of icy fiction, concocted **narrative**, and spurious biography of Arctic voyagers, it is pleasant to meet with a real and genuine volume. . . . He shows much tact in recounting his adventures, and they are so interspersed with anecdotes and information as to make them anything but wearisome. . . . The book, as a whole, is the most important addition made to our Arctic literature for a long time.*"—ATHENÆUM.

Crown 8vo, cloth, full gilt, 7s. 6d.
Latter-Day Lyrics:
Poems of Sentiment and Reflection by Living Writers; selected and arranged, with Notes, by W. DAVENPORT ADAMS. With a Note on some Foreign Forms of Verse, by AUSTIN DOBSON.

Crown 8vo, cloth, full gilt, 6s.
Leigh's A Town Garland.
By HENRY S. LEIGH, Author of "Carols of Cockayne."

"*If Mr. Leigh's verse survive to a future generation—and there is no reason why that honour should not be accorded productions so delicate, so finished, and so full of humour—their author will probably be remembered as the Poet of the Strand. . . . Very whimsically does Mr. Leigh treat the subjects which commend themselves to him. His verse is always admirable in rhythm, and his rhymes are happy enough to deserve a place by the best of Barham. . . . The entire contents of the volume are equally noteworthy for humour and for daintiness of workmanship.*"—ATHENÆUM.

SECOND EDITION.—Crown 8vo, cloth extra, with Illustrations, 10s. 6d.
Leisure-Time Studies, chiefly Biological.
By ANDREW WILSON, Ph.D., Lecturer on Zoology and Comparative Anatomy in the Edinburgh Medical School.

"*It is well when we can take up the work of a really qualified investigator, who in the intervals of his more serious professional labours sets himself to impart knowledge in such a simple and elementary form as may attract and instruct, with no danger of misleading the tyro in natural science. Such a work is this little volume, made up of essays and addresses written and delivered by Dr. Andrew Wilson, lecturer and examiner in science at Edinburgh and Glasgow, at leisure intervals in a busy professional life. . . . Dr. Wilson's pages teem with matter stimulating to a healthy love of science and a reverence for the truths of nature.*"—SATURDAY REVIEW.

Crown 8vo, cloth extra, with Illustrations, 7s. 6d.

Life in London;
or, The History of Jerry Hawthorn and Corinthian Tom. With the whole of CRUIKSHANK'S Illustrations, in Colours, after the Originals.

Crown 8vo, cloth extra, 6s.

Lights on the Way:
Some Tales within a Tale. By the late J. H. ALEXANDER, B.A. Edited, with an Explanatory Note, by H. A. PAGE, Author of "Thoreau: A Study."

Crown 8vo, cloth extra, with Illustrations, 7s. 6d.

Longfellow's Complete Prose Works.
Including "Outre Mer," "Hyperion," "Kavanagh," "The Poets and Poetry of Europe," and "Driftwood." With Portrait and Illustrations by VALENTINE BROMLEY.

Crown 8vo, cloth extra, gilt, with Illustrations, 7s. 6d.

Longfellow's Poetical Works.
Carefully Reprinted from the Original Editions. With numerous fine Illustrations on Steel and Wood.

"*Mr. Longfellow has for many years been the best known and the most read of American poets; and his popularity is of the right kind, and rightly and fairly won. He has not stooped to catch attention by artifice, nor striven to force it by violence. His works have faced the test of parody and burlesque (which in these days is almost the common lot of writings of any mark), and have come off unharmed.*"—SATURDAY REVIEW.

Crown 8vo, cloth extra, 5s.

Lunatic Asylum, My Experiences in a.
By a SANE PATIENT.

"*The story is clever and interesting, sad beyond measure though the subject be. There is no personal bitterness, and no violence or anger. Whatever may have been the evidence for our author's madness when he was consigned to an asylum, nothing can be clearer than his sanity when he wrote this book; it is bright, calm, and to the point.*"—SPECTATOR.

A NORMAN AND BRETON TOUR.
Square 8vo, cloth gilt, gilt top, profusely Illustrated, 10s. 6d.

Macquoid's Pictures and Legends from
Normandy and Brittany. By KATHARINE S. MACQUOID. With numerous Illustrations by THOMAS R. MACQUOID.

"*Mr. and Mrs. Macquoid have been strolling in Normandy and Brittany, and the result of their observations and researches in that picturesque land of romantic associations is an attractive volume, which is neither a work of travel nor a collection of stories, but a book partaking almost in equal degree of each of these characters. . . . The wanderings of the tourists, their sojournings in old inns, their explorations of ancient towns, and loiterings by rivers and other pleasant spots, are all related in a fresh and lively style. . . . The illustrations, which are numerous, are drawn, as a rule, with remarkable delicacy as well as with true artistic feeling.*"—DAILY NEWS.

Crown 8vo, cloth extra, with Illustrations, 2s. 6d.

Madre Natura v. The Moloch of Fashion.
By LUKE LIMNER. With 32 Illustrations by the Author. FOURTH EDITION, revised and enlarged.

Handsomely printed in facsimile, price 5s.
Magna Charta.
An exact Facsimile of the Original Document in the British Museum, printed on fine plate paper, nearly 3 feet long by 2 feet wide, with the Arms and Seals emblazoned in Gold and Colours.

₊ A full Translation, with Notes, on a large sheet, 6d.

NEW WORK BY THE AUTHOR OF "THE NEW REPUBLIC."
Demy 8vo, cloth extra, 12s. 6d.
Mallock's Is Life Worth Living?
By WILLIAM HURRELL MALLOCK.

"*This deeply interesting volume. .... It is the most powerful vindication of religion, both natural and revealed, that has appeared since Bishop Butler wrote, and is much more useful than either the Analogy or the Sermons of that great divine, as a refutation of the peculiar form assumed by the infidelity of the present day. .... Deeply philosophical as the book is, there is not a heavy page in it. The writer is 'possessed,' so to speak, with his great subject, has sounded its depths, surveyed it in all its extent, and brought to bear on it all the resources of a vivid, rich, and impassioned style, as well as an adequate acquaintance with the science, the philosophy, and the literature of the day.*"—IRISH DAILY NEWS.

Mark Twain's Works:

The Choice Works of Mark Twain. Revised and Corrected throughout by the Author. With Life, Portrait, and numerous Illustrations. Crown 8vo, cloth extra, 7s. 6d.

The Adventures of Tom Sawyer. By MARK TWAIN. With One Hundred Illustrations. Small 8vo, cloth extra, 7s. 6d.

₊ Also a Cheap Edition, in illustrated boards, at 2s.

"*A book to be read. There is a certain freshness and novelty about it, a practically romantic character, so to speak, which will make it very attractive.*"—SPECTATOR.

A Pleasure Trip on the Continent of Europe: The Innocents Abroad, and The New Pilgrim's Progress. By MARK TWAIN. Post 8vo, illustrated boards, 2s.

An Idle Excursion, and other Sketches. By MARK TWAIN. Post 8vo, illustrated boards, 2s.

Small 8vo, 1s.; cloth extra, 1s. 6d.
Milton's The Hygiene of the Skin.
A Concise Set of Rules for the Management of the Skin; with Directions for Diet, Wines, Soaps, Baths, &c. By J. L. MILTON, Senior Surgeon to St. John's Hospital.

Crown 8vo, cloth extra, with Frontispiece, 7s. 6d.
Moore's (Thos.) Prose and Verse—Humorous,
Satirical, and Sentimental. Including Suppressed Passages from the Memoirs of Lord Byron. Chiefly from the Author's MSS., and all hitherto Inedited and Uncollected. Edited, with Notes, by RICHARD HERNE SHEPHERD.

Mayfair Library, The:

Post 8vo, cloth limp, 2s. 6d. per vol.

The New Republic. By W. H. MALLOCK.

The New Paul and Virginia. By W. H. MALLOCK.

The True History of Joshua Davidson. By E. LYNN LINTON.

Old Stories Re-told. By WALTER THORNBURY.

Thoreau: His Life and Aims. By H. A. PAGE.

By Stream and Sea. By WILLIAM SENIOR.

Jeux d'Esprit. Edited by HENRY S. LEIGH.

Puniana. By the Hon. HUGH ROWLEY.

More Puniana. By the Hon. HUGH ROWLEY.

Puck on Pegasus. By H. CHOLMONDELEY-PENNELL.

Muses of Mayfair. Edited by H. CHOLMONDELEY-PENNELL.

Gastronomy as a Fine Art. By BRILLAT-SAVARIN.

Original Plays. By W. S. GILBERT.

⁎ *Other Volumes are in preparation.*

New Novels at every Library.

THE FALLEN LEAVES. By WILKIE COLLINS. Three Vols., crown 8vo.

"*The natural vigour and brightness of Mr. Wilkie Collins's work, which have helped to win him his well-deserved reputation, are as noticeable in his last book as in any. It would be hardly possible for anybody who begins the book not to read on to the end without a moment's weariness. . . . It is, perhaps, the chief triumph of the book that the reader leaves off with his appetite whetted instead of dulled.*"—ATHENÆUM.

UNDER ONE ROOF. By JAMES PAYN, Author of "By Proxy," &c. Three Vols., crown 8vo.

"*The title of this novel is more than usually happy and significant. . . . The author deserves thanks for his charming sketch of the German governess, for his portraits of the two natural, graceful English girls, and for the scenes in which these three girls are wooed and eventually won. With a few delicate and happy touches, and a dash of humour to colour the picture, he presents us with many an exhilarating piece of love-making which we at once acknowledge to be hit off to the life, and of which we can easily fill up the mere outline either from the imagination or, peradventure, from memory. . . . The irrepressible spirit of drollery prevails. . . . The story is pretty sure to be found attractive.*"—PALL MALL GAZETTE.

MAID, WIFE, OR WIDOW? By Mrs. ALEXANDER, Author of "The Wooing o't." SECOND EDITION. Crown 8vo, cloth extra, 10s. 6d.

"*It would be difficult, and certainly ungracious, to pick out the blemishes which may possibly exist in Mrs. Alexander's pretty, pathetic, well-modulated little romance. As a matter of fact, the story cannot be read without pleasure; and it is written with so much delicacy as well as correctness, that criticism is disarmed from the outset. . . . Humanity at its truest and tenderest, youthful affection and faith at their purest and simplest, circumstance and detail in their most natural form: these are the materials out of which Mrs. Alexander has woven a charming tale of German life. The thorough ease of the narrative is one of the best proofs of the fidelity of the pictures which it brings before our eyes.*"—ATHENÆUM.

NEW NOVELS—*continued*.

THE CURE OF SOULS: A Novel. By MACLAREN COBBAN. Crown 8vo, cloth extra, 10s. 6d.

"*It is long since we have seen a more promising début. . . . He has force, a certain rude pathos and realistic intensity of sentiment, and a remarkable faculty for inventing natural dialogue. It is refreshing to come upon a novel by a new hand which is neither silly, weak, nor flighty, and which shows proof of thought and care in the writer.*"—SATURDAY REVIEW.

MR. PAYN'S NEW NOVEL.

HIGH SPIRITS: Being Stories written in them. By JAMES PAYN, Author of "By Proxy," &c. Three Vols., crown 8vo.

"*In those comic historiettes of which Mr. Payn only among living writers has the secret, there is as much occasion for good, honest, sociable laughter, as in any three volumes we remember during the last ten years to have read.*"—ATHENÆUM.

MRS. LINTON'S NEW NOVEL.

UNDER WHICH LORD? By E. LYNN LINTON, Author of "Patricia Kemball," &c. Three Vols., crown 8vo.

MR. JUSTIN McCARTHY'S NEW NOVEL.

DONNA QUIXOTE. By JUSTIN McCARTHY, Author of "Dear Lady Disdain," &c. Three Vols., crown 8vo. [*Nov.* 15.

CHARLES GIBBON'S NEW NOVEL.

QUEEN OF THE MEADOW. By CHARLES GIBBON, Author of "Robin Gray," &c. Three Vols., crown 8vo. [*Dec.* 12.

OUIDA'S NEW NOVEL.

MOTHS. By OUIDA, Author of "Puck," "Ariadne," &c. Three Vols., crown 8vo. [*Shortly.*

NEW AND CHEAPER EDITION.

THORNICROFT'S MODEL. By Mrs. A. W. HUNT. Crown 8vo, cloth extra, 6s.

Square 8vo, cloth extra, with numerous Illustrations, 9s.

North Italian Folk.

By Mrs. COMYNS CARR. Illustrations by RANDOLPH CALDECOTT.

"*A delightful book, of a kind which is far too rare. If anyone wants to really know the North Italian folk, we can honestly advise him to omit the journey, and sit down to read Mrs. Carr's pages instead. . . . Description with Mrs. Carr is a real gift. . . . It is rarely that a book is so happily illustrated.*"—CONTEMPORARY REVIEW.

Crown 8vo, cloth extra, with Vignette Portraits, price 6s. per Vol.

Old Dramatists, The:

Ben Jonson's Works.
With Notes, Critical and Explanatory, and a Biographical Memoir by WILLIAM GIFFORD. Edited by Colonel CUNNINGHAM. Three Vols.

Chapman's Works.
Now First Collected. Complete in Three Vols. Vol. I. contains the Plays complete, including the doubtful ones; Vol. II. the Poems and Minor Translations, with an Introductory Essay by ALGERNON CHARLES SWINBURNE; Vol. III. the Translations of the Iliad and Odyssey.

Marlowe's Works.
Including his Translations. Edited, with Notes and Introduction, by Col. CUNNINGHAM. One Vol.

Massinger's Plays.
From the Text of WILLIAM GIFFORD. With the addition of the Tragedy of "Believe as you List." Edited by Col. CUNNINGHAM. One Vol.

Crown 8vo, red cloth extra, 5s. each.

Ouida's Novels.—Library Edition.

Held in Bondage.	By OUIDA.	Folle Farine.	By OUIDA.
Strathmore.	By OUIDA.	Dog of Flanders.	By OUIDA.
Chandos.	By OUIDA.	Pascarel.	By OUIDA.
Under Two Flags.	By OUIDA.	Two Wooden Shoes.	By OUIDA.
Idalia.	By OUIDA.	Signa.	By OUIDA.
Cecil Castlemaine.	By OUIDA.	In a Winter City.	By OUIDA.
Tricotrin.	By OUIDA.	Ariadne.	By OUIDA.
Puck.	By OUIDA.	Friendship.	By OUIDA.

CHEAP EDITION OF OUIDA'S NOVELS.
Post 8vo, illustrated boards, 2s. each.

Held in Bondage.	By OUIDA.	Under Two Flags.	By OUIDA.
Strathmore.	By OUIDA.	Idalia.	By OUIDA.
Chandos.	By OUIDA.	Cecil Castlemaine.	By OUIDA.

The other Novels will follow in Monthly Volumes.

Two Vols. 8vo, cloth extra, with Illustrations, 10s. 6d.
Plutarch's Lives of Illustrious Men.
Translated from the Greek, with Notes, Critical and Historical, and a Life of Plutarch, by JOHN and WILLIAM LANGHORNE. New Edition, with Medallion Portraits.

Crown 8vo, cloth extra, with Portrait and Illustrations, 7s. 6d.
Poe's Choice Prose and Poetical Works.
With BAUDELAIRE'S "Essay."

Crown 8vo, cloth extra, Illustrated, 7s. 6d.
Poe, The Life of Edgar Allan.
By W. F. GILL. With numerous Illustrations and Facsimiles.

Crown 8vo, cloth extra, 7s. 6d.
Primitive Manners and Customs.
By JAMES A. FARRER.

"*A book which is really both instructive and amusing, and which will open a new field of thought to many readers.*"—ATHENÆUM.

An admirable example of the application of the scientific method and the rking of the truly scientific spirit."—SATURDAY REVIEW.

Small 8vo, cloth extra, with Illustrations, 3s. 6d.
Prince of Argolis, The:
A Story of the Old Greek Fairy Time. By J. MOYR SMITH. With 130 Illustrations by the Author.

Crown 8vo, carefully printed on creamy paper, and tastefully bound in cloth for the Library, price 6s. each.

Piccadilly Novels, The.
Popular Stories by the Best Authors.

READY-MONEY MORTIBOY. By W. BESANT and JAMES RICE.

MY LITTLE GIRL. By W. BESANT and JAMES RICE.

THE CASE OF MR. LUCRAFT. By W. BESANT and JAMES RICE.

THIS SON OF VULCAN. By W. BESANT and JAMES RICE.

WITH HARP AND CROWN. By W. BESANT and JAMES RICE.

THE GOLDEN BUTTERFLY. By W. BESANT and JAMES RICE. With a Frontispiece by F. S. WALKER.

BY CELIA'S ARBOUR. By W. BESANT and JAMES RICE.

THE MONKS OF THELEMA. By W. BESANT and JAMES RICE.

'TWAS IN TRAFALGAR'S BAY. By W. BESANT & JAMES RICE.

ANTONINA. By WILKIE COLLINS. Illustrated by Sir J. GILBERT and ALFRED CONCANEN.

BASIL. By WILKIE COLLINS. Illustrated by Sir JOHN GILBERT and J. MAHONEY.

HIDE AND SEEK. By WILKIE COLLINS. Illustrated by Sir JOHN GILBERT and J. MAHONEY.

THE DEAD SECRET. By WILKIE COLLINS. Illustrated by Sir JOHN GILBERT and H. FURNISS.

QUEEN OF HEARTS. By WILKIE COLLINS. Illustrated by Sir JOHN GILBERT and A. CONCANEN.

MY MISCELLANIES. By WILKIE COLLINS. With Steel Portrait, and Illustrations by A. CONCANEN.

THE WOMAN IN WHITE. By WILKIE COLLINS. Illustrated by Sir J. GILBERT and F. A. FRASER.

THE MOONSTONE. By WILKIE COLLINS. Illustrated by G. DU MAURIER and F. A. FRASER.

MAN AND WIFE. By WILKIE COLLINS. Illust. by WM. SMALL.

POOR MISS FINCH. By WILKIE COLLINS. Illustrated by G. DU MAURIER and EDWARD HUGHES.

MISS OR MRS. ? By WILKIE COLLINS. Illustrated by S. L. FILDES and HENRY WOODS.

THE NEW MAGDALEN. By WILKIE COLLINS. Illustrated by G. DU MAURIER and C. S. RANDS.

THE FROZEN DEEP. By WILKIE COLLINS. Illustrated by G. DU MAURIER and J. MAHONEY.

THE LAW AND THE LADY. By WILKIE COLLINS. Illustrated by S. L. FILDES and SYDNEY HALL.

PICCADILLY NOVELS—*continued*.

THE TWO DESTINIES. By WILKIE COLLINS.

THE HAUNTED HOTEL. By WILKIE COLLINS. Illustrated by ARTHUR HOPKINS.

DECEIVERS EVER. By Mrs. H. LOVETT CAMERON.

JULIET'S GUARDIAN. By Mrs. H. LOVETT CAMERON. Illustrated by VALENTINE BROMLEY.

FELICIA. By M. BETHAM-EDWARDS. Frontispiece by W. BOWLES.

OLYMPIA. By R. E. FRANCILLON.

UNDER THE GREENWOOD TREE. By THOMAS HARDY.

THORNICROFT'S MODEL. By Mrs. A. W. HUNT.

FATED TO BE FREE. By JEAN INGELOW.

THE QUEEN OF CONNAUGHT. By HARRIETT JAY.

THE DARK COLLEEN. By HARRIETT JAY.

NUMBER SEVENTEEN. By HENRY KINGSLEY.

OAKSHOTT CASTLE. By HENRY KINGSLEY. With a Frontispiece by SHIRLEY HODSON.

THE WORLD WELL LOST. By E. LYNN LINTON. Illustrated by J. LAWSON and HENRY FRENCH.

THE ATONEMENT OF LEAM DUNDAS. By E. LYNN LINTON. With a Frontispiece by HENRY WOODS.

PATRICIA KEMBALL. By E. LYNN LINTON. With a Frontispiece by G. DU MAURIER.

THE WATERDALE NEIGHBOURS. By JUSTIN MCCARTHY.

MY ENEMY'S DAUGHTER. By JUSTIN MCCARTHY.

LINLEY ROCHFORD. By JUSTIN MCCARTHY.

A FAIR SAXON. By JUSTIN MCCARTHY.

DEAR LADY DISDAIN. By JUSTIN MCCARTHY.

MISS MISANTHROPE. By JUSTIN MCCARTHY. Illustrated by ARTHUR HOPKINS.

LOST ROSE. By KATHARINE S. MACQUOID.

THE EVIL EYE, and other Stories. By KATHARINE S. MACQUOID. Illustrated by THOMAS R. MACQUOID and PERCY MACQUOID.

OPEN! SESAME! By FLORENCE MARRYAT. Illustrated by F. A. FRASER.

TOUCH AND GO. By JEAN MIDDLEMASS.

WHITELADIES. By Mrs. OLIPHANT. With Illustrations by A. HOPKINS and H. WOODS.

THE BEST OF HUSBANDS. By JAMES PAYN. Illustrated by J. MOYR SMITH.

PICCADILLY NOVELS—*continued.*
FALLEN FORTUNES. By JAMES PAYN.
HALVES. By JAMES PAYN. With a Frontispiece by J. MAHONEY.
WALTER'S WORD. By JAMES PAYN. Illust. by J. MOYR SMITH.
WHAT HE COST HER. By JAMES PAYN.
LESS BLACK THAN WE'RE PAINTED. By JAMES PAYN.
BY PROXY. By JAMES PAYN. Illustrated by ARTHUR HOPKINS.
HER MOTHER'S DARLING. By Mrs. J. H. RIDDELL.
BOUND TO THE WHEEL. By JOHN SAUNDERS.
GUY WATERMAN. By JOHN SAUNDERS.
ONE AGAINST THE WORLD. By JOHN SAUNDERS.
THE LION IN THE PATH. By JOHN SAUNDERS.
THE WAY WE LIVE NOW. By ANTHONY TROLLOPE. Illust.
THE AMERICAN SENATOR. By ANTHONY TROLLOPE.
DIAMOND CUT DIAMOND. By T. A. TROLLOPE.

Post 8vo, illustrated boards, 2*s.* each.
Popular Novels, Cheap Editions of.

[WILKIE COLLINS' NOVELS and BESANT and RICE'S NOVELS may also be had in cloth limp at 2*s.* 6*d. See, too, the* PICCADILLY NOVELS, *for Library Editions.*]

Ready-Money Mortiboy. By WALTER BESANT and JAMES RICE.
The Golden Butterfly. By Authors of "Ready-Money Mortiboy."
This Son of Vulcan. By the same.
My Little Girl. By the same.
The Case of Mr. Lucraft. By Authors of "Ready-Money Mortiboy."
With Harp and Crown. By Authors of "Ready-Money Mortiboy."
Surly Tim. By F. H. BURNETT.
The Woman in White. By WILKIE COLLINS.
Antonina. By WILKIE COLLINS.
Basil. By WILKIE COLLINS.
Hide and Seek. By the same.
The Dead Secret. By the same.
The Queen of Hearts. By WILKIE COLLINS.
My Miscellanies. By the same.
The Moonstone. By the same.
Man and Wife. By WILKIE COLLINS.
Poor Miss Finch. By the same.
Miss or Mrs.? By the same.
The New Magdalen. By WILKIE COLLINS.
The Frozen Deep. By the same.
The Law and the Lady. By WILKIE COLLINS.
The Two Destinies. By WILKIE COLLINS.
Roxy. By EDWARD EGGLESTON.
Felicia. M. BETHAM-EDWARDS.
Filthy Lucre. By ALBANY DE FONBLANQUE.
Olympia. By R. E. FRANCILLON.
Dick Temple. By JAMES GREENWOOD.
Under the Greenwood Tree. By THOMAS HARDY.
An Heiress of Red Dog. By BRET HARTE.

POPULAR NOVELS—*continued*.

The Luck of Roaring Camp. By BRET HARTE.
Fated to be Free. By JEAN INGELOW.
The Queen of Connaught. By HARRIETT JAY.
The Dark Colleen. By HARRIETT JAY.
Number Seventeen. By HENRY KINGSLEY.
Oakshott Castle. By the same.
The Waterdale Neighbours. By JUSTIN MCCARTHY.
My Enemy's Daughter. By JUSTIN MCCARTHY.
Linley Rochford. By the same.
A Fair Saxon. By the same.
Dear Lady Disdain. By the same.
The Evil Eye. By KATHARINE S. MACQUOID.
Open! Sesame! By FLORENCE MARRYAT.
Whiteladies. Mrs. OLIPHANT.
Held in Bondage. By OUIDA.
Strathmore. By OUIDA.
Chandos. By OUIDA.
Under Two Flags. By OUIDA.
Idalia. By OUIDA.
Cecil Castlemaine. By OUIDA.

The Best of Husbands. By JAMES PAYN.
Walter's Word. By J. PAYN.
The Mystery of Marie Roget. By EDGAR A. POE.
Her Mother's Darling. By Mrs. J. H. RIDDELL.
Gaslight and Daylight. By GEORGE AUGUSTUS SALA.
Bound to the Wheel. By JOHN SAUNDERS.
Guy Waterman. J. SAUNDERS.
One Against the World. By JOHN SAUNDERS.
The Lion in the Path. By JOHN and KATHERINE SAUNDERS.
Tales for the Marines. By WALTER THORNBURY.
The Way we Live Now. By ANTHONY TROLLOPE.
The American Senator. By ANTHONY TROLLOPE.
Diamond Cut Diamond. By T. A. TROLLOPE.
An Idle Excursion. By MARK TWAIN.
Adventures of Tom Sawyer. By MARK TWAIN.
A Pleasure Trip on the Continent of Europe. By MARK TWAIN.

Fcap. 8vo, picture covers, 1s. each.

The Twins of Table Mountain. By BRET HARTE.
Mrs. Gainsborough's Diamonds. By JULIAN HAWTHORNE.
Kathleen Mavourneen. By the Author of "That Lass o' Lowrie's."
Lindsay's Luck. By the Author of "That Lass o' Lowrie's."
Pretty Polly Pemberton. By Author of "That Lass o' Lowrie's."

Crown 8vo, cloth extra, with Portrait and Facsimile, 7s. 6d.

Prout (Father), The Final Reliques of.
Collected and Edited, from MSS. supplied by the family of the Rev. FRANCIS MAHONY, by BLANCHARD JERROLD.

Proctor's (R. A.) Works:

Myths and Marvels of Astronomy. By RICH. A. PROCTOR, Author of "Other Worlds than Ours," &c. Demy 8vo, cloth extra, 12s. 6d.

"*Mr. Proctor, who is well and widely known for his faculty of popularising the latest results of the science of which he is a master, has brought together in these fascinating chapters a curious collection of popular beliefs concerning divination by the stars, the influences of the moon, the destination of the comets, he constellation figures, and the habitation of other worlds than ours.*"—DAILY NEWS.

Pleasant Ways in Science. By RICHARD A. PROCTOR. Crown 8vo, cloth extra, 10s. 6d.

"*When scientific problems of an abstruse and difficult character are presented to the unscientific mind, something more than mere knowledge is necessary in order to achieve success. The ability to trace such problems through the several stages of observation and experiment to their successful solution, without once suffering the reader's attention to flag, or his interest in the issue of the investigation to abate, argues the possession by the writer, not only of a thorough acquaintance with his subject, but also of that rare gift, the power of readily imparting his knowledge to those who have not the aptitude to acquire it, undivested of scientific formulæ. Now, such a writer is Mr. R. A. Proctor.*"—SCOTSMAN.

Rough Ways made Smooth. By RICHARD A. PROCTOR. Crown 8vo, cloth extra, 10s. 6d. [*In the press.*

Crown 8vo, cloth extra, gilt, 7s. 6d.

Pursuivant of Arms, The;

or, Heraldry founded upon Facts. A Popular Guide to the Science of Heraldry. By J. R. PLANCHE, Esq., Somerset Herald. With Coloured Frontispiece, Plates, and 200 Illustrations.

Crown 8vo, cloth extra, with Illustrations, 7s. 6d.

Rabelais' Works.

Faithfully Translated from the French, with variorum Notes, and numerous characteristic Illustrations by GUSTAVE DORE.

"*His buffoonery was not merely Brutus's rough skin, which contained a rod of gold: it was necessary as an amulet against the monks and legates; and he must be classed with the greatest creative minds in the world—with Shakespeare, with Dante, and with Cervantes.*"—S. T. COLERIDGE.

Crown 8vo, cloth gilt, with numerous Illustrations, and a beautifully executed Chart of the various Spectra, 7s. 6d.

Rambosson's Astronomy.

By J. RAMBOSSON, Laureate of the Institute of France. Translated by C. B. PITMAN. Profusely Illustrated.

Crown 8vo, cloth extra, with Illustrations, 7s. 6d.

Regalia: Crowns, Coronations, and Inaugura-

tions, in various Ages and Countries. By W. JONES, F.S.A., Author of "Finger-Ring Lore," &c. With very numerous Illustrations. [*In preparation.*

Crown 8vo, cloth extra, 10s. 6d.

Richardson's (Dr.) A Ministry of Health,
and other Papers. By BENJAMIN WARD RICHARDSON, M.D., &c.

"*This highly interesting volume contains upwards of nine addresses, writte in the author's well-known style, and full of great and good thoughts. . . . The work is, like all those of the author, that of a man of genius, of great power, of experience, and noble independence of thought.*"—POPULAR SCIENCE REVIEW.

Handsomely printed, price 5s.

Roll of Battle Abbey, The;
or, A List of the Principal Warriors who came over from Normandy with William the Conqueror, and Settled in this Country, A.D. 1066-7. Printed on fine plate paper, nearly three feet by two, with the principal Arms emblazoned in Gold and Colours.

Two Vols., large 4to, profusely Illustrated, half-morocco, £2 16s.

Rowlandson, the Caricaturist.
A Selection from his Works, with Anecdotal Descriptions of his Famous Caricatures, and a Sketch of his Life, Times, and Contemporaries. With nearly 400 Illustrations, mostly in Facsimile of the Originals. By JOSEPH GREGO, Author of "James Gillray, the Caricaturist; his Life, Works, and Times." [*In the press.*

Crown 8vo, cloth extra, profusely Illustrated, 4s. 6d. each.

"Secret Out" Series, The.

The Pyrotechnist's Treasury; or, Complete Art of Making Fireworks. By THOMAS KENTISH. With numerous Illustrations.

The Art of Amusing: A Collection of Graceful Arts, Games, Tricks, Puzzles, and Charades. By FRANK BELLEW. 300 Illustrations.

Hanky-Panky: Very Easy Tricks, Very Difficult Tricks, White Magic, Sleight of Hand. Edited by W. H. CREMER. 200 Illustrations.

The Merry Circle: A Book of New Intellectual Games and Amusements. By CLARA BELLEW. Many Illustrations.

Magician's Own Book: Performances with Cups and Balls. Eggs, Hats, Handkerchiefs, &c. All from Actual Experience. Edited by W. H. CREMER. 200 Illustrations.

Magic No Mystery: Tricks with Cards, Dice, Balls, &c., with fully descriptive Directions; the Art of Secret Writing; the Training of Performing Animals, &c. With Coloured Frontispiece and many Illustrations.

The Secret Out: One Thousand Tricks with Cards, and other Recreations; with Entertaining Experiments in Drawing-room or "White Magic." By W. H. CREMER. 300 Engravings.

Crown 8vo, cloth extra, 7s. 6d.

Sanson Family, Memoirs of the:
Seven Generations of Executioners. By HENRI SANSON. Translated from the French, with Introduction, by CAMILLE BARRERE.

"*A faithful translation of this curious work, which will certainly repay perusal—not on the ground of its being full of horrors, for the original author seems to be rather ashamed of the technical aspect of his profession, and is commendably reticent as to its details, but because it contains a lucid account of the most notable causes célèbres from the time of Louis XIV. to a period within the memory of persons still living. . . . Extremely entertaining.*"—DAILY TELEGRAPH.

Crown 8vo, cloth extra, 6s.
Senior's Travel and Trout in the Antipodes.
An Angler's Sketches in Tasmania and New Zealand. By WILLIAM SENIOR ("Red Spinner"), Author of "Stream and Sea." [*In the press.*

Shakespeare and Shakespeareana:
Shakespeare, The First Folio. Mr. WILLIAM SHAKESPEARE'S Comedies, Histories, and Tragedies. Published according to the true Originall Copies. London, Printed by ISAAC IAGGARD and ED. BLOUNT, 1623.—A Reproduction of the extremely rare original, in reduced facsimile by a photographic process—ensuring the strictest accuracy in every detail. Small 8vo, half-Roxburghe, 10s. 6d.

"*To Messrs. Chatto and Windus belongs the merit of having done more to facilitate the critical study of the text of our great dramatist than all the Shakespeare clubs and societies put together. A complete facsimile of the celebrated First Folio edition of 1623 for half-a-guinea is at once a miracle of cheapness and enterprise. Being in a reduced form, the type is necessarily rather diminutive, but it is as distinct as in a genuine copy of the original, and will be found to be as useful and far more handy to the student than the latter.*"—ATHENÆUM.

Shakespeare, The Lansdowne. Beautifully printed in red and black, in small but very clear type. With engraved facsimile of DROESHOUT'S Portrait. Post 8vo, cloth extra, 7s. 6d.

Shakspere's Dramatic Works, Poems. Doubtful Plays, and Biography.—CHARLES KNIGHT'S PICTORIAL EDITION, with many hundred beautiful Engravings on Wood of Views, Costumes, Old Buildings, Antiquities, Portraits, &c. Eight Vols., royal 8vo, cloth extra, £3 12s.

Shakespeare for Children: Tales from Shakespeare. By CHARLES and MARY LAMB. With numerous Illustrations, coloured and plain, by J. MOYR SMITH. Crown 4to, cloth gilt, 10s. 6d.

Shakspere, The School of. Including "The Life and Death of Captain Thomas Stukeley," "Nobody and Somebody," "Histriomastix," "The Prodigal Son," "Jack Drum's Entertainment," "A Warning for Fair Women," and "Fair Em." Edited, with Notes, by RICHARD SIMPSON. Introduction by F. J. FURNIVALL. Two Vols., crown 8vo, cloth extra, 18s.

Shakespeare Music, The Handbook of. Being an Account of Three Hundred and Fifty Pieces of Music, set to Words taken from the Plays and Poems of Shakespeare, the compositions ranging from the Elizabethan Age to the Present Time. By ALFRED ROFFE. 4to, half-Roxburghe, 7s.

Shakespeare, A Study of. By ALGERNON CHARLES SWINBURNE. Crown 8vo, cloth extra, 8s. [*In the press.*

Crown 8vo, cloth extra, gilt, with 10 full-page Tinted Illustrations, 7s. 6d.
Sheridan's Complete Works,
with Life and Anecdotes. Including his Dramatic Writings, printed from the Original Editions, his Works in Prose and Poetry, Translations, Speeches, Jokes, Puns, &c.; with a Collection of Sheridaniana.

"*The editor has brought together within a manageable compass not only the seven plays by which Sheridan is best known, but a collection also of his poetical pieces which are less familiar to the public, sketches of unfinished dramas, selections from his reported witticisms, and extracts from his principal speeches. To these is prefixed a short but well-written memoir, giving the chief facts in Sheridan's literary and political career; so that, with this volume in his hand, the student may consider himself tolerably well furnished with all that is necessary for a general comprehension of the subject of it.*"—PALL MALL GAZETTE.

Crown 8vo, cloth extra, with Illustrations, 7s. 6d.

Signboards:
Their History. With Anecdotes of Famous Taverns and Remarkable Characters. By JACOB LARWOOD and JOHN CAMDEN HOTTEN. With nearly 100 Illustrations.

"*Even if we were ever so maliciously inclined, we could not pick out all Messrs. Larwood and Hotten's plums, because the good things are so numerous as to defy the most wholesale depredation.*"—TIMES.

Crown 8vo, cloth extra, gilt, 6s. 6d.

Slang Dictionary, The:
Etymological, Historical, and Anecdotal. An ENTIRELY NEW EDITION, revised throughout, and considerably Enlarged.

"*We are glad to see the Slang Dictionary reprinted and enlarged. From a high scientific point of view this book is not to be despised. Of course it cannot fail to be amusing also. It contains the very vocabulary of unrestrained humour, and oddity, and grotesqueness. In a word, it provides valuable material both for the student of language and the student of human nature.*"—ACADEMY.

Exquisitely printed in miniature, cloth extra, gilt edges, 2s. 6d.

Smoker's Text-Book, The.
By J. HAMER, F.R.S.L.

Crown 8vo, cloth extra, 5s.

Spalding's Elizabethan Demonology:
An Essay in Illustration of the Belief in the Existence of Devils, and the Powers possessed by them, as it was generally held during the period of the Reformation, and the times immediately succeeding; with Special Reference to Shakspere and his Works. By T. ALFRED SPALDING, LL.B. [*In the press.*

Crown 4to, uniform with "Chaucer for Children," with Coloured Illustrations, cloth gilt, 10s. 6d.

Spenser for Children.
By M. H. TOWRY. With Illustrations in Colours by WALTER J. MORGAN.

"*Spenser has simply been transferred into plain prose, with here and there a line or stanza quoted, where the meaning and the diction are within a child's comprehension, and additional point is thus given to the narrative without the cost of obscurity. . . . Altogether the work has been well and carefully done.*"—THE TIMES.

Crown 8vo, cloth extra, 9s.

Stedman's Victorian Poets:
Critical Essays. By EDMUND CLARENCE STEDMAN.

"*We ought to be thankful to those who do critical work with competent skill and understanding, with honesty of purpose, and with diligence and thoroughness of execution. And Mr. Stedman, having chosen to work in this line, deserves the thanks of English scholars by these qualities and by something more; . . . . he is faithful, studious, and discerning.*"—SATURDAY REVIEW.

Crown 8vo, cloth extra, with Illustrations, 7s. 6d.
Strutt's Sports and Pastimes of the People
of England; including the Rural and Domestic Recreations, May Games, Mummeries, Shows, Processions, Pageants, and Pompous Spectacles, from the Earliest Period to the Present Time. With 140 Illustrations. Edited by WILLIAM HONE.

Crown 8vo, cloth extra, with Illustrations, 7s. 6d.
Swift's Choice Works,
In Prose and Verse. With Memoir, Portrait, and Facsimiles of the Maps in the Original Edition of "Gulliver's Travels."

"*If he had never written either the 'Tale of a Tub' or 'Gulliver's Travels,' his name merely as a poet would have come down to us, and have gone down to posterity, with well-earned honours.*"—HAZLITT.

Swinburne's Works:

The Queen Mother and Rosamond. Fcap. 8vo, 5s.
Atalanta in Calydon.
A New Edition. Crown 8vo, 6s.
Chastelard.
A Tragedy. Crown 8vo, 7s.
Poems and Ballads.
FIRST SERIES. Fcap. 8vo, 9s. Also in crown 8vo, at same price.
Poems and Ballads.
SECOND SERIES. Fcap. 8vo, 9s. Also in crown 8vo, at same price.
Notes on "Poems and Ballads." 8vo, 1s.
William Blake:
A Critical Essay. With Facsimile Paintings. Demy 8vo, 16s.
Songs before Sunrise.
Crown 8vo, 10s. 6d.
Bothwell:
A Tragedy. Crown 8vo, 12s. 6d.
George Chapman:
An Essay. Crown 8vo, 7s.
Songs of Two Nations.
Crown 8vo, 6s.
Essays and Studies.
Crown 8vo, 12s.
Erechtheus:
A Tragedy. Crown 8vo, 6s.
Note of an English Republican on the Muscovite Crusade. 8vo, 1s.
A Note on Charlotte Brontë.
Crown 8vo, 6s.
A Study of Shakespeare.
Crown 8vo, 8s. [*In the press.*

Medium 8vo, cloth extra, with Illustrations, 7s. 6d.
Syntax's (Dr.) Three Tours,
in Search of the Picturesque, in Search of Consolation, and in Search of a Wife. With the whole of ROWLANDSON'S droll page Illustrations, in Colours, and Life of the Author by J. C. HOTTEN.

Four Vols. small 8vo, cloth boards, 30s.
Taine's History of English Literature.
Translated by HENRY VAN LAUN.

*** Also a POPULAR EDITION, in Two Vols. crown 8vo, cloth extra, 15s.

Crown 8vo, cloth gilt, profusely Illustrated, 6s.
Tales of Old Thule.
Collected and Illustrated by J. MOYR SMITH.

One Vol. crown 8vo, cloth extra, 7s. 6d.
Taylor's (Tom) Historical Dramas:
"Clancarty," "Jeanne Darc," "'Twixt Axe and Crown," "The Fool's Revenge," "Arkwright's Wife," "Anne Boleyn," "Plot and Passion."

*** The Plays may also be had separately, at 1s. each.

Crown 8vo, cloth extra, with Coloured Frontispiece and numerous Illustrations, 7s. 6d.
Thackerayana:
Notes and Anecdotes. Illustrated by a profusion of Sketches by WILLIAM MAKEPEACE THACKERAY, depicting Humorous Incidents in his School-life, and Favourite Characters in the books of his every-day reading. With Hundreds of Wood Engravings, facsimiled from Mr. Thackeray's Original Drawings.

"It would have been a real loss to bibliographical literature had copyright difficulties deprived the general public of this very amusing collection. One of Thackeray's habits, from his schoolboy days, was to ornament the margins and blank pages of the books he had in use with caricature illustrations of their contents. This gave special value to the sale of his library, and is almost cause for regret that it could not have been preserved in its integrity. Thackeray's place in literature is eminent enough to have made this an interest to future generations. The anonymous editor has done the best that he could to compensate for the lack of this. It is an admirable addendum, not only to his collected works, but also to any memoir of him that has been, or that is likely to be, written."—BRITISH QUARTERLY REVIEW.

Crown 8vo, cloth extra, gilt edges, with Illustrations, 7s. 6d.
Thomson's Seasons and Castle of Indolence.
With a Biographical and Critical Introduction by ALLAN CUNNINGHAM, and over 50 fine Illustrations on Steel and Wood.

Crown 8vo, cloth extra, with numerous Illustrations, 7s. 6d.
Thornbury's (Walter) Haunted London.
A New Edition, Revised and Corrected, with numerous Illustrations by F. W. FAIRHOLT, F.S.A. [In the press.

Crown 8vo, cloth extra, with Illustrations, 7s. 6d.
Timbs' Clubs and Club Life in London.
With Anecdotes of its famous Coffee-houses, Hostelries, and Taverns. By JOHN TIMBS, F.S.A. With numerous Illustrations.

Crown 8vo, cloth extra, with Illustrations, 7s. 6d.

Timbs' English Eccentrics and Eccentricities: Stories of Wealth and Fashion, Delusions, Impostures, and Fanatic Missions, Strange Sights and Sporting Scenes, Eccentric Artists, Theatrical Folks, Men of Letters, &c. By JOHN TIMBS, F.S.A. With nearly 50 Illustrations.

Demy 8vo, cloth extra, 14s.

Torrens' The Marquess Wellesley,
Architect of Empire. An Historic Portrait. By W. M. TORRENS, M.P.
[*In the press.*

---

*Crown 8vo, cloth extra, with Coloured Illustrations, 7s. 6d.

Turner's (J. M. W.) Life and Correspondence.
Founded upon Letters and Papers furnished by his Friends and fellow-Academicians. By WALTER THORNBURY. A New Edition, considerably Enlarged. With numerous Illustrations in Colours, facsimiled from Turner's original Drawings.

Two Vols., crown 8vo, cloth extra, with Map and Ground-Plans, 14s.

Walcott's Church Work and Life in English
Minsters; and the English Student's Monasticon. By the Rev. MACKENZIE E. C. WALCOTT, B.D.

The 20th Annual Edition, for 1880, elegantly bound, cloth, full gilt, price 50s.

Walford's County Families of the United
Kingdom. A Royal Manual of the Titled and Untitled Aristocracy of Great Britain and Ireland. By EDWARD WALFORD, M.A., late Scholar of Balliol College, Oxford. Containing Notices of the Descent, Birth, Marriage, Education, &c., of more than 12,000 distinguished Heads of Families in the United Kingdom, their Heirs Apparent or Presumptive, together with a Record of the Patronage at their disposal, the Offices which they hold or have held, their Town Addresses, Country Residences, Clubs, &c. [*In the press.*

"*What would the gossips of old have given for a book which opened to them the recesses of every County Family in the Three Kingdoms? . . . This work, however, will serve other purposes besides those of mere curiosity, envy, or malice. It is just the book for the lady of the house to have at hand when making up the County dinner, as it gives exactly that information which punctilious and particular people are so desirous of obtaining—the exact standing of every person in the county. To the business man, 'The County Families' stands in the place of directory and biographical dictionary. The fund of information it affords respecting the Upper Ten Thousand must give it a place in the lawyer's library; and to the money-lender, who is so interested in finding out the difference between a gentleman and a 'gent,' between heirs-at-law and younger sons, Mr. Walford has been a real benefactor. In this splendid volume he has managed to meet a universal want—one which cannot fail to be felt by the lady in her drawing-room, the peer in his library, the tradesman in his counting-house, and the gentleman in his club.*"—TIMES.

Large crown 8vo, cloth antique, with Illustrations, 7s. 6d.

Walton and Cotton's Complete Angler;
or, The Contemplative Man's Recreation : being a Discourse of Rivers, Fishponds, Fish and Fishing, written by IZAAK WALTON ; and Instructions how to Angle for a Trout or Grayling in a clear Stream, by CHARLES COTTON. With Original Memoirs and Notes by Sir HARRIS NICOLAS, and 61 Copperplate Illustrations.

Carefully printed on paper to imitate the Original, 22 in. by 14 in., 2s.

Warrant to Execute Charles I.
An exact Facsimile of this important Document, with the Fifty-nine Signatures of the Regicides, and corresponding Seals.

Beautifully printed on paper to imitate the Original MS., price 2s.

Warrant to Execute Mary Queen of Scots.
An exact Facsimile, including the Signature of Queen Elizabeth, and a Facsimile of the Great Seal.

Post 8vo, cloth limp, with numerous Illustrations, 2s. 6d.

Westropp's Handbook of Pottery and Porcelain; or, History of those Arts from the Earliest Period. By HODDER M. WESTROPP, Author of " Handbook of Archæology," &c. With numerous beautiful Illustrations, and a List of Marks. [*In the press.*

SEVENTH EDITION. Square 8vo, 1s.

Whistler v. Ruskin : Art and Art Critics.
By J. A. MACNEILL WHISTLER.

Crown 8vo, cloth extra, with Illustrations, 7s. 6d.

Wright's Caricature History of the Georges.
(The House of Hanover.) With 400 Pictures, Caricatures, Squibs, Broadsides, Window Pictures, &c. By THOMAS WRIGHT, Esq., M.A., F.S.A.

Large post 8vo, cloth extra, gilt, with Illustrations, 7s. 6d.

Wright's History of Caricature and of the
Grotesque in Art, Literature, Sculpture, and Painting, from the Earliest Times to the Present Day. By THOMAS WRIGHT, M.A., F.S.A. Profusely Illustrated by F. W. FAIRHOLT, F.S.A.

J. OGDEN AND CO., PRINTERS, 172, ST. JOHN STREET, E.C.

www.ingramcontent.com/pod-product-compliance
Lightning Source LLC
Chambersburg PA
CBHW031942290426
44108CB00011B/645